# Turkish Literature as World Literature

## Literatures as World Literature

Can the literature of a specific country, author, or genre be used to approach the elusive concept of "world literature"? **Literatures as World Literature** takes a novel approach to world literature by analyzing specific constellations—according to language, nation, form, or theme—of literary texts and authors in their own world-literary dimensions. World literature is obviously so vast that any view of it cannot help but be partial; the question then becomes how to reduce the complex task of understanding and describing world literature. Most treatments of world literature so far either have been theoretical and thus abstract, or else have made broad use of exemplary texts from a variety of languages and epochs. The majority of critical work, the filling in of what has been traced, lies ahead of us. **Literatures as World Literature** fills in the devilish details by allowing scholars to move outward from their own areas of specialization, fostering scholarly writing that approaches more closely the polyphonic, multiperspectival nature of world literature.

*Series Editor:*
Thomas O. Beebee

*Editorial Board:*
Eduardo Coutinho, Federal University of Rio de Janeiro, Brazil
Hsinya Huang, National Sun-yat Sen University, Taiwan
Meg Samuelson, University of Cape Town, South Africa
Ken Seigneurie, Simon Fraser University, Canada
Mads Rosendahl Thomsen, Aarhus University, Denmark

*Volumes in the Series*
*German Literature as World Literature*, edited by Thomas O. Beebee
*Roberto Bolaño as World Literature*, edited by Nicholas Birns and
Juan E. De Castro
*Crime Fiction as World Literature*, edited by David Damrosch,
Theo D'haen, and Louise Nilsson
*Danish Literature as World Literature*, edited by Dan Ringgaard and Mads
Rosendahl Thomsen
*From Paris to Tlön: Surrealism as World Literature*, by Delia Ungureanu
*American Literature as World Literature*, edited by Jeffrey R. Di Leo
*Romanian Literature as World Literature*, edited by Mircea Martin,
Christian Moraru, and Andrei Terian
*Brazilian Literature as World Literature*, edited by Eduardo F. Coutinho
*Dutch and Flemish Literature as World Literature*, edited by Theo D'haen
*Afropolitan Literature as World Literature*, edited by James Hodapp
*Francophone Literature as World Literature*, edited by Christian Moraru,
Nicole Simek, and Bertrand Westphal
*Bulgarian Literature as World Literature*, edited by Mihaela P. Harper
and Dimitar Kambourov
*Philosophy as World Literature*, edited by Jeffrey R. Di Leo
*Turkish Literature as World Literature*, edited by Burcu Alkan and
Çimen Günay-Erkol
*Elena Ferrante as World Literature*, by Stiliana Milkova (forthcoming)
*Modern Indian Literature as World Literature: Going Beyond English*,
by Bhavya Tiwari (forthcoming)
*Multilingual Literature as World Literature*, edited by Jane Hiddleston
and Wen-chin Ouyang (forthcoming)
*Persian Literature as World Literature*, edited by Mostafa Abedinifard,
Omid Azadibougar, and Amirhossein Vafa (forthcoming)
*Mexican Literature as World Literature*, edited by Ignacio M. Sánchez Prado
(forthcoming)
*Modern Irish Literature as World Literature*, edited by Christopher Langlois
(forthcoming)

# Turkish Literature as World Literature

*Edited by*
*Burcu Alkan and*
*Çimen Günay-Erkol*

BLOOMSBURY ACADEMIC
NEW YORK • LONDON • OXFORD • NEW DELHI • SYDNEY

BLOOMSBURY ACADEMIC
Bloomsbury Publishing Inc
1385 Broadway, New York, NY 10018, USA
50 Bedford Square, London, WC1B 3DP, UK
29 Earlsfort Terrace, Dublin 2, Ireland

BLOOMSBURY, BLOOMSBURY ACADEMIC and the Diana logo are trademarks of
Bloomsbury Publishing Plc

First published in the United States of America 2021
This paperback edition published 2022

Volume Editor's Part of the Work © Burcu Alkan and Çimen Günay-Erkol, 2021
Each chapter © Contributors, 2021

Cover design by Simon Levy

All rights reserved. No part of this publication may be reproduced or transmitted in any form or by any means, electronic or mechanical, including photocopying, recording, or any information storage or retrieval system, without prior permission in writing from the publishers.

Bloomsbury Publishing Inc does not have any control over, or responsibility for, any third-party websites referred to or in this book. All internet addresses given in this book were correct at the time of going to press. The author and publisher regret any inconvenience caused if addresses have changed or sites have ceased to exist, but can accept no responsibility for any such changes.

Library of Congress Cataloging-in-Publication Data
Names: Alkan, Burcu, editor. | Günay-Erkol, Çimen, editor.
Title: Turkish literature as world literature / edited by Burcu Alkan and Çimen Günay-Erkol.
Description: New York: Bloomsbury Academic, 2021. | Series: Literatures as world literature | Includes bibliographical references and index.
Identifiers: LCCN 2020030093 (print) | LCCN 2020030094 (ebook) | ISBN 9781501358012 (hardback) | ISBN 9781501371639 (paperback) | ISBN 9781501358029 (epub) | ISBN 9781501358036 (pdf)
Subjects: LCSH: Turkish literature–20th century–History and criticism. | Turkish literature–21st century–History and criticism. | Literature, Modern–Turkish influences. | Turkish literature–Appreciation.
Classification: LCC PL208 .T87 2021 (print) | LCC PL208 (ebook) | DDC 894/.3509–dc23
LC record available at https://lccn.loc.gov/2020030093
LC ebook record available at https://lccn.loc.gov/2020030094

ISBN: HB: 978-1-5013-5801-2
PB: 978-1-5013-7163-9
ePDF: 978-1-5013-5803-6
eBook: 978-1-5013-5802-9

Series: Literatures as World Literature

Typeset by Deanta Global Publishing Services, Chennai, India

To find out more about our authors and books visit www.bloomsbury.com and sign up for our newsletters.

*To Talât Sait Halman and Terry Eagleton*

# CONTENTS

*List of Figures* xi
*Acknowledgments* xii
*A Note on the Text* xiii

Introduction: "Turkish Literature as World Literature"? What Is in a Preposition? *Burcu Alkan and Çimen Günay-Erkol* 1

**PART I** Breathing Turkish in the World Stage 17

1. The Entangled History of Cosmopolitanism and Nationalism in Modern Turkish Literature *Fatih Altuğ* 19

2. Translation, Transcription, and the Making of World Literature: On Late Ottoman and Modern Turkish Scriptworlds *Etienne E. Charrière* 36

3. Translating Yunus Emre, Translating the Self, Translating Islam: Zafer Şenocak's Turkish-German Path to Modernity *Joseph Twist* 55

**PART II** Turkish Literature in Transnational Waters 73

4. World Literature as Performance: Turkish and British Women's Writing in Transcultural Dialogue at the Turn of the Twentieth Century *Peter Cherry* 75

5. "The Living Link between India and Turkey": Halide Edib on the Subcontinent *Anirudha Dhanawade and Şima İmşir* 93

6  Nâzım Hikmet's Reception as a World Poet
   *Mediha Göbenli* 112

7  The Internationalist Left and World Literature: The Case
   of Nâzım Hikmet in Greece  *Kenan Behzat Sharpe* 129

8  The Influence of Nâzım Hikmet on Arab Poetry  *Mehmet
   Hakkı Suçin* 148

**PART III** Contemporary Forms and Cosmopolitanism  169

9  World Literary Refractions: Orhan Pamuk and Juan
   Goytisolo  *Başak Çandar* 171

10  Teaching *The Museum of Innocence* in Arts and Design
    Context  *Irmak Ertuna Howison* 188

11  Elif Şafak and Her Fiction: Cultural Commodities of the
    Global Capital  *Simla Doğangün* 204

12  For/Against the World: Literary Prizes and Political
    Culture in the "New Turkey"  *Kaitlin Staudt* 221

*Notes on Contributors* 239
*Index* 243

# FIGURES

2.1  Scriptural coexistence in the Ottoman Empire  43
2.2  *Sınırdışı Saatler* by Mehmet Yaşın (p. 135, YKY 2015)  48
10.1  "Corn flakes" panel from *Dare to Disappoint*  195
10.2  Narrative layers of *The Museum of Innocence*, a class diagram  199

# ACKNOWLEDGMENTS

Some of the key ideas that gave this book its final shape came from the conversations Burcu Alkan had at Harvard University's Institute for World Literature in 2019. She benefited greatly from her discussions with David Damrosch, Irvin Cemil Schick, Thomas Claviez, Ferda Keskin, Aysim Türkmen, Deniz Gündoğan İbrişim, and many other members of the seminars and colloquia. She would also like to thank the International Graduate Center for the Study of Culture (GCSC) at Justus Liebig University for the funding that was made available to her to attend the Institute in Boston and Jens Kugele of the GCSC for his advice and support regarding the trip. She is also indebted to her family, friends, and colleagues for their support. Birte Christ and Papatya Alkan-Genca in particular were extremely helpful in the final, demanding stages of this volume.

Among many intellectual mentors who made valuable contributions to the field, Çimen Günay-Erkol would like to express her gratitude to Talât Sait Halman, who played a pioneering role in introducing Turkish writers to audiences worldwide, for being a genuine source of inspiration. She would like to acknowledge Burcu Karahan for her help in reaching some of the references, and Wendy Wiseman and John Stonor for their diligent proofreading of the Introduction. She is also indebted to her family and friends for their support during the preparation of this volume. She would also like to gratefully acknowledge institutional funding provided by Özyeğin University toward the final phase of the book for the index.

# A NOTE ON THE TEXT

Turkish transcription is preferred where necessary and the References list follows an alphabetical order based on Turkish. The letters *c*, *g*, *o*, *s*, *u* are followed by *ç*, *ğ*, *ö*, *ş*, *ü*, respectively, and the letter *i* is preceded by *ı*.

# Introduction

# "Turkish Literature as World Literature"? What Is in a Preposition?

*Burcu Alkan and Çimen Günay-Erkol*

Thinking about a volume on "Turkish literature as world literature" introduces some seemingly simple questions. What is "Turkish literature as world literature?" Is not Turkish literature naturally *a* world literature? The qualification created by the addition of the preposition "as" is suggestive of a difference between Turkish literature on its own and Turkish literature within a collective proposition. Since the materials that constitute Turkish literature do not change with or without the "as," this preposition seems to refer to a qualification toward not Turkish literature but what world literature is in its relation to national literary traditions. Accordingly, the singular within the collective comes into focus and both gain reciprocal value and meaning in association with one another. The question to be asked then is this: What is this "world literature" that changes the perception of a national literature and is itself redefined when they interact? What is this third literary body that emerges out of the convergence of the singular and the collective spheres by means of an "as"? What is in a preposition?

This volume seeks to elaborate on the definitions and delineations of world literature from a geographical and cultural threshold, a transit-space both literally and metaphorically, while introducing a "national" literature in its "world literary-ness." Yet, it also acknowledges and highlights the "negative freedom" from the boundaries of the "national traditions" that essentially culminates in a global interdependence determined by certain illusions of world literature along the lines Pheng Cheah defines (309). Moreover, the chapters are selected with the aim of challenging and reformulating the conventional ways of thinking about modern Turkish literature that often emphasize how it is influenced by "Western" traditions. Instead, they examine the impact of Turkish literature on literatures and cultures of the world on both the "eastern" and the "western" side of the threshold. This reversed perspective also challenges the prevalent discourses on world literature that still—more often than not—maintain the predominance of the "west" and the "center" over the "not-west" and the "periphery."

In "World Literature in a Postcanonical, Hypercanonical Age," David Damrosch examines the transformation of the field of world literature from a two-tiered model to a three-tiered one following the development of postcolonial studies. He notes that what used to be a "major vs. minor works" understanding of world literature has become a system of "a *hypercanon*, a *countercanon*, and a *shadow canon*." He argues that while new works from the periphery are introduced into the system to form a *countercanon*, the major works of the old system still make up the *hypercanon* and do not necessarily lose their status. In fact, they "gain new vitality from association with [the countercanon]" (45). This relational structure, instead, pushes out the "old 'minor'" authors, rendering them the *shadows* of what they once were as remembered but not necessarily passed on.

This hierarchical structure within the world literary canon not only persists but different versions of it are also reproduced in the other integrated systems that maintain the world literary canon. For example, a tiered system not so different from the one Damrosch describes maintains the sphere of translated works as a fundamental access point to "world literature." Most of the time only certain works—major and/or popular—of a national literature make it through this gateway with the "minor" alternatives lining up in decreasing order of interest, awaiting translation and publication. The foundational texts of a national literary tradition are often left behind as a shadow canon, important but not necessarily relevant to or interesting enough for a global audience. Essentially, demands and sales determine what gets to be translated and published, and what thus forms a good portion of the texts available as "world literature." These translated works in turn might find themselves in the various world and comparative literature syllabi and achieve some canonical status.

This impact of global capitalism on the publication (and translation) industry forms the basis of most world literature debates. At its earlier stages, for instance, Erich Auerbach had signaled the extent and potential outcomes of such an impact in his "Philology and 'Weltliteratur'" through his concerns regarding the sameness that has taken over the world and its literary spheres. While globalization has rendered the access of different voices to broader audiences possible and thus somewhat counteracted Auerbach's concerns, in essence the threat of standardization that so concerned him could be argued to have merely changed form. The global book market allows different voices, but it does so primarily along the lines that maintain and perpetuate certain patterns deciding what is worthy of being deemed world literature and translated to be published for a broader readership.

Naturally not all the works of a national literary tradition can be made accessible to a world audience and probably not all of them need to be. Still, what gets to be translated and published is defined by various economic concerns and political influences. In such a decision-making process, not always shaped by the most idealistic intellectual and literary drives, a significant work of a national tradition that would present a key picture of the said tradition might be overlooked among the more popular texts for the sake of reaching higher sales figures. In short, the translation-publication access point is a key agent in the construction of the world literary canon, as it is directly interlinked to the "countercanon" tier of the world literary system. In the broad expansion of temporal and spatial possibilities, only a limited number of names get a chance to coexist alongside the major works of the global market as a result of the interlocked set of hierarchical sorting processes in the making of what is promoted as world literature.

Discussing what "Turkish literature as world literature" means, then, is about examining how the multitude of works within the Turkish literary tradition fares in relation to the dynamics of such processes. How is Turkish literature situated in the *countercanon* of world literature and its translation-publication access point? While the *countercanon* introduces many alternative, challenging, and unique voices to the world literary sphere, what they establish is still a canon and as such naturally leaves many works out. Talking about Turkish literature as world literature is therefore about how much and what elements of Turkish literature make it through the gateway of the world literary sphere and why. What do the works and the names that manage to join the ranks of the *countercanon* (but still not the *hypercanon*) tell us about not only the Turkish but also the world literary sphere?

Accessibility is undoubtedly a key point of discussion in world literature. In addition to the issues of a literary work's achieving world literariness along the lines of translation and publication practices, another even more overlooked problem of accessibility prevails. The (peripheral) scholarship on the said (peripheral) literatures is rarely translated. So little of the scholarly discussions on national literatures outside the "major," "Western" languages, and even less on their engagement with the comparative world literary scholarship, reach a broader audience. Are we to assume that no such discussions take place elsewhere? Or are we to recognize once again that the domination of the designated lingua francas of academia has as great a role in shaping world literary discourses as the literatures themselves do? How then do we reconcile with the reality of building this discussion on Turkish literature in English in this collection of chapters so that the idea of Turkish literature as world literature may enter into scholarly circulation?

Resistance against the lingua francas of literary scholarship would be counterproductive and, in this case, self-defeating. Just like the sphere of literary works themselves, there are linguistic dominions in the world of literary scholarship. These dominions are similarly linked to economic, political, and intellectual determinants that cannot be so easily eradicated. Yet these lingua francas also enable international dialogues. As such, while the expansion of the modes of conversation and the diversification of languages as contact zones are imperative for the development of the field, the question of how achievable overcoming such linguistic dominions is continues to haunt any associated discussion and theorization. It seems that however much progress is made in the humanities, the power relations among social, political, and economic structures are intact and our progress is relatively small. While not disregarding the pathways that are opened and that this book is yet another attempt as such, it is important not to get too comfortable in our small triumphs and keep our eyes on the core issues of equity and equality in literature and literary scholarship.

World literature is an immense field that reaches over a great temporal and spatial realm. It also bears internal complexities arising from the mobile, multicultural, and cosmopolitan nature of texts, peoples, cultures, and languages. This immense and complex territory is, of course, not easy to chart, and even at its most modest, exploring it requires the efforts of many people. As Franco Moretti says, "reading more is always a good thing, but not the solution" (55). Moretti builds his argument against close reading to promote his distant reading as a more effective methodology for a theory of world literature. Close reading, for Moretti, is not only besides the point of world literature, which for him is the big picture, but he also considers it methodologically counterproductive. Most literary scholarship focuses on very limited subjects of very few major texts and authors, and using years of other people's analysis to be synthesized into a system achieves a "second hand" literary history. While he has a valid point in terms of knowing a lot about a very small canon, like many Western or Western-oriented scholars of the field, he is speaking from the perspective of the center.

The scholars of the various national literatures, who provide the material for "distant reading," become sideliners for Moretti's centric theorization. Close reading practices of the scholars of peripheral national literatures, combined with the relational focus of the comparativists, make possible a composite picture of interconnections. However daunting a task, a scholar of world literature needs to be able to move through the diverse traditions, establish networks of meaning, and constantly negotiate relationships between the home base and the wider world with the limited resources that are available to each individual. It is not a methodological choice but an undeniable reality that needs to be tackled. As Pheng Cheah relates, translation, and comparative and world literary practices are all interconnected in the very "being" of "world literature" (304). Moretti's "distant reading" is a key theoretical and methodological position for world literature and it contributes greatly to world literary scholarship, but is it really "the way" for world literature as he promotes? Seeing world literature as the big, composite picture that it is, indeed, necessitates a distance, a "distant reading." The thematic and formalistic patterns, "the waves and the trees" and the like, are effective and invaluable in providing telling and informative understandings for broader audiences. However, it is hard to ignore the underlying centric presumptions regarding the theorization of world literature in such an argumentation.

In the case of non-center world literatures, close readings and comparative discussions are often methodological pathways that enable visibility and build dialogic relationships between not just the center and the periphery but within the periphery as well. Moretti is correct in saying that no one can read all the works in all the languages of the world, not even close. However, instead of an ideologically fraught methodology as the way to move forward, one could also argue that *doing world literature has to be a collaborative affair*. Emphasizing and encouraging collaboration with the so-called periphery—beyond references to a couple of names in passing and promoting their global accessibility in the worlds of publication and scholarship, where certain strongholds are acquired by the so-called center—would achieve a more lateral distribution of world literary attention. The question to ask might be whether a true change to the center-periphery model is really desired or whether it is assumed that acknowledging and criticizing such a model while continuing to maintain its structures is enough. Building theories and methodologies from a perspective of collaboration, a highly exigent necessity that is alas beyond the scope of a work of this kind, would encourage a more lateral possibility and might manage to push against the persistent core-periphery systems that seem to prevail even in the "pro-periphery" theorizations.

The urge to understand what appeals most to the international literary sphere accelerates the theoretical discussions among world literature scholars, regardless of their conflicting views in modeling world literature and its commercial globalization. The way Pascale Casanova mapped the literary system, the "world republic of letters," foregrounds the hegemony of the founders of major European literatures that made it possible for them to control the means of cultural legitimation for centuries. With Paris at the center, this map presents a conflictual literary history, over which Casanova discusses the dependence of literary production on the politics of nation-making, the (im)possibility to emancipate texts from their national, transnational, and political constraints, and whether the mechanisms of domination that marginalize some texts can be hacked. Similar to Moretti, Casanova points to the unequal state of affairs in the world literary sphere and argues that "a genuinely literary history of literature can be written only by taking into account the unequal states of the players in the literary game and the specific mechanisms of domination that are manifested in it" (352). Forces in this theory of literature, the specificity of the national paradigm, and the idea of a literary universality that transcends the national borders provide the productive tensions with which this volume attempts to enrich the dialectical understanding of relations within world literature, by presenting perspectives from Turkey to support the effort to write "a genuinely literary history of literature."

In his "Philology and 'Weltliteratur'" Auerbach, who wrote his magnum opus *Mimesis* in Istanbul, says "our philological home is the earth." The predominant scholarship focusing on world literature has failed to a great extent to envision Turkish literature at this *philological home* and as a part of the discussions due to the very limited number of works available in translation. In her address during a 2002 roundtable in Stockholm organized by the Swedish PEN, Müge Gürsoy Sökmen, an experienced publisher who has been involved in the sector since 1982, cites "the lack of competent translators from the Turkish and editors who can read Turkish" to explain the initial scarcity of Turkish authors in translation. She adds, however, that some European publishers interested in Turkish literature searched for "good literary documentaries of family violence, wife beating, harassment from the violent Orient" in the proposals to fulfill the role expected from Turkey in literature. According to Gürsoy Sökmen, not coming from major European languages builds a high barrier for writers from Turkey, a barrier that is maintained if not raised higher with active as well as dormant Orientalist beliefs in the publishing sector.

After the "prejudice barrier," comes the "quota barrier," says Sökmen. Several publishers tended to turn down second proposals from Turkey, saying they had already published one author from Turkey. Sökmen's speech includes a critical warning about the inherent assumptions on works that succeed in making their way to the center of the world literary sphere. Putting on display what the center of the world literature ecosystem finds exotic has been a strategy to make writers from Turkey eligible for translation and carry them across borders. Several works from Turkey found their way into world literature with their "local colors" promoted as their distinguishing features, diminishing the importance of their aesthetic and technical strategies.

Language might still be an obstacle for writers from Turkey, but rules of the game are subject to change. It is now commonplace to say, for example, that Anglophony no longer defines the literary cultures of Britain and the commonwealth but, rather, refers to "linguistic contact zones all over the world," as Emily Apter notes (55). Similar to Apter, Gayatri Spivak reminds us that "the sources of literary agency have expanded beyond the old European national literatures" and calls for the study of long-marginalized voices as "active cultural media rather than as objects of cultural study by the sanctioned ignorance of the metropolitan migrant" (6–9). In tandem with globalization, the literary agency of Europe, indeed, expanded beyond its origin and diversified. It is even harder today to accept the Eurocentrism in Pascale Casanova's Paris-centered "World Republic of Letters" as a comprehensive model to explain the complicated dynamics of world literature. As Rossen Djagalov suggests in "People's Republic of Letters," there have been competing centers of world literature, the Soviet Union being one for the international left, for instance (26). "The Greenwich meridian" of Casanova's map is being shifted with numerous works of literature that simultaneously occupy different linguistic milieux or claim a transnational status. We, therefore, suggest a return to Auerbach's dictum as a new beginning.

"Bibliomigrancy" of Turkish literature is the product of a collegial effort that also includes the historical traces of Auerbach (Mani 2017: 10). During his stint in Istanbul, Auerbach's assistant at Istanbul University was Güzin Dino, who, in 1973, published one of the pioneering works on nineteenth-century Turkish literature, *La genèse du roman turc au XIXe siècle.* In those years, while at Princeton University, Talât Sait Halman was publishing articles in English on modern Turkish literature, with a wide range of interest from epic dramas to lyric poetry (Halman 1976). While Halman acted as a translator and ambassador of Turkish literature in the United States, several other acclaimed translators were trying to make Turkish literature visible in the UK (Menemencioğlu and İz 1978). Turkish literature as a phenomenon thus crossed the national boundaries more visibly in the 1970s with the joint efforts of the translators, critics, and academics. New books of historical criticism followed in the 1980s, such as Ahmet Ö. Evin's *The Origins and Development of the Turkish Novel* (1983) that explored the complexities of Ottoman-Turkish literature at the turn of the century.

However, texts do not become part of world literature when analyses of them appear in other languages—it is necessary that they themselves cross-linguistic borders. When the critical works by Dino, Halman, and Evin appeared in French and English, not all of the literary works they discussed were accessible in those languages; a discussion on the foundational elements of Turkish literature started to travel globally before the material itself arrived in translation at the world scene in the 1970s. When anthologies (Sılay 1996), surveys (Halman and Warner 2008, Moran 2012), and books with comparative perspectives (Seyhan 2008) arrived in later years, it was possible to refer to a greater number of works in translation. Lately, in 2005–9, 2,389 works were translated and published in several languages with the support of the TEDA Project (Translation and Publication Grant Program of Turkey). According to the statistics announced on TEDA's website, among the languages that received support, the top six are Bulgarian, Arabic, German, Albanian, Persian, and English. Translations into German are twice as numerous as translations into English in the given timeframe.

The TEDA Project brings Turkish literature in conversation with languages other than Turkish, but despite the growing number of translations, the availability of Turkish texts in major world languages is still very limited when compared to the output. Some very important, canonical texts either have been translated only very recently or are still waiting to be translated. For instance, two of the highly significant and provocative writers whose works critically deal with Turkey's modernization are Oğuz Atay and Leyla Erbil. Atay's *The Disconnected* (*Tutunamayanlar*, originally published in 1972) has been translated into English by Sevin Seydi and the translation was printed in 2017, a year after its German translation *Die Haltlosen* and forty-five years after the publication of the novel in Turkey. This book was Atay's introduction to the English-speaking world, but it was available only as a limited edition from the publisher, Olric Press. One of the most important books in modern Turkish literature is still seeking a commercial publisher, as Olric Press was subsidized by the copyright holder and its translation was done on a voluntary basis. Erbil's *A Strange Woman* (*Tuhaf Bir Kadın*, originally published in 1971) came out in 2020 in Nermin Menemencioğlu's translation and was published by Deep Vellum. While the time gap of almost fifty years between the book's publication in Turkish and its translations highlights the "hierarchized universe" in which translation occurs (Casanova 2010: 287–8), that the English translation came one year after its French counterpart by Belleville Editions is suggestive of the interactive dynamics among the publishing sectors of major languages and the impact of such dynamics on the "hierarchized universe" of world literature.

In *Turkish Literature as World Literature*, we focused on the post-interlingual movement of Turkish literature into the hierarchies of today's globalized world and sought to examine its multifaceted dynamics, rather than envisioning the volume as a history of Turkish literature in the world scene. The particular interest of the volume is the "process" of Turkish literature's becoming world literature, in which it becomes possible to look closely at writers who had a global impact. *Turkish Literature as World Literature* overall is a plea to return to the earlier discussions in the field on the history of world literature to critically explore how they were inspired by political hierarchies frozen in the Cold War era that informed and sustained the center-periphery model, and to discuss the susceptibility of the concept of world literature to the ups and downs in global politics. Our aim has been to divert the attention from a sense of narrativity based, only or primarily, on culture, history, and tints of "local colors" toward one that acknowledges a well-established and heterogeneous tradition with its unique forms and aesthetics. By shedding light on Turkish literature as world literature and exploring its trajectories, we question the tense relationship between the center and the periphery in the "World Republic of Letters" (Casanova 2005), bringing them into dialogue with each other in a new manner that encourages a more lateral layout by challenging the inherent (and oftentimes openly) binary model of the field even, or especially, when the discussions on its decolonization also seem to be entangled with that model.

In a wide timeframe that expands from the modernization of the Ottoman Empire to the rise of the neo-Ottomanism proposed by the current government in Turkey, this volume traces a variety of works, writers, and trends in Turkish literature that had a global impact. The primary material mentioned in this volume is largely comprised of works that have been translated into major European languages. We started out with an important change of paradigm, and in contrast to the conventional comparativist exercise that moves from the European center to the peripheries, we traversed it in the reverse direction, to explore how Turkey's literature, from the peripheries of Europe, influenced the literatures of the world. Understanding the impact of Turkish literature on the world literary sphere requires a meta-analysis of several different but interrelated subjects, such as the market dynamics of translation, mobility of theories and theoretical concepts, and the geopolitics of the literary enterprise, all of which necessitate an awareness of the production processes of literature. Such a grand analytical exercise is, of course, not limited to the topics, writers, and texts included in this volume. Many names with international reputations like Yaşar Kemal, as well as the broader diasporic Turkish literature in countries such as Germany (Emine Sevgi Özdamar, Esmahan Aykol), France (Nedim Gürsel), the United Kingdom (Aysel Özakın, Moris Farhi), and the United States (Erje Ayden, Elif Batuman) among others, would have a welcome place in this book. Their absence is, indeed, a shortcoming of the volume, but as in any edited collection of this kind, our choices were shaped by limitations of time, space, and material availability.

Part I, "Breathing Turkish in the World Stage," is comprised of chapters that negotiate the core-periphery dichotomy. These chapters examine the "peripheral" position of Turkish literature on the world stage and evaluate the history that gave a specific character to the peripheral locality and national particularity of Turkish literature. Part I discusses Turkish literature as world literature by exploring figures of a period before the birth of modern Turkey and linking this period, retrospectively, to contemporary times, in which resonances between "national literature" and "world literature" require closer examination with novel perspectives. Overall, this part includes discussions of how the concept of world literature is negotiated in the Ottoman Empire, a multi-language and multi-script macrocosm, and in which ways the times before the birth of the secular Republic influenced the literature of the following era, connecting the historical specificities with the idea of the world as a cosmopolitan place. We intended this part to provide a basis for readers unfamiliar with the history of late Ottoman-early Republican literature.

Firmly grounded in Chapter 1 of this volume is a discussion on the local characteristics of Ottoman-Turkish literature and questions addressed in it about the concept of world literature. Several topics articulated by this opening chapter contribute to the analytical perspective aimed by the following chapters, which are built on the full recognition of the complex history of Ottoman-Turkish literature. Fatih Altuğ's chapter "The Entangled History of Cosmopolitanism and Nationalism in Modern Turkish Literature" delineates the beginnings of Ottoman literary modernity, which was born to a multiethnic empire with multiple scripts in use, creating a pluralistic literary field. Altuğ claims that "a new literature" is taken as an objective by the literary elites in Istanbul, the capital of the empire, where Turkish, Armenian, Greek, Bulgarian, and other ethnic literatures intersected with French literature, that is, the *prima materia* of world literature at the time. He elaborates on how certain tendencies and antinomies continued to haunt the world literature discussions from the times of the prominent Tanzimat intellectuals, such as Namık Kemal and Ahmed Mithat, until the national awakening in the Second Constitutional era when figures such as Fuad Köprülü presented the basic tenets of how a national literature should be.

Etienne Charrière in his chapter "Translation, Transcription, and the Making of World Literature: On Late Ottoman Scriptworlds" builds on the pluralism in the Ottoman Empire in terms of scripts to dwell, more pointedly, on the "cultural-political role of scripts," as Damrosch coins it, in world literature discussions. Charrière shows that there is a complicated history behind the Turkish script revolution of 1928 that led to the transition from the Arabic script to the Latin. In the pluralistic scripts' world of the Ottoman Empire, he maintains that there was not only coexistence but also competition. When literary histories of the Ottoman era were written by the Republican elites, the canon excluded Armenian- and Greek-scripted works of the nineteenth century and thus *nationalized* a cosmopolitan history. Still, Charrière shows that heterographics survive and surface in the works from the borders, such as the works of the Turkish-Cypriot writer and poet Mehmet Yaşın.

Joseph Twist expands on border-crossing by focusing on the prominent Turkish-German writer Zafer Şenocak in his chapter "Translating Yunus Emre, Translating the Self, and Translating Islam: Zafer Şenocak's Turkish-German Path to Modernity." He discusses how the writings of the Sufi humanist Yunus Emre, who has been aligned with Bektashism, served as a key inspiration for Şenocak and how Şenocak, in turn, translated Yunus Emre's works and carried his influence beyond the Turkish context. Twist elaborates on Şenocak's attempts to challenge stereotypical images and assumptions present in Germany about Turkey and Islam via bringing the teachings of Yunus Emre into dialogue with German writers and philosophers within his own essays and poetry. The chapter argues that Şenocak makes a call to an unpolarized spirituality by pulling Yunus Emre's brand of humanism to the center of the cosmopolitan and secular German society and he seeks to challenge the Western biases on the stage of world literature against what is often neatly categorized non-Western or peripheral.

The Republican era that followed the disintegration of the Ottoman Empire established a literary canon that prioritizes Turkish language over the other languages of the empire, and hence by regulating what counts and does not count as "Turkish literature" formed the internal basis of which authors from Turkey are to join the world literature canon as members of Turkish literature. In Part II of the volume, "Turkish Literature in Transnational Waters," there are chapters that explore Ottoman-Turkish subjects of the empire during the turn of the century in dialogue with their counterparts from the "center" and the "peripheries" of the world literature ecosystem. This second part delivers a discussion of how Turkish literature influenced its counterparts not only in the West but also in the North (the Soviet Union) and the East (India and the Arab world), along the rising tides of nationalism and socialist internationalism, and created hybrid localities that mark Emily Apter's "translation zone."

The first two chapters focus on the turn of the century and show how discourses of the harem, female empowerment, and national awakening are rehabilitated in literature in the form of a transnational cultural exchange. Peter Cherry in his chapter "World Literature as Performance: Turkish and British Women's Writing in Transcultural Dialogue at the Turn of the Twentieth Century" deals with the harem as the prolific producer in world literature of stereotypical images of women, appealing to Western readership. Cherry argues that travelogues by women of the nineteenth century, such as those of Grace Ellison and Zeyneb Hanım, reveal much information on the cultural hegemonies and dynamics between Britain and Turkey. He notes how the Imperial Harem, decorated with European furniture and artwork, served as a potential game changer for Ellison, a visitor in Istanbul who disguised herself as a Muslim Turk and compared and contrasted British discourses of domesticity and marriage with those in the Ottoman lands to talk about the disadvantages of women in both places. In an opposite vein, Zeynep Hanım, in London, observed British society and played with their expectancy to affirm the exoticism of the harem. Cherry critically elaborates on their performing Turkishness for the British audience and positions this role-playing on the world literature scene.

Şima İmşir and Anirudha Dhanawade focus on writer, feminist political activist, and spokesperson of Turkish nationalism Halide Edip (Adıvar) (1884–1964) in their chapter "'The Living Link between India and Turkey': Halide Edip on the Subcontinent." İmşir and Dhanawade argue that a close-up view of the turbulences caused by Halide Edip's 1935 trip to India can yield provocative insights to understand the influences of Turkish literature as world literature in India before independence. As a country struggling under European colonialism, India welcomed Halide Edip enthusiastically as a powerful symbol of a nation which had recently gained independence. Analyzing the Lahori translation of her 1922 novel *Ateşten Gömlek* (*The Shirt of Flame*), her lectures during her trip to India in 1935, and, finally, her 1937 book *Inside India*, İmşir and Dhanawade show how the appeal of Halide Edip in India revoked anxieties which characterized Indian culture and politics during the 1930s.

The three complementary chapters on Nâzım Hikmet in Part II of this volume point to an era wherein internationalism was a natural aspect of literary intellectual circles, particularly of those with left-aligned political engagements. Nâzım Hikmet, like many of his kind, is part of an international, transnational world of letters with highly mobile and oftentimes exilic members. What stand out in the chapters in this part are consistent references to friendship and solidarity, marking this particular "republic of letters" one of joined forces in a romantic battle for the improvement of the world order. That almost every international reference to Nâzım Hikmet's work passes through his poem "Angina Pectoris" is no coincidence, as poetry and revolutionary struggle is a matter of the heart for the poets of the era and Nâzım Hikmet, "the romantic communist," is a shining figure, a true representative of "Turkish literature as world literature."

Mediha Göbenli in her chapter "Nâzım Hikmet's Reception as World Poet" explores the two different phases in the reception of Nâzım Hikmet's poetry. The first phase is from the 1930s until the 1990s, in which Nâzım Hikmet's ideology was inseparable from his poetry. The second phase is Hikmet's later reception as a romantic poet that stresses the poetic and stylistic elements in his oeuvre. Tracing the circumstances around Nâzım Hikmet's becoming a prominent figure of world literature via the increasing popularity of his translated works in different parts of the world, such as Germany, France, the United Kingdom, and the United States, Göbenli charts the history of the Cold War, in which literature also served as a tool for the peace movement. Göbenli argues that Nâzım Hikmet's poetic voice of the Turkish left found resonances all around the world and his legacy is still alive in the freedom and peace movements.

Kenan Behzat Sharpe, in his chapter "The Internationalist Left and World Literature: The Case of Nâzım Hikmet in Greece," writes about Nâzım Hikmet's reception in Greece and the transnational relationships that are established through political engagement and solidarity. Also, more importantly, he refers to the Eurocentric limitations of Casanova's "republic of letters" and supplements it with voices from its periphery in communication with one another: Greece and Turkey. This circle, of course, has links to Europe via Paris, but their convergence hub is often primarily Moscow in dialogue with Paris, shifting the geographic weight along the lines of political relevance. Sharpe discusses how the world communist movement contributed to the popularity of Nâzım Hikmet, and explores more closely his domestication in Greece via translations by Yannis Ritsos, Stelios Mayiopoulos, and Aris Diktaios.

Mehmet Hakkı Suçin turns to the Arabic peninsula in his chapter "Nâzım Hikmet's Influence on Arabic Poetry" and focuses, exclusively, on the influence of Nâzım Hikmet on Palestinian poets Tawfiq Zayyād, Mahmoud Darwish, Samīh al-Qasīm, and Mu'īn Bseiso, in addition to the Egyptian poet Salah Abdel Sabour and the Iraqi poet Abd al-Wahhab al-Bayati. He discusses the impact of Nâzım Hikmet at the height of the rise of Arab socialism through the image of the poet as the advocate of the oppressed. He shows how Arab poets, with their primary interest and concern being on the side of the poor and the common people, adopted and reproduced Nâzım's themes and techniques. Suçin also turns to requiems written following the death of the poet to illustrate how Nâzım formed a haunting image for the Arab poets, as well as to the quality of the translations, to question whether they succeed in matching a similar dynamic rhythm in Arabic, in order to elaborate on how Nâzım Hikmet kept crossing national boundaries.

Chapters in Part III turn to the complicated problem of the political internationalization of literature and explore how translation goes hand in hand with the "domestication" of literary works. The third part of the volume, "Contemporary Forms and Cosmopolitanism," brings four chapters together that deal with contemporary works and figures of Turkish literature in the neoliberal period of media convergence, mass marketing, and international literary prizes, a period that requires closer examination for one to be able to talk about the recent dynamics of world literature. Two chapters in this last part turn to Orhan Pamuk, Turkey's 2006 (and only) Nobel Laureate and one of the most translated writers of Turkish literature, to discuss how works of literature can be well provided with national symbols while at the same time allowing a multiplicity that challenges the singularity attributed to the idea of the nation, and to elaborate on how such global works find their places in the world literature curriculum.

Başak Çandar shows the ways in which literary practice challenges and advances literary theory in her chapter "World Literary Refractions: Orhan Pamuk and Juan Goytisolo." She discusses Pamuk and Goytisolo as both national and global writers, whose works can be evaluated within the elliptical model of circulation postulated by Damrosch. She, however, argues that both Pamuk and Goytisolo denationalize the history and culture of their native countries and thus complicate the notion of cultural negotiation that underlies the idea of world literature, which assumes fixed national points in the elliptical trajectory. The national space in Pamuk and Goytisolo, Çandar shows is diversified and unstable and poses challenges to the elliptical model. With works indicating the multiplicity and syncretism of the national context, Çandar notes that world literature's reliance on the national as a category is *a priori* questionable.

Irmak Ertuna Howison in her chapter "Teaching *The Museum of Innocence* in Arts and Design Context" discusses Pamuk's securing a place in the world literature curriculum and elaborates on her experiences as an instructor in the classroom with Pamuk's 2008 novel *The Museum of Innocence* put in dialogue with two graphic novels, Özge Samancı's *Dare to Disappoint* (2015) and Marjane Satrapi's *Persepolis* (2000). She elaborates on how *The Museum of Innocence* served as a gateway for her students to understand global issues and cosmopolitanism, in a period marked by the rise of Donald Trump's anti-immigrant rhetoric and the looming global consequences of the climate crisis. Discussing how the trajectory of objects in the novels and the concept of museums helped the students grasp the ways in which objects are imbued with personal and cultural meanings, Ertuna Howison shows how literature helps us view the everyday world in its global connections.

The final two chapters of the volume turn to institutions, such as literary academies, honors, and prizes, and focus on the ways in which certain themes appeal to the world literary market and help writers position themselves as world literature in relation to the contemporary wave of authoritarian nationalism across the globe. These chapters also reveal how the power of literature and the popularity of literary figures are recognized by the market. Starting from the 1960s, the European intellectual impact on Turkish literature is replaced by the increasing domination of the United States in the spheres of arts and culture, while the publishing sector is transformed from a low-budget form of artistic endeavor to an industry with a much higher budget. Discussions in the last two chapters reflect that transformation and elaborate on how the industrialization of literature influenced literary institutions, honors, and prizes in Turkey and abroad. They point to the pressure on writers who attempt to resist the market hegemony, and highlight the new critical spaces these writers create through literature as a result.

Simla Doğangün's chapter "Elif Şafak and Her Fiction: Cultural Commodities of the Global Capital" elaborates on hybridity and cosmopolitanism, two popular concepts frequently used by the influential British-Turkish writer Elif Şafak to articulate both her identity and works and bring them into discussions with world literature. Traversing Şafak's literary universe, Doğangün explores *The Saint of Incipient Insanities* (2004) and *The Forty Rules of Love: A Novel of Rumi* (2010) in detail to discuss the ways in which these novels allude to major issues in world literature, and analyzes to what extent Şafak and her works themselves have become cultural commodities of the global capital.

Kaitlin Staudt in her chapter "For/Against the World: Literary Prizes and Political Culture in the 'New Turkey'" elaborates on "Ottoman Islamist" policies that resuscitate the cultural ties between Turkey and the former Ottoman lands. It explores how these policies treat literature as a means to political power which is expected to re-establish Turkey as a cultural center in the former Ottoman periphery. Staudt argues, however, that in the West, literary prizes treat writers from Turkey as human rights defenders under attack. Moving from conflicts in literary prizes as institutions to the case of Aslı Erdoğan, Staudt examines how Turkey's polarized culture is reflected in the world literature system.

While this volume was in development, several other texts of Turkish literature have been translated into English and other languages, a slow but invaluable enterprise. As more and more works reach out from their national literary space, it will be possible to assess the evolving position of Turkish literature as world literature. We hope this volume contributes to the steadily increasing number of discussions and inspires even more literary translations of Turkish literature, as well as further scholarly interest toward a more complex world literature system. We expect the border-crossings, cosmopolitanism, and hybridity that are explored in different contexts in this volume to produce generative insights and to inspire multiple works on Turkish literature as world literature in the near future. We expect our intervention to be supported by a widening of the scopes of both literary translations from Turkish and the scholarly discussions on them in the near future, in order for Turkish literature to appear on the world literary stage with all its complexities. While acknowledging the popular authors and texts of Turkish literature that traveled globally and discussing the ways they moved from the margins to the center, this volume is intended to flag the rich diversity of those left behind but equally make Turkish literature a world literature.

# References

Apter, Emily. (2006), *The Translation Zone: A New Comparative Literature*, Princeton, NJ: Princeton University Press.

Auerbach, Erich. (1969), "Philology and 'Weltliteratur'," Tr. Maire and Edward Said, *The Centennial Review* 13 (1): 1–17.

Casanova, Pascale. (2005), *The World Republic of Letters*, Tr. M. B. DeBevoise, Cambridge: Harvard University Press.

Casanova, Pascale. (2010), "Consecration and Accumulation of Literary Capital: Translation as Unequal Exchange," in M. Baker (ed.), *Critical Readings in Translation Studies*, 287–303, New York: Routledge.

Cheah, Pheng. (2014), "World Against Globe: Toward a Normative Conception of World Literature," *New Literary History* 45: 303–29.

Damrosch, David. (2006), "World Literature in a Postcanonical, Hypercanonical Age," in H. Saussy (ed.), *Comparative Literature in an Age of Globalization*, 43–53, Baltimore: The Johns Hopkins University Press.

Dino, Güzin. (1973), *La genèse du roman turc au XIXe siècle*, Paris: Publications orientalistes de France.

Djagalov, Rossen. (2017), "Literary Monopolists and the Forging of the Post-WWII People's Republic of Letters," in N. Skradol and E. Dobrenko (eds.), *Socialist Realism in Central and Eastern European Literatures under Stalin: Institutions, Dynamics, Discourses*, 25–37, London: Anthem Press.

Evin, Ahmet Ö. (1983), *The Origins and Development of the Turkish Novel*, Minneapolis: University of Minneapolis Press.

Halman, Talât Sait. (ed.), (1976), *Modern Turkish Drama: An Anthology of Plays in Translation*, Minneapolis and Chicago: Bibliotheca Islamica.
Halman, Talât Sait and Jayne L. Warner. (2008), *A Millennium of Turkish Literature: A Concise History*, New York: Syracuse University Press.
Mani, Venkat B. (2017), *Recoding World Literature: Libraries, Print Culture and Germany's Pact with Books*, New York: Fordham University Press.
Menemencioğlu, Nermin and Fahir İz. (1978), *Penguin Book of Turkish Verse*, Harmondsworth: Penguin.
Moran, Berna. (2012), *Der türkische Roman Eine Literaturgeschichte in Essays: Von Ahmet Mithat Bis A. H. Tanpınar*, Tr. Béatrice Hendrich, Wiesbaden: Harrassowitz Verlag.
Moretti, Franco. (2000), "Conjectures on World Literature," *New Left Review* 1: 54–68.
Seyhan, Azade. (2008), *Tales of Crossed Destinies: The Modern Turkish Novel in a Comparative Context*, New York: MLA.
Sılay, Kemal. (ed.) (1996), *An Anthology of Turkish Literature*, Bloomington: Indiana University Press.
Sökmen, Müge Gürsoy. (2020), "Being a Woman Publisher in Islamist Country," Bianet http://bianet.org/english/people/14841-being-a-woman-publisher-in-islamist-country (accessed January 20, 2020).
Spivak, Gayatri. (2003), *Death of a Discipline*, New York: Columbia University Press.

# PART I

# Breathing Turkish in the World Stage

# 1

# The Entangled History of Cosmopolitanism and Nationalism in Modern Turkish Literature

## *Fatih Altuğ*

The dominant vein in literary historiography in Turkey dates the beginning of modern Turkish literature to the 1860s. The first examples of modern poetry, drama, and criticism emerged in those years, and the genres of the novel and drama became central in the literary field shortly thereafter, in the 1870s. At the same time, traditional genres weakened, and after the 1870s the novel became the dominant genre in the different literatures of the Ottoman people (Ayaydın-Cebe 2009: 321; Charrière 2016: 40). The first novels of Turkish literature were published in Istanbul using Armenian, Greek, and Arabic scripts, and the first Armenian and Bulgarian novels were published there as well. Citizens of Istanbul created literary texts in Turkish, Greek, Armenian, Bulgarian, French, and Ladino. These modern literatures, which developed simultaneously and used different languages and scripts, made Istanbul an exceptional city for world literature. Peoples who had been living in the same city for centuries constructed a new literature in their own languages during these years.

In this milieu, Turkish was the main language of three distinct literatures, each of which used a different script and none of which interacted much with the others. Of these three literatures, the first novel written in Turkish using the Arabic script was *Taaşşuk-ı Talât u Fıtnat* (The Romance of Talât and Fitnat) (1872), written by Şemsettin Sami [Fraşeri] (Sâmi Frashëri), a lexicographer and prominent scholar of literature whose native language was Albanian. His publisher was Faris Shidyaq, who was also the author of the first Arabic novel, which had been published in Paris in 1855 (Strauss 2003: 56). The first novel written in Turkish using the Armenian script was *Akabi Hikayesi* (Akabi's Story) by Hovsep Vartanian, published in 1851, several years before Şemsettin Sami's novel. A third body of literature was written in Turkish using the Greek script, as epitomized by Evangelinos Misailidis's 1871 novel *Temaşa-i Dünya* (*Theatrum Mundi*).

Modern literary practices emerged simultaneously among different groups of Ottoman subjects. Literary translations between these languages were few, and each language formed its modern literature through translations from French. The paucity of interaction between the different literatures of the city meant that the plural literary field of nineteenth-century Istanbul failed to form a multilayered network of literature. That said, modern Ottoman literatures in different languages and scripts often had connections with one another through French literature, which served as a kind of mediator. This means that any effort to interpret the similarities and parallels between these literatures must also take French literature into account (Strauss 2003: 51). Etienne Charrière states that 95 percent of translated novels published in Istanbul were originally written in French: "In fact, in late-nineteenth-century Constantinople, translating a foreign literary work almost always meant translating a novel, and translating a novel almost always meant translating a French novel" (Charrière 2016: 40).

Istanbul was the locus of negotiation between French literature and Turkish, Armenian, Greek, and Bulgarian literatures. David Damrosch's elliptical model (2003: 283) can be useful in order to understand the literary dynamics of this period. We can think of each Istanbulite literature and French literature as two foci that generate an elliptical space, with nineteenth-century Istanbul becoming the intersection point of these literary ellipses. Speaking of this intersection, Namık Kemal, who is regarded as the "founding father" of modern Turkish literature, attributed the need for a new literature to the encounter between Ottoman literature (his writings rarely mention other literatures in the empire) and Western literature. This encounter weakened classical Ottoman literature, and the traditional genres of the *ghazal*, *mathnawi*, and *qasida* experienced rapid declines (Ayaydın Cebe 2009: 327). Namık Kemal called this incapacitating encounter a "shock" (*sadme*), and he looked to the basic dynamics of classical Ottoman and Western literatures to design a new literature.

In 1866, Namık Kemal penned a manifesto containing the basic principles of modern Turkish literature: "Lisan-ı Osmaninin Edebiyatı Hakkında Bazı Mülahazatı Şamildir" (Some Considerations about the Literature of the Ottoman Language). In this article, he lays out the basic principles of modern Turkish literature and discusses the encounter with Western literature, the deficiencies of classical Ottoman literature compared to ideal literature, and the things to be done to form a new literature (Namık Kemal 1866). Through the intense globalization of Western literature, Namık Kemal and his generation became aware of the weaknesses of their own literature. When they looked at classical literature from this new perspective, old school texts appeared unrealistic, anti-representational, and bombastic. Namık Kemal described classical literature as a dead carcass, a corpse. The enervating experience of the literary encounter with the West weakened the old literature, but it also empowered the agents of the new. They sought to jettison the old literature from the body of the nation and thus imagined the literary field as an empty space without any value. The emergence of a new literature required a fundamental rupture with, and an absolute devaluation of, the past.

Although they trivialized the classical literature, Namık Kemal and his generation were also forced to grapple with the problems inherent in using a foreign model to construct a new literature. In doing so, Namık Kemal used various universalization and localization tactics. According to Namık Kemal, literature was universal, and its basic principles were not bound by historical and geographical conditions. He believed that this universal literature was formed at a certain place in every age: first India, then ancient Greece, then the Abbasid Caliphate. In each, universal literature had flowered. Over time, however, Muslims abandoned the principles of verisimilitude and transparency which had given rise to this literature, and these were taken up by the West, which became the new locus of universal literature. This entangled logic of universalization and localization allowed Namık Kemal to efface the foreignness of Western literature (Altuğ 2007: 87–132).

The consistency of this model, in which both classical Arab and modern Western literature were representatives of a broader universal literature, involved a devaluation of classical Persian literature. Arabs, in Namık Kemal's theory, were estranged from their own literature over time, which had been rational and realistic, and the Ottomans were later influenced instead by Persian literature, which was corrupt, bombastic, unrealistic, and abject. The goal, as he presented it, was thus to eliminate the Persian influence and to construct a modern literature subject to the universal model represented by both classical Arabic and modern Western literature.

In Namık Kemal's view, modern Ottoman literature was not based on an absolute idea of Turkishness and a homogeneous center, but was a combination of classical Arabic literature, modern French literature, and Turkish. In the "garden" of Ottoman literature, the positive aspects of Eastern and Western literatures could come together; however, there was no place for other Ottoman literatures—including those with a non-Arabic script—in that garden. His model, while constructing a modern Turkish literature, also obliterated the literary space for other languages and alphabets, as well as the marks of classical Ottoman literature. Greek and Arabic literatures were precious only for their classical examples; the contemporary Greek and Arab peoples were followers of a corrupt literature far behind that of their forebears.

Namık Kemal conceived of legitimate literary relations as occurring only between the dominant languages, and this was connected to his notion of national sovereignty. Though a host of languages were used in Ottoman lands, Namık Kemal ignored virtually everything other than Turkish. He did not say even a single word about Armenian, Bulgarian, French, and Ladino literatures, though examples of them abounded in the very city around him. When he did mention other literatures, he did so in a derogatory way, as in the case of modern Greek and Arabic literature, which for him were characterized by backwardness. This derogatory tone was even more evident when it came to the Albanians and the Laz: he believed Turkish was so weak that it could not make even these peoples, who lacked so much as their own alphabets, forget their respective languages. From this example, one sees how closely the construction of a new literature was, for Namık Kemal, related to the domination of the other peoples in the empire. This is an important point where Namık Kemal's ideas of literary and political sovereignty intertwined.

Naoki Sakai's concept of "the schema of cofiguration" helps shed some light on the politics of inclusion and exclusion in these closely connected spheres of sovereignty:

> [T]he schema of *cofiguration* is a means by which a national community represents itself to itself, thereby constituting itself as a subject. But this auto-constitution of the national subject would not proceed unitarily, on the contrary, it would constitute itself only by making visible the figure of another with which it engages in a translational relationship. (1997: 15)

In this light, modern Turkish literature was constructed through a relational assemblage of modern French literature and classical Arab literature, but also through the exclusion of literatures of others under Ottoman rule, who were made invisible and thereby devalued.

Until recently, Turkish literary historiography has stuck to the principles and discourse of Namık Kemal. However, his was not the only model. Another was offered by his contemporary Ahmet Mithat, who was one of the most productive and influential writers of his time, with around two hundred works to his name. His novels often bear traces of the multicultural and cosmopolitan lives of the empire, especially in Istanbul. In his 1891 *Müşahedat* (The Observations), one of the most important literary experiments of the century, he classified the Turkish novel into two types: the national (*milli*) and the local (*yerli*) (Ahmet Mithat 1891). While the national novel speaks only of Muslims, the local novel involves people from different religions, ethnicities, and languages. *Müşahedat* was a local novel, and in it, Armenians, Arabs, Turks, and Catholics often interact with one another. The author himself is a character in the novel, and the processes of writing and reading the novel are included in its plot. Through this metafiction, we follow the plurality of the city and the layering of the novel; but at the end of the novel, all the protagonists unite under Islam, and the religious difference between them is eliminated.

Ahmet Mithat was not just a prolific author, but also one whose novels were widely transliterated and published in the Armenian and Greek scripts. *Müşahedat* testifies to this through one of its main characters, an Armenian woman named Siranush, who has read Ahmet Mithat's *Felatun Bey ile Rakım Efendi* (Felatun Bey and Rakım Efendi) in the Armeno-Turkish script. His works were also translated into other languages, including Tatar, and he was one of the most important actors in the literary relations between Istanbul and Kazan (Bargan 2016). The wide dissemination of his novels in different scripts and languages, and thus among different communities, made him perhaps the most influential Ottoman author. Although he does not give up his authorial sovereignty in the novels and sees Muslim Turks as dominant, Ahmet Mithat nevertheless presents a completely different perspective from Namık Kemal in terms of representing the plurality of Ottoman society and the relations among the Turkish languages with different languages and scripts.

## The New Relations and Tensions of the 1890s

In the 1890s, three groups emerged in modern Turkish literature. In the first were prolific writers in the field of popular literature, including Ahmet Mithat, Ahmet Rasim, Mehmet Celal, and Vecihi. In the decade when book publishing was on the rise (Ayaydın Cebe 2009: 128), these writers became the bestseller authors of their day—it was their work that ordinary people read the most. In the second group were a group of writers gathered around the journal *Servet-i Fünun* (Wealth of Sciences), which began to be published in 1896. This group included such writers as Tevfik Fikret, Halid Ziya, and Mehmet Rauf. They radically changed the schema of Namık Kemal, replacing classical Arabic literature, which he had held in high esteem, with a new form of literature connected to the symbolist, decadent, and Parnassian movements of French literature. One of the first experiments with the stream-of-consciousness technique in world literature occurred in Recaizade Ekrem's novel *Araba Sevdası* (A Carriage Affair), which was serialized in this journal. Tevfik Fikret's poem "La danse serpentine" (Serpentine Dance) and Halid Ziya's story "Mösyö Kanguru" (Monsieur Kangaroo), which were published there as well, were both influenced by the serpentine dance which had been invented and popularized by Loie Fuller and which Mallarme had taken as a model for his poems (Altuğ 2019).

Relations between these two groups were anything but cordial. In the debates over the dichotomies of popularity and excellence, localness and foreignness, and intelligibility and ambiguity, the first group accused *Servet-i Fünun* of cosmopolitanism, which connoted excessive openness to the French, while *Servet-i Fünun* found the popular authors literarily and aesthetically outdated and reactionary (Gökçek 2014: 15–27). Although the Turkish poems of Jewish poets such as Avram Naon and Isak Ferera appeared in *Servet-i Fünun*, the journal was far from representative of the linguistic and literary diversity of the empire.

Although both of these groups were dominated by men, and although *Servet-i Fünun* was basically a men's journal, a generation of female writers also emerged in the closing years of the 1890s, and these constitute the third group in modern Turkish literature during the period. Some of the writers in this group, such as Zafer Hanım and Fatma Aliye, had published novels before. But it was with the publication of *Hanımlara Mahsus Gazete* (Newspaper for Ladies) that the poems, stories, and novels of such other female authors as Nigâr Hanım, Makbule Leman, Fatma Fahrünnisa, Emine Semiye, and Güzide Sabri began to appear one after another. This community defined itself as women's literature: "woman writers" addressing their work to "woman readers." The increase in the number of educated women during the period caused a rapid increase in the number of female writers and readers. Moreover, although the literature of *Servet-i Fünun* established a much more intense relationship with French literature, female writers were more frequently translated into other languages. Some works of Fatma Aliye were translated into English for the Chicago World's Fair, her *Udi* (Lute Player) was translated into French, and her *Nisvan-ı İslam* (Women of Islam) was translated into French and Arabic. It was also possible to read the novels of Fatma Aliye, Emine Semiye, and Güzide Sabri in Serbian (Taşçıoğlu 2006: 435). The French, English, and German newspapers of the time published articles by a number of Ottoman female writers, especially Nigâr Hanım and Fatma Aliye. This group contacted European female writers such as Carmen Sylva, whose novels were translated into Turkish.

Since they did not conform to the stereotypical images of Ottoman women held by the European literary community, the female Ottoman writers of the 1890s attracted more acclaim in world literature than their male counterparts. However, among the almost 16,000 texts listed in the *İstanbul Kütüphanelerindeki Eski Harfli Türkçe Kadın Dergileri Bibliyografyası (1869–1927)* (Bibliography of Women's Magazines in Turkish in the Old Script in the Libraries of Istanbul), no more than twenty were written by non-Muslim Ottoman female writers (Toska et al. 1993). Although women who wrote in Turkish had the opportunity to reach readers who knew French, English, Arabic, and Serbian through translations, the readers of these journals encountered hardly anything written by other female writers in the same empire. However, there were some exceptions, such as Theodossia

Sartinska, who published sixteen issues of the journal *Marifet* (Merit), beginning in 1898. Theodossia, a native Greek, published this magazine in Turkish and French and was the first Ottoman woman to obtain a license for magazine publication.

The fin de siècle was also the period in which the term "world literature" (*cihan edebiyatı*) first appeared in the Ottoman literary public. Halid Ziya Uşaklıgil, the most prominent novelist of *Servet-i Fünun*, wrote essays during the early 1890s on Sanskrit, Hebrew, Russian, Finnish, and Swedish literatures in the journal *Mekteb* (The School). He also later published books on French, German, and Spanish literatures, in the 1910s. The *Tableau de l'histoire littéraire du monde* (1899) of Frederic Loliée, one of the early historians of world literature (D'haen 2011: 18, 171), was translated into Turkish by Mehmet Ali Ayni in 1902 as *Tarih-i Edebî-i Âlem* (Literary History of the World). But it was Mehmet Rauf, one of the most important critics writing for *Servet-i Fünun*, who did the most to popularize the term.

In his 1901 article "Edebiyatımız ve Avrupa" (Our literature and Europe), Mehmet Rauf attributed the existence of national literatures to limitations in the relations among nations. He argued that the idea of a single European literature arose because of the freedom of exchange among European literatures, but for him, the idea of world literature should be the ideal in the twentieth century (Mehmet Rauf 1901). This desire, expressed in economic terms, was tantamount to the elimination of protectionism and the rise to dominance of free exchange in literature. When the process of translating all Far Eastern literature into European literature had been completed, he believed, it would then be possible to have a world literature in which the similarities between different literatures increased and the whole world effectively became a single continent (Damak 2018: 120–1). Mehmet Rauf's ideas played an important role in the emergence of the notion of "world literature," although he put Europe at the center of the relationship and thought of translation as a one-way street.

## The Literature of the Second Constitutional Era: The Tide of Cosmopolitanism and Nationalism

In 1908, Sultan Abdülhamid II was dethroned and the Second Constitution was declared, marking a new era of burgeoning literary encounters. More Turkish books were published in the five years after 1908 than had been published in the entire nineteenth century. Detective stories and erotic texts began to dominate the literature market and were associated with this boom in publication (Schick 2011: 198). Moreover, literary interactions among the different Ottoman national communities increased to an unprecedented level. The 600-page novel *Abdülhamid ve Sherlock Holmes* (Abdülhamid and Sherlock Holmes), written by Yervant Odyan and marked by literary score-settling with the old regime, was serialized in Armenian and Turkish in 1911. In 1912, Greek, French, Albanian, and Bulgarian translations of the novel were also published (Şahin 2017: 10–11). This detective novel, which was published in six languages spoken in the empire within a single year, illustrates one of the highest points of literary interaction in the Ottoman Empire. Literary translations between languages also increased. Although there had been literary translations from Turkish to Armenian before, there were previously very few translations from Armenian to Turkish.

In the 1913 *Ermeni Edebiyatı Numuneleri* (Samples from Armenian literature), Turkish translations of the stories of the leading Armenian writers of the time were presented with prefaces written by such writers as Süleyman Nazif, Şahabettin Süleyman, and Abdullah Cevdet, who said they regretted not knowing enough Armenian literature (Srents 1913). The same period witnessed the diversification of women's journalism and literature. Where between 1895 and 1908 the *Hanımlara Mahsus Gazete* was the sole women's periodical, by 1908 there were four different women's magazines, and by 1914 there were eight. Moreover, this period also saw an intensification of relations among the different women's literatures of the empire. For example, the journal *Demet* (Bouquet) prepared issues around special themes, introducing Zabel Asadur, Srpouhi Dussap, and Zabel Yesayan, the leading female writers of modern Armenian literature, and presenting examples of their works.

Another trend in this period was an increase in the number of bilingual journals. The first modern literary works in languages such as Syriac, Kurdish, and Circassian were produced only after the dawn of the twentieth century, and these languages became visible in the world of publication and literature through a number of bilingual journals after 1908, including *Mürşid-i Asuriyun* (1909–14) and *Kevkeb Mednbo* (1910–12) in Syriac and Turkish, *Kürt Teavün ve Terakki Gazetesi* (1908–9) and *Rojî Kurd* (1913) in Kurdish and Turkish, and *Ğuaze* (1911–14) in Circassian and Turkish (Yekdeş and Erdem 2014; Trigona-Harany 2008; Besleney 2014). These journals sought ways to be both Ottoman and Assyrian, Kurdish, and Circassian, and they published work from well-known intellectuals and writers such as Abdullah Cevdet and Süleyman Nazif.

Fuad Köprülü, the founder of the discipline of Turkish literature at the Darülfünun (House of Sciences, now Istanbul University), offered a manifesto and summary of the basic principles of the historiography of national literature in an article titled "Türk Edebiyatı Tarihinde Usul" (Method in the History of Turkish literature) in 1913, the same year he became a professor at the university. The pioneer of the nationalist literary imagination, however, had been a complete anti-nationalist in the period between 1908 and 1913, when he defended literary cosmopolitanism. In 1913, during the Balkan

Wars, the Ottoman Empire was defeated by the Balkan states, which had only recently broken from its rule. Before this traumatic event, Köprülü, who saw Ottomanness as a heterogeneous assemblage of various peoples, ethnicities, and religions, had clashed with the rising Turkish nationalism of those years. He had opposed attempts to simplify and localize the language, emphasizing that the Ottoman language was heterogeneous, just like the Ottomans. In his article "Edebiyatlar Arasında" (Between Literatures), he argued that a purely national literature was impossible, and that literature was necessarily comparative and transnational. According to him, national literature emerged as a derivative of the complex networks of relations constructed among literatures (Köprülü 1911).

Although he had a heterogeneous and plural understanding of Ottomanism and Ottoman language, Köprülü's agenda in this period nevertheless lacked any trace of the other literatures of the empire. Köprülü assessed the development of Scandinavian literatures by writing in-depth analyses of writers and critics such as Henrik Ibsen and Georg Brandes, but he had no interest in the Armenian, Greek, Bulgarian, Arab, and Persian literatures of his time. While the relationality between classical Arabic and modern French literature was central to Namık Kemal's formula for Ottoman literature, Köprülü regarded modern Ottoman literature as a part of European literature. In this respect, he focused on Norwegian, Danish, and Russian literature and attempted to think about how literatures on the periphery of Europe strengthened and influenced the center. Taking the influence of writers such as Ibsen, Dostoevsky, and Tolstoy and of critics such as Brandes on French literature as an example, he offered models for Ottoman literature to move from the periphery to the center.

In his model, however, literary Europeanization based on the dynamics of center-periphery relations did not include neighboring literatures. In any event, the Balkan Wars precluded any more inclusive literary approach and pushed Köprülü to embrace the national literature paradigm, whose founding representative he became at the university. The trauma of the Balkan Wars led other writers down a similar path, including Yakup Kadri Karaosmanoğlu, Refik Halid Karay, and Halide Edib Adıvar, all of whom became more nationalist and joined the national literature group. In the words of the historian Erik Jan Zürcher, describing the role of the Balkan Wars in the rise of nationalism, "Pan-Turkism gained a certain amount of support among Young Turk intellectuals, but it received no official blessing until the Balkan War of 1913 had made Ottomanism a dead letter anyway. Even then, however, it remained more of a romantic dream offering an escape from the disasters of day-to-day politics than a concrete policy" (2004: 130).

The relationship between cosmopolitanism and nationalism is not based on a binary opposition. In Köprülü's discourse, cosmopolitanism in literature is a prerequisite for national literature. These are not mutually exclusive but entangled. Köprülü's favorite critic Georg Brandes, one of the earliest theoreticians of world literature, explained this entanglement in his article "World Literature" (1899):

> When Goethe coined the term "world literature," humanism and cosmopolitanism were still ideas that everyone held in honour. In the last years of the nineteenth century, an ever stronger and more jealous national sentiment has caused these ideas to recede almost everywhere. Today literature is becoming more and more national. But I do not believe that nationality and cosmopolitanism are incompatible. The world literature of the future will be all the more interesting, the more strongly its national stamp is pronounced and the more distinctive it is, even if, as art, it also has its international side; for that which is written directly for the world will hardly appear as a work of art. (D'haen 2011: 156)

The tension between cosmopolitanism and nationalism may vary depending on the historical context, but cosmopolitanism and nationalism are always intertwined. This was also true for the national literature paradigm, which had been on the rise since 1908. The journal *Genç Kalemler* (Young Pens) (1910–12) presented the basic ideas of the national literature. In this journal, Ziya Gökalp, Ali Canip Yöntem, and Ömer Seyfettin explained their projects for nationalizing language and literature. According to Ali Canip, since the literature of *Servet-i Fünun* could not bond with Turkishness, and because a scratch of the surface revealed an underlying Frenchness, it was "cosmopolitan." He and his fellows at *Genç Kalemler* had themselves been followers of Western literature and had not sought out a national literature, which suddenly emerged on its own (Ali Canip [1911] 1999: 64). In this perspective, national literature was also related to the external and was influenced by the cosmopolitan; however, unlike the cosmopolitan, the national can appropriate this influence.

The article "Yeni Lisan" (New language), written by Ali Canip and Ziya Gökalp and one of the main texts of the national literature paradigm in Turkey, exemplifies the differentiation of internationalization, nation, and ethnicity and the opposition between the national and the cosmopolitan. Bekir Fahri, an opponent of national literature, claimed that he felt Turkish, Albanian, Armenian, Bulgarian, Greek, Kurdish, and even "French and English" at the same time; he argued that there could not be a national literature, and that literature could only be international, universal (Ali Canip and Ziya Gökalp [1911] 1999: 108). However, *Genç Kalemler* thought that science was international, that politics was national, and that language was about ethnicity. In this context, the national expressed a political commitment: the citizens of the Ottoman Empire constituted the Ottoman nation. However, literature and language were not about being

Ottoman; there was no Ottoman literature surrounding and addressing every citizen—each community had its own literature and language.

In the approach laid out in "Yeni Lisan," it was wrong in politics to prioritize ethnicity over the Ottoman nation; but in language and literature, it was wrong to prioritize the nation over ethnicity. Members of the Ottoman nation had their own Turkish, Arabic, Armenian, Bulgarian, and Greek literatures, and therefore the concept of Ottoman literature carried the potential danger of eliminating these ethnic literatures. While the Ottoman ethnicities gathered around the concept of the Ottoman nation politically, they ought to continue to protect their ethnic languages and literatures (Ali Canip and Ziya Gökalp [1911] 1999: 108). In this article, mainstream men of letters recognized the literatures of neighboring peoples, but paradoxically, they did so only to prevent the idea of a future cosmopolitan literature. In their conception of Ottoman literature, hybridity and cosmopolitanism were either impossible or dangerous, and the intertwining of literatures inevitably led to the death of national literatures.

In the article "Milli, Daha Doğrusu Kavmi Edebiyat Ne Demektir" (What is National, or rather, What is Ethnic Literature?), Ali Canip, writing against Fuad Köprülü, notes that cosmopolitanism increased after the downfall of Abdülhamid II and the start of the Second Constitutional Period (Ali Canip [1912] 1999). While all the nations of the world—Germans, Russians, the Japanese, Italians, Spaniards, and "even" Greeks, Armenians, Arabs, and Albanians—were proud of their ethnicities, the Turks were deprived of theirs. Ali Canip thus proposed a national literature that availed itself fully of the resources of the outside but that was original and authentic in doing so. It was the city, mainly Istanbul, which was "the nest of the cosmopolitan, partly looking . . . like China and partly belonging to the West, and, like monkeys in our homeland, imitating—good or bad—everything, all the ins and outs of which have gotten Byzantine" (Ali Canip 1927: 167). While the globalism of the city had led to the destruction of the empire, the worldview of the provinces of the empire had given rise to a patriotic spirit. Although the peoples of the provinces were originally Circassians, Kurds, Albanians, and various mixings thereof, they united under the ideal of Turkishness. Ali Canip imagines Turkishness as a supra-identity. For him, being a Turk in the present day was an example of the "new person," the Nietzschean *Übermensch* (Ali Canip 1927: 167), regardless of ethnicities.

In *Genç Kalemler*, Turkishness had an ambivalent status. On the one hand, it expressed an existing ethnic characteristic; on the other, it pointed to an ideal. While each society's right to its own literature implied an already evident national difference, the producers of the anti-cosmopolitan literature of the Turkish *Übermensch* ideal were themselves a heterogeneous group. When the Muslim peoples of the empire were gathered together under the umbrella of Turkishness, the difference between the ethnic and the national blurred, as can be seen in the title of Ali Canip's article. While Turkish literature was the literature of one of the many ethnicities that constituted the Ottoman nation, it broadened into a form of national literature in its own right, in line with the broadening of the notion of Turkishness itself, as the literature of all Muslim Anatolian peoples working together. That said, this conception of Turkish literature excluded Arabs in addition to non-Muslims, for in Ali Canip's mind, while non-Muslims were cosmopolitan elements who did not rightfully belong, Arabs were not native residents of Anatolia. So universal Turkish identity became an umbrella category only for the non-Arab Muslim peoples of Anatolia.

## The Triumph of National Literature

The national literature paradigm became the main paradigm after the collapse of the Ottoman Empire. A decade of war (1912–22) had radically changed the population of the region, and wars, massacres, forced migrations, and population exchange shattered the material basis of alternative literary imaginations, leaving only national literature. Ziya Gökalp, the ideological pioneer of both the late Union and Progress Party and the early republic, was the most important agent of this transition period. Gökalp appointed Fuad Köprülü as professor of literature at the Darülfünun in 1913, and he was also the founding figure of Turkish nationalism. In his presentation of the ideal national position in every aspect of life in his *Türkçülüğün Esasları* (The Principles of Turkism), the main enemy was, again, cosmopolitanism (Ziya Gökalp 1968). Cosmopolitanism was considered dangerous because it did not accept the nation as the necessary intermediary between the individual and civilization; both nationalism and internationalism, in contrast, put the nation at the center of life.

However, according to Gökalp's nationalism, the individual was only meaningful as a member of a biological species, and it was the relationship between the nation and the individual that determined the national social life. In this respect, the Ottomans, being cosmopolitan in all respects, despised the Turks. Gökalp's approach was based on easy distinctions between individuals, nations, and internationalism, as if there were no contexts where different nations lived side by side and intertwined with one another. Therefore, although cosmopolitanism was represented and criticized as a direct relationship between the individual and civilization, what was really excluded was a heterogeneous network that did not fit into the definition of a pure nation and that was produced by the entangled relations of people of different religions, languages, and nations.

For Gökalp, constructing a national literature would be possible by modeling Turkish folk literature and classical Western literature simultaneously. The long-term aim of a national literature would be realized by excluding contemporary European and classical Ottoman literature—it would be a literature under which Azerbaijanis, Uzbeks, Tatars, and

Kazakhs could merge. Gökalp revealed his utopia as a kind of Turkic internationalism. In terms of the short-term goal, Gökalp stated that the aesthetic values of European civilization would be used to destroy the classical Ottoman aesthetics, which had been under the influence of Iran, but added that European values would not be allowed to replace national values. As Orhan Koçak claims, this formula would be the official policy of the state in the 1940s (2001: 370).

In his 1927 article "Edebiyat Tedrisatının Yeni Veçhesi Çocukları Kozmopolit Yapar mı?" (Will the New Direction in Literary Education Make Children Cosmopolitan?), Ali Canip addressed concerns over whether the reading of Greek, Latin, English, German, French, and Italian literature would make students cosmopolitan, for European literature had not been included in literature textbooks before the republic. Ali Canip attributed universality to European literature by referring to the literatures above as "world literatures," and he believed these literatures were superior to the national literature; he thus argued that education which employed these world literatures would not have a "negative" influence.

In the writings of this period, one sees a dual process at work. On the one hand, the desire for a national literature took on a more concrete shape, and an answer was sought to the question of "what the literature of Turkish reform should be." On the other hand, the backwardness of Turkish literature vis-à-vis "world literatures" was accepted as a given, and it was thought that there was both a qualitative and a temporal difference between national literature and world literatures. Therefore, contemporary Turkish literature was always treated as somewhat deficient, lacking a single work that met the criteria of nationality and literariness. Therefore, since world literatures were accepted as being in a position of dominance, the severity and permissible extent of their influence on Turkish literature was always a subject of debate.

In 1936, Nusret Safa Coşkun asked the writers of the period, "Can we create national literature?" (Coşkun [1936] 2019). Most of the answers to this question emphasized that the pressure to be national did harm to literature. Good literature, it was argued, was naturally national in character; but literary efforts that aimed primarily to be national often made poor literature. The entangled tensions between literariness, nationality, and worldliness would go on to produce a variety of positions in the cultural atmosphere of the following years. And while cosmopolitanism lost ground as an overt "threat," it continued to exist as an accusation. For example, in Hikmet Kıvılcımlı's *Edebiyat-ı Cedide'nin Otopsisi* (The Autopsy of the New Literature), one of the first examples of socialist literary critique in Turkey, cosmopolitanism was a part of the character of the bourgeois *Servet-i Fünun* (Kıvılcımlı 1935). Kıvılcımlı positioned cosmopolitanism, considered along with passivity, as being opposed to universal thought and international ideals, reformulating cosmopolitan literature as emulating the West by eliminating and demeaning its own local reality.

## Conclusion

Beginning in the 1940s, the literary and cultural policy of the republic became slightly more open to the outside and the past. Hasan Âli Yücel, the minister of national education, initiated a project to translate into Turkish a wide repertoire of works ranging from Greek and Latin classics to twentieth-century literature. Reading the classics was encouraged, and these translations were included in the curriculum (Koçak 2001: 393–8). A few examples of classical Arabic and Persian literature even made their way in; and while classical Islamic poems were translated into prose, losing much of their aesthetic appeal in the process, these translations point to a change in the long-standing rejection of classical Islamic literature. Under the project, a more complex cultural assemblage was established, one that was still Western-centered but that also made some room for other literatures of the past. Most of the new writers of the period worked as translators at the Tercüme Bürosu (Translation Office), and their translations played a great role in introducing the next generations to world literature. Şehnaz Tahir Gürçağlar refers to the increasing frequency in the use of the title "world literature" during the period:

> One interesting difference between the series of canonical and of semi and non-canonical literary works lay in their titles. Throughout the 1940s and 1950s, series with a claim to canonical literature adopted names that identified them with "world literature." "Translations from World Literature," "Translations from World Authors" and "Selected Works from World Literature" (...) are only three examples among many. In my view, these series intended to highlight the universal appeal and prestige of their books. (Gürçağlar 2008: 172–3)

In 1948, the first original history of world literature, Fehmi Yahya Tuna's *Dünya Edebiyatı Tarihi*, was published. Tuna had been a student of Professor Erich Kunze at the *Deutsche Akademie* in Munich in 1943 and learned a new methodology of literary history from Kunze. Although he did not give specific details about that methodology, his book is one of the most comprehensive literary histories written in Turkish. He classified national literatures according to geographical region, from Africa to Europe, and presented historical periods and literary figures of almost all national literatures, including Burmese, Tibetan, Manchurian, Thai, Nepalese, Caucasian, Georgian, Ethiopian, Syriac, Armenian, Arabic, Albanian, and Romanian literatures (Tuna 2019).

In the 1950s, the literary field in Turkey began to polarize between two camps, that of modernist, aesthetic-autonomist writers and those with various leftist inclinations. Especially between 1960 and 1980, the leftists enjoyed great cultural power and the texts of socially and politically oriented writers led the translations from Turkish literature into other languages in these years. The works of Nâzım Hikmet, Aziz Nesin, and Orhan Kemal were translated not only into the languages of the socialist bloc and Western Europe but also into Arabic and Persian. Following the establishment of the Afro-Asian Writers Association, Turkish left-aligned writers participated in its meetings and in 1982 Ataol Behramoğlu won the association's Lotus Prize. Yet, even in these years, when a growing number of Turkish poems extolled anti-imperialist movements and men of letters from Turkey established relationships with the litterateurs of Africa and Asia, little if anything was written about international socialist literary ideals.

Turkey's prominent leftist critics defined themselves as nationalists and the mainstream Turkish leftists of the 1960s incorporated nationalism into their political and literary discourses (Doğan 2010). Although there were many differences among them, the writers of this group all retained Turkey's long-standing opposition to cosmopolitanism. According to Attilâ İlhan, a left-aligned author of poems, novels, and critiques active from the 1950s onward, there were two obstacles: Islamism and comprador cosmopolitanism. For İlhan, the 1940s, which saw the expansion of Turkish literature's cultural boundaries and its partial opening to other literatures, were a period in which support for cultural cosmopolitanism had led to an estrangement from Atatürk's national-cultural policy and the rise of the so-called Garip poetry (İlhan 1993: 233).

For Asım Bezirci, one of the most productive socialist critics of the period, capitalism proposed a cosmopolitan culture against the national culture. According to him, cosmopolitanism acted as if it would unite all the people and the world, but in doing so actually sought to destroy patriotism and national values and erase them from memory, thus providing a cover for the expansionism of imperialism (Bezirci [1979] 1997: 87). For Kemal Tahir, another left-aligned novelist and thinker, nineteenth-century modernization and the Tanzimat reform era had created a Turkish cosmopolite: it was impossible to find true Turkishness in Istanbul, where the Byzantine spirit lived on. True Turks remained only in the rural areas but had no place in the corrupt urban culture (Tahir 1989: 109). This was an almost exact repetition of *Genç Kalemler*'s argument from the beginning of the century.

From the 1850s, the dawn of the Ottoman publishing era, to the 1980s, when modern literary works began to be published in more than one language and script, one sees that as monolingualism strengthened, nationalism became an indispensable intermediary in people's relationship with world literature. The national literary discourse, which became the basic paradigm after 1913, frequently accused its rivals of being cosmopolitan. While the multilingual literary modernizations of the various communities in the nineteenth-century Ottoman Empire had rich potential for world literature discussions, the lack of interaction between these communities meant that a literary cosmopolitanism was never fully realized. Nevertheless, the ghost of this possibility, in the caricatured form of rootlessness and excessive admiration for and imitation of the French, continued to haunt national literature. With the rise of multiculturalism in the 1980s, attempts to better understand the other literatures of Turkey and to better appreciate the relationship between these literatures and Turkish literature have increased. The national literature paradigm continues to struggle with these attempts. Purely nationalist and purely cosmopolitan literary projects always run the risk of eliminating literary pluralism and heterogeneity. Accepting and exploring the entanglement of nationalism and cosmopolitanism in the history of Turkish literature is a prerequisite for better understanding both Turkish literature as a world literature and the inner worlds of this intricate literary field.

# References

Ahmet Mithat. ([1891] 2000), *Müşahedat*, Ankara: Türk Dil Kurumu.
Ali Canip. ([1911] 1999), "Düne Nazaran Bugün," in İ. Parlatır and N. Çetin (eds.), *Genç Kalemler Dergisi*, 61-4, Ankara: Türk Dil Kurumu.
Ali Canip. ([1912] 1999), "Milli, Daha Doğrusu Kavmi Edebiyat Ne Demektir," in İ. Parlatır and N. Çetin (eds.), *Genç Kalemler Dergisi*, 162-67, Ankara: Türk Dil Kurumu.
Ali Canip. (1927), "Edebiyat Tedrisatının Yeni Veçhesi Çocukları Kozmopolit Yapar mı?" *Hayat* 3 (3): 164-7.
Ali Canip and Ziya Gökalp. ([1911] 1999), "Yeni Lisan," in İ. Parlatır and N. Çetin (eds.), *Genç Kalemler Dergisi*, 105-9, Ankara: Türk Dil Kurumu.
Altuğ, Fatih. (2007), "Namık Kemal'in Edebiyat Eleştirisinde Modernlik ve Öznellik," PhD diss., Turkish Language and Literature, Boğaziçi University.
Altuğ, Fatih. (2019), "Mecralar Arasında Hareket, Beden ve Şiddet: 'La Danse Serpentine' ve 'Mösyö Kanguru'yu Birlikte Okumak," in D. Küçük and M. Narcı (eds.), *Siyah Endişe: Bir Asır Sonu Anlatısı Olarak Halit Ziya Anlatısı*, 161-88, İstanbul: İletişim.
Ayaydın Cebe, Günil Özlem. (2009), "19. Yüzyılda Osmanlı Toplumu ve Basılı Türkçe Edebiyat: Etkileşimler, Değişimler, Çeşitlilik," PhD diss., Turkish Literature, Bilkent University.
Bargan, Hüseyin. (2016), "Şemseddin Sami ve İdil-Ural Tatarları," *Türkiyat Mecmuası* 26 (1): 51-60.
Besleney, Zeynel Abidin. (2014), *The Circassian Diaspora in Turkey*, London: Routledge.
Bezirci, Asım. ([1979] 1997), *Halk ve Sosyalizm için Kültür ve Edebiyat*, İstanbul: Evrensel.
Charrière, Etienne. (2016), "'We Must Ourselves Write About Ourselves': The Trans-Communal Rise of the Novel in the Late Ottoman Empire," PhD diss., Comparative Literature, University of Michigan.
Coşkun, Nusret Safa. ([1936] 2019), *Milli Bir Edebiyat Yaratabilir miyiz?* Ankara: Çolpan.
D'haen, Theo. (2011), *The Routledge Concise History of World Literature*, London: Routledge.

Damak, Fatma. (2018), "Servet-i Fünundan 'Cihanî' Edebiyata," MA diss., Turkish Language and Literature, Boğaziçi University.
Damrosch, David. (2003), *What Is World Literature?* Princeton: Princeton University Press.
Doğan, Erkan. (2010), "Articulating Socialism with Nationalism: A Critical Analysis of Nationalism in the Turkish Leftist Tradition in the 1960s," PhD diss., Political Science, Bilkent University.
Gökçek, Fazıl. (2014), *Bir Tartışmanın Hikâyesi Dekadanlar*, İstanbul: Dergâh.
Gürçağlar, Şehnaz Tahir. (2008), *The Politics and Poetics of Translation in Turkey: 1923-1960*, Amsterdam: Rodopi Publishing.
İlhan, Attilâ. (1993), *Hangi Edebiyat*, Ankara: Bilgi.
Kıvılcımlı, Hikmet. (1935), *Edebiyat-ı Cedide'nin Otopsisi*, İstanbul: Necm-i İstiklal.
Koçak, Orhan. (2001), "1920lerden 1970lere Kültür Politikaları," in *Kemalizm*, 370-418, İstanbul: İletişim.
Köprülü, Fuad. (1911), "Edebiyatlar Arasında," *Servet-i Fünun* 41 (1043): 54-58.
Mehmet Rauf. (1901), "Edebiyatımız ve Avrupa," *Servet-i Fünun* 523: 38-44.
Namık Kemal. (1866), "Lisan-ı Osmaninin Edebiyatı Hakkında Bazı Mülahazatı Şamildir," *Tasvir-i Efkâr* 417 (1866): 1-3.
Şahin, Seval. (2017), "Önsöz," in Y. Odyan, *Abdülhamid ve Sherlock Holmes*, 7-11, İstanbul: Everest.
Sakai, Naoki. (1997), *Translation and Subjectivity*, Minnesota: University of Minnesota Press.
Schick, Irvin Cemil. (2011), "Print Capitalism and Women's Sexual Agency in the Late Ottoman Empire," *Comparative Studies of South Asia, Africa and the Middle East* 31 (1): 196-216.
Srents, Sarkis. ([1913] 2012), *Ermeni Edebiyatı Numuneleri*, İstanbul: Aras.
Strauss, Johann. (2003), "Who Read What in the Ottoman Empire (19th-20th Centuries)?" *Middle Eastern Literatures* 6 (1): 39-76.
Tahir, Kemal. (1989), *Notlar: Sanat Edebiyat 1*, İstanbul: Bağlam.
Taşçıoğlu, Yılmaz. (2006), "Balkanlarda Yeni Türk Edebiyatı Literatürü," *Türkiye Araştırmaları Literatür Dergisi* 4 (7): 429-77.
Toska, Zehra, et al. (1993), *İstanbul Kütüphanelerindeki Eski Harfli Türkçe Kadın Dergileri Bibliyografyası* (1869-1927), İstanbul: Metis.
Trigona-Harany, Benjamin Oliver Sunny. (2008), "İntibâh or Hâb-ı Gaflet: Âşûr Yûsuf, Naûm Fâik and the Ottoman Süryânî," MA diss., History, Boğaziçi University.
Tuna, Fehmi Yahya. ([1948] 2019), *Dünya Edebiyatı Tarihi*, İstanbul: Kesit.
Yekdeş, Ömer Faruk and Erdem, Servet. (2014), "Bölücü Bir Edebiyat mı Bölünmüş bir Edebiyat mı?: Geç Osmanlı Dönemi Kürt Edebiyat(lar)ı," in M. F. Uslu and F. Altuğ (eds.), *Tanzimat ve Edebiyat*, 327-58, İstanbul: Türkiye İş Bankası Yayınları.
Ziya Gökalp. (1968), *Türkçülüğün Esasları*, İstanbul: Varlık.
Zürcher, Erik Jan. (2004), *Turkey: A Modern History*, London: I. B. Tauris.

# 2

# Translation, Transcription, and the Making of World Literature

# On Late Ottoman and Modern Turkish Scriptworlds

*Etienne E. Charrière*

As reported in the press (Taştekin 2015), protesters stood in front of the Ministry of National Education in Ankara in April 2015, holding banners that read *Alfabeme dokunma!* (Hands off my alphabet!). Few in number but firm in their resolve, the protesters belonged to one of modern Turkey's largest ethnic minorities, the group somewhat improperly known as "Circassians"[1] and had gathered to protest a recent decision of the Ministry of Education, which ruled that the Cyrillic alphabet, the writing system most commonly used to write the Adyghe ("Circassian") language, would be replaced by the Latin script in the language courses offered in a number of Turkish schools. Although it remained largely contained within the Circassian community, this acrimonious dispute was but a mere symptom of the broader tensions that have emerged within this community in recent years.

On one side of a divide that threatened to durably poison intracommunal relations, the Federation of Caucasian Associations (*Kafkas Dernekleri Federasyonu* or KAFFED) opposed the switch to the Latin alphabet in which it saw an undue encroachment of the Turkish state upon the internal affairs of a minority community. KAFFED's arguments mostly focused on the threat posed by the proposed script reform to the cultural ties between the Turkish-Circassian community and its ancestral homeland, the modern republics of Adygea, Kabardino-Balkaria and Karachay-Cherkessia, autonomous entities in the Russian Federation where the different varieties of the Circassian languages have all been written in the Cyrillic alphabet since the 1930s (Papşu 2015). On the other end of the spectrum, a Konya-based group, religiously more conservative and significantly closer to the government of the Justice and Development Party (AKP), the Adyghe Language Association (*Adıge Dili Derneği*, ADDER) used the same argument of language conservation to promote the switch to the Latin alphabet and emphasized that the adoption of the Latin script would remove the burden of having to teach the Cyrillic alphabet, thereby raising literacy among Turkish youth of Circassian descent (Dönmez 2012).

This recent instance of an "alphabet crisis" in the context of modern Turkey can serve as a particularly apt *Ansatzpunkt* to a broader discussion of the intersections of script, identity, and literacy in the *longue durée* of the region, from the final decades of the Ottoman Empire to the present day. Additionally, the fact that this script debate took place in a minority community and concerned a language other than Turkish turns it into a helpful point of entry into a study of script issues that precisely seeks to go beyond the Arabic-to-Latin paradigm in an effort to decenter the "Script Revolution" of 1928 and to pay attention to a much broader range of tensions around modes of writing in the late Ottoman Empire and in the Republic of Turkey. In the present chapter, I start by surveying what can be described as the late Ottoman "traffic in scripts," with a special attention to script shifts, script crises, and script debates. Taking stock of recent developments in world literature scholarship that have drawn attention to the ways in which script constitutes a crucial, yet often overlooked category of analysis in comparative literary studies, I conceptualize the dense range of transcultural and transcommunal textual contacts that characterized the late Ottoman literary realm by mobilizing the concept of "scriptworld" proposed by David Damrosch to describe "a broad literary system" (2007: 195) bound together by the common use of a given writing system. Making use of the nuanced connotations of the concept of script (taken to denote at once a typeface and a template), I then analyze, within the context of the rich multilingual literary ecosystem of the late Ottoman Empire, instances where the notions of transcription, translation, and transliteration intersected in complex ways, often with palimpsestic results. Finally, I move to a much more recent period and to a case of "heterographics"—the intermixture of different scripts in a single text—used as a literary device in a Turkish-Cypriot work published in the 1990s in order to show how the cultural memory of the script issues of the Ottoman past continues to haunt modern Turkish literature. In doing so, I show how a script-focused approach to late Ottoman and modern Turkish literature—and in particular one that emphasizes the type of transcommunal contacts that are enabled by shared or hybrid modes of writing—contributes to recent discussions around world literature and simultaneously offers a reappraisal of Turkey's position within the field.

The language now commonly identified as "Ottoman-Turkish" developed as the dominant language of political power in Anatolia during the thirteenth and fourteenth centuries when the gradual Turkicization of the region paralleled the dawn of the Seljuk Empire, whose court language was Persian. Mostly known as *lisan-ı (Türkî-i) Rum* (literally, "the Turkish tongue of the former Byzantine lands") until at least the mid-nineteenth century (Ertürk 2011: 8–9), Ottoman-Turkish was primarily written in the Arabic script, with the addition of a small number of letters, almost all also used in Persian and that rendered sounds absent in Arabic. In addition, other linguistic communities used their own scripts, such as the Armenian, Greek, Syriac, and Cyrillic alphabets, while Sephardic Jews wrote their tongue (known under different names such as Ladino, Judezmo, or Judeo-Spanish) in the so-called Rashi script, a cursive version of the Hebrew alphabet. However, because there existed no absolute correspondence between "ethno-religious" and linguistic communities, a certain number of groups developed various practices that can be designated under the general name of "minor-scripting," that is, the recourse to another script than the one primarily used to render their language. The most well-documented cases include what we now call "Armeno-Turkish" and *karamanlidika*, respectively, Armenian- and Greek-scripted Turkish used in the written production of Christian Ottomans who had adopted Turkish as their main language of communication in daily life yet retained the corresponding scripts as markers of their identification with Armenian and Greek Orthodox culture. As Murat Cankara has convincingly demonstrated (Cankara 2015), engagement with "minor-scripting" practices was not entirely limited to the communities where it originated. Indeed, in the case of Armeno-Turkish, a number of non-Armenian Turkish literati acquired a degree of familiarity with the Armenian script and learned to read Turkish texts written in it for a number of reasons that included, among others, an interest in the potential for a greater degree of vernacularization of Turkish afforded by the vocalic capabilities of the Armenian script or the desire to access Western sources yet unavailable in Arabic-scripted Ottoman-Turkish (10–12).

While Ottoman-Turkish remained the most markedly pluriscriptic of all the languages in use in the empire and was also written, in more localized contexts, in the Syriac, Hebrew, and Cyrillic scripts, reverse phenomena are also attested, in particular the writing of Greek in the Arabo-Persian scripts by the Muslims of Crete or Ladino texts written in the Greek script. In parallel, a discourse around the perceived unsuitedness of the Arabo-Persian script to represent the rich vocalic nuances of Turkish—a process that Nergis Ertürk has framed as the rise of phonocentrism (Ertürk 2011)—started to crystallize in the second half of the nineteenth century, leading to scriptural debates and experimentations that would later lead to the adoption of the Latin alphabet to write Turkish in 1928 (Aytürk 2010).

## From "Scriptworlds" to "Scripts' World"

In his discussion of Armeno-Turkish writing, Murat Cankara makes a brief reference to the notion of "scriptworlds," in the margins of which he locates the emergence of "multiple hybridities" (2018: 190). In the present section, I follow this lead and use the same notion as a productive framework to conceptualize cultural and literary practices cutting across communal boundaries in the Ottoman Empire. At the same time, however, I argue that the idea of scriptworld can only be applied to the present context in a nuanced fashion and that the late Ottoman case does, in fact, put this notion to a test, which in turn reveals a number of unsuspected aspects of the intersections of script and literature, opening up new possibilities for further study along this line of inquiry in comparative literary studies.

In his first article devoted to the concept of "scriptworld," the inaugural example of the "cultural-political role of scripts" mentioned by Damrosch is none other than the Turkish "Script Revolution" of 1928, which enacted the switch from the Arabo-Persian to the Latin alphabet (Damrosch 2007). Beyond this initial example, most of the scriptworlds described by Damrosch belong to the pre- and early-modern periods, from the cuneiform world of ancient Mesopotamia to medieval Iceland and Mesoamerica in the early colonial era (Damrosch 2016). In the wake of Damrosch's initial discussion of scriptworlds, a number of scholars have, in recent years, turned to the concept and used it to highlight the part that script has historically played in facilitating and/or hindering the cross-linguistic diffusion of literary texts within supra-national regions in various areas of the globe. In her introduction to a 2016 special issue of the *Journal of World Literature* entirely dedicated to scriptworlds, Sowon S. Park emphasizes the need to recognize "the scriptworld as a useful analytical unit for world literature" (2016: 129). The turn toward script in comparative literary studies should constitute, as Park underlines, a necessary complement to the earlier rise of transnational, language-based approaches, which themselves constituted an effort to disentangle area studies from the boundaries imposed by modern political borders: "the label that is '-phone' tends to inhibit the development of another substantial foundation upon which to build the literary model of the world: script" (132). The majority of the essays included in the special issue are concerned with various case studies rooted in the Chinese scriptworld, which comprises not only the modern Sinophone world but also countries where Chinese characters were either historically used before being replaced by other scripts (Korea, Vietnam) or where they remain in use as part of a composite writing system (Japan) (Lim 2016; Chozick 2016; Thornber 2016; Bachner 2016).

In contradistinction with the Chinese scriptworld, where cases of script shift and script intermixture happened across very fundamental divides between writing systems—from logographic to alphabetic (Vietnamese), from logographic to featural alphabetic (Korean), or the combination of logographic characters with multiple syllabaries (Japanese) —the late Ottoman script issues all remained confined within the boundaries of an exclusively alphabetic conception of writing. Thus, the essential tensions that structure the traffic in scripts of East Asia—starting with the opposition between predominantly logographic and exclusively phonographic writing—are transposed, in the Ottoman case, onto an entirely different plane, that of the divide between vocalization and nonvocalization, as well as of the frictions between the cultural, symbolic, and religious investments into a range of scripts all intrinsically linked to Abrahamic religious traditions.

Another range of features of the late Ottoman scriptural landscape, notably the ones that arise from the cultural practices that I have described earlier as "minor-scripting" (such as the use of Armenian or Greek letters to write Turkish) further set it apart from the most frequently analyzed scriptworlds. Describing the adoption by the Akkadians of the cuneiform and the prestige that the Sumerian language—for the writing of which the cuneiform had been originally devised—continued to enjoy after the Akkadians prevailed politically and culturally, Damrosch contends that "[a] writing system is often the centerpiece of a program of education and employment, and in learning a script one absorbs key elements of a broad literary history: its terms of reference, habits of style, and poetics, often transcending those of any one language or country" (2007: 200). Damrosch also notes that "writers who use the new script [. . .] for their native vernacular frequently show deep awareness of the culture that brought forth the script, sometimes appropriating its stories, sometimes parodying or contesting them, often doing both at once" (208–9). If that is certainly the case with the use by Turks of the Arabo-Persian script and its corresponding cultural baggage, Ottoman "minor-scripting" practices could not be further removed from this description. Indeed, in the case of Greek-Orthodox Turkish speakers of central Anatolia, what was at stake in the writing of Turkish in Greek letters was not the adoption of a foreign, more prestigious script but, rather, the retention of a "native" writing system whose religious and symbolic charge allowed it to survive the gradual shift to Turkish as the medium of daily communication.

Correspondingly, those Ottoman-Turkish intellectuals that learned the Armenian script did so primarily for practical or even purely strategic reasons, such as those identified by Cankara. As much as Ahmet Mithat found the Armenian script to be "a rather excellent one" (Cankara 2015: 6), it would undoubtedly be an exaggeration to interpret these instances of a marked interest in the Armenian script or pedagogical achievements on the part of Ottoman Turks as the wholesale adoption of the "terms of reference, habits of style, and poetics" associated with the Armenian script. Similarly, if there existed, at times, a degree of awareness and even a true interest in Armenian cultural production beyond the Armenian script, the various functions of the Armenian alphabet within Ottoman-Turkish letters never came close to the prestige enjoyed by the Sumerian cuneiform in Akkadian culture or by Chinese characters in early-modern Japan, Korea, and Vietnam (McDonald 2016).

In fact, if the Armenian script was invested with any kind of prestige among non-Armenian intellectuals in the late Ottoman Empire, it was, very paradoxically, because it has afforded them access to the prestige—or at least the enjoyment—of Western, primarily French cultural products, such as, for instance, contemporary popular fiction, which started to be translated into Armenian-scripted Ottoman-Turkish before it appeared in the Arabo-Persian script. Symptomatically, Ahmet İhsan Tokgöz writes in his memoirs published after the establishment of the Turkish Republic that "[he] read most of Xavier de Montépin's crime novels in the Armenian letters" (Cankara 2015: 8). Thus, late Ottoman "minor-scripting" practices have very little in common with the instances described by Damrosch (such as the gradual adoption of Chinese characters by different groups in pre-modern China or the rapid diffusion of the Latin alphabet among Mesoamerican native cultures in the colonial era) where "the leading edge of a global language is its globalizing script" (2007: 206). Indeed, far from being the written expression of a "global language," the Armenian script had a relatively localized usage within the empire and the Middle East at large. At the same time, the language for which it had been designed and which it primarily served to render in written form was spoken by a substantially smaller number of individuals than the sum of those who spoke all the languages primarily written in the Arabic (or Arabo-Persian) script. Unlike Damrosch's "Babylonian scribes [who] freely translated back and forth between Sumerian and Akkadian," (2007: 202), the practice of the Ottoman-Turkish literati who acquired a knowledge of the Armenian script was not one of "monoscriptural bilingualism" but, rather, of its exact opposite, "biscriptural monolingualism."

As these considerations seem to indicate, the late Ottoman case puts existing definitions of the scriptworld to a test. In particular, the potential of scriptworlds to bind together, through the use of a common script, cultures separated by language, was not at play in the Ottoman case where there existed no single "scribal culture" (Damrosch 2007: 202) unifying the different components of the empire's complex demographic makeup. However, I argue that the notion of scriptworld remains partially operative in the context of the late Ottoman Empire provided that we leave open the possibility that there exists next to—or rather, in an extension of—the scriptworld, another conceptual space which constitutes its more elusive, quasi-spectral double, a world borne not out of a unity through script but out of the common participation of various cultural, linguistic, and literary communities into a complex traffic in script, as well as out of a shared experience of script-shifting and scriptural dysphoria.

I call this space a "scripts' world" rather than a "scriptworld" to acknowledge, through lexical split, the points of ruptures that punctuate the former more fundamentally than the latter, particularly the fact that the literatures that belong to a scripts' world, do not necessarily "tend to stay in their respective scriptworlds" (Damrosch 2007: 199). In the late Ottoman Empire, we are thus in the presence of an eminently fragmented scripts' world: part of it coincides with a portion of a much larger scriptworld, which binds together speakers of different languages within the broader Islamicate world through a common use of Arabic letters. In parallel with this portion of the Arabo-Persian scriptworld that overlaps with part of the Ottoman scripts' world, smaller segments of other transnational scriptworlds (Greek, Armenian, Hebrew, Cyrillic, etc.) are present in this scriptural ecosystem, marked by practices of script exchange or script substitution (as in the case of "minor-scripting"), as well as by various forms of anxieties over the desirable script (Ottoman Turks, Sephardic Jews), which often result in the eventual adoption of an "imported" script (for instance, the Latin alphabet). In these instances—and this constitutes another crucial feature of the scripts' world—the logic of writing is transferred onto the choice of script itself. When the available script is construed as incomplete, lacking, or entirely unsuited, the aspiration to *another* script, to a script-to-come becomes "the very *différance* for which a remedy must be sought" (Johnson 1990: 45), calling for the advent of a scriptural supplement, in the Derridian sense, that will function first as addition and later as substitute.

Thus, in a scripts' world, individual writing systems never enjoy an absolute cultural monopoly but are, instead, always in a situation of coexistence and competition with other ones, in a configuration where script divides as much as it unites. In the late Ottoman Empire, scriptural division resulted, for instance, in multilingual and pluriscriptic signs that proliferated notably in print media and in advertisement (see Figure 2.1), thereby turning public spaces into a typographically fragmented and apportioned visual landscape experienced by each individual through the prism of a partial illiteracy predicated upon one's personal script-reading skills. Conversely, practices such as "minor-scripting" and other forms of script-swapping brought communities closer, not by "unifying" them but by creating the conditions of possibility for hybrid modes of *lire-et écrire-ensemble*. As for literature, the implications of the very structure of a scripts' world are, as well-documented instances in the case of the Ottoman Empire and modern Turkey demonstrate, of both an enabling and a hindering nature: on the one hand, the crossings of scriptural boundaries that the

FIGURE 2.1 *Scriptural coexistence in the Ottoman Empire.*

scripts' world fosters allow for a degree of cultural hybridity and for a dense circulation of texts between linguistic communities (as evidenced, for instance, by the case of Ottoman-Turkish literature composed and/or printed in the Armenian alphabet). On the other, the same phenomenon interferes with the *a posteriori* construction of a unified "national" literary canon—as evidenced, for instance, by the non-inclusion of Armenian- and Greek-scripted novels in the canon of nineteenth-century Ottoman prose fiction—while script shifts complicate diachronic literacy and access to a literary past rendered "illegible" and in perpetual need of transcription and translation (Mignon 2005; Stepanyan 2005).

## Translation as Transcription

It is precisely when it is applied to a discussion of this articulation between transcription and translation that the notion of scriptworld retains most of its potency in the study of the late Ottoman scriptural and literary landscape. Notably in that, it allows for an inquiry into the boundaries between the two terms, while revealing their conceptual porosity—a move which brings much-needed complexity to oft-repeated conceptualizations of translational practices, as pointed by Sowon S. Park who asserts that "[e]tymologically, translation is the 'carrying across' of meaning from one language to another [but] this description does not take into account script as a factor in the practice of translation" (2016: 132). At first glance, script—or, rather, the boundaries of scriptworlds—are often described in the scholarship as a hindrance to the circulation of texts through direct translations, a phenomenon observed by Damrosch in the reception of *Gilgamesh* outside of the cuneiform scriptworld (2007: 199–200). Other scriptworlds, however, seem to offer counterexamples that reveal the more complex role played by script in translational practices.

As Judy Wakabayashi notes, "[t]ranslators usually pay little or no heed to the script embodying the meaning of a text, yet at times the script itself makes a significant contribution to the text's meaning, aesthetics or ideology" (2016: 173). Wakabayashi uses the context of Japan and its hybrid writing system to emphasize the ways in which script often "transcends [the] auxiliary function" (174) it is commonly thought to perform to acquire a range of additional functions that come to the forefront when translation is mobilized. As she points out, the composite nature of Japan's writing system (which combines Chinese characters with two indigenous syllabaries) "gives rise to the question of mutual 'translation' among these scripts, each of which has not only a different appearance but also a different 'feel'" (175) which shows, as she argues, the power of script to "shape writing and translation" (194). Although Wakabayashi is concerned with a hybrid, non-alphabetic scriptural culture within the Sinographic scriptworld, I argue that reading the traffic in scripts in the late Ottoman scripts' world in light of her findings allows for a renewed understanding of the relationship between script and translation in that context.

Needless to say, the Japanese examples analyzed by Wakabayashi do present particularities that are difficult and even impossible to verify in the Ottoman case. For instance, the possibility for Japanese authors to combine Chinese characters with the Japanese *katakana* and *hiragana* syllabaries or even with *romaji* (the Latin characters used for the phonetic Romanization of Japanese) in unusual ways within one single text and to diverge from their respective codified use for graphic and/or poetic reasons has no equivalent in Ottoman texts. Yet, it is possible to productively use this framework that sparks from an East-Asian scriptworld to make sense, *a contrario*, of a number of distinctively Ottoman phenomena.

First, the interplay of script and translation analyzed by Wakabayashi serves as a useful reference point to think about the circulation of literary texts in the "translating communities" of the late Ottoman Empire (Charrière 2019). Such a feature is particularly visible in the case of the various translations of foreign, primarily French novels, often extant in multiple different Ottoman Turkish versions in the Arabo-Persian, Armenian, and Greek alphabets, in parallel with other translations into Armenian, Greek, or Ladino.[2]

Second, the ways in which script shifts and permutations effectively put to a test commonly held notions of what "translation" truly entails are apparent in a number of cases of late Ottoman cross-script intralingual translation where the palimpsestic nature of the practice is particularly evident. For instance, Ioannis Gavriilidis, a Turkish-speaking Ottoman Greek published two versions in Greek-scripted Ottoman-Turkish of works by novelist Ahmet Mithat originally composed in the Arabo-Persian script. In some parts almost identical to its prototype but markedly different in others, *The Janissaries* (serialized in 1890–1) is based on Ahmet Mithat's *Yeniçeriler* (1871) and constitutes at once a transcription of the original text (from Arabic to Greek letters), an adaptation (with the addition by Gavriilidis of explanatory comments and direct addresses to the reader not found in Ahmet Mithat's text), and a translation (with a notable effort on the part of Gavriilidis to simplify Mithat's Ottoman-Turkish and bring it closer to the vernacular) (Şişmanoğlu Şimşek 2011).

Symptomatically, the ambiguity of Gavriilidis's position vis-à-vis Ahmet Mithat is clearly visible in the terms used to describe his role in paratextual notations, calling himself alternatively a "conveyor" (*nakili*) and a "translator" (*mütercim*) (Şişmanoğlu Şimşek 2011: 258; Berk Albachten 2018: 175). This example of intralingual translation/transcription (i.e., one language in two scripts) that results in two differently scripted versions of a text written in the same language yet partially different in terms of register can be contrasted with its quasi-polar opposite, the Japanese practice, evoked by Wakabayashi, of *kanbun kundoku* ("Japanese reading of Chinese writing") in which diacritical markers added to a text in Chinese characters allow it to be read in Japanese (i.e., one script in two languages).

In that it implies the partial word-for-word copy of certain passages of the original text and the transformation through vernacularization and adaptation of others, a case like Gavriilidis's translation as transcription of Ahmet Mithat's novels brings to mind ideas of both textual cannibalization and a scriptural form of appropriative *braconnage* (poaching) in the sense given to the term by Michel de Certeau (1980). In turn, following this metaphor through the example of yet another text within the "minor-scripted" corpus of late Ottoman prose fiction reveals new complexities in the interplay of transcription and translation, by bringing up another range of broader connotations embedded in the notion of script.

In 1871–2, the same newspaper that would publish Gavriilidis's version of Ahmet Mithat's novel twenty years later serialized *Temaşa-i Dünya ve Cefakar-u Cefakeş* (*Theatrum Mundi, and Tyrants and Tyrannised*), a novel by Evangelinos Misailidis. Like Gavriilidis's *Yeniçeriler*, Misailidis's *Temaşa-i Dünya* was, in fact, the Greek-scripted Ottoman-Turkish version of an earlier text, originally written in Greek, Gregorios Palaiologos's *O Polypathis* (1839) (Karra 2010). As in *Yeniçeriler*, there were notable differences between the two versions and Misailidis's work is more of an adaptation than a direct translation of Palaiologos (Şişmanoğlu Şimşek 2014). Unlike Gavriilidis's *Yeniçeriler*, which constituted the differently scripted double of Ahmet Mithat's novel, *Temaşa-i Dünya* and *O Polypathis* were thus written in the same script but in different languages.

However, the intricate relationship between the two texts is further complicated by the fact that Palaiologos's 1839 novel was itself an adaptation of *Gil Blas de Santillane* (1715–35), a French picaresque novel by Alain-René Lesage (Farinou-Malamatari 1991; Tziovas 2003). An eighteenth-century French reworking of the earlier Spanish picaresque tradition, *Gil Blas* itself partially reproduces the plot of Vicente Estivel's *Marcos de Obregon* (1618), modifying the specifics of its plot while retaining the basic template, or "script," of picaresque fiction (Garguilo 1991). Thus, the Misailidis/Palaiologos pair (i.e., a Greek-scripted Ottoman-Turkish text partially translated from a Greek text) is situated at the end of a long concatenation of textual transfers that conjure up the notions of both translation and script. Furthermore, the trajectory of the spatial and textual movement of *translatio* (from Spanish to French, from French to Greek, from Greek to Greek-scripted Ottoman Turkish), which ultimately finds its outcome in Misailidis's *Temaşa-i Dünya*, mobilizes a dual notion of script, which encompasses both the idea of writing system or typeface, and that of a set of patterns acquired and refracted through transcultural contact (as in the concept of "cultural script" in the field of ethnopragmatics)[3] (Goddard 2006).

## Heterographics as Border-Thinking: The Case of Mehmet Yaşın

Much of what once was the fabric of the complex late Ottoman scripts' world progressively unraveled as the empire disintegrated. In particular, the "minor-scripting" practices that included Armenian-, Greek-, Cyrillic-, or Hebrew-scripted Ottoman-Turkish, and Arabic-scripted Greek shared the fate of the communities where they had originated and rapidly became quasi-extinct. Although its tradition was therefore largely interrupted, "minor-scripting" somewhat unexpectedly resurfaces, this time in the form of what scholarship has dubbed "heterographics" (Lock 2006; Bodin 2018), in the work of Turkish-Cypriot author Mehmet Yaşın, where it becomes a site for probing the lasting legacy of the defunct late Ottoman scripts' world and of the transcommunal trauma that resulted from its violent demise.

The literary career of Mehmet Yaşın (born 1958) began in the immediate aftermath of the de facto partition of the island in 1974. Due to the author's critical stance on Turkish policies in Cyprus, his works were suppressed during the 1980s and he was expelled from Turkey in 1986. Since then, Yaşın has lived between England and Greece, as well as episodically in Cyprus and Turkey, where he was allowed to return in 1993. Published in 2003, *Deportation Hours* (*Sınırdışı Saatler*) was Yaşın's second novel and came after numerous publications that included, among others, poetry and essay collections. Described by its author as a novel, the text is, in fact, a rather hybrid and genre-bending work, where the boundaries of fiction, poetic prose, autobiographical essay, and experimental metanarrative become blurred.

The author himself plays a prominent part in a multilayered narrative that also incorporates documentary digressions complete with detailed bibliographic footnotes, on the history of *karamanlidika* literature, reproductions of the cover pages of *karamanlidika* books, as well as, most importantly, passages entirely composed in Turkish but using the Greek alphabet. These heterographic passages include segments of the fragmented narrative itself, some—but not all—transliterated in Latin-scripted Turkish. The book opens with the epigraph "'Dilin kemiği yok,' derler. Alfabe kıkırdaktır" ("'A tongue has no bone,' they say. The alphabet is a cartilage" Yaşın 2015: 5), immediately followed by a chart (see Figure 2.2) that places the letters of the Greek alphabet next to their equivalents in the Turkish version of the Latin alphabet[4] and is meant to help Turkish readers unfamiliar with the Greek alphabet decipher the passages of the text composed in Greek letters. The deciphering process that the chart permits is immediately mobilized at the very beginning of the first chapter of the novel (titled Πιρινιζι Παπ/ *Birinci Bâb*) which begins as follows:

Κιταπην ιλκ ιζουμλεσινε βουγουκ πιρ ωζεν κωστερεν γαζαρλαρα ωγκουνουγορυμ: Οκυρλαρη παστανζηκαρηιζη βαατλερδε πυλυναιζακ βε –σανκι πεν πωγλε πιρ οκυρα κατλαναπιλιρμισιμ κιπι- ονλαρην πανα κατλανμασηνη δαχα ιλκ ιζουμλε ιλε καραντιγε αλαιζακ πιρ γολ αρηγορδυμ κι, (Kitabın ilk cümlesine büyük bir özen gösteren yazarlara öykünüyorum: Okurları baştan çıkarıcı vaatlerde bulunacak ve -sanki ben böyle bir okura katlanabilirmişim gibi- onların bana katlanmasını daha ilk cümleyle garantiye alacak bir yol arıyorum ki), dönerkapı gene açılmış ve getirenler içeri geçmeye başlamıştı. (Yaşın 2015: 11)

'Αι φολό δε ληδ οφ δε άουθορς χου τρητ δε φερστ σέντενς οφ ε μπουκ γουίθ γκρέιτ κέιρ: ας άι γούαζ λουκίνγκ φορ αν ινίσιαλ σέντενς δατ γούντ μέικ εντάισινγκ πρόμισιζ του δε ρίντερζ έντ – ας ιφ άι κουντ μάισελφ πυτ απ γουίθ σάτς ε ρίντερ- δατ γούντ ενσούρ δατ δέι πυτ απ γουίθ μι (I follow the lead of the authors who treat the first sentence of a book with great care: as I was looking for an initial sentence that would make enticing promises to the readers and—as if I could myself put up with such a reader—that would ensure that they put up with me), the turnstile opened again and what it brought started to come in.⁵

"Dilin kemiği yok," derler. Alfabe kikirdaktır.*

| | |
|---|---|
| A α | A a |
| ΙΑ ια | Â â ve AE ae |
| Π̇ π̇ | B b |
| Ιζ ιζ | C c |
| Τζ τζ | Ç ç |
| Δ δ | D d |
| Ε ε | E e |
| Φ φ | F f |
| Κ̇ κ̇ | G g |
| Γ̇ γ̇ | Ğ ğ |
| Χ χ | H h |
| Η η | I ı |
| Ι ι | İ i |
| Ψ ψ | J j |
| Κ κ | K k |
| Λ λ | L l |
| Μ μ | M m |
| Ν ν | N n |
| Ν̇ ν̇ | NG ng |
| Ο ο | O o |
| Ω ω | Ö ö |
| Π π | P p |
| Ρ ρ | R r |
| Σ σ (sözcük sonu ς) | S s |
| Σ̇ σ̇ (sözcük sonu ς̇) | Ş ş |
| T t | T t |
| U u | U u |
| ΟΥ ου | ω Ü |
| Β β | V v |
| Γ γ | Y y |
| Ζ ζ | Z z |

* Elinizdeki romanın 154–155. sayfalarından.

FIGURE 2.2 *Sınırdışı Saatler* by *Mehmet Yaşın (p. 135, YKY 2015).*

This device, the intermixture of Greek-scripted, mostly non-transliterated Turkish with Latin-scripted Turkish, continues throughout the text, thus creating a constant tension around legibility which requires that the reader non-familiar with the Greek alphabet constantly return to the beginning of the book to consult the alphabetic chart, thereby echoing Helena Bodin's observation that "the occasional use of heterographics in literary texts influences readers' experiences of cultural affinity or alterity, that is, of inclusion or exclusion" (2018: 198).

I do not suggest that there exists an unbroken continuity between the pluriscriptic late- Ottoman literary milieu and the largely monolingual and mono-scriptic Turkish literary field. Afterall, Yaşın's œuvre —and, by extension, his occasional use of heterographics—occupies a largely marginal position within modern Turkish literature, not least due to the "ultraminor" situation of Turkish-Cypriot literature within world literature (Moberg and Damrosch 2017). Although Will Stroebel (2018) has recently shown that, contrary to a long-held belief, literature in Greek-scripted Turkish continued to be written and occasionally published after the Greek-Turkish population exchange of 1923, notably in the Greek diaspora in the United States, it is precisely the fact that he reactivates an obsolete mode of writing and confers to it new meanings and new functions that gives potency to his authorial gesture. In addition, because it is not a literary gimmick but, rather, a way for the author to signal his commitment to both represent and overcome the multilayered tensions between communities that have plagued his native island over the past decades, Yaşın's use of heterographics also refracts older intersections of script and literature in the broader region, recasting them as an inquiry into the politics of borders, both scriptural and geographic.

In this context, Emily Apter's notion of "translation at the border" is useful to make sense of Yaşın's heterographics in the context of divided Cyprus. Building upon Walter Mignolo's concept of "border gnosis," Apter's exploration of poetics of borders in contemporary culture ultimately leads her to question what she sees as an implicit weakening of the political potential of the recourse, in discourses on translation and cultural circulation, to the metaphor of border-crossing, which, she writes, "has become such an all-purpose, ubiquitous way of talking about translation that its purchase on the politics of actual borders—whether linguistic or territorial—has become attenuated" (Apter 2014: 56).

As a response to this depoliticization of "border gnosis," Apter calls for a renewed attention to border incidents, (bio)-politically charged encounters taking place along actual territorial divides and that compel the critic to "treat translation as a set of performative and politically volatile interactions that happen at checkpoints" (72). In her invocation of the checkpoint as a powerful image that displaces and unsettles entrenched conceptualizations and institutionalized expressions of "border thinking" by shifting the focus to the "line" (the border) to the "dot" (the checkpoint), the actual point where identities are subjected to often oppressive forms or control and where entry and non-entry are determined, Apter invites us to simultaneously refine and critique the metaphoric language of "border thinking" and to use it against its own depoliticized imprecision, as a way to reveal the forgotten possibilities of translation as a counter-hegemonic practice.

I argue that, far from being limited to mere postmodern typographic experimentation, Yaşın's recourse to "minor-scripting" in *Deportation Hours*—a work whose very title evokes images of border violence, territorial loss, and displacement—can be read as an instance, embedded in script, of Apter's notion of the checkpoint. In *Deportation Hours*, script changes function as a form of double checkpoint: on the one hand, the reader is confronted, through its reactivation in a postmodern text of a long-lost mode of hybrid written expression borrowed virtually unattested since the 1920s, with the reemergence from the mist of history of the textured cultural landscape of the broader Ottoman space formerly marked by an intense traffic in scripts. On the other, Yaşın's use of Greek-scripted Turkish and its material, practical implications for the Turkish reader unfamiliar with the Greek script can also be read as a form of physical checkpoint: by compelling readers to return, again and again, to the alphabetic chart printed at the beginning of the book in order to cross the scriptural border, the author seems to stage a process of constant "checking" and "re-checking" metaphorically akin to the rituals (body scan, searching, frisking, identity check) enforced by the state apparatus at actual checkpoints.

In addition, Yaşın's idiosyncratic bending of the unstable *karamanlidika* orthography evokes, through the interplay of typographic glyphs and supplemental diacritical dots, the dialectics of the line and the (check)point at work in Apter's rethinking of border-crossings. Furthermore, by situating this "checkpoint" not on the linguistic *limes* proper but within the grey zone of scriptural hybridity, Yaşın also probes another conceptually contentious border, the one which separates translation from transcription. Here the two categories become ultimately blurred and the mechanisms of transcription mobilized are not, as during Turkey's coming of age as a modern, Westernized, and ethnically "cohesive" nation-state, from the Arabic/Islamic to the Latin/secular script, but from the latter to the script of a different (Greek) "Other." As a result, the text effectively repositions the Turkish- Cypriot self into an undetermined zone where the suffix "trans-" is, quite paradoxically, the only stable element, where the "transit area" becomes the locus of a durable and uneasy settlement.

As Ronit Ricci writes, "scripts can illuminate questions of heritage and history in their capacity both as concrete, tangible artifacts and conveyors of echoes of radical change from an intangible past . . . [their study] offers new ways of exploring and understanding the practices and politics of writing, reading, and cultural transformation" (Ricci 2015: 432). In my own exploration of the manifold intersections of writing systems and literary expression, and of the ways they complicate commonly held notions around translation in the larger Turkish context—from practices of "minor-scripting" in the late Ottoman scripts' world to their resurgence and reinvention, among the ruins of empire, in contemporary Turkish-Cypriot literature—I have mobilized the complexities of the notion of script. In doing so, I wish to situate contemporary Turkish literary studies in a position that echoes Wai-chew Sim's recent definition of Sinophone studies, as an "externalist oriented set of assemblages [that] is similarly an enjoinment to cultivate . . . capacities . . . to interact with other entities [and] other literary systems." As Sim points out, "[t]his means, among other things, attending to literary multilingualism" (Sim 2019: 8). In the case of Turkish literature, this reorientation, which participates in much-needed efforts to further articulate the field within contemporary discussions around world literature, also means attending to the multiplicity of scripts and of the lasting traces they leave.

## Notes

1 Strictly speaking, the term "Circassian" designates the Northwestern Caucasus group that refers to itself and to its language as "Adyghe." However, in the context of the late Ottoman Empire and of modern Turkey, where the descendants of Muslims forced out of the broader Caucasus region as a result of Russian expansionism and resettled in Anatolia continue to live in large numbers, the term "Circassian" (*Çerkes*) has acquired a broader meaning. Although the more precise term of "Adyghe" (alternatively rendered as *Adige* or as *Adığe* in Turkish) seems to have, in recent years, found its way back into the terminology used by a number of community organizations in Turkey, "Circassian/*Çerkes*" remains very widely used.

2 There exist at least three prominent examples of a foreign novel translated into Ottoman-Turkish in three separate versions (Arabic-, Armenian-, and Greek-scripted): Alexandre Dumas's *Count of Monte Cristo* (Arabic-scripted Ottoman: 1872; Armenian-scripted Ottoman: 1882; Greek-scripted Ottoman: 1882), Xavier de Montépin's *Simone et Marie* (Armenian-scripted Ottoman: 1885; Arabic-scripted Ottoman: 1889; Greek-scripted Ottoman: 1890) and, by the same author, *La Porteuse de pain* (Greek-scripted Ottoman: 1885; Armenian-scripted Ottoman: 1886; Arabic-scripted Ottoman: 1890). See (Charrière 2016: 103) and on the third novel (de Tapia 2014).

3 The depth of meaning of the Latin word *scriptum* has become somewhat obscured in modern English. In Latin, the *scriptum* is at once graphic (a line and its trace) and legal (the law and its letter)—and, in both cases, something that one is invited to follow. Some of this ambiguity resurfaces in Spanish, where script (in the modern sense of "scenario") is rendered as *guión* (derived from *guiar*, "to guide"). Incidentally, *guión* is also used, in the vocabulary of printing, for a metallic frame that guides the hand of the typesetter on the page, as well

as, in the lexicon of writing, for the hyphen—that marker of hybrid identities that I use when I type the words "Armeno-Turkish" or "Ottoman-Turkish."

4 Interestingly, as Yaşın notes later in the text, next to a second iteration of the chart printed at the beginning of the book, his version of the Greek alphabet is a modified one, with diacritics added to render certain Turkish letters such as *c*, *ğ*, or *ş*. As the rules of *karamanlidika* orthography were never standardized when the practice was still commonly used, Yaşın's version—which he calls "yeni Karamanlıca" (new *karamanlidika*)—is as much a reactivation of a tradition as a form of departure from it (Yaşın 2015: 134).

5 Although it has circulated in an Italian translation (where the passages in Greek letters are rendered in uppercase Latin letters) (Yashin 2008), *Deportation Hours* poses a nearly insurmountable challenge to the translator who struggles to render the author's play with scripts. In my quotation, I resort to "Greeklish," the macaronic and entirely unregulated practice of phonetically rendering English in Greek letters. However, in its original context, "Greeklish" has quasi-comedic connotations that run counter to the meaning of Yaşın's text.

# References

Apter, Emily. (2014), "Translation at the Checkpoint," *Journal of Postcolonial Writing* 50 (1): 56–74.
Aytürk, İlker. (2010), "Script Charisma in Hebrew and Turkish: A Comparative. Framework for Explaining Success and Failure of Romanization," *Journal of World History* 21 (1): 97–130.
Bachner Andrea. (2016), "Cultural Margins, Hybrid Scripts: Bigraphism and Translation in Taiwanese Indigenous Writing," *Journal of World Literature* 1: 226–44.
Berk Albachten, Özlem. (2018), "Challenging the Boundaries of Translation and Filling the Gaps in Translation History: Two Cases of Intralingual Translation from the 19th Century Ottoman Literary Scene," in H. V. Dam, K. K. Zethsen, and M. N. Brøgger (eds.), *Moving Boundaries in Translation Studies*, 168–80, London and New York: Routledge.
Bodin, Helena. (2018), "Heterographics as a Literary Device: Auditory, Visual, and Cultural Features," *Journal of World Literature* 3: 196–216.
Cankara, Murat. (2015), "Rethinking Ottoman Cross-Cultural Encounters: Turks and the Armenian Alphabet," *Middle Eastern Studies* 51 (1): 1–16.
Cankara, Murat. (2018), "Armeno-Turkish Writing and the Question of Hybridity," in K. Babayan and M. Pifer (eds.), *An Armenian Mediterranean*, 173–91, London: Palgrave McMillan.
"Çerkeslerden anadil eylemi," (2015), *Evrensel*, April 16. Available online: www.evrensel.net/haber/110533/cerkeslerden-anadil-eylemi (accessed August 7, 2019).
de Certeau, Michel. (1980), *L'invention du quotidian*, Paris: Gallimard.
Charrière, Etienne. 2016. //deepblue.lib.umich.edu/bitstream/handle/2027.42/135833/etiechar_1.pdf?sequence=1.

Charrière, Etienne. (2019), "Translating Communities: Reading Foreign Fiction Across Communal Boundaries in the Tanzimat Period," in M. Ringer and E. Charrière (eds.), *Ottoman Culture and the Project of Modernity: Reform and the Tanzimat Novel*, London: I.B. Tauris.

Chozick, Matthew. (2016), "Eating Murasaki Shikibu: Scriptworlds, Reverse-Importation, and *The Tale of Genji*," *Journal of World Literature* 1: 259-74.

Damrosch, David. (2007), "Scriptworlds: Writing Systems and the Formation of World Literature," *Modern Language Quarterly* 68 (2): 195-219.

Damrosch, David. (2016), "Scriptworlds Lost and Found," *Journal of World Literature* 1: 143-57.

Dönmez, Yılmaz. (2012), "Niçin Adige Latin Alfabesi?," *kafkasevi.com*, 25 December. www.kafkasevi.com/index.php/article/detail/471 (accessed January 13, 2020).

Ertürk, Nergis. (2011), *Grammatology and Literary Modernity in Turkey*, Oxford and New York: Oxford University Press.

Farinou-Malamatari, Georgia. (1991), "'Ἑλληνικός Ζιλβλάσιος.' *Ο Πολυπαθής του Γρ. Παλαιολόγου*," *Επιστημονική Επετηρίδα της Φιλοσοφικής Σχολής ΑΠΘ* 1: 297-324.

Garguilo, René. (1991), "Le Diable *boiteux* et *Gil de Santillane* de Lesage: manipulations culturelles ou créations originales?" in M. L. Donaire and F. Lafarga (eds.), *Traducción y adaptación cultural: España-Francia*, 221-30, Oviedo: Servicio de Publicaciones de la Universidad de Oviedo.

Goddard, Cliff (ed.) (2006), *Ethnopragmatics*, Berlin: de Gruyter.

Johnson, Barbara. (1990), "Writing," in F. Lentricchia and T. McLaughlin (eds.), *Critical Terms for Literary Study*, 39-49, Chicago: The University of Chicago Press.

Karra, Anthi. (2010), "From *Polypathis* to *Temaşa-i Dünya*, from the Safe Port of Translation to the Open Sea of Creation," in E. Balta and M. Kappler (eds.), *Cries and Whispers in Karamanlidika Books: Proceedings of the First International Conference on Karamanlidika Studies*, 201-18, Wiesbaden: Harrasowitz.

Lim, Hyung Taek. (2016), "From the Universal to the National: The Question of Language and Writing in Twentieth-Century Korea," *Journal of World Literature* 1: 245-58.

Lock, Charles. (2006), "Heterographics: Towards a History and Theory of Other Lettering," in I. Klitgard (ed.), *Literary Translation: World Literature or 'Worlding' Literature?*, 158-72, Copenhagen: Museum Tusculanum Press.

McDonald, Edward. (2016), "The Chinese Script in the Chinese Scriptworld: Chinese Characters in Native and Borrowed Traditions," *Journal of World Literature* 1: 195-211.

Mignon, Laurent. (2005), "Lost Voices: Religious Minorities and the Literary Canon in Turkey," in Laurent Mignon, *Neither Shiraz nor Paris: Papers on Modern Turkish Literature*, 15-26, Istanbul: The Isis Press.

Moberg, Bergur Ronne, and David Damrosch. (2017), "Introduction: Defining the Ultraminor," *Journal of World Literature* 2: 133-7.

Papşu, Murat. (2015), "Çerkeslerin Yeni Sorunu: Adığe Dil Derneği (ADDER)." *kaffed.org*, April 15. Available online: http://www.kaffed.org/kose-buc

ak-yazilari/item/2592-çerkeslerin-yeni-sorunu-adiġe-dil-derneği-adder.html (accessed August 6, 2019)

Park, Sowon S. (2016), "Introduction: Transnational Scriptworlds," *Journal of World Literature* 1: 129–41.

Ricci, Ronit. (2015), "Reading a History of Writing: Heritage, Religion, and Script Change in Java," *Itinerario* 39 (3): 419–35.

Sim, Wai-chew. (2019), "Overlapping Scriptworlds: Chinese Literature as a Global Assemblage," *CLCWeb: Comparative Literature and Culture* 21 (4). Available online. https://doi.org/10.7771/1481-4374.3206 (accessed August 4, 2019).

Şişmanoğlu Şimşek, Şehnaz. (2011), "The *Yeniçeriler* of Ioannis Gavriilidis: A Palimpsest in Karamanlidika," in E. Balta and M. Ölmez (eds.), *Turkish-Speaking Christians, Jews and Greek-Speaking Muslims and Catholics in the Ottoman Empire*, 245–75, Istanbul: Eren.

Şişmanoğlu Şimşek, Şehnaz. (2014), "Evangelinos Misailidis'in Karamanlıca Başyapıtı: *Temaşa-i Dünya ve Cefakar u Cefakeş* ya da 'İki Kelise Arasında Bînamaz' Olmak," in M. F. Uslu and F. Altuğ (eds.), *Tanzimat ve Edebiyat*, 193–230, Istanbul: İş Bankası Kültür Yayınları.

Stepanyan, Hasmik. (2005), *Ermeni Harfli Türkçe Kitaplar ve Süreli Yayınlar Bibliyografyası (1727–1968) – Bibliographie des livres et de la presse arméno-turque*, Istanbul: Turkuaz.

Stroebel, William. (2018), "The Hyphenated Hyphen: Turkish-in-the-Greek-Script American Literature," *Ergon*. Available online: https://ergon.scienzine.com/article/articles/the-hyphenated-hyphen-turkish-in-the-greek-script-american-literature (accessed August 12, 2019).

de Tapia, Aude Aylin. (2014), "De *La Porteuse de Pain* (1884) à *l'Ekmekçi Hatun* (1885), un roman populaire français chez les Karamanlis," in E. Balta and M. Ölmez (eds.), *Cultural Encounters in The Turkish-Speaking Communities of The Late Ottoman Empire*, 223–56, Istanbul: The Isis Press.

Taştekin, Fehim. (2015), "Turkey's Circassians in uproar over alphabet." *Al Monitor*, April 22. Available online: www.al-monitor.com/pulse/originals/2015/04/turkey-circassians-in-uproar-over-latin-alphabet.html (accessed August 6, 2019).

Thornber, Karen L. (2016), "The Many Scripts of the Chinese Scriptworld, the *Epic of King Gesar*, and World Literature," *Journal of World Literature* 1: 212–25.

Tziovas, Dimitris. (2003), "Palaiologos' *O Polypathis*: Picaresque (Auto)biography as a National Romance," in *The Other Self: Selfhood and Society in Modern Greek Fiction*, 55–82, Lanham, MD: Lexington Books.

Wakabayashi, Judy. (2016), "Script as a Factor in Translation," *Journal of World Literature* 1: 173–94.

Yashin, Mehmet. (2008), *Le ore del confine*. Tr. R. d'Amora, Lucera: Mediterraneo è cultura.

Yaşın, Mehmet (ed.) (2000), *Step-Mothertongue: From Nationalism to Multiculturalism: Literatures of Cyprus, Greece and Turkey*, Middlesex: Middlesex University Press.

Yaşın, Mehmet. (2015), *Sınırdışı Saatler*, Istanbul: Yapı Kredi Yayınları.

# 3

# Translating Yunus Emre, Translating the Self, Translating Islam

## Zafer Şenocak's Turkish-German Path to Modernity[1]

*Joseph Twist*

> Turkish writers know Goethe, Schiller, Hölderlin,
> Benn, Trakl, Eich, Celan, Bachmann, Kafka, Camus.
> And German writers? Do they know
> Cansever, Uyar, Süreya? (Şenocak 1994: 31)[2]

The writer and public intellectual Zafer Şenocak (b. 1961 in Ankara) is well aware of the imbalances in today's globalized literary markets. Mass migration is, however, bringing about processes of cultural cross-pollination that challenge traditional ideas of center and periphery. If, with David Damrosch, we regard world literature as encompassing "all literary works that circulate beyond their culture of origin, either in translation or in their original language" (2003: 199), it can be argued that Turkish literature is increasingly playing such a role in Germany, where Turks currently form the largest ethnic minority (Statistisches Bundesamt 2018). As one-sided as the cultural exchanges between Germany and Turkey may appear, Şenocak's own publications demonstrate that there is movement in both directions.³ He has written essays on Turkish and Ottoman literature, such as "Einen anderen Duft als den der Rose: Über türkische Volks- und Diwandichtung" (Another Scent than that of the Rose: On Turkish Folk and Divan Poetry, Şenocak 1993), and he has translated the poetry of Pir Sultan Abdal (Şenocak 1988) and Yunus Emre (Yunus Emre 1986) into German. Moreover, his own literary and essayistic writing (in both German and Turkish) is inspired by authors and thinkers from both cultural spheres.

An exploration of the enlightenment credentials of Islamic societies throughout history has been a central aspect of Şenocak's writing from the beginning of his literary career in the 1980s. The varied developments in culture, religion, and society during the "Islamic Golden Age" (dated from the eighth to the fourteenth century) are particularly formative for his thinking. He views this period as a process of enlightenment in its own right, one that not only predated and contributed toward the so-called "European Enlightenment," but that is also relevant again now, as it can provide a corrective to the wholly rationalist mindset that prevails in the West. In this regard, Yunus Emre's brand of mysticism is a key inspiration for Şenocak. At a time when Islam is being viewed in an increasingly demonized, Orientalizing way, Şenocak's work demonstrates that Yunus Emre's writing has much to offer beyond the Turkish context and warrants being treated as world literature.

His translations of Yunus Emre's poems in *Das Kummerrad/Dertli Dolap* (Wheel of Misery, 1986, republished in 2005) constitute, to use Lawrence Venuti's terminology, both a "domesticating" gesture, in that he wants to make Yunus Emre German, and also a "foreignizing" one, since he deploys Yunus Emre to challenge Orientalist assumptions that exclude Turks and Muslims from modernity. This act of translation was also a journey of self-discovery for Şenocak, as it allowed him to reflect on his position as a Turkish-German with a Muslim background. Ethnic, racial, and religious divisions have become ever more entangled in debates around the Turkish minority in Germany, but rather than becoming trapped in the binaries of this discourse, Yunus Emre enables Şenocak to think through them. By translating Yunus Emre and bringing him into dialogue with German writers and philosophers, especially the Frankfurt School and the Romantics, within his own essays and poetry, Şenocak demonstrates the benefits of redressing the Eurocentric bias of world literature. He argues that an engagement with Turkey's mystical heritage can bring about a shift toward a more reflective process of enlightenment, which can also revitalize Islamic thought and culture. An analysis that similarly uses a methodological framework indebted to the Frankfurt School can provide a comprehensive picture of Şenocak's nuanced and at times seemingly contradictory positions within these debates, as he explores alternative forms of modernity with both Turkish and German roots. As Eduardo Mendieta states, for the thinkers of the Frankfurt School "religion can be both a source of reification and opium, but just the same of memory, hope, and yearning that may from within instigate new forms of Enlightenment and Cosmopolitanism" (2005: 11).

## Translating Yunus Emre

Translation is central to the circulation of world literature. Yet, as Venuti indicates, translations are a complex negotiation between the foreign norms of the source culture and the domestic ones of the target culture, which are both heterogeneous entities themselves (2000: 468). Venuti views an approach that tends to foreignize as a more ethical method, as the translator is visible and readers experience a destabilizing encounter with the foreign, rather than having their own values affirmed. Hence, for Turkish literature to have a transformative effect on other cultures as world literature, its translations must be more than "an ethnocentric reduction of the foreign text to target-language cultural values" (Venuti 1995: 20). The domesticating/foreignizing process "begins with the very choice of a text for translation" (Venuti 2000: 468), and the decision to translate Yunus Emre challenges both the market forces that govern publishing and German readers' assumptions about Turkey and Islam.

Below is an example poem from *Das Kummerrad/Dertli Dolap* with the Turkish original and Şenocak's translation into German, here with the addition of an English translation:

Mâna evine daldık vücudu seyran kıldık
İki cihan seyrini cümle vücudda bulduk

Bu çizginen görkleri tahtesserâ yerleri
Yetmişbin hicabları cümle vücudda bulduk

Yedi yer yedi göğü dağları denizleri
Uçmağ ile Tamu'yu cümle vücudda bulduk

Gece ile gündüzü gökde yedi yıldızı
Levhde yazılı sözü cümle vücudda bulduk

Tevrât ile İncili Furkan ile Zeburu
Bunlardaki beyânı cümle vücudda bulduk

Yunus'un sözleri hak cümlemiz dedik saddak
Kand'istersen anda Hak cümle vücudda bulduk

Hereinspaziert ins Sinngebäude wir schauen uns die Körper an
Denn Dies- und Jenseits sind in allen Körpern zu finden
Die Himmel voller Prunk die tiefgeschnittnen [sic] Erden
Die siebzigtausend Scheidewände in allen Körpern zu finden

Die siebenfache Erde die siebenfache Sphäre der Berg das Meer
Der Himmel die Hölle in allen Körpern zu finden
Der Tag wie auch die Nacht am Firmament die sieben Sterne
Was auf Gottes Tafel hingeschrieben in allen Körpern zu finden
Die Bibel und die Thora der Koran und der Psalter
Was dargelegt in ihnen in allen Körpern zu finden
Wahr sind Yunus Worte bezeugt wird was er spricht
Wo du hinschaust ist Gott in allen Körpern zu finden.

(Yunus Emre 1986: 40–1)

(We entered the house of realization, we witnessed the bodies,
for the two worlds are to be found in all bodies

The whirling skies, the many-layered earth,
the seventy-thousand veils, we found in all bodies.

Seven earths, seven spheres, the mountain and the sea,
Heaven and earth, we found in all bodies

The night and the day, the planets,
the words inscribed on the Holy Tablets, we observed in all bodies.

*Torah, Psalms, Gospel, Quran—*
what these books have to say, we found in all bodies.

Everybody says these words of Yunus are true.
Truth is wherever you want it. We found it within all bodies.)

(Yunus Emre 1989: 20; translation adapted by the author)

When reflecting on his translation strategy in his essay collection *Das Fremde, das in jedem wohnt: Wie Unterschiede unsere Gesellschaft zusammenhalten* (The Foreign that Resides in Everyone: How Differences Hold our Society Together, 2018), Şenocak states: "It is important for a translation that its language no longer appears as a foreign language" (2018: 65). This would suggest a domesticating translation, and there are certain aspects of his translation that suggest an adherence to the norms of the target culture. For instance, the word "Furkan" in the poem above is a reference to the twenty-fifth surah ("Al-Furqan," meaning "The Criterion"), but this was rendered as "der Koran" in order to be meaningful to non-Muslims. Moreover, the word "hicabları" has been translated as "Scheidewände" (partition walls), rather than as "Scheier" (veils) or even as the Arabic loanword "hijab," which can mean "partition wall," "screen," "curtain," or "veil." In the wake of the Iranian Revolution, there was an increased tendency in Western Europe to view the Islamic veil as a tool of patriarchal oppression. Thus the decision to choose "partition walls" can be viewed as domesticating, suggesting that Şenocak would view a reference to the veil as diluting the modern image of Yunus Emre he wishes to project.

Perhaps the most striking change is on a structural level, as the Oriental *ghazel* form is dropped. Although the repetition has been maintained, rhyme has also been lost, replaced with the sibilance of "Sterne," "Psalter," and "spricht." The effect is that the poem appears more modern and more Western to the contemporary German reader, which is reinforced by the lack of punctuation, which replicates the original as it appears in this edition. Nevertheless, when the age of the source text is considered, making it appear so modern can be viewed as a foreignizing tactic; it does not appear like a medieval German text and hence the translator is highly visible. The decision to include the source text, positioned to the left of the translation, equally makes it clear that we are dealing with a translation. Further complexity is evident when we consider that, according to Şenocak, for a German to read a Turkish text is not the overwhelming encounter with the foreign that stereotypes would suggest. Part of Şenocak's aim is to demonstrate that Turkish culture, even from Yunus Emre's era, can be just as, if not more "modern" than, contemporary German culture, in that it evidences a reflective process of enlightenment that challenges the authority both of organized religion and of instrumentalizing reason. Therefore, the translation is, paradoxically, foreignizing in that it appears so close to domestic norms, as this defies reader expectations. This translation therefore blurs distinctions between the foreign and the domestic, but nevertheless leaves Şenocak open to criticism for effacing Yunus Emre's foreignness to a certain degree.

The translation's main foreignizing function is its challenge to Orientalist assumptions about Turkish culture, in that it employs "discursive strategies where the hierarchies that rank the values in the domestic culture are disarranged to set going processes of defamiliarization, canon reformation, ideological critique, and institutional change" (Venuti 2000: 469). This poem is emblematic of many others in the collection that convey a non-dualist spirituality, religious tolerance, and a love of humanity and nature. To use the postcolonial theorist Dipesh Chakrabarty's term, these translations "provincialize Europe," defying the inward-looking Western narratives of the so-called "Orient" as being in the "waiting room of history," anticipating the inevitable progress that has already happened in European societies (2008: 9). As Şenocak mentions in his 1991 essay "'Orient' und 'Okzident': am Scheideweg?" ("'Orient' and 'Occident': At the Crossroads?" 2000): "The fruits of the Enlightenment were planted and cultivated jointly, in Andalusian Spain in Seljukian Anatolia, in the Córdoba of Averroës [Ibn Rushd] and in the Konya of the mystic Jalal al-Din Rumi" (2000: 16–17).

Şenocak further encourages the reader to interpret Yunus Emre as a progressive figure through the accompanying postface, "Yunus Emre: Unser Zeitgenosse" (Yunus Emre: Our Contemporary). Here, partly following trends in Turkish Republican scholarship that characterize Yunus Emre as a humanist,[4] he refers to him as "the preacher of those values that the Islamic Enlightenment had cultivated: love, tolerance and peace" (Şenocak 1986: 89–95). Şenocak cites the cosmopolitan makeup of Anatolia as important for understanding Yunus Emre's writing: "Yes these Turks already saw themselves as Muslim, but the culture they brought with them exhibited clear traces of pre-Islamic, shamanist modes of faith. [. . .] This synthesis resulted in fertile soils for many eclectic, heretical, and very tolerant religious orientations, which quickly came under a mystical umbrella" (1986: 90). Yunus Emre is aligned with Bektashism (Türer 2005: 248) and Annemarie Schimmel outlines the pluricultural composition of this order:

> In addition to the Shia trend, which is one of the peculiarities of the Bektashi order, Christian influences have been seen in the ritual (which would not be astonishing, in view of the strong Christian substratum in Anatolia). There are, in fact, certain similarities, like penitence or the sacramental meal of bread and wine, but one should not press these similarities too far. The communal meal is much older than the Christian sacrament. In modern, nationalistic Turkish research, a certain "shamanist" aspect of Bektashism has been emphasized; this would connect the order with old Turkish, Central Asian forms of mystical life. (1975: 340)

This Kemalist perspective that emphasizes the cultural legacy of pre-Islamic Anatolia in order to diminish the importance of Islam and the Ottoman Empire has seemingly influenced Şenocak's understanding of Yunus Emre and Turkish branches of Sufism, such as Bektashism, whose military role also afforded it a privileged position during much of the Ottoman period. Indeed, Alevis faced persecution despite sharing many beliefs with Bektashism (Türer 2005: 248). Nevertheless, Şenocak stresses the importance of the religious dimension of Yunus Emre's thought, rather than regarding it as part of a proto-secularizing movement. For him, Islam need not secularize to become compatible with modernity and nor should it, if it is to challenge the limitations of a wholly secularized process of enlightenment.

Thus, if Şenocak values the idea of enlightenment, he does so with some caveats. In "'Orient' and 'Occident,'" he refutes the assumption that modernization is an inherently positive force, identifying two interconnected branches within modern thought involving "humanism and Enlightenment" on one side, and the "absolute claim by humans to domination of nature, and Europe's colonialism" on the other (Şenocak 2000: 17). Although Şenocak uses enlightenment in a positive sense here, the distinction he makes resonates with Max Horkheimer and Theodor W. Adorno's argument that instances of extreme brutality such as colonialism and the Holocaust not only happened in spite of enlightenment, but also because of it, since the concept of enlightenment is embedded in a dialectical relationship with myth (Horkheimer and Adorno 1997). If, as these thinkers contend, the central drive of enlightenment, and by extension the eighteenth-century philosophical movement of the same name, is fear of the unknown, then its mission to scientifically and rationally explain the material world can fall back into the utilitarian domination of both nature and humanity. Throughout much of his writing, Şenocak seeks to salvage the self-critical qualities of enlightenment from its instrumental aspects.

David N. Coury maintains that Şenocak "argues strongly for the values of the Enlightenment, noting that the church was not the driving force behind industrialization, rationalism, or positivism; rather, secular forces brought about these developments" (2013: 147). These developments are all, however, instrumentalizing aspects of enlightenment that can be linked to myth and barbarism. Conversely, Şenocak's praise for Yunus Emre focuses on his enlightened brand of humanism that does not result in anthropocentrism: "The modern understanding that science and art is to be practiced as an end in itself has raised many questions. [. . .] Yunus Emre's philosophy represents a counter-image to this European view. It does not link human freedom to the level of knowledge over nature, but rather to the level of knowledge over the self" (Şenocak 1986: 94). Here, Şenocak makes clear that Yunus Emre's mystical outlook can act as a counterbalance to the instrumental understanding of enlightenment that currently dominates the globe, and in line with Yunus Emre's teachings, this cross-cultural undertaking did, indeed, have a profound impact on Şenocak's understanding of himself.

## Translating the Self

It was the act of translating Yunus Emre that allowed Şenocak to come to terms with his multifaceted identity: "Had I not been working on Yunus Emre's oeuvre, [. . .] I would have fallen victim to the irreconcilable contradictions between the Sex Pistols and the Koran" (Şenocak 2007a: 238). Through Yunus Emre, he was able to make unexpected connections between his political and social views, and a previously unfamiliar dimension of Islam, a religion he continues to criticize for its lack of cultural vitality: "Islam has always been a religion of regulations, with the aspiration to govern life and the everyday in every detail. Yet this world religion also had a spiritual, even poetic dimension, that has completely faded into the background today, which is why only the skeleton of commandments and prohibitions seems to have remained intact" (Şenocak 2006: 53).

Religious, ethnic, racial and national differences have become increasingly entangled in Germany's multiculturalism debates and Şenocak identified this growing tension before 9/11 in the wake of the Iranian Revolution and the First Gulf War (2000: 1–9). As Coury affirms, Islamophobia in contemporary

Germany is often coupled with an uncritical affirmation of the Enlightenment (2013: 140). Despite debates from the Frankfurt School that outline the mythic and regressive aspects of enlightenment, ideas of progress tied to the philosophical movement the Enlightenment—such as democracy, human rights, a secular public sphere, and tolerance—are praised as cornerstones of European and German identity, while negative aspects—such as colonialism and the environmental damage wrought by industrialization—are often viewed as unrelated issues, or banished onto an Other. In this regard, it is argued that Islam, often viewed as a monolithic entity, never underwent the process of secularization that the Western Christian denominations did, and hence threatens post-Enlightenment European modernity, which is also often viewed as a monolithic entity. The normative sense of Germanness—referred to as "Leitkultur" (guiding culture)—that has developed within German political discourse often affirms this uncritical link between German ethnic identity and Enlightenment values, which blurs the divide between the universal and the particular and excludes (perceived) Muslims from wider society. In his 2011 essay "Die atonale Welt: Wie viel Vielfalt ertragen wir?" (The Atonal World: How much Diversity Can We Take?), Şenocak criticizes how the "civilizational"[5] principles of the Enlightenment are being co-opted and distorted by a narrow German nationalism:[6]

> [The ideals of the Enlightenment] can [. . .] also be instrumentalized in order to construct cultural milieus with the aim of excluding foreigners. A gulf opens up between the usurpation of the Enlightenment as a label for a specific culture and its use in social life. This gulf can only be overcome through the universal character of the Enlightenment that is common to all humankind. The incompatibility of others, for example Muslims, with Enlightenment values becomes, by contrast, a stigmatizing judgement through formulaic repetition, and consequently becomes a prejudice. (Şenocak 2011: 46)

In the essay "Deutschland – Heimat für Türken?: Ein Plädoyer für die Überwindung der Krise zwischen Okzident und Orient" (1990; "Germany – Home for Turks?: A Plea for Overcoming the Crisis between Orient and Occident," 2000), Şenocak describes Humanism and Enlightenment thought as "twilight creatures of West and East," which means that "[p]racticing and cultivating them would not be alienating for Muslims. On the contrary, this would be the discovery of a lost Muslim tradition" (2000: 9). This is important, as it offers Muslims a route to reform from within their own traditions. It would be the rekindling of the cooperation that first led to the Enlightenment, in which Yunus Emre, "a wunderkind of the Islamic Enlightenment" (Şenocak 1986: 90), played an important role. It is perhaps due to the shared heritage of the Enlightenment's ideals that Şenocak regards them as a universal binding force, particularly in his

2011 essay collection *Deutschsein: Eine Aufklärungsschrift* (Being German: An Educational Pamphlet)—the pun in the subtitle calls to mind the philosophical Enlightenment (*die Aufklärung*) and its central importance for Germany's sense of self.

Şenocak argues here that Enlightenment principles, especially human rights, would be "a solid foundation to give a heterogeneous society identity. For these values do not have ethnic groups, nations and religious orientations as their base, but rather the individual as the elementary particle of society" (2011: 45). He therefore sides with the cosmopolitan thinker Jürgen Habermas, who also argues that "the universalist project of the political Enlightenment by no means contradicts the particularist sensibilities of a correctly conceived multiculturalism" (2008). As Coury indicates (2013: 148–9), Şenocak also advocates Habermas's idea of a politically neutral, secular, and post-national "constitutional patriotism" in the 2007 article "Islam and Enlightenment: Of Culture Clash and Constitution": "[The Basic Law] documents the core values that bind the society together. Whenever it comes to conflict between this Basic Law and any religious book, it is the Basic Law, the constitution, which must always, always take precedence" (Şenocak 2007b: n.p.). Şenocak therefore makes a distinction between the particularism of the *Leitkultur* debate and the neutral values of Germany's constitution, which he regards as the heir of cross-cultural work between East and West. Şenocak's engagement with Yunus Emre's poetry led him to realize that Islam is compatible with such constitutional patriotism, as it can be much more than just a religious ideology that determines how one lives (Şenocak 2006: 31). In the abovementioned poem, the divine is located "in all bodies" rather than in holy books.[7] Such a spirituality without clearly defined rules cannot enter into conflict with temporal laws, and hence it allows space for someone like Şenocak, a Turkish-German with a Muslim background, to fit within a German society whose neutral constitution allows for a plurality of voices.

## Translating Islam

Şenocak laments that many Muslim countries have chosen to ignore the positive aspects of this joint enlightenment heritage but embrace the instrumental aspects, such as industrialization and military technology, albeit under threat from Western powers. In this regard, the founding reforms undertaken by the revolutionary leader and first president of Turkey, Mustafa Kemal Atatürk, were inspired by European politics and secularism and sought to distance Turkey from its Ottoman past and orientate it away from its neighbors in the East, relegating Islam to a cultural, rather than religious identity. Rather than undergoing "a foundational process of modernization within Islam," Turks, instead, "saw themselves forced to import modernity like a replacement part" (Şenocak 1994: 13). In the essay "Islam Übersetzen"

(Translating Islam: 2006), Şenocak argues that another form of "translation" is necessary to instill a "new dynamism in Islamic thought [...], so that it can act in tandem with the thought structures of its time and world" (2006: 54). Rather than viewing Islam as a static set of religious rules and practices, he recommends a creative engagement with Sufism (itself a diverse grouping of orders and philosophical schools, many of which have suffered persecution)[8] to both update Islamic thought and rediscover the religion's eclectic aspects. This creative act of translation would have the potential to contribute toward a form of Islam that fits with today's diverse world by being both accepting of alterity and subordinate to supposedly cosmopolitan constitutional laws. Whereas various essays outline Şenocak's criticisms of contemporary Islamic thought, his attempts to "translate" Islam can be found in his poetry. Poem "XV" from the cycle "Istanbuler Tango" (Istanbul Tango) in the collection *Ritual der Jugend* (Ritual of Youth, 1987) is a salient example, since it has the most overt associations with the Sufi tradition of all Şenocak's poetry:

als wir gingen kam der Wein
als wir kamen ging der Wein

unberührt von unserem zagen Durst
ein roter Schleier war der Wein

ein Erker verband uns zwei Fenster
uns Architekten der Laster

uns Menschen erwartet nicht viel
froh sind wir um etwas Brot und Wein

ein Jüngling brachte die volle Karaffe
war er der Hübsche oder war es die Karaffe

später holte ein anderer die Karaffe ab
unberührt von unserem zagen Durst

ein anderer Schenk legte seine betörende Spur
blieb er unberührt oder blieb es die Karaffe

uns Menschen erwartet nicht viel
froh sind wir um etwas Brot und Wein

(Şenocak 1987: 77)

(as we went the wine came
as we came the wine went

untouched by our timid thirst
a red veil was the wine

we two windows joined by an oriel
we architects of vice

not much awaits us mortals
happy are we with a little bread and wine

a lad brought the full decanter
was he the beautiful one or was it the decanter

later someone else picked the decanter up
untouched by our timid thirst

another butler laid his beguiling trace
did he stay untouched or was it the decanter

not much awaits us mortals
happy are we with a little bread and wine)

As Karin E. Yeşilada asserts, this poem's imagery and loose *ghazel* form indicate a clear link with Sufi poetry. She regards its praise of wine, "whose coming and going reflects the world's transience," and its homoerotic content, particularly the playful ambiguity between the young man and the decanter, as a specific reference to Rumi (Yeşilada 2012: 209).[9] This imagery, with the same coming and going of people, is also found in Yunus Emre's poetry, albeit not in a poem featured in Şenocak's translated anthology:[10]

I have seen—those who attained flew away
They drank from the full cup of Love.
Their whims are tolerated at the level of Truth,
Their heads are bowed.

Yunus, if you are the servant of the wise,
don't forget your death.
So many of the attained have come and gone,
now our turn has come.

(Yunus Emre 1989: 84)

The themes of wine and homosexuality are linked in Şenocak's poem, suggesting a clear break from orthodox forms of Islam and a turn toward a Sufi understanding of divine love. Many Sufis link both drunkenness and sexual passion to spiritual ecstasy and to temporarily escaping rational thought (Schimmel 1997: 284), and it is through alcohol that the inhibitions of the poetic persona and the young man are overcome and they can, presumably, become intimately acquainted. This imagery can function on a symbolic level, but some Sufis also consider beauty and sexual passion as providing access to the divine on a material level within "a model of religious personhood that is liberated from the binaries of spirit and matter, piety and desire, sanctity and carnality" (Shaikh 2014: 189). Islam's supposed incompatibility with contemporary German attitudes toward gender and sexuality, a prominent feature of integration debates,[11] is therefore challenged in this poem.

Moreover, this poem not only suggests an Islam that dispenses with heteronormativity, but equally one without clear boundaries to other religions, as the bread and wine allude to both Sufi ideas of asceticism and the Christian Eucharist. Thus, the ambiguity of the abovementioned poem and its acceptance of heterodox Muslim identities can be regarded as a creative reinterpretation of the Anatolian mysticism of Yunus Emre's era, with its porosity of religious boundaries and its mixing of Islamic and shamanist traditions. This reference to bread and wine also establishes a connection with the German poet Friedrich Hölderlin's elegy "Brod und Wein" (c. 1800, "Bread and Wine"), in which the bread and wine symbolize a trace left behind by the absenting Gods. Şenocak's poem thus "translates" Islam and undermines the East-West dichotomy in various ways: by favoring the body over doctrine; by demonstrating the compatibility of Yunus Emre's Bektashism with liberal attitudes to gender and sexuality; through ambiguous allusions to both Islam and Christianity; and by conflating Turkish and German literature.

Reading German Romantics alongside Turkish mystical poetry was an important source of inspiration for Şenocak that "unleashed the very creativity in [him] that enabled [him] to write poetry" (Şenocak 2018: 70), and Hölderlin's spirituality, particularly his thought around the lack of divine names, resonates with Şenocak's engagement with Sufism. The dilemma surrounding the inability to express the divine in language can be seen most obviously in verse VI of the elegy "Heimkunft" (1802, "Homecoming"): "Ihn zu fassen, ist fast unsere Freude zu klein. / Schweigen müssen wir oft; es fehlen heilige Nahmen, / Herzen schlagen und doch bleibet die Rede zurük?" ("Him to embrace and to hold our joy is too small. / Silence often behooves us: deficient in names that are holy, / Hearts may beat high, while lips hesitate, wary of speech?") (Hölderlin 1994: 280–1). This theme of a distant divinity is also present in "Brod und Wein," as bread and wine symbolize a trace left behind by the absenting gods: "Brod ist der Erde Frucht, doch ists vom Lichte gesegnet, / Und vom donnernden Gott kommet die Freude des Weins. / Darum denken wir auch dabei der Himmlischen, die sonst / Da gewesen und die kehren in richtiger Zeit" ("Bread is a fruit of Earth, yet touched by the blessing of sunlight, / From the thundering god issues the gladness of wine. / Therefore in tasting them we think of the Heavenly who once were / Here and shall come again, come when their advent is due") (Hölderlin 1994: 270–1). To return to the Frankfurt School, Adorno pointed out that Hölderlin must work with abstractions and semblances as the divine is ultimately something beyond human understanding (Adorno 1992: 125). Hölderlin can therefore be linked to mystics, such as Yunus Emre, who seek a personal relationship with the divine outside of institutionalized rituals that name god and presume to act on his behalf, thus minimizing his divinity.

Şenocak's own attempts to evoke a mystical relationship with the divine that avoids dogma and group identities has a similar paradoxical sense of the divine that is both distant and near. The abovementioned poem from "Istanbuler Tango," too, leaves the matter of divine presence—symbolized here through erotic encounter—unanswered, as drunkenness not only leads to the loss of inhibitions and of rational thought, but also of memory, casting doubt on the events. This problem is emphasized by the structure of the poem, as the chiasmus in the opening couplet suggests confusion and the repetitions, forgetfulness. Was it the decanter or the butler that remained untouched? Either way, an orthodox interpretation of Islam has been contravened, but doubt nevertheless surrounds any potential *unio mystica*. Thus, guided by both Yunus Emre and Hölderlin, Şenocak's poem evokes an Islam based on affective experience rather than rules that could enter into conflict with temporal laws.

Şenocak acknowledges in "Die Atonale Welt" that "humans are not only rational beings" (2011: 42), and that we, in fact, suffer under "a world that is only submitted to reason" (2011: 38). He therefore sees positive enlightenment values as worth striving toward and seeks to separate these from other tendencies, such as the control of nature, that are also arguably the result of a process of enlightenment. The verb "to submit to something" (*sich etwas unterwerfen*) used in the above statement alludes to the Arabic etymology of "Islam," implying the shared potential of both religion and reason to be either instrumentalizing or self-critical. There are, then, much broader implications resulting from Şenocak's engagement with Yunus Emre than the mere subordination of Islam to Germany's Basic Law; his open-ended spirituality calls both metaphysical projects into question. The spirituality of poem "XV" from "Istanbuler Tango" is not only compatible with constitutional patriotism and secularized Europe's model of modernity, but also plots an alternative path to modernity that can perhaps overcome the shortcomings that resulted from installing Man on God's vacated throne. In this regard, Şenocak compares his engagement with Turkey's mystical heritage with German-Jewish writers and intellectuals, such as Gershom Scholem, Martin Buber, Franz Rosenzweig, and Walter Benjamin: "The pupils of Hebrew among the German-Jewish youth of the time were especially interesting to me. Universalism's 'religion of reason,' the liberal way of thinking, was certainly not dismissed by them. Yet there was resistance against rationalism's absolute claims and against the extent to which the intellectual world was determined by positivism" (2018: 66). Indeed, the abovementioned poem's ambiguous presentation of an ineffable sense of the divine rejects instrumentalizing aspects of this Eurocentric paradigm, embracing the irrational, the unknowable, and the undecidable, turning its back on the enlightenment demand to know and name, which often also means to control and exploit.

Thus, whereas Şenocak's essays, at times, seem to regard a universal sense of reason in the Enlightenment tradition as the way of safeguarding a religiously and culturally pluralist society, his poetry can also suggest a spirituality that emerges from escaping rational thought and enlightenment's fear of the unknown. Rather than seeking to disenchant the material world through a process of enlightenment, Şenocak's understanding of enlightenment also aims to re-enchant it, just as "Yunus Emre views humans as being embedded in an overall context that is at the same time divine" (Şenocak 1986: 94): "Şol cennetin ırmakları akar Allah deyu deyu / Çıkmış İslâm bülbülleri öter Allah deyu deyu"; "Die Flüsse aus dem Paradies fließen Allah rufen Allah / Die Nachtigallen des Islam zwitschen Allah rufen Allah" (Yunus Emre 1986: 26–7) ("The rivers of paradise flow, chanting Allah, Allah. / The nightingales of Islam are perched all around, /singing, Allah, Allah") (Yunus Emre 1989: 72). Şenocak therefore disrupts a polarized understanding of the temporal and the spiritual worlds, placing both beyond the bounds of the instrumentalizing rational thought that allows enlightenment to revert to myth. The ambiguity of his poem serves to hint at a connection with divinity, while simultaneously undermining it, and hence the poem does not overcome the ineffable nature of god, but hints at the abstractness of the divine. In contrast to literalists who presume to possess the only valid interpretation of the Koran, Şenocak emphasizes the centrality of doubt.

## Conclusion

The two seemingly contradictory poles of Şenocak's thought (on the one hand, the universalist claim of enlightenment values; on the other, the unknowable nature of god and the world) counterbalance each other. Just as Habermas states that "[b]oth religious and secular mentalities must be open to a complementary learning process if we are to balance shared citizenship and cultural difference" (Habermas 2008: n.p.), Şenocak speaks of the human desire for both reason and the irrational. This embrace of paradox is something Şenocak shares with many Sufis, such as Yunus Emre, who inspire him: "Sufis are drawn to paradoxes as skillful means to convey spiritual teachings. Baffling our senses of analytic reason is precisely their power! Without sidestepping our self-centered reasoning, how could we ever taste of the transformational mystery of spiritual experience?" (Kugel 2007: 127).

Through Şenocak's engagement with Yunus Emre he seeks to challenge the Western biases of world literature and to defy the Eurocentric, teleological understanding of the world, in which modernity is viewed as being inherently positive and involves an inevitable process of secularization. While his translations of Yunus Emre and his reworking of Yunus Emre's ideas in his own essays and poetry intimate a non-prescriptive spiritual outlook that is "metaphysically weak" (Henkel 2008: 121) and hence compatible with contemporary Germany's neutral constitution, he does not merely relegate Islam to a dispensable aspect of the private sphere in line with Enlightenment secularization. He equally implies that the skeptical and questioning sense of the divine found in Yunus Emre's writing is *needed* as a counterbalance to the wholly rationalist worldview that has spread from Western Europe to dominate the globe.

By bringing Islamic thought, here in the form of Yunus Emre, back into enlightenment debates, Şenocak points beyond the enlightenment-myth dialectic through a positive emphasis on the unknowable and the uncontrollable. Hence faith and reason exist in tension and complement one another, and do not exist as binary opposites. In his own words, Şenocak's literary project revolves around this constant interaction between the irrational and the rational, religion and enlightenment, using both to question the boundaries of knowledge, rather than separating them into opposing camps with totalizing claims: "[My writing myth] came into being at the breaking point between reason and mysticism, at the railway station of Eros, where coming and going is the elixir of life for all who haven't believed in the advent of angels for a long while" (Şenocak 2001: 101). His thinking is influenced by Yunus Emre, Adorno, Horkheimer, Hölderlin, Habermas, Kemalist thought, and much more, without being neatly categorized as German/rational and Turkish/irrational. Consequently, Şenocak challenges the binaries of faith and reason, Islam and enlightenment, and German and Turkish culture, demonstrating the transformative potential of Turkish literature as world literature for our understanding of modernity and enlightenment.

# Notes

1 I am grateful to the National University of Ireland, Galway, for supporting this research through the Moore Fellowship.
2 All translations, unless otherwise stated, are my own. I thank the editors and reviewers for all their help with the Turkish originals.
3 Other important writers and translators from Turkish into German include Yüksel Pazarkaya, Aras Ören, Nevfel Cumart, and Özlem Özgül Dündar.
4 See (Halman 1968).
5 Şenocak's use of the term "civilization" is similar to revolutionary leader and first president of Turkey Mustafa Kemal Atatürk's notion of a universal world civilization with multiple origins, including in the Islamic civilization (Turfan 1998: 16).
6 For example, Katherine Pratt Ewing's study reveals the anger over Muslim girls' exemptions from physical education on the grounds of modesty as being

less about the constitutional right to education and more about German "body culture," in which "[e]xposure of the human body and even full nudity continue to be associated with openness, purity, and a healthy sexuality" (2008: 193).

7  For more on the theoretical implications of this aspect of Şenocak's work, see (Littler 2012: 139–52) and (Twist 2018: 25–55).
8  For a discussion of the historic variety in Anatolian Sufism, see (Uludağ 2005).
9  The symbolism of the oriel window could be a reference to the *mashrabiya*, a decoratively screened bay window that is an architectural feature of many Arabic residences, which serves to create privacy from the street.
10  The mystical praise of wine is also present among Şenocak's translations: "Hak'dan inen şerbeti içtik Elhamdü lillah," "Des Himmels Wein tranken wir Gottlob" (Yunus Emre 1986: 68–9) ("The drink sent down from Truth, / we drank it, glory be to God") (Yunus Emre 1989: 21). For analyses of other intertextual links to Yunus Emre in Şenocak's poetry, see Joseph Twist (2016: 336–7; 2018: 36–7 and 43).
11  As Pratt Ewing points out, nationalist politicians uncharacteristically become gay rights activists and defenders of gender equality during discussions about integration, as the questions of the so-called "Muslim Test" used for citizenship applications in Baden-Württemberg suggest (Pratt Ewing 2008: 181–4).

# References

Adorno, Theodor W. (1992), *Notes to Literature*, Vol. 2, R. Tiedermann (ed.). Tr. Shierry Weber Nicholsen, New York: Columbia University Press.
Chakrabarty, Dipesh. (2008), *Provincializing Europe: Postcolonial Thought and Historical Difference*, Princeton: Princeton University.
Coury, David N. (2013), "Enlightenment Fundamentalism: Zafer Şenocak, Navid Kermani, and Multiculturalism in Germany Today," in E. Jeremiah and F. Matthes (eds.), *Edinburgh German Yearbook 7: Ethical Approaches in Contemporary German-Language Literature and Culture*, 139–57, Rochester, NY: Camden House.
Damrosch, David. (2003), "What Is World Literature?" in T. D'haen, C. Domínguez, and M. Rosendahl Thomsen (eds.), *World Literature: A Reader*, 198–206, Abingdon, NY: Routledge.
Habermas, Jürgen. (2008), "Notes on a Post-Secular Society," *signandsight*, June 18, 2008. Available online: http://www.signandsight.com/features/1714.html (accessed March 22, 2019).
Halman, Talât Sait. (1968), "Turkish Humanism and the Poetry of Yunus Emre," *Tarih Araştırmaları Dergisi* 10: 231-40.
Henkel, Heiko. (2008) "Turkish Islam in Germany: A Problematic Tradition or the Fifth Project of Constitutional Patriotism?" *Journal of Muslim Minority Affairs* 28 (1): 113-23.
Hölderlin, Friedrich. (1994), *Poems and Fragments*. Tr. Michael Hamburger, London: Anvil Press Poetry.

Horkheimer, Max and Theodor W. Adorno. (1997), *Dialectic of Enlightenment*. Tr. John Cumming, London: Verso.
Kugel, Scott. (2007), *Sufis and Saints' Bodies: Mysticism, Corporeality, and Sacred Power in Islam*, Chapel Hill: University of North Carolina Press.
Littler, Margaret. (2012), "Der Islam im Werk von Zafer Şenocak: Der *Pavillon*," in M. Hofmann and K. von Stosch (eds.), *Islam in der deutschen und türkischen Literatur*, 139–52, Paderborn: Schöningh.
Mendieta, Eduardo. (2005), "Religion as Critique: Theology as Social Critique and Enlightened Reason," in E. Mendieta (ed.), *The Frankfurt School on Religion: Key Writings by the Major Thinkers*, 1–17, New York and London: Routledge.
Pratt Ewing, Katherine. (2008), *Stolen Honor: Stigmatizing Muslim Men in Berlin*, Stanford: Stanford University Press.
Schimmel, Annemarie. (1975), *Mystical Dimensions of Islam*, Chapel Hill: The University of North Carolina Press.
Schimmel, Annemarie. (1997), "'I Take Off the Dress of the Body': Eros in Sufi Literature and Life," in S. Coakley (ed.), *Religion and the Body*, 262–88, Cambridge: Cambridge University.
Şenocak, Zafer. (1986), "Yunus Emre: Unser Zeitgenosse," in Yunus Emre, *Das Kummerrad/Dertli Dolap*. Tr. Zafer Şenocak, 89–95, Frankfurt am Main: Dağyeli.
Şenocak, Zafer. (1987), *Ritual der Jugend*, Frankfurt am Main: Dağyeli.
Şenocak, Zafer. (1988), "Ein Lied auf des Volkes Zunge: Anmerkungen zu Pir Sultan Abdal (ca. 1520-1560)," *Sirene* 1: 52–83.
Şenocak, Zafer. (1993) "Einen anderen Duft als den der Rose: Über türkische Volks - und Diwandichtung," *Der Deutschunterricht* 5: 18–31.
Şenocak, Zafer. (1994), *War Hitler Araber? IrreFührungen an den Rand Europas*, Berlin: Babel.
Şenocak, Zafer. (2000), *Atlas of a Tropical Germany: Essays on Politics and Culture, 1990-1998*. Tr. L. A. Adelson, Lincoln: University of Nabraska Press.
Şenocak, Zafer. (2001), *Zungenentfernung: Bericht aus der Quarantänestation*, Munich: Babel.
Şenocak, Zafer. (2006), *Das Land hinter den Buchstaben: Deutschland und der Islam im Umbruch*, Munich: Babel.
Şenocak, Zafer. (2007a), "Between the Sex Pistols and the Koran," Tr. Lucy Powel, in D. Göktürk, D. Gramling and A. Kaes (eds.), *Germany in Transit: Nation and Migration, 1955-2005*, 136–39, Berkeley: University of California Press.
Şenocak, Zafer. (2007b), "Islam and Enlightenment: Of Culture Clash and Constitution," Tr. Ron Walker. *Qantara*, April 13, 2007. Available online: http://en.qantara.de/content/islam-and-enlightenment-of-culture-clash-and-constitution (accessed March 22, 2019).
Şenocak, Zafer. (2011), *Deutschsein: Eine Aufklärungsschrift*, Hamburg: Edition Körber.
Şenocak, Zafer. (2018), *Das Fremde das in jedem wohnt: Wie Unterschiede unsere Gesellschaft zusammenhalten*, Hamburg: Edition Körber.
Shaikh, Sa'diyya. (2014), *Sufi Narratives of Intimacy: Ibn 'Arabī, Gender, and Sexuality*, Chapel Hill: The University of North Carolina Press.
Statistisches Bundesamt. (2018), "Migration und Integration: Ausländische Bevölkerung nach ausgewählten Staatsangehörigkeiten," Available online:

https://www.destatis.de/DE/Themen/Gesellschaft-Umwelt/Bevoelkerung/Migration-Integration/Tabellen/auslaendische-bevoelkerung-staatsangehoerigkeit-jahre.html (accessed March 22, 2019).

Türer, Osman. (2005), "General Distribution of the Sufi Orders in Ottoman Anatolia," in A. Y. Ocak (ed.), *Sufism and Sufis in Ottoman Society: Sources-Doctrine-Rituals-Turuq-Architecture Literature and Fine Arts-Modernism*, 219–56, Ankara: Turkish Historical Society.

Turfan, M. Naim. (1998), "Mustafa Kemal Atatürk," in R. Benewick and P. Green (eds.), *The Routledge Dictionary of Twentieth-Century Political Thinkers*, 15–18, London and New York: Routledge.

Twist, Joseph. (2016), "'Es kostet Sinn und Zeit / die Sphären zu einen': Das Selbst und der Andere, der Himmel und die Erde in Zafer Şenocaks *Übergang*," in E. Binder, S. Klettenhammer, and B. Mertz-Baumgartner (eds.), *Lyrik Transkulturell*, 333–51, Würzburg: Könighausen & Neumann.

Twist, Joseph. (2018), *Mystical Islam and Cosmopolitanism in Contemporary German Literature: Openness to Alterity*, Rochester, NY: Camden House.

Uludağ, Süleyman. (2005), "Basic Sources for Mystical Thought in the Ottoman Period," in A. Y. Ocak (ed.), *Sufism and Sufis in Ottoman Society: Sources-Doctrine-Rituals-Turuq-Architecture Literature and Fine Arts-Modernism*, 21–50, Ankara: Turkish Historical Society.

Venuti, Lawrence. (1995), *The Translator's Invisibility: A History of Translation*, London and New York: Routledge.

Venuti, Lawrence. (2000), "Translation, Community, Utopia," in L. Venuti and M. Baker (eds.), *The Translation Studies Reader*, 468–88, London and New York: Routledge.

Yeşilada, Karin E. (2012), *Poesie der dritten Sprache: Türkisch-deutsche Lyrik der zweiten Generation*, Tübingen: Stauffenburg.

Yunus Emre. (1986), *Das Kummerrad/Dertli Dolap*. Tr. Zafer Şenocak, Frankfurt am Main: Dağyeli.

Yunus Emre. (1989), *The Drop That Became the Sea*. Tr. Kabir Helminisji and Refik Algan, Boston and London: Shambhala.

# PART II

# Turkish Literature in Transnational Waters

# 4

# World Literature as Performance

## Turkish and British Women's Writing in Transcultural Dialogue at the Turn of the Twentieth Century

*Peter Cherry*

There is a striking moment in Zeyneb Hanım's account of her time traveling in Europe, *A Turkish Woman's European Impressions* (1913), when the writer describes visiting the British Houses of Parliament.[1] Writing to her interlocutor, the British travel writer Grace Ellison, she details being taken to a special chamber called "The Ladies Gallery" where female visitors were obligated to sit if they wished to watch parliamentary debates. Zeyneb Hanım sarcastically regales the experience:

> But, my dear, why have you never told me that the Ladies' Gallery is a harem? A harem with its latticed windows! The harem of the government! No wonder the women cried through the windows of that harem that they wanted to be free! I felt inclined to shout out too. "Is it in free England that you dare to have a harem? How inconsistent are you English! You send your women out unprotected all over the world, and here in the workshop where your laws are made, you cover them with a symbol of protection." (Zeyneb Hanım 1913: 194)

In the passage, Zeyneb Hanım both observes a significant hypocrisy in British Orientalist discourse and poses a vital question which has ramifications for how British readers perceived the Ottoman Turkish Orient. To put it simply: What is a harem and why is it that female-only spaces in Britain are exceptionally different from a harem? As evidenced by Zeyneb Hanım's questioning of whether a "harem" is axiomatically a feature of Orientalized societies and not also found within places like Britain, I read the travel writing of Grace Ellison and Zeyneb Hanım as a cultural exchange through which definitions of "Turkishness" are critiqued but ultimately reduced to a series of performative expectations relating to gender, notably shown in each writer's participation in identity hoaxes, that each writer needs to navigate in order to be consumed by non-Turkish European readers. In so doing, this chapter proposes a materialist approach to world literature discourses that calls for greater awareness of how travel writing reinforces global hierarchies rather than posing a way for reading transnational exchanges apolitically.

The locus of Ellison and Zeyneb Hanım's engagements with Turkishness is the concept of the harem. The harem refers literally to three things: first, to "an inviolable space that women and only close male relatives can enter"; second, "to a woman or wife (in the singular or plural)"; and, third, to a "certain arrangement of domestic space common to a wide variety of Islamicate societies across many centuries" (Booth 2010: 5). Yet, understandings of the harem have often been very different in the West. Stereotyped images of what Reina Lewis refers to as the "phantasmagorical harem," a space of cruelty and sexual deviance where secluded, hapless women were forced to be imprisoned against their will, loomed large in the British (and Euro-American) cultural imagination (Lewis 2004: 101). These abstracted ideas of the harem "animated some of the West's best-known examples of dominant Orientalism from fine art, to operas, to novels and popular literature" (Lewis 2004: 12). Immensely popular cultural productions such as Voltaire's play *Zaïre* (1732) and operas such as Mozart's *Abduction from the Seraglio* (1782) drew on myths of subjugated women in cloistered spaces living according to the depraved whims of Ottoman noblemen. Furthermore, these hyperbolic understandings of the harem keyed into political discourses justifying European colonial interests in Ottoman (and Orientalized) lands as "the (inevitably sexualised) tyrannies of Oriental despotism provided a foil to Europe's own image of just governance [. . .] the veiled, secluded Oriental woman became the perfect image of the non-citizen" (Lewis 2004: 96).

Within this context, the political power of Zeyneb Hanım's description of the British House of Commons is even more radical as she was not only drawing attention to Britain's own cultural practices of gender segregation but also exposing how Britain's use of women's rights as a front for political policy was bogus. However, Zeyneb Hanım's humorous episode also necessitates a deeper conceptual rethinking into meanings of the "harem" and how it often came to symbolize the Orientalized "other"—in this instance, Ottoman Turkey. Lewis's extensive work on a range of female-authored travelogues and exchanges led her to develop a critical framework for reading so-called harem literature—a genre in which women writers used the sexual allure of the harem to attract prurient, often male, Western readers and, as with Zeyneb Hanım's example, frequently forced them to confront their own Orientalist attitudes and anti-feminist views. Lewis evocatively describes the selling power of these texts in the following manner:

> There is no denying it—as a topic, the harem sold books. From the eighteenth century on, whether you wrote about living in one, visiting one, or escaping from one, any book that had anything to do with the harem sold. Publishers knew it, booksellers knew it, readers knew it and authors knew it. And women the world over who had lived within the harem's segregating system knew it too. Not so entirely divorced from the conventions of Western culture as stereotypes of the isolated odalisque suggested, they cannily entitled their books with the evocative words "harem," "Turkish," "Arabian" or "princess," and pictured themselves in veils or *yaşmaks* on the front cover. All this even as they wrote about lives that were the opposite of what the curious West expected to find. (Lewis 2004: 12)

In this chapter, I am in dialogue with Lewis's output on the textual commerce between British and Ottoman-Turkish women writers at the turn of the century, developing it by bringing harem literature into conversation with developments in the field of world literature. In recent debates surrounding world literature, the notion has been explored either as a *corpus* of texts bound together by their ability to cross national and linguistic boundaries through translation or as a *methodology* for reading literature transnationally (Damrosch 2003: 1–39). In this chapter, against the grain of this binary conception, I argue that harem literature achieves neither of these functions. Instead, I argue that these texts offer a new reading of "world literature" as a performative gesture borne out of transnational encounters that mobilize identities shaped by parameters such as national belonging and practices of gender.

In particular, I argue that the "harem," as conceived in the literary output of Zeyneb Hanım and the British writer Grace Ellison, marks a fruitful case study for Emily Apter's theorization of what she terms the "translation zone" (Apter 2006). In creating the term "translation zone," Apter was broadening Mary Louise Pratt's influential work on "contact zones" (Pratt 1992). For Pratt, "contact zones" refers to spaces or situations of cultural encounter in which two or multiple cultures are forced to engage and position themselves in relation to one another. These confrontations can take place in contexts with highly asymmetrical power relations, such as colonialism, but necessarily result in both cultures transforming themselves, thereby enabling new possibilities and fusions to occur due to this moment of contact, a process she terms "transculturation." Pratt's model has been used extensively to read the ways in which cultures are shaped by contact and Lewis herself uses Pratt's theory to read how writers such as Ellison and Zeyneb Hanım are influenced by one another in their textual production. However, Apter expands Pratt's model by bringing language into the picture therein, suggesting that sometimes cultures can misread, misunderstand, or even allow for a cultural encounter that is more *critical* than Pratt's model allows. As Apter explains:

> In fastening the term "zone" as a theoretical mainstay, the intention has been to imagine a broad intellectual topography that is neither the property of a single nation, nor an amorphous condition associated with post-nationalism, but rather a zone of critical engagement that connects the "l" and "n" of transLation and transNation. (Apter 2006: 5)

With the word and concept "harem" then, I contend that Ellison and Zeyneb Hanım are entering a form of translation zone which is not only transcultural in Pratt's sense but also, crucially, *critical* of the dynamics of gender in both cultural contexts. Ellison and Zeyneb Hanım's writing pulls them out of the comfort of their cultures and forces them to look afresh at their status as women travel writers in both Britain and Turkey. Of course, these discourses of the harem are not specific to the Turkish context, as single-sex spaces in Islamicate societies across the Balkans, the Middle East, and South Asia were also Orientalized and resisted by women writers from areas like Egypt, Palestine, and the Indian subcontinent in a similar manner, but they acquire a particular relevance to world literature by delineating the kinds of stereotyped images that women writers from Turkey had to navigate and sometimes embody when appealing to Western readers.

As will be seen in the following pages, the two writers frequently "perform" Turkishness either in dress, in writing, or in adopting hoax identities. In due course, I will be exploring how decades after the publishing of Zeyneb Hanım's travelogue, publications appeared that exposed her identity as falsely constructed and showed her posing as a fictional figure from the novel *Les désenchantées* (1906) by the French writer Pierre Loti, whose real name was Louis Marie-Julien Vaud. These performances are, I contend, not merely forms of transculturation as Lewis interprets, but actually a form of critique that combines Apter's conception of the translation zone with Judith Butler's work on gender performativity.

In Butler's early work on gender performativity, she argued that gender is performative in that it is the "repeated stylization of the body, a set of repeated acts within a highly rigid regulatory frame that congeal over time to produce the appearance of substance, of a natural form of being"

(Butler 1990: 43–4). In line with Butler's writing on how gender identities are performative and therefore subject to continual cultural construction and reconstruction, Ellison and Zeyneb Hanım often dress up as "Turkish" or alternatively claim different cultural identities and consequently call attention to the ways that gender, and national and cultural identities are discursively constructed. The majority of British readers, however, were only interested in having their notion of the Ottoman-Turkish harem reaffirmed precisely within a highly rigid regulatory frame.

Therefore, in my chapter, I want to draw attention to an important tension that has significant import on definitions of world literature. While both Ellison and Zeyneb Hanım challenge identity discourses and subject them to a process of critical reassessment with the word/concept of the "harem" at the center of this process, their success as travel writers depended on how well they followed the expectations of their genre and audience. For scholars of world literature, travel writing is of obvious interest as it is a genre which, although varying significantly in style, represents journeys around the world, engages discursively with constructions of "worlding," and records subsequent encounters with "foreign" peoples and cultures. However, drawing on the theoretical questions posed by Edward Said, travel writing critics such as Debbie Lisle have observed how realistic, non-prejudiced, and unbiased depictions of unfamiliar places are impossible. Indeed, Lisle argues that in satisfying the reader's interest with all that is "foreign," travel writing is a genre that generally seeks not to challenge perceptions of cultures but, rather, support and even preserve global hegemonies.

Lisle's work dovetails with Grace Ellison and Zeyneb Hanım's travel writing production in that cultural hegemonies and dynamics between Britain and Turkey are observed, subtly critiqued, but ultimately maintained. In this sense, this chapter is making an argument not only for foregrounding the role of performative identities in scholarship on world literature but also for pointing out that travel writing provides a fruitful literary genre from which to make materialist arguments against world literature's tendency to ignore questions of global power and inequality. Rather than supporting world literature's aim to show how literature gains in translation then, Ellison and Zeyneb Hanım's work suggests that quite often readers actually want stereotyped ideas of cultures reaffirmed rather than rewritten.

I turn first to the writing of Grace Ellison. Most of the biographical information that we know about Ellison is from Lewis's work; however, there are still intriguing gaps (Lewis 2004: 42–51). For example, Lewis writes that we do not know the year or situation of Ellison's birth except that she was born in Scotland. Curiously, Lewis does not offer any references for this information and I have been unable to find any corroborative evidence. Lewis states that Ellison first came to Turkey in 1905 but returned as a journalist in 1908 to report on the inauguration of the constitutional government under Sultan Abdülhamit II. Unable to speak Turkish, Ellison communicated in French while she was in Istanbul. French was a common feature of upper to upper-middle class education in turn-of-the-century Britain and Ottoman Anatolia. Ellison, however, was exceptionally proficient in the language as she had spent a number of years at a school in the northern French city of Lille. Through her French language skills we can also surmise that she spoke almost exclusively with the upper echelons of Ottoman society. Notably then, she came into contact with Kamil Paşa, the grand vizier to Abdülhamit II, and developed good relations with his daughter Makboulé. It is her friendship with Makboulé, renamed with the pseudonym Fatima by Ellison, that is crucial in the development of her writing career in Turkey as she invites Ellison to stay during the end of 1913 and beginning of 1914.

Her stay with the renamed Fatima formed the basis of a regular column for *The Daily Telegraph* entitled "Life in the Harem," which, in 1915, was collected, edited, and published in book form as the suggestively titled *An Englishwoman in a Turkish Harem*. In her work, Ellison demonstrates a shrewd understanding of the exotic and titillating allure that the harem evoked in her British readers. Teresa Heffernan and Reina Lewis eloquently summarize this as follows:

> Classifications like "Englishwoman" and "Turkish harem" do not simply indicate geographical locations: the fruitful contrast of gender, religions, and nationality keyed into a set of knowledges about the presumed differences between East and West, Christianity and Islam, whose imagined incompatability Ellison set out to disprove. (Heffernan and Lewis 2007: ix)

Emphasizing that this book had cultural merit rather than being another lascivious account of the goings-on in an all-female space, *An Englishwoman in a Turkish Harem* opened with a foreword written by Edward Granville-Browne, a scholar of Ottoman and Persian literature at Cambridge University, and closed with an afterword by the author herself who, writing during the First World War when the Ottoman Empire and Britain were at war with one another, demonstrates a large amount of sympathy for Turkey and suggests that Britain should forge an alliance with the country. Even while making political overtures, Ellison clearly understood that the most effective way to get her message across to the British public was to use the appeal of the "harem." There are many examples in the text where Ellison shows a reflexive understanding of how to use the exoticism of the harem to subvert dominant Orientalist stereotypes. In the first chapter of her book, she addresses the issue directly, commenting that "a chapter, at least, on harem life will always add to the value of the book," many of which "are written, not to extend the truth about a people, but only to sell" (Ellison

1915: 15). She also contrasts Western expectations with the "quiet harem existence" she experienced:

> To the Western ear, to be staying in a Turkish harem sounds alarming, and not a little—yes, let us confess it—improper. When, before I left this country, I had the impudence to tell a newspaper correspondent that I was longing to get back to the harem experience, I was accused of "advocating polygamy," for to the uninitiated the word "harem" means a collection of wives legitimate or otherwise, and even the initiated prefers to pretend he knows no other meaning. (Ellison 1915: 2)

Ellison continually frustrates prurient Western assumptions by naming chapters "The Prophet and Polygamy" and "The Man with Two Wives," then, as in the first chapter, remarks that "the Turk loves his home and he loves his wife. He is an indulgent husband and a kind father" (Ellison 1915: 15), thereby completely destroying British Orientalist desire for salacious details of concubinage and polygamy.

However, in one chapter, Ellison does give many Western readers what they might expect, as Fatima procures Ellison clearance to visit the Imperial Harem in Istanbul's Dolmabahçe Palace. Ellison describes the experience as "the first time that I have felt myself really within a harem" (Ellison 1915: 36) and recalls a scene of excess which was closely guarded by eunuchs. Even so, Ellison regards the Harem with a culturally relativist perspective:

> It is true, Fatima explains to me, that all these women are solemnly asked four times at the end of the year whether they would like to marry and leave the harem. I say to myself, then, if they stay it is because they wish to stay, and are therefore happy [. . .] I longed to break down for them the lattice-work which is always there between them and the sun, to fling the windows wide open, so that they could breathe the fresh air, and open the doors so that they, too, might go out. And yet not one of these women seemed in the least to feel her slavery, and, no doubt, they would turn their backs in horror on the ugly, unprotected existence of some of the women of my country. (Ellison 1915: 37)

At once inviting sexualized stereotypes and then frustrating them, Ellison encourages the reader to assess the harem code on its own cultural terms and also goes on to suggest that the harem inhabitants may find criticism with British gender orders. But still, her account is remarkably superficial. Ellison's inability to converse in Turkish means that she can only assume that these women want to stay and that she must accept what Fatima tells her as fact which, given Fatima's social standing as the daughter of a minister, could hardly be considered unbiased.

Lewis is right, however, to point out that Ellison's inclusion of the Imperial Harem in her text also serves as a fruitful contrast to the other harem spaces she visits. Ellison emphasizes that the Imperial Harem is an exception and, rather, for the most part, the harem is actually a domestic space. In the previous chapter to the Imperial Harem episode, she records how

> [t]he Turkish home in which I'm staying has little in common with the harem described by most Western writers, and no doubt those readers accustomed to the *usual* notions of harem life will consider my surroundings disappointingly Western. (Ellison 1915: 19)

More familiar than foreign for her readers, Ellison casts an ethnographic eye over her surroundings. The harem she finds herself in is actually a domestic space that is decorated with European furniture, artwork, and *objets d'art*. The mythical nature of the harem is therefore repeatedly contested in Ellison's work and this is especially the case when she attends a feminist meeting in Istanbul:

> I asked Halide-Hanoum [Halide Edip], perhaps the most active and best known of modern Turkish women, in the name of one of our prominent suffrage societies, how we English women could help the Turkish women in their advancement. "Ask them," she said, "to delete for ever that misunderstood word 'harem,' and speak of us in our Turkish 'homes.' Ask them to try and dispel the nasty atmosphere which a wrong meaning of the word has cast over our lives. Tell them what our existence really is." (Ellison 1915: 17)

Thus, Ellison entices her readers by using the titillating connotations of the harem, then exposes and critiques the Orientalist assumptions underpinning this prurient fascination

But the harem signifies more than this in Ellison's writing: in her discussion of harems as domestic same-sex spaces, Ellison makes comparisons and critiques how British discourses of domesticity and marriage disadvantage women in the UK. On the topic of polygamy, for example, Ellison finds two women who are married to a Sufi dervish and, after asking them why they are too "proud" not to divorce their husband, she reflects on how their resistance to seek alimony is matched by the number of unhappy British women who are insistent on suffering rather than leaving their marriages. In both instances, she argues, more divorces would set a normalizing precedent in which leaving unhealthy marriages would become acceptable for all women. Patronizingly, she summarizes how "[t]hey [. . .] like other women of Turkey, will learn as the women of the West are learning, that they must as individuals, insist on their rights for the benefit of the community, and reserve their pride for something else" (Ellison 1915: 136). Another key point is how Ellison is incredulous at the support Turkish women receive from men. At the aforementioned women's rights meeting, Ellison finds it "almost incomprehensible" (Ellison 1915: 65) that men are in attendance and offering supportive speeches and comments. This is something that contrasts sharply with the way that men in Britain oversaw the jailing and force-feeding of suffragettes who engaged in public rallies and demonstrations.

Ellison's work is also unique in that it provides space for women "from the Harem" to speak, thereby enabling them to actively engage and reshape the Orientalizing forces that silence them. For the purposes of this chapter, the most important is Zeyneb Hanım whose recollections of the British Houses of Parliament opened this chapter. Her real name Hadidje Zennour, Zeyneb was the daughter of Noury Bey, the foreign minister under Sultan Adülhamit II, and the granddaughter of a French military officer who had converted to Islam after falling in love with an Ottoman Circassian woman (Lewis 2004: 19). Ellison, Zeyneb Hanım, and Zeyneb's sister Melek Hanım (real name Neyr) were friends and collaborators who met sometime in the early twentieth century.[2] Lewis explains that there is some confusion and "bewildering self-contradiction" (Lewis 2004: 21) with regard to when exactly the three women met. Initially, Zeyneb Hanım dates the trio's crossing paths in the French town of Fontainebleau to 1906, thereby dating their meeting before Ellison's stint as a correspondent in Turkey and before her lengthy stay in 1913–14. However, Ellison later describes first becoming acquainted with the sisters during her 1905 visit to Turkey. Either way, this is the beginning of a series of perplexing details about the relationship between Grace Ellison and Zeyneb Hanım which I mention not to be pedantic but to set the scene for a series of ambiguities that shape the writers' literary output and exchange to which I will return in due course.

Ellison was instrumental in the publication of Zeyneb Hanım's travelogue *A Turkish Woman's Impressions*, which came out two years before Ellison's *An Englishwoman in a Turkish Harem*. Zeyneb Hanım's book consists of a series of letters addressed to Ellison written during her travels across Italy, Switzerland, France, and Britain. These letters were heavily, and sometimes obstructively, edited by Ellison and published with an introduction by her. An indicative example of this editing process occurs when Zeyneb Hanım writes of her visit to London. Ellison intervenes in the text to disassociate herself from Zeyneb Hanım's criticism of Christianity. Nevertheless, like Ellison, Zeyneb Hanım is interested in deconstructing the Orientalist gaze that stereotypes Ottoman women. Yet, in Zeyneb Hanım's writing this takes a different direction. Rather than Ellison's rejection of Western abstractions, Zeyneb Hanım perceives plenty of harem spaces within Britain—as shown by her visit to the Houses of Parliament. Another fascinating example is when she stays at a Ladies' Club in London. Opening in the late nineteenth century, Ladies' Clubs were places of refuge and rest for, as the journalist Dora Jones put it in 1899, "the evolution of the independent professional woman" (Rappaport 2000: 96). Zeyneb Hanım's choice of residence in London, then, situates her within an upper to upper-middle class milieu of educated women, much like Ellison's company in Istanbul. Crucially, though, to Zeyneb Hanım's eyes, the Ladies' Club also closely resembles that mysterious female-only space of such erotic enchantment to the West (Zeyneb Hanım 1913: 182–6). As with her observations of the Ladies' Gallery in Parliament, Lewis reads this as a form of "haremisation in reverse" whereby Western Orientalist discourses are sent back to their "place of origin" (Lewis 2004: 223). But I think this interpretation underplays the critical power of Zeyneb Hanım's use of harem terminology. Consonant with Apter's theorizations of a translation zone as a critical space of encounter, which throw up the values of a culture to fresh scrutiny, here the notion of the "harem" is displaced from an Orientalized setting and used both to mock British expectations and to offer critical readings of British economies of gender (Apter 1996). In other words, Zeyneb Hanım is using "the harem" to argue that actually Britain also has an unhealthy attitude toward women in public space.

It is worth noting here that Zeyneb Hanım, like Ellison, is also quite clearly playing with her British audience. Her book's title *A Turkish Woman's European Impressions*, for instance, mirrors Ellison's astute reading of vocabulary that would excite British readers— the words "Turkish Woman" signifying the exotic and foreign. However, there is another crucial aspect that piqued British interest in the text, as the title page claims that the book is by "Zeyneb Hanım, heroine of Pierre Loti's novel *Les Désenchantées*" (Loti 1906). Lewis explains that Zeyneb and her sister Melek were using pseudonyms that they took from the lead protagonists in Pierre Loti's 1906 novel *Les désenchantées* (*The Disenchanted*) which was allegedly based on the sisters themselves. The perplexing story is that Zeyneb and her sister Melek were long-term fans of Loti, who had penned two Orientalist Romance novels set in Istanbul, and so, when they heard that the writer was visiting the city in 1904, they wrote to him to arrange a meeting. The sisters viewed him as "a friend of the Turks," and such was their enjoyment of his novel *Aziyade* (Loti 1879) that Zeyneb had even written him a fan letter (Lewis 2004: 19–20; Nakai 2015: 25). The sisters believed that Loti could use his influence to write a novel that would incite European intellectual favor toward the cause of female liberation in Ottoman Anatolia and, in particular, against the practice of arranged marriages at a time when Zeyneb Hanım's father was organizing a suitor for her. Of course, it should be noted here that in both nineteenth-century France and Britain, arranged marriages existed among the landed gentry anyway.

Zeyneb and Melek's plan, however, turned out quite differently and Loti took considerable artistic license. In Loti's novel, three Turkish women approach a French novelist and ask him to write about their fathers' attempts to force them into marriage against their will. However, the writer falls in love with one of these women and, when she briefly lifts her veil, he sees that her face is the mirror image of his former lover. In a ridiculous melodramatic denouement, the woman then dies of unfulfilled love for the French novelist. Quite obviously, then, Loti's novel contradicts the sort of narrative the sisters had wanted from the author. Even though Loti had changed their names in his novel (Hadidje Zennour became Zeyneb and Neyr became Melek), the sisters still felt sufficiently unsafe and, for reasons still not known, they fled Turkey for Europe shortly before the novel was even published in 1906.

Nevertheless, there is an added complication as in Loti's novel, Zeyneb and Melek had a third sister. In 1923, an expose entitled *Le secret des "Désenchantées"* was published by a French journalist called Marie-Amélie Léra (or Lerat), under the male pseudonym Marc Hélys, in which she confesses that the third sister named Djenane was based on her as she had provided Zeyneb with contact details for Loti and acted as an intermediary (Hélys 1923). By this time, the novel had been translated into a number of languages, and was still popular with British readers. Léra's confession appeared shortly after the translation of Loti's original novel into Turkish in 1921 as *Naşad Kızlar* and, although there is no evidence to suggest Léra was aware of this publication, her decision to write under a fake male name can reasonably be assumed to be a tactic for protection against reproach, thereby emphasizing the controversial nature of this confusing episode.

No scholar has ever been able to get to the bottom of this bewildering story, yet it presents a number of fascinating insights into the ways Ottoman Turkishness was marketed and conceptualized in turn-of-the-century Britain (and France). *Les désenchantées* is a paradigmatic example of a global novel that was written in French, consumed by French-reading audiences outside of France's borders, quickly translated into English by Clara Bell, and which also fit in with common Orientalizing discourses shared by both Britain and France during the late nineteenth and early twentieth centuries. As Lewis points out, the novel "remained a touchstone for arguments about the representation of the Ottoman woman and female emancipation" (2004: 23) and a number of British and American women travel writers in the period, such as Hester Donaldson Jenkins and Demetra Vaka Brown, invoked the novel to decry the supposedly poor situation of women in Turkey (Lewis 2004: 23). In both Zeyneb Hanım's *A Turkish Woman's European Impressions* and Ellison's *An Englishwoman in a Turkish Harem*, there are frequent references to Loti's novel and Zeyneb's alleged background which are mentioned in a matter-of-fact way; Zeyneb refers to herself as a "désenchantée" and Ellison describes staying with Zeyneb and her sister who are "the heroines of Pierre Loti's 'Désenchantées'" (Zeyneb Hanım 1913: 116). Whatever the truth of Zeyneb's identity, both she and Ellison were able to use British Orientalist tropes to their advantage to gain readers and garner attention through a novel that Orientalized Istanbul and circulated across Europe.

In all likelihood then, Zeyneb was not who she or Ellison said she was. However, in both Zeyneb and Ellison's "performances" of identity, the two were also intervening into gendered and national-cultural parameters of what or who could be represented as Turkish. For example, on the title page of Ellison's book *An Englishwoman in a Turkish Harem*, the reader is faced with a photographic image of Ellison accompanied by the caption "the Author in Turkish costume" (Ellison 1915: frontispiece). As Lewis puts it, this caption would have "simultaneously enacted and frustrated" her British readers' expectations by both aligning her, in an ethnographic sense, with the people she was writing about, thereby proving that she was able to gain entry into Turkish spaces, and also pointing to the instability of national-cultural identity labels such as "Turkish" (and English). Kader Konuk in her influential 2004 article on ethno-masquerade in Ottoman and British encounters, however, demonstrates that Ellison's attempts to pass as Turkish frequently backfire on Ottoman subjects.[3] At one point in the text, Ellison disguises herself as a Muslim Turk in order to gain entry to the holy mosque in Istanbul's Eyüp neighborhood which, she reports, refuses entry to Christians. However, suggesting that her costume was not foolproof, she confesses to an Islamic preacher at the mosque that she is a Christian. For Konuk, this demonstrates that Ellison's attempts at ethno-masquerade failed but they still thrilled her.

Writing on Loti who was also fond of dressing up as Turkish, Apter contends that passing "undermines previous conventions of absolute difference" and "serves as an example of the fluidity of boundaries" (Lewis 2004: 213). Intriguingly though, for Ellison, the thrill of "passing" as Turkish was rarely directed at Turks but, rather, at her British compatriots who are the arbiters of whether she successfully performs Turkishness; as Konuk writes, this "might say something about the difficulty of passing in the eyes of natives, as well as the main addressee of Ellison's ethnomasquerade, namely English men" (Konuk 2004: 399). Konuk's argument is proved by Ellison's visit to Eyüp:

> Just before we reached our carriage, I saw a dear friend with her accustomed unselfishness escorting some English visitors round as much as they, Christians, could see of the holy city of Eyoub. She recognised my voice, and I was introduced as a Turkish lady to my compatriots.
>
> I felt just a little guilty at their delight in meeting a real Turkish woman, but it was too dangerous to undeceive them in those fantastical surroundings. "And how well you speak English too!" they said. "English was the first language I spoke," I answered truthfully. I wonder whether Miss A. ever told them who I really was. (Ellison 1915: 169)

I believe that photographically, and in her walks around Istanbul, Ellison was "performing" Turkishness for a British audience and, as her joking in the above quotation demonstrates, she was seeking to expose the ridiculousness of their Orientalist expectations and judgments. Such a view then corresponds to Apter's work on the translation zone as a space in which cross-cultural concepts are encountered, but also critiqued.

For Zeyneb Hanım, photography and clothing work to "validate" her identity as a Turkish woman in British eyes but, as Konuk attests, Zeyneb's writing and captured image reveal a far more ambivalent subject positioning. Particularly indicative of Konuk's point are the two photographs that frame *A Turkish Woman's European Impressions*. Her book opens in a similar manner to Ellison's text with a picture depicting Zeyneb Hanım in Ottoman dress with the caption "Zeyneb in her Paris Dressing Room" and underneath this, it reads "She is wearing the Yashmak and Feradjè, or cloak" (Zeyneb Hanım 1913: frontispiece). The opening picture therefore explicates the book's title by showing a stereotypical image of a veiled woman. Her background comprises of objects that her readers would associate far more closely with Istanbul than with Paris, such as carpets with Koranic inscriptions. At the end of the book, however, is an image of Zeyneb's sister Melek in nineteenth-century European dress on the veranda of a house in Fontainebleau. Likewise, throughout the text, Zeyneb Hanım presents alternate images of herself and her sister in both Ottoman-Turkish and European attire. Zeyneb's discourse on the common turn-of-the-twentieth-century European practice of wearing hats is also significant. Whereas Ellison dislikes the veil but enjoys having an Englishman mistake her veiled appearance as Turkish and "paying compliments to our 'silhouttes'" (Ellison 1915: 69), Zeyneb views the hat as "curious, but charming all the same" and so dons the numerous hats which are bought for her as a gift while in Switzerland with little feeling either way. Konuk contends that her ambivalent attitudes to hats imply that "[s]elf-Orientalization as well as ethno-masquerade is employed to strengthen the narrative authority of Zeyneb Hanım's letters" (Konuk 2004: 404).

I would argue, however, that Zeyneb Hanım is unsuccessful precisely because of this ambivalence. In a review from the *Times Literary Supplement* published in 1913, the reviewer judges Zeyneb Hanım's book negatively and draws particular attention to her claims of Turkishness:

> She is no typical Turkish lady, but the granddaughter of a Frenchman, who, to use Mr. Pickthall's coinage, "islamed," and her upbringing and the political unrest encouraged her inherited disposition to revolt. She is apparently one of those women who belong by temperament to the rebels. She detests the suffragettes; yet, but for her high breeding and traditional fastidiousness, she has the making of one. For, however much she differs from and excels the average woman of her race, she possesses

to the full that characteristic of clear vision and independent thought which Mr. Pickthall sets first among the virtues of the harem. (Konuk 2004: 406)[4]

This review highlights that Zeyneb Hanım was unable to convince British readers of her Turkish subjectivity precisely because she did not completely engage in the kinds of performative Turkishness that Ellison so clearly reveled in. At one point in the book, Zeyneb Hanım includes photographs of a harem space; however, these images completely contradict Orientalist expectations. In contrast to her carpeted backdrop in Paris, these are depictions of domesticated interiors of the kind Ellison wrote about staying in. Zeyneb Hanım herself notes underneath one of these pictures:

> This photograph was taken expressly for a London paper. It was returned with this comment: "The British public would not accept this as a picture of a Turkish Harem." As a matter of fact, in the smartest Turkish houses European furniture is much in evidence. (Zeyneb Hanoum 1913: 192)

As is inferred from the review, Zeyneb's attempts to critique these misconceptions fail as they do not accord with received ideas of latticed windows and thick patterned carpets. However, Ellison in her book, despite writing about similar spaces and critiquing Western stereotypes, still included an account of the Imperial Harem which she emphatically described as "the harem in a real sense of the word, the harem about which Western readers expect to hear" (Ellison 1915: 36). Zeyneb's ambivalence, then, means she does not correlate with what the British public understood "Turkish" to be whereas Ellison, for all her criticism of British abstracted ideas of Turkishness, was able to deliver satisfyingly Orientalized preconceptions.

As I wrote at the beginning of this chapter, Damrosch (2003) understands "world literature" as the study of texts that, no matter where they were written or what context they were published in, can gain in translation, thereby crossing linguistic and cultural barriers. The relevance of Ellison and Zeyneb Hanım's work is that it problematizes and necessitates a rethinking of Damrosch's model. These texts do not gain in translation nor offer a way of reading gender transnationally, but actually show that for their British readers, "Turkishness" consisted of a series of gender and cultural stereotypes that, in their ability to perform and claim authenticity to, meant regurgitating certain stereotypes even as Ellison and Zeyneb Hanım worked to criticize them. Ultimately, then, turn-of-the-century British readers had a fixed idea of what being Turkish was and the success of Ellison and Zeyneb Hanım's texts depended on how well they followed these abstractions and "performed" Turkishness.

Reading and critically unpacking what Turkishness, and the harem as a term that connoted Orientalized gender identities, means in these two turn-of-the-century travelogues makes clear that notions of world literature need to be reformulated to accommodate conceptions of cultural translation and performative identity. The kinds of cultural translation proposed by Homi Bhabha (1994), Rey Chow (1995), and Emily Apter (2006) draw attention to how cultures, as fluid and unstable entities by definition, are constructed according to global hegemonic power dynamics. Theories such as Apter's "the translation zone," then, identify where cultures misread, misinterpret, or subtly critique one another. This is vital critical apparatus in a historical and lived reality where culture is used to uphold or reflect patterns of global power, as true now as it was at the turn of the century. Rey Chow's work on "coercive mimeticism" is worth calling to mind at this juncture. For Chow, cultural production by those deemed an "ethnic subject" is doomed to "resemble and replicate the very banal preconceptions that have been appended to them, a process in which they are expected to objectify themselves in accordance with the already seen and thus to authenticate the familiar imaginings of them as ethnics" (Chow 1995: 107). It is my contention that world literature too frequently bypasses this kind of crucial political questioning and fails to shine a light on texts which merely engage in the repetition of received ideas, such as Ellison's and Zeyneb Hanım's performed Turkishness. Understandings of world literature, then, should be expanded to include texts that engage in forms of performative identity in which cultures are reduced to regurgitated stereotype or exposed as contingent and constructed.

To this end, travel writing is a valuable ground to make world literature's theoretical shortcomings apparent. As critics such as Robyn Davidson (1980), Lisle (2006), Patrick Holland, and Graham Huggan (1998) have demonstrated, travel writing is often invested in reinstating a sense of rigid difference between cultures in order to sell and satisfy curiosity. In so doing, the genre is often complicit with global sociopolitical orders as the texts are frequently "fashioned over and against a series of others who are denied the power of representing themselves" (Lisle 2006: 69). Far from emphasizing that which is similar, travel writing has often sought to reaffirm cultural stereotypes about Orientalized societies and even suggest a degree of moral or intellectual superiority on the part of the writer's national or cultural background. Clearly, then, travel writing is a form of literary and cultural production that definitively and generically seeks to represent the world, yet not always in a manner that fits Damrosch's reading of world literature, and often comes closer to resembling the kinds of representational straitjacketing that Chow observes.

In relation to Turkish Literature as world literature, my case study shows the hurdles which writers, particularly women writers, had to navigate through in order to be read by an audience outside Turkey. Transcultural discourses on the harem, as well as what visually and textually resembled an imagined idea of a "Turkish woman," loomed large in the British (and Euro-American) cultural imagination, largely fueled by travel narratives. Zeyneb Hanım's ambivalence about these discourses and her failure to give in to coercive mimeticism meant she never gained a large readership whereas Ellison's work went on to be cited by writers well after the declaration of the Turkish Republic in 1923. The notion of "performing" Turkishness is even reflected in the author (and employee of the British government's Ministry of Propaganda) John Buchan's highly popular 1916 novel *Greenmantle* which, against the backdrop of the First World War, tracks a British spy's attempts to terminate the influence of a charismatic Turkish Islamic preacher named Greenmantle (Buchan 1916).[5] Greenmantle's aim was to appeal to the Muslim subjects of the British Empire and convince them that supporting the Ottoman Empire (and Germany) against Britain was a religious calling. When the spy Richard Hannay manages to locate Greenmantle, he finds that he's a British defector dressed in a stereotyped notion of Turkish clothing and pretending to be Turkish. With this in mind, Ellison and Zeyneb Hanım's performances do not appear in a vacuum but also relate to political connections between Britain and Turkey.

Nevertheless, it is perversely these performances and mistranslations that connect depictions of Turkishness with other cultures in the Middle East, North Africa, and South Asia. Edward Said (1978) famously wrote of the role of travel writing in the European colonial project, emphasizing a culture's backwardness in distinction to a dominant culture's superiority. In the discursive production of British India, for instance, the harem was fundamental in showing the supposedly exceptional difference of how women lived in South Asia compared to Britain, thereby seeking to justify colonization and build a sense of British moral superiority over Islamicate cultures in India. In her work on how China was perceived in Western cultural production, Chow argues that countries that were Orientalized in a manner analogous to Said's model but remained "territorially independent" from the West "offer even better illustrations of how imperialism works—i.e., how imperialism as ideological domination succeeds best without physical coercion, without actually capturing the body and the land" (Chow 2003: 8). Turkey offers one such comparative case: a country that was not colonized and was actually a colonizing power but, in relation to the harem at least, the writing strategies and representations that Britain employed to present the Ottoman Empire were remarkably similar to those used in relation to India and were used to comparable ends.

## Notes

1 As there were no surnames in Ottoman-era Turkey, Zeyneb Hanoum's letters were published under the name Zeyneb Hanoum. "Hanoum" is an Anglicized version of the term "Hanım" meaning "lady." In line with Konuk (2004) and Lewis (2004), I have chosen to use the modern Turkish version of "Hanım."

2 Melek Hanım is also the author of an Orientalist novel entitled *Abdul Hamid's Daughter: The Tragedy of an Orientalist Princess* which was edited by Ellison (Melek Hanoum 1913). For more information on this, consult (Lewis 2004).
3 By ethno-masquerade, I am referring to "the performance of an ethnic identity through the mimicking of clothes, gestures, appearance, language, cultural codes, or other components of identity formation" (Konuk 2004: 393).
4 Muhammad Marmeduke Pickthall, to whom the review refers, was a renowned Islamic scholar and British convert to Islam. He published a number of travel narratives about the Middle East, books on Islamic scholarship and a translation of the Koran in 1930.
5 For more information on Buchan's role in the Ministry of Propaganda and the role of Greenmantle, see (Katz 2016: 199–233).

# References

Apter, Emily. (1996), "Acting Out Orientalism: Sapphic Theatricality in Turn-of-the-Century Paris," in E. Diamond (ed.), *Performance and Cultural Politics*, 102–16, London: Routledge.
Apter, Emily. (2006), *The Translation Zone: A New Comparative Literature*, Princeton, NJ: Princeton University Press.
Bhabha, Homi K. (1994), *The Location of Culture*, London: Routledge.
Booth, Marilyn. (2010), "Introduction," in M. Booth (ed.), *Harem Histories: Envisioning Places and Living Spaces*, 1–23, Durham, NC: Duke University Press.
Buchan, John. ([1916] 1999), *Greenmantle*, Oxford: Oxford University Press.
Butler, Judith. ([1990] 2014), *Gender Trouble: Feminism and the Subversion of Identity*, London: Routledge.
Chow, Rey. (1995), *The Protestant Ethnic and the Spirit of Capitalism*, New York: Columbia University Press.
Chow, Rey. (2003), *Writing Diaspora: Tactics of Intervention in Contemporary Cultural Studies*, Bloomington: Indiana Press.
Damrosch, David. (2003), *What Is World Literature?*, Princeton: Princeton University Press.
Davidson, Robyn. ([1980] 1998), *Tracks*, London: Picador.
Ellison, Grace. ([1915] 2007), *An Englishwoman in a Turkish Harem*, Piscataway, NJ: Gorgias Press.
Heffernan, Teresa and Lewis, Reina. (2007), "Feminist Dialogues Across Cultures: An English Woman in a Turkish Harem and the Turkish Harem in an English Woman," in Ellison Grace, *An Englishwoman in a Turkish Harem*, Piscataway, NJ: Gorgias Press.
Hélys, Marc. (1923), *Les secrets de "Désenchantées,"* Paris: Perren.
Holland, Patrick and Graham Huggan. (1998), *Tourists with Typewriters: Critical Reflections on Contemporary Travel Writing*, Ann Arbor: University of Michigan Press.
Katz, David. S. (2016), *The Shaping of Turkey in the British Cultural Imagination, 1776–1923*, Basingstoke: Palgrave Macmillan.

Konuk, Kader. (2004), "Ethnomasquerade in Ottoman-European Encounters: Reenacting Lady Mary Wortley Montagu," *Criticism* 46 (3): 393–414.
Loti, Pierre. ([1879] 1989), *Aziyadé*. Tr. Marjorie Laurie, London: Routledge.
Loti, Pierre. (1906), *Les Désenchantées. Romans des harems turcs contemprains*, Paris: Calmann-Levy.
Lewis, Reina. (2004), *Rethinking Orientalism: Women, Travel and the Ottoman Harem*, London: I.B. Tauris.
Lisle, Debbie. (2006), *The Global Politics of Contemporary Travel Writing*, Cambridge: Cambridge University Press.
Melek Hanoum. (1913), *Abdul Hamid's Daughter: The Tragedy of an Ottoman Princess*, London: Meuthen Press.
Nakai, Asako. (2015), "Shakespeare's Sisters in Istanbul: Grace Ellison and the Politics of Feminist Friendship," *Journal of Postcolonial Writing* 51 (1): 22–33.
Pratt, Mary L. (1992), *Imperial Eyes: Travel Writing and Transculturation*, Abingdon: Routledge.
Rappaport, Erika Diane. (2000), *Shopping for Pleasure: Women in the Making of London's West End*, Princeton, NJ: Princeton University Press.
Said, Edward W. ([1978] 2003), *Orientalism*, London: Penguin.
Voltaire. ([1732] 2004), *Zaïre*, Paris: Éditions Flammarion.
Zeyneb Hanoum. ([1913] 2013), *A Turkish Woman's European Impressions*, Cambridge: Cambridge University Press.

# 5

# "The Living Link between India and Turkey"

# Halide Edib on the Subcontinent

*Anirudha Dhanawade
and Şima İmşir*

In 1912 a team of Indian doctors took ship from Bombay for the Ottoman Empire. Their mission, organized under the auspices of the Indian Red Crescent, was to provide medical assistance to the Ottoman army as the empire fought against the forces of Bulgaria, Greece, Serbia, and Montenegro in the First Balkan War and they were led by one Mukhtar Ahmed Ansari, a distinguished physician with a long-standing involvement in the politics of Indian nationalism.[1] Ansari described his travels throughout the empire in a series of letters published in the Indian newspaper *Comrade*, and it was in one such letter that he described meeting a certain Turkish writer in Istanbul in 1913: a woman who was "considered one of the leading lights of the Party of Union and Progress" (Akçapar 2014: 238). For the first time, the Indian public had been introduced to the figure of Halide Edib.

Well known as a writer, political activist, and nationalist, both in the last years of the Ottoman Empire and in the early years of the Turkish Republic, Halide Edib was a prolific author who wrote twenty-one novels in addition to short story collections, plays, scholarly works, and two autobiographies. Producing her first works during the Young Turk revolution in 1908, which would result in the restoration of the constitutional monarchy by Sultan

Abdul Hamid II and a parliamentary majority for the Committee of Union and Progress, she asserted throughout her life that her political activism and literary production were intertwined with one another (Halide Edib 2005: 260). Yet Edib's politics were also rather protean, and her ideas concerning nationalism, republicanism, and feminism—as well as her understanding of Islam—were all subject to frequent and substantial change. In 1912, for example, she published a novel entitled *Yeni Turan* (New Turan), in which she shared her utopian beliefs in Turanism, an ideology that aimed to unite Ural-Altaic people inside and outside the borders of the Ottoman Empire, and which had found substantial support within the Committee of Union and Progress. A national and international success, the novel was translated into German in 1916 by Friedrich Schrader under the title *Das neue Turan: ein türkisches Frauenschicksal*. Yet Edib's enthusiasm for Turanism, and by extension for the CUP, came to an end when she began to openly criticize their policies toward the Armenian population of the Ottoman Empire. Indeed, after 1915, her disappointment was such that she distanced herself not only from the Unionists but also from her own writing.

Perhaps the most volatile phase in Edib's political life came in the aftermath of the First World War, when she became a vocal proponent of the American mandate, believing that it would "prevent the Ottoman Empire from further territory loss . . . protect Turkey from the influence and rivalries of Europe through an alliance with a power stronger than Europe, and . . . strengthen the nation against the threats of the Christian minorities" (Adak 2005: xi). Less than two years later, however, she found herself fleeing to Anatolia with her husband to join the Turkish Independence War as a member of Mustafa Kemal's National Army.[2] Yet her time as a Kemalist revolutionary was also short-lived, and after victory in the War of Independence she would be increasingly critical of Atatürk's leadership. Her growing antipathy toward him is especially evident in her memoirs, in which she emphasizes the evils of totalitarianism and dictatorship, observing that nations tend to suffer most in the hands of self-centered leaders (Halide Edib 2005: 268).

Edib's estrangement from Atatürk would lead her reputation in Turkey to become complicated, especially after she went into self-imposed exile in 1926 in London and Paris. She was subsequently condemned by him in his epic 1927 speech *Nutuk* (in which her previous support for the American mandate was used to call her nationalist fervor into question).[3] Eventually however, she returned to her native country in 1939, a year after Atatürk's death, and in 1950 became an MP for the Democrat Party which formed the opposition to the Republican People's Party founded under his leadership. After serving for four years as an MP, she likewise accused the Democrat Party of authoritarianism and resigned, warning people not to become the victims of politicians who were incapable of moving beyond their personal interests (Halide Edib 1954).

Edib's feminism is another aspect of her politics which defies simple definition or description. While she was always fervent and outspoken on the issue of women's rights, her literary works in particular portrayed female characters in an idealistic fashion, which arguably affirmed and reinforced normative gender definitions. As Hülya Adak has argued, sexuality in particular functions in Edib's works as a trap for female protagonists, who are unable to find happiness or fulfilment if they find themselves "transgressing socially acceptable modes of conduct" (Adak 2005: ix).

Despite (or perhaps because of) her changeable politics, throughout her life Edib placed herself at the heart of political turmoil and change. Her role as an author, an intellectual, and even a soldier during Turkey's War of Independence, as well as her work and activism on the issue of women's emancipation, gave her an important and quite distinctive position at a time when Turkey's anti-colonial independence movement was closely observed across the world. For instance, an article published in *The New York Times* in 1928 was entitled "A Woman Speaks for the New Turkey: Halide Edib Hanum Comes to America as a Striking Symbol of the Changed Life of the Near East – A Woman of the New Turkey" (Price 1928). Edib's significant role in the independence movement, as well as the fact that she was seen as a symbol of women's emancipated position in the "new Turkey," marked her literature as world literature.

Accordingly, during her years of exile, Edib acquired a certain eminence in pre-independence India. Her 1922 novel *Ateşten Gömlek* (*The Shirt of Flame*), for example, was published in English in the city of Lahore in 1932 under the title *The Daughter of Smyrna*, the only English edition to appear since Edib herself had translated the text for publication in 1924 (Halide Edib 1924). In 1935, moreover, Edib traveled to India at Ansari's invitation to deliver a series of lectures about Turkish history and culture at the Jamia Millia Islamia University in New Delhi, which were attended by many of the leading figures in Indian politics including Mahatma Gandhi. Edib was described as a "fighter in the cause of freedom" and a "choice spirit of the age," by Mahadev Desai, Gandhi's personal secretary, and her popularity extended beyond intellectuals, writers, and independence campaigners (Desai 1935: 12). In Hyderabad, as the Indian historian Mushirul Hasan recounts, "disorderly scenes marred her talk, with 5,000 people jostling each other to gain entry into the Town Hall," while "over 10,000 people attended her lectures in Calcutta" (Hasan 2002: xxi).

This chapter offers a critical analysis and explanation of Edib's appeal in India in the decades before independence, and thus offers a case study of the reception of a canonical Turkish writer in a historically very significant non-European context, thereby marking her as a figure of world literature. The chapter explores some of the complicated ways in which Halide Edib's work manifests as world literature in the Indian context by looking at meanings which could be given to Turkish nationalism and the early history of the

Turkish Republic in a country which was itself struggling with the effects of European colonialism, as well as with ideas concerning nationalism, secularism, and modernization.

The chapter is divided into three sections, considering in turn the Lahori translation of *Ateşten Gömlek*, Edib's lectures of 1935, and, finally, her 1937 book *Inside India*, which chronicled her travels across the subcontinent as well as her reflections on Indian politics. In each instance we try to give a sense of how and why these individual texts, and Edib's work as a whole, might have been attractive to audiences in colonial India. In addition, we attend to the differences *between* texts, showing how the reception of Turkish literature might illuminate some of the conflicting desires and anxieties which characterized Indian culture and politics during the 1930s.

## *Ateşten Gömlek* and *The Daughter of Smyrna*

In 1935 India's independence from British rule was still twelve years away, and the people of India were acutely aware of the realities of imperial violence. In 1932 the new viceroy of India Lord Willingdon had instituted the draconian Indian Emergency Powers Act, imprisoning over 100,000 Indians affiliated with the leading nationalist organization, the Indian National Congress; those imprisoned included Gandhi and Jawaharlal Nehru, who would become India's first prime minister. By 1934, however, the British government had also agreed to push through the constitutional reforms discussed in the so-called Round Table Conferences of 1930–2, and scheduled elections for 1935 and 1937. Thus, when Halide Edib arrived in Bombay in 1935, the politics of Indian nationalism stood at a delicate juncture. If it was possible to discern a liberalization of British policy, and perhaps even to glimpse independence upon the horizon, most Indians involved in the struggle for independence knew very well that the future of an independent India was far from assured and that in the meantime they still stood under threat from an oppressive colonial administration.[4]

In this context it is easy to see how and why Edib herself might have appealed to an Indian audience. Desai (1935: 12) wrote that Edib "has laboured and suffered all her life, written great books and striven to bring her people nearer to that freedom," emphasizing that her literary production went hand in hand with political praxis and with her significant role in the Turkish nationalist movement which would lead one nationalist periodical to call her "the mother of the Turk." Praised by Ansari (1934) as "a great world figure . . . whether you look on her as a Turkish feminist leader, as a world-renowned authority on education or as a great writer," Edib struck Indian observers too as the embodiment of a nation which had recently (and successfully) asserted its independence in the face of European aggression.

Both Edib and the Turkish Republic served as a screen for many of the desires and dreams of Indian nationalists.

The attraction of Edib's own life, redolent of a heroism born of nationalist enthusiasm, helps to explain why *Ateşten Gömlek* in particular was selected for translation by an Indian publishing house. For in 1919, when news of the Greek occupation of Izmir reached Istanbul, Edib delivered a now-famous speech in Sultanahmet which decried the invasion and electrified her audience. Her criticism of European governments for their "aggressive policy" applied "unjustly [and] sometimes even treacherously" suggests how her patriotism grew stronger after the occupation of the empire by the allied forces (Adıvar 1981: 134). Edib also made a differentiation between people and governments, warning her listeners not to confuse the two, while criticizing the European governments for not missing any opportunities "to break to pieces the last empire ruled by the crescent" (Adıvar 1981: 134).

This same speech would later appear in *Ateşten Gömlek*, delivered by the character of Ayesha, and the novel's translator Muhammad Yakub Khan was keen to draw his readers' attention to the fact. "[U]nder the garb of Aysha [sic]," he wrote, Edib "depicts her own patriotic fervour and her own adventures during the Turco-Greek War" (1940: vii). Khan also tellingly transformed the title of the novel from *The Shirt of Flame* to *The Daughter of Smyrna: A Story of the Rise of Modern Turkey, on the Ashes of the Ottoman Empire – the Turk's Revolt Against Western Domination, His Thrilling Adventures, Sufferings and Sacrifices in the Cause of National Honour and Independence*. Edib's novel, and the autobiographical representation of Edib *within* the novel, almost seems designed to show colonial readers precisely what patriotic subjects can achieve against "Western domination."

In his introduction to *The Daughter of Smyrna*, Khan (1940: viii) ventured his hope that the "sufferings and sacrifices of our Turkish brothers and sisters in the cause of national freedom ... may kindle something of that noble spark in the bosoms of the sons and daughters of India which is just now passing through the travail of a re-birth." Like others in the Raj he saw Turkish nationalism as an example for Indians to follow. But what is most striking about *The Daughter of Smyrna* is the fact that Khan took drastic liberties with Edib's original novel. In doing so, he reshaped the text and its portrayal of the Turkish War of Independence according to the concerns of Indian nationalism. His work thus demonstrates the difficulties involved in translating and mediating between different historical conditions, different national contexts, and divergent forms of nationalist ideology.

Set during the Turkish War of Independence, *Ateşten Gömlek* begins and ends in a hospital ward, as a mortally wounded soldier named Peyami recounts the story of the war through the burgeoning romance between Ayesha and his friend Ihsan. Upon Peyami's death, however, his doctors are unable to find any evidence that either Ihsan or Ayesha ever actually existed. Aside from ignoring the structure of Edib's original chapters, *The Daughter of Smyrna* erases this framing narrative from the text entirely, giving its Indian readers a quite different and arguably less sophisticated text as a result. But why should Khan have decided to transform *Ateşten Gömlek* so radically, rather than producing a more faithful translation of his source material?

In an article of 2013, Erdağ Göknar has argued that in the story of Ihsan and Ayesha, *Ateşten Gömlek* enacts for its readers the narration of the new Turkish nation-state. Ihsan, a major in the nationalist army, serves as an emblem of military resistance to foreign invasion, while throughout the course of the novel Ayesha is increasingly identified with Turkey itself: in Edib's words, she is "a symbol of [the] suffering country" (1924: 236). Ayesha and Peyami's relationship, according to Göknar, is thus a "symbolic union": it represents a new "imagined community" of freedom fighters devoted to and at one with their national ideal. Moreover, the fact that the two lovers seem to be figments of Peyami's imagination—literally, a fiction—demonstrates that this community must be actively produced, and that "Peyami's duty does not end on the battlefield, but also includes a struggle of intellect, imagination, and authorship in the construction of the national self/subject." As a consequence, Göknar asserts that "[t]he story of Peyami, Ayesha, and Ihsan . . . is above all the account of a psycho-social transformation from cosmopolitan Ottoman to national-secular 'Turk'" (2013: 42–4). Indeed, as Erol Köroğlu (2007) has pointed out, while *Ateşten Gömlek* describes the liberation of Izmir from Greek forces and Turkish victory in the War of Independence, it was actually written and published before the war came to an end. It is a proleptic novel of the nation-to-come, depicting not only the martial and imaginative struggle to create the new nation but also an image of what that nation will look like.

But while *Ateşten Gömlek* is fundamentally concerned with the narration of the future nation-state, *The Daughter of Smyrna* is rather more preoccupied with the iniquities of the Indian present, adapting Edib's novel in order to picture colonial injustice and the *emergence* of anti-colonial nationalism in response to it. If Edib's Ayesha is the symbol of a "suffering country," then she is also transfigured not only in her death but also in the defeat of the Greek army and the reconquest of Izmir. Khan, however, adds to his translation and in doing so emphasizes the portrayal of national humiliation and injury at the hands of a foreign power; as Ayesha delivers her speech at Sultanahmet in *The Daughter of Smyrna*, we read that she "was in fact a symbol . . . of the whole of the nation in mourning." In yet another addition, Khan writes that "[t]he nation had donned the crown of thorns" (Khan 1940: 13, 18). At the same time, his alterations to Edib's text accentuate the sense of a nationalist enthusiasm coming into being. For example, as Köroğlu (2007) observes, while Edib's own translation of a sentence in *Ateşten Gömlek* gives us the dry, procedural "A propaganda office with the name of Defence of Smyrna was organized in Istamboul,"

Khan renders this passage in rather more fervid terms: "there was but one cry that resounded all over—the defence of Smyrna! This magic expression attracted everybody" (Khan 1940: 18).

Köroğlu (2007) has argued that Khan's erasure of Edib's framing narrative, and his perhaps all-too-liberal translation, transforms the nationalist romance of *Ateşten Gömlek* into a kind of heroic epic. To this it might be added that Khan's rewriting of the novel focuses attention on a different moment in the nationalist struggle and in the development of a nationalist consciousness. For, as he wrote in his introduction, "India *is just now* passing through the travail of a re-birth." Crucially, this metaphor of parturition reappears in a lengthy passage of Khan's own invention, which describes the faces of Ihsan and another character, Cemal:

> On their oval faces played a strange ray of light.... This was the ray of confidence and hope. Apparently there was no reason for this new-born feeling.... It was this new-born sense of national suffering that inspired confidence. (Khan 1940: 18)

Here, as elsewhere, there is little pretense about the fact that Khan is using Edib's Turkish novel to describe an Indian scenario. If *The Daughter of Smyrna* amounts to a radical editorializing of *Ateşten Gömlek*, then that is of interest because it throws light upon the anxieties, as well as the hopes and dreams, that the example of Turkey and the figure of Edib could provoke in the Indian context. For while the original novel looks forward to a victory which was in fact achieved, amid the tumult of the 1930s the possibility of an independent India could still seem like a precarious possibility which was also as vulnerable as a newborn baby.

In addition, the way in which Khan adapted *Ateşten Gömlek* for his audience may betray some of the ambiguities in both Indian nationalist politics of the 1930s and Indian attitudes toward Turkey. If, as Göknar has argued, Edib used her novel to valorize the ideological transition from a composite Ottoman identity to "national-secular 'Turk,'" it would be far more difficult for an Indian writer to be quite so sanguine or sure about the outlines of self and society in an independent India. While the Congress had managed to gather together a broad coalition of forces, and in the 1937 elections had asserted its dominant position in Indian politics, what historian Maria Misra (2007: 182) has described as the "bewildering profusion of nationalist ideologies ... all competing to challenge the Raj to its last great fight" would have made it difficult for Khan to allude confidently to a single vision of the India yet-to-come (or at least one which would have been sure to satisfy all of his readers). And Indian Muslims may not have been entirely comfortable with a novel in which, according to Göknar, "the sect of nationalism ... supersedes no-longer relevant beliefs such as Ottomanism and Islamism" (Göknar 2013: 44).

After all, an important aspect of an earlier phase of Indian nationalism from 1919 to 1924 had been the *Khilafat* movement, created by Muslim leaders in India to defend the position of the Ottoman sultan as leader of the caliphate.

Appropriating Turkey and Turkish nationalism for his own purposes, Khan produces a text that is at once a simplification of his source material and a way of seeing through to some of the complexities and indeterminacies which plagued the imagination of Indian nationalism nine years before independence was finally declared. It is in this broader sense of the term, perhaps, that his work is best understood as a "translation" of Edib and her work into an Indian context: mobilizing them as emblems of incipient victory against the forces of colonial domination, yet unable to define exactly what that victory might look like or to forego consciousness of the fact that—in India at least—the success of the anti-colonial project was still far from inevitable.

## *Conflict of East and West in Turkey*

Halide Edib's lecture series at the Jamia Islamia University, delivered in 1935, offered its audience an introduction to the history of the Ottoman Empire, the Turkish War of Independence, and the early years of the Turkish Republic. The series thus demonstrates how an important writer and nationalist sought to explain and frame Turkish history, as well as the importance of Turkish nationalism, to a foreign audience. This section seeks to uncover a rather more complex aspect to Edib's lectures (which were later published in book format by the Jamia Islamia Press under the title *Conflict of East and West in Turkey*) and their appeal: one which presents the histories of India and Turkey as mirrors of one another, which suggests how non-European pasts might be reconceptualized in order to build or imagine a postcolonial future, and which questions rather than affirms the right of western civilization to a proprietary claim upon the nature of the modern.

Perhaps the most obvious appeal of Edib's lectures, at least to an Indian audience, lies in her description of the Turkish War of Independence. Listeners were surely enthused by her description of a small, ill-equipped army of freedom fighters defeating a numerically and logistically superior force of European occupation. They would have responded, too, to her insistence that practical obstacles were no match for nationalist fervor and that despite the "enormous" difficulties facing the Turkish troops, "the will of thousands of patriotic men and women found a way" (Halide Edib 1935: 114, 113). Indians would also have found acknowledgment that the trauma of domination at the hands of a foreign power is as much existential as it is material and economic. Edib describes the Treaty of Sèvres, for example, as a spiritual maiming, "a sentence of mutilation and death on the Turkish people," while her description of the Allies' decision "to create a Greek Empire in the Near East" evokes the image of a new Byzantium, resurrected by Britain and France in order to humiliate the descendants of the Ottoman Empire (Halide Edib 1935: 112, 104).

Edib's lectures do not just give their audience a glimpse of future liberation but also a means of creatively reimagining India's past. For if recent Turkish history proved that colonialism could, indeed, be defeated, then it also asked Indians to consider what *might have been* if previous struggles against British rule had been successful. Most notably, Edib's depiction of the War of Independence in Turkey (and, indeed, the figure of Edib herself) would have invited comparison with the ill-fated 1857 rebellion against the British, which the colonial administration described as a "mutiny," but which certain nationalists had begun to call "the Indian War of Independence."[5]

In his introduction to the printed edition of the lectures, Ansari stressed Edib's role as a female combatant who had "served at the headquarters of the nationalist army, with the din and smoke of a grim battle around her" (Halide Edib 1935: iii). In India this description which would have been an ineluctable reminder of the famed Rani (queen) Lakshmi Bai of Jhansi, who died fighting against the British in 1857. Turned posthumously into an idol of the independence movement, the Rani was routinely pictured in the thick of battle by early twentieth-century Indian visual culture, in much the same way as Ansari described Edib.[6] Edib thus appears in Ansari's words as a modern and *victorious* version of the Rani of Jhansi, portraying India's future as an image of its own history transformed in and through the example of her Turkish nationalism. Much the same can be said of the content of Edib's lectures, too. For when she describes the machinations of the European powers, intent upon the dismemberment of Turkey so that "[it] would have become an altogether abstract term," quotes Arnold Toynbee on the destruction caused by the Greek invasion, and recollects the Turkish people's success in their "struggle . . . for life and liberty," Indians would at one and the same time have seen their past and its potential redemption playing out in front of them (Halide Edib 1935: 105–6, 116). What has not been properly acknowledged is her insistence that the future of nations such as Turkey and India need not be overly or anxiously indebted to the West, and her ideas in this regard are most clearly visible in her discussion of "the Ottoman mind" and its attitude to state-building, an attitude which she claims is re-emerging or "recurring" in the world of the 1930s.

In her overview of the Ottoman Empire, Edib describes the training of a "governing Caste" recruited by means of the *devşirme* system. As a part of that training, she tells her audience that "the individual had to be free of family ties, of old customs, and any tradition which would attach him to his particular milieu in order to create an ideal Ottoman subject" (Halide Edib 1935: 21). Edib suggests that the education of *devşirme* recruits may have been inspired by Plato's *Republic*, demonstrating that Ottoman rulers were as conversant with the European classical tradition as with that of Islam. Rather more strikingly and much more boldly, however, she also argues that the Ottoman framework provides an antecedent to certain nation states in the early twentieth century:

> Now we bear witness to the rise of dictatorships which try to apply a plan in its entirety on nations. Though they differ widely in their aim and principle, their procedure and their organizations are the same. The first parallel to this sort of mind and action appears in history with the Ottomans. (Halide Edib 1935: 29)

In particular, Edib compares the Ottoman system with that of Soviet Russia. "Like the Ottomans," she opines, "Communist state-builders are of mixed origins" and "[r]ace is utterly discarded." Moreover, she claims that the molding of *devşirme* recruits constitutes the "prototyp[e]" of communist education in the Soviet Union, since "[b]oth attempts signify this —to fabricate a new mind in the human unity according to state conception" (Halide Edib 1935: 29–30).

Clearly the modern states to which Edib alludes are totalitarian. Indeed, she freely admits her distaste for the "Ottoman system," quoting and concurring with Toynbee's assessment that it "was contrary to human nature." But the point is that if "[i]n the West states are rising which want to fabricate not only the ruling caste but nations wholesale," then not only the precedent but also the *prototype* of these efforts is to be found in the ideology and institutions of a non-Western state. Even Edib's moral opprobrium is couched in language which underlines the achievement of the Ottoman Empire: "[i]t is somewhat distasteful to me," she wrote, "that . . . the Ottomans tried to fabricate a mind as one would fabricate a robot" (Halide Edib 1935: 31). It is worth noting that the word "robot," at least as far as it refers to mechanical automata, had entered the English language only in the early 1920s and would have signified the kind of technological accomplishment which was still confined to the realm of science fiction. Again, though, the accomplishment discussed here—no matter how "distasteful" it might be—has its origins not in the development of European totalitarianism but in the history of a non-European culture.

Edib notes at a much later point in the lectures that conceptions of an independent India based around racial or religious unity simply will not work (Halide Edib 1935: 243–4). She thus implies that any Indian nation-state would have to discard such categories as criteria of national belonging. Her talks assert that in doing so, and in imagining a postcolonial future, Indians need not necessarily look for inspiration to the culture, history, or politics of Europe. Edib also mentions Mahatma Gandhi as living proof of this principle, since his effort to transform India reminds her "very much of the economic and moral organization of the Turkish society by the mystic-economic orders called 'Ahiler' in Anatolia in the thirteenth century" (Halide Edib 1935: 246). As the Turkish War of Independence gave Indians a redemptive version of their own history, fulfilling the anti-colonial potential of 1857, so in turn does Gandhi bring to fruition the utopian promise of this medieval Turkish fraternity and what Edib calls its "passionate drive to serve the people and uplift them morally" (Halide Edib 1935: 143).

According to Edib (1935: 144), the Ahiler[7] were characterized by a belief in "a supreme, a real democracy." Here, as elsewhere, her lectures suggest that what was seen as the hallmarks of "Western" modernity can actually be found, for good or ill, in pre- or early-modern non-European traditions, and that, in other words, it is far too simplistic to think of modernity purely as a product of western civilization. Such argument was aligned with the opinions and writings of Ziya Gökalp, a key ideologist behind the Young Turk movement as well as the primary formulator of Turkish nationalism during the foundation of the Turkish Republic. Halide Edib was an avid follower of his ideas despite their fallout in later years. Ziya Gökalp formulated a combination of Sufism, European corporatism, and Turkic ideas with which he aimed to portray Turkishness with an inert tendency toward notions such as democracy or feminism. This is exemplified in his *The Principles of Turkism* in which he writes, "The ancient Turks were not only the world's most democratic ethnic group but also its most feminist" (104). In his writings, he differentiates between civilization and culture, and argues that while the former is international and consists of knowledge, the latter is the unique essence of every community that is unchanging and consists of emotions (29). Civilization is an act of will, while culture is natural, inert, and unique to communities. With these arguments, he formulated a future for the Turkish nation that would be progressive without losing its cultural characteristics, and reforms applied by the new Republic did not mean an abandonment of unique Turkish characteristics but, on the contrary, a return to them.

Echoing Gökalp's ideas, Halide Edib's talks serve as a kind of laboratory to show how non-European cultures and histories can reflect and draw inspiration from one another. Certainly, there are more straightforward reasons to account for the popularity of the talks, most notably their forthright support for Gandhian nationalism, which would have been warmly received in the climate of the Jamia Islamia.[8] Yet, working behind the scenes, in a rather more subtle manner, is a certain reading of ancient and recent history, and the relations between them, which rubs Eurocentric notions about the modern world against the grain, and which affirms that its modernity belongs to the peoples of the "east" as much as it does to those of the "west."

## *Inside India*[9]

Mention has already been made of the ideological conflicts which characterized Indian nationalism before 1947. This is a topic of forbidding complexity and doing proper justice to it lies beyond the scope of the present chapter. However, *Inside India* attests to Edib's awareness of some of the principal debates taking place in nationalist circles at this time. Her chapter on Nehru, for example, offers readers an overview of the role played by socialist politics in Indian nationalism. Noting that Nehru's "creed" is "Socialism, a less maximalist form than that of present Russia, but nevertheless based on Marxism," Edib contrasts his politics with those of Gandhi, rooted as they were in "the continuation of the nineteenth-century Hindu reform movements." While "Gandhi proposes to keep the original pattern of Hinduism with some alterations . . . Nehru wants the whole system to go, root and branch." Yet, Edib also stresses that the unique circumstances of the Indian independence movement bring these two divergent ideologies into synthesis with one another, for "in spite of the basic differences in principle, [Mahatma Gandhi and Nehru] are still in close co-operation." Indeed, "Jawaharlal Nehru would not break [with Gandhi] even if he could" (Halide Edib 1937: 305–7). *Inside India* also touches upon the importance and divisive nature of sectarian movements, discussing the Hindu chauvinism of groups who mean "to extirpate both Christianity and Islam" and detailing an interview conducted by Edib with Choudhry Rahmat Ali, who is credited with the invention of "Pakistan" as the name of a separate nation-state for South Asian Muslims (Halide Edib 1937: 204, 352–62).

As these latter details suggest, in *Inside India* Edib addressed the most fraught question facing Indian nationalists in the 1930s, namely, whether a unified India could hope to mediate successfully between the conflicting desires and anxieties of Hindu and Muslim communities, or whether "India [would] be led by Communalists who believe in two Indian nations" (Halide Edib 1937: 351). Edib emphasizes that she is simply an observer in such debates and underlines her desire to create a "truthful and objective" account of her time on the subcontinent (Halide Edib 1937: 10). However, it is clear that her sympathies lie with the political ideals of Mahatma Gandhi, who believed in a unified independent India and in the importance of Hindu-Muslim cooperation.[10] In fact, *Inside India* depicts Gandhi as a kind of historical force working for the good of all humanity and as someone who possesses a "unique significance, not just for India, but for the whole world" (Halide Edib 1937: 248). This universal significance, moreover, derives from the fact that Gandhi is the incarnation of a particularly Indian ethos, which seeks constantly to synthesize different identities and bring them into harmony with one another. "On the surface," Edib wrote, "India is, and always was a minutely divided humanity; but below the surface there has always been an unbroken urge for unity" (Halide Edib 1937: 181). According to Edib, the "genius" of India, embodied in Gandhi and his politics, is filled with a utopian potential, demonstrating the possibility of a nationalism which leads not to conflict between countries, cultures, and communities but, rather, to concord between them. Indeed, she writes that the Indians of the 1930s seem "born to set right a time that is out of joint, the cursed spite of centuries," predestined to transform a world and global history tragically marred by exploitation and domination (Halide Edib 1937: 32).

In a chapter devoted to the history of Islam in India, Edib offers an account of the cross-cultural encounter between Hindus and Muslims in the medieval period:

[T]he Muslem *élite* fell under the spell of Hinduism. A synthesis of Hindu and Muslem culture was soon created and a distinctly new art came into being on Indian soil. The very languages the conquerors spoke, Mongolic, Arabic, Persian, Turkish, etc., amalgamated with the Sanscrit, took its grammar, and came into being under the name of Urdu. (Halide Edib 1937: 314)

This narrative of "synthesis" mirrors the picture of medieval and early-modern Indian history depicted in the work of contemporary scholars such as Finbarr Flood (2009) and Audrey Truschke (2015). In *Inside India*, however, that narrative appears as an exemplary expression of the "unbroken urge for unity" described earlier by Edib, which she also calls "a perpetual longing which runs throughout Indian history from the very beginning" (Halide Edib 1937: 181). She found this longing not just in the example of historical figures such as the Mughal emperor Akbar, who attempted to blend Hinduism and Islam together into a new universal religion, but also in many of the Indians encountered during the course of her travels. There is Zohra Ansari, for whom the ancient Indian emperor Ashoka "was a part of her past history just as much as Humayun or Babur," the first rulers and founders of the Mughal dynasty (Halide Edib 1937: 33). There is Lady Amina Tyabji, an "Orthodox Muslim" who "listen[s] to any enthusiast of Hinduism or to any depreciation of Islam, with equal serenity" (Halide Edib 1937: 220). There are the Hindus and Muslims of Calcutta, who stand together in the same crowd crying *Vande Mataram* and *Allahu Akbar* and whom Edib compares rather bathetically to a bickering married couple who could never live without each other (Halide Edib 1937: 206). And there is Mahatma Gandhi.

In her discussion of Gandhi, Edib acknowledges that his ideas were rooted in Hindu philosophy, going so far as to call him "the Hindu of Hindus, the essence of oldest India" (Edib 1937: 54). She remarks, too, that he was "above all concerned with remaking Hindu society" and emphasizes that Gandhi "is less acquainted with the philosophy of Islam than he is with the philosophy of other religions" (Halide Edib 1937: 258). Even so, amid the bitter sectarian divisions of Indian politics, Gandhi's ideal of equal respect for all religions meant that his leadership was "sincerely accepted by the Muslims as much as by the Hindus" (Halide Edib 1937: 320) so that "Hindu and Muslim were merely Indians struggling hand in hand for the ultimate independence of their common motherland." This, Edib writes, was an "ideal brotherhood" (Halide Edib 1937: 322).

As would become clear throughout the course of the struggle for independence, the unity between Hindus and Muslims was extraordinarily fragile. Edib herself suggested that relations between the two communities might always be troubled and disjunctive because their respective religions were so dissimilar: when Islam arrived in India, she wrote, "Hinduism . . . had to devise a means of living side by side with a society based on an utterly different conception from its own" (Halide Edib 1937: 250). Mahatma Gandhi, however, brought these two profoundly different "societies" together to contest the colonial order, and thus in *Inside India* he represents the crystallization in a politically urgent, nationalist form of the "urge for unity" at the core of Indian culture.

Gandhi is also proof of the fact that this special Indian appetite for synthesis and syncretism has utopian implications for all of humanity. In Gandhi's most prominent Muslim supporters, for example, Edib asserted that she could see not just a "bridge between Hindus and Muslims" but also "the symbol of a new political conception." Gandhi's Muslim disciples [Edib adds] "represent two fundamental principles in Islam towards which the world is moving," namely democracy and egalitarianism (Halide Edib 1937: 339). They come to express this aspect of their Muslim faith, however, through adherence to the teachings and leadership of a man who—as Edib herself stresses—was in many respects a quintessential Hindu. Similarly, Edib notes, in their thoughts on moral and theological education, the ideas of the faculty at Jamia Islamia University display a "nearness to Mahatma Gandhi, that is to the Hindu conception" (Halide Edib 1937: 110). It is this [cosmopolitan] "political conception," perhaps, which had allowed Edib to rather provocatively describe Gandhi in her lectures as an "ideal neo-Muslim," a non-Muslim in whom the social idealism of Islam might be best realized (Halide Edib 1935: 247).

Edib also opines that Gandhi's fundamental beliefs "represent a trend in the writings of the world intelligentsia, and the secret longings of a large number of inarticulate human beings" (Halide Edib 1937: 287). It seems that the "essence of oldest India" is also the spirit of the early twentieth-century dreaming of a better tomorrow. And, strikingly, Edib writes about Western examples of emancipatory politics and international cooperation as explicitly Gandhian phenomena. "The League of Nations, strikes, blockades, boycotts, are the early signs of Satyagraha in the West," she asserts, referring to Gandhi's Sanskrit description of his political mission as a "struggle for truth." "The general strike in England in 1926," she continues, "was . . . an admirably organised and carried out Western Satyagraha" (Halide Edib 1937: 297). Thus, while Indian nationalism was in many respects inspired by and dependent upon European intellectual traditions, Edib casts those aspects of Western politics which possess utopian potential as specifically Indian.

## Conclusion

It should go without saying, perhaps, that Edib's ideas concerning the spirit or "essence" of Indian identity and culture are themselves rather problematic. Yet there is an undeniable power to the way in which she attributes the potential salvation of Europe to a quintessentially "Indian ideology." This sly reversal of the logic of colonialism—which claimed that European rule was an act of benevolence designed to save the benighted peoples of Africa and Asia from themselves—may well be attributed to Edib's long-standing antipathy to the policies of the continent's colonial powers. More broadly, however, she also suggests that as the distillation of a particular subcontinental "urge for unity," Gandhi's ideas have a truly universal application. In fact, the "new political conception" of universal and non-violent cooperation based on a common humanity offers the only way to avoid disaster on a global scale. "[T]he realisation that war does not pay . . . may eventually lead to a more hopeful organisation, and the application of Satyagraha between nations . . . the alternative is that of interdestruction, which means nations being wiped off the face of the earth" (Halide Edib 1937: 297). Gandhian satyagraha, according to Edib, has the power not only to free India but to liberate all of us from our own murderous instincts.

There is little concrete evidence about the way in which *Inside India* was read and received in India, and, indeed, Edib writes as one addressing herself to a well-intentioned foreigner with no specialist knowledge of the country. Nevertheless, the fact that it was written in English made the book available to an Indian audience, and at the same time offered them an enticing opportunity for national and cultural self-aggrandizement. For in this text Edib argues that there is an extraordinary promise encrypted in the heart of Indian history and culture: the promise not just of a better world but of a world that is better because it has been made over on Indian terms, because it has been transformed for the better by India and by Indians. The book thus affirms the value of Indian culture and asserts a form of "Indian exceptionalism," assuring the people of India not only that they can save themselves from colonial oppression, but also that they have the power to save humanity itself.

By the time Halide Edib left India, its press was in no doubt about her significance. "[W]herever she went," wrote an anonymous journalist for *The Bombay Chronicle* (1935: 7), "she interpreted the secret of Turkey's Renaissance epitomized in the stirring slogan: 'No individual, but the nation; no rights but duties' . . . millions of young men and women of India will worthily respond."[11] As this language suggests, the principal importance of Edib and her work lay in their ability to "interpret" Turkey and Turkish history to the people of British India, particularly in relation to the Turkish War of Independence and the nature of the Turkish Republic.

However, aside from their obvious appeal Edib's works also contained a set of complex ideas about both Turkish and Indian nationalism and history. Some of these ideas could pose a problem in the Indian context, as Khan's translation of *Ateşten Gömlek* makes clear. But they also offered resources to an Indian audience with which they could conceptualize their struggle for independence and imagine the possibilities of a postcolonial future (assuring readers, for example, that an independent India could successfully harmonize Gandhi's religiously inspired nationalism with Nehru's socialist ideology). In the translation of *Ateşten Gömlek*, for example, we detect uncertainty about the future nature of an independent India, made visible by the conspicuous alterations made to the novel by the translator. By contrast, Edib's lectures assured Indians that a postcolonial future could, indeed, be grasped by rethinking and reimagining the past, implying that it was possible to conceive of a modernity beyond the coordinates of colonial domination. Finally, *Inside India* affirms a triumphal vision of Indian nationalism, in which the very nature of India and its culture promises not only to create a new nation-state based on tolerance and pluralism, but also to save the world from human destructiveness. Described by Mahatma Gandhi as "the living link between India and Turkey," in his introduction to one of her lectures at the Jamia Islamia, Edib's work thus demonstrates how Turkish literature as world literature contributed to, and can help us to understand, some of the extraordinary complexities of nationalist politics and culture in India before independence (Gandhi 1935).

# Notes

1 For a detailed account of the Indian medical mission, see (Akçapar 2014).
2 For an overview of Edib's participation in nationalist politics, her activism, and her involvement in the Turkish War of Independence, see (Adak 2005).
3 On this issue, see (Adak 2003).
4 For a recent analysis of this period, see (Muldon 2016: 87–122).
5 The term "Indian War of Independence" used to describe the rebellion of 1857 was coined by the Hindu nationalist Vinayak Savarkar in a text of

1909 which was promptly banned by the British authorities. For more information on this controversial text see (Sharma 2007).

6  For an overview of the life of the Rani of Jhansi, and her afterlife in the Indian nationalist imagination, see (Singh 2014).

7  In her lecture, Halide Edib defines "ahiler" as follows: "Ahiler came into existence during the age of Seljuk decline. They are said to have established a regular state in Angora [. . .]. It was the organisation of guilds and corporations among small traders and originated with the association of tanners. It is an organisation symptomatic of the thirteenth century in general, if one considers the guilds and city corporations of Europe and similar corporate bodies in the Islamic world. But in Turkish Anatolia they seem to have been very firmly rooted and to have had a very particular complexion" (171–72).

8  As Mushirul Hasan (2010) notes, the atmosphere of the university was at once Islamic and cosmopolitan, with an emphasis on amity and cooperation between Hindus and Muslims. For Edib this atmosphere offered a welcome contrast to the Muslim's League's politics of Muslim exceptionalism: as Hasan writes, "Halide could not . . . make much of the Muslim League's demands in India's multicultural and multireligious landscape. Gandhi, Nehru, Ghaffar Khan and the Jamia men made much more sense to her."

9  *Inside India* was not published in Turkish in book format until 2014, but was partially serialized by *Tan* newspaper in 1938, and in its entirety by *Yeni Sabah* in 1940–1. The Turkish text, however, is not entirely a faithful translation but, rather, a rewriting of the English original. In the course of her revisions Edib removed (among other things) her criticism of the British Empire and colonialism. While a comparative analysis between the English original and the Turkish text would be a valuable project to pursue in order to reveal the role of India in the Turkish political imagination during the Second World War, it is outside the scope of this chapter, which focuses on the reception of Halide Edib's lectures and works in India before 1938. It is, however, worth noting that Edib's decision to remove her criticism of Britain and colonialism may well have had something to do with the timing of the Turkish text's publication. For, as Hülya Adak points out, Edib might have felt that it was not entirely the best time to be a fiery critic of the empire as Britain fought against Nazi Germany, Fascist Italy, and the empire of Japan (Adak 2014: 209).

10  Gandhi wrote and spoke on many occasions about the importance of Hindu-Muslim cooperation. On this topic, see (Nanda 2002).

11  The collectivist slogan quoted here was, of course, coined by Ziya Gökalp, who exerted a powerful influence upon Edib (Edib 2005: 319).

# References

Adak, Hülya. (2003), "National Myths and Self-Na(rra)tions: Mustafa Kemal's *Nutuk* and Edib's *Memoirs* and *The Turkish Ordeal*," *South Atlantic Quarterly* 102 (23): 510–12.

Adak, Hülya. (2005), "An Epic for Peace," in Halide Edib, *Memoirs of Halide Edib*, v–xvii, Piscataway, NJ: Gorgias Press.
Adak, Hülya. (2014), "İkinci Dünya Savaşı Esnasında Hint Bağımsızlık Hareketi: Hindistan'a Dair'in Sessizlikleri," in *Hindistan'a Dair*, 205–10, Istanbul: Can Publishing.
Akçapar, Burak. (2014), *People's Mission to the Ottoman Empire: MA Ansari and the Indian Medical Mission, 1912-1913*, New Delhi: Oxford University Press.
Ansari, Mukhtar Ahmed. (1934), Letter to Seth Jamal Mohamed, October 20, 1934, Ansari Papers, Jamia Millia Islamia, New Delhi.
Desai, Mahadev. (1935), "Masques and Souls: Halide Hanum's Discussion with Gandhiji," *The Hindustan Times*, January 19, 2019.
Flood, Finbarr. (2009), *Objects of Translation: Material Culture and Medieval 'Hindu-Muslim' Encounter*, London: Princeton University Press.
Gandhi, Mahatma. (1935), "Gandhiji's Glowing Tribute to Halide's Service: 'Musalmans, Bones of Our Bones', Indissoluble Tie Between Two Nations," *The Bombay Chronicle*, January 21, 1935.
Göknar, Erdağ. (2013), "Turkish-Islamic Feminism Confronts Patriarchy: Halide Edib's Divided Self," *Journal of Middle East Women's Studies* 9 (2): 32–57.
Halide Edib. (1924), *The Shirt of Flame*, New York: Duffield and Company.
Halide Edib. (1935), *Conflict of East and West in Turkey*, Delhi: Maktaba Jamia Millia Islamia.
Halide Edib. (1937), *Inside India*, London: Allen and Unwin.
Halide Edib. (1954), "Siyasi Vedaname," *Cumhuriyet*, January 5, 1954.
Halide Edib. (1981), *The Turkish Ordeal*, Westport: Hyperion Press.
Halide Edib. (2005), *Memoirs of Halide Edib*, Piscataway, NJ: Gorgias Press.
Hasan, Mushirul. (2002), "Enduring Encounters: Halide Edib's Image of India and Turkey," in Halide Edib, *Inside India*, New Delhi: Oxford University Press.
Hasan, Mushirul. (2010), *Between Modernity and Nationalism: Halide Edip's Encounter with Gandhi's India*, New Delhi: Oxford University Press.
Khan, Muhammed Yakub. (tr.) (1940), *The Daughter of Smyrna: A Story of the Rise of Modern Turkey, on the Ashes of the Ottoman Empire – the Turk's Revolt Against Western Domination, His Thrilling Adventures, Sufferings and Sacrifices in the Cause of National Honour and Independence*, Halide Edib, Lahore: Dar-ul-kutub Islamia.
Köroğlu, Erol. (2007), "Lost in Nationalist Translation: Configurations, Appropriations, and Translations of History in H. E. Adıvar's *The Shirt of Flame*," (unpublished article, 2007), pdf.
Misra, Maria. (2007), *Vishnu's Crowded Temple: India Since the Great Rebellion*, London: Penguin.
Muldon, Andrew. (2016), *Empire, Politics, and the Creation of the 1935 India Act: Last Act of the Raj*, Oxford: Routledge.
Nanda, Bal Ram. (2002), *Gandhi: Pan-Islamism, Imperialism, and Nationalism*, Oxford: Oxford University Press.
Price, Clair. (1928), "A Woman Speaks for the New Turkey: Halide Edib Hanum Comes to America as a Striking Symbol of the Changed Life of the Near East – A Woman of the New Turkey," *The New York Times*, July 29, 1928.
Sharma, Jyotirmaya. (2007), "History as Revenge and Retaliation: Rereading Savarkar's *The War of Independence of 1857*," *Economic and Political Weekly* 42 (19): 1717–19.

Singh, Harleen. (2014), *The Rani of Jhansi: Gender, History, and Fable in India*, Cambridge: Cambridge University Press.
Truschke, Audrey and Adamjee, Qamar. (2015), "Re-imagining 'the Idol Temple of Hindustan': Textual and Visual Translation of Sanskrit Texts in Mughal India," in C. Lefèvre, I. G. Zupanov and J. Flores (eds.), *Cosmopolitismes en Asie de Sud. Sources, intinéraires, langues (XVIe-XVIIIe siècle)*, 251–74, Paris: Editions de l'EHESS.

# 6

# Nâzım Hikmet's Reception as a World Poet[1]

## *Mediha Göbenli*[2]

Nâzım Hikmet (Ran) is acknowledged worldwide as a poet who revolutionized Turkish poetry. His work has been translated into more than fifty languages, and in many European countries, such as Italy, Greece, Spain, England, and Germany, he is undoubtedly also the most widely translated and read of Turkish poets (Mignon 2017: 85; Akbatur and Tekgül 2013: 24). This chapter aims at analyzing Nâzım Hikmet's contribution to "world literature,"[3] as well as the manifold ways of his reception by other national literatures, especially European and North American. There is a vast array of literary resources which feature Nâzım Hikmet: they range from memoirs, such as those by Ilja Ehrenburg (Ehrenburg 1968), Pablo Neruda (Neruda 1977), and Simone de Beauvoir; biographies by Ekber Babayev and Rady Fish; talks by Pablo Neruda, Jean-Paul Sartre, and Tristan Tzara; and anthologies of literature/poetry, to literary works such as novels by Peter-Paul Zahl, Emine Sevgi Özdamar, Aras Ören, and Nedim Gürsel and poetry by Pablo Neruda, Howard Fast, Peter Blackman, Yannis Ritsos, and Yevgeny Yevtushenko.

As I intend to show in this chapter Nâzım Hikmet's poetry was shaped "in response to national and world events" (Konuk Blasing 2013: 7), and there are two different phases in the reception of Hikmet's poetry: the first phase, from the 1930s until the 1990s, considers Nâzım Hikmet a political poet, his ideology inseparable from his poetry; the second phase consists of Hikmet's reception as a romantic poet or "the romantic communist," stressing the poetic and stylistic elements in his poetry. Nevertheless, even in the second phase there are writers such as Güzin Dino, Saime Göksu and Edward Timms, Erhan Turgut and Peter-Paul Zahl, who stressed the inseparability of the content and style of Hikmet's poetry from his worldview or politics. Başak Ergil emphasizes the political dynamics as a reason why the reception of Nâzım Hikmet as a communist poet changed, whereby he became a romantic, mystic and lyric figure. The collapse of the Soviet Union is responsible for the alteration in the reception of Nâzım Hikmet as a political poet. "The image of Hikmet as 'communist' poet and the selection of his politically engaged poems might therefore have been excluded towards the end of the 20th century" (Ergil 2008: 101).

During his lifetime, translations of Nâzım Hikmet's poems were published in various countries, such as Bulgaria, Britain, East Germany, France, Greece, Poland, Spain, and Italy. The first to dedicate a poem to Nâzım Hikmet was the American director Howard Fast:

And there came to me that day in prison,
speaking in the prison whisper you know so well,
that gentle writer, Albert Maltz—
Like you, his crime was words that sang of life,
of peace and hope and the things men cherish—
and told me you were free.

(Fast 1950: n.p)

Fast penned the abovementioned poem when he learned that Nâzım Hikmet had been released after a prison sentence of thirteen years. Later, in 2002, on the occasion of Nâzım Hikmet's hundredth birthday celebration, Fast would comment on his poem: "[I] called him my brother because his life was connected to my life, his thoughts connected with mine and his suffering had come out of doing what I would have done were I a part of his community" (Fast 2002: 247). Significantly, Fast points out that Nâzım Hikmet shared many similarities with poets and authors who fought for social justice and freedom worldwide.

The poem comments on Nâzım Hikmet and the American writer Albert Maltz, both of whom suffered political persecution because of ideological reasons. The latter was accused of and prosecuted for anti-American activities during the Cold War period. He was one of the "Hollywood Ten" of directors and screenwriters who appeared before the House Un-American Activities Committee (HUAC) in October 1947, sent to prison, and later blacklisted. As Frances Stonor Saunders details, under McCarthy's chairmanship of the House Un-American Activities Committee, "hearings, accusations and blacklists became the order of the day" (Saunders 2000: 191). Various investigations against intellectuals and writers were initiated. Among the targets were Bertolt Brecht (in exile on American soil), the folk singer Peter Seeger, Howard Fast, Arthur Miller, Charlie Chaplin, Marlon

Brando, and Henry Wallace, all "accused of toying with Communism" (Saunders 2000: 52) and blacklisted after refusing to answer the HUAC's interrogations.

In those "dark times" (ironically, given Brecht's comments on Hitler's totalitarian regime which he had managed to escape), it was a crime to sing of "life, of peace and hope" (Fast 1950: n.p.). Poets such as Nâzım Hikmet established themselves as spokesmen and advocates of humanity, resisting the rule of "dark times" and uniting their voices to promote brotherhood and peace. The key terms "singing"/ "song" feature in many writings and poems on Nâzım Hikmet, written by different international world literature figures such as Samuel Sillen, Pablo Neruda, Simone de Beauvoir, and Claude Roy. In Azade Seyhan's words, singing symbolizes "the power of Hikmet's words to fire his audiences and enlist them in the fight against tyranny" (Seyhan 2003: 168).

Another significant poet who was influenced by "Turkey's poet" and who wrote poetry dedicated to him was Pablo Neruda; the two had met for the first time at the Youth Festival, which was held in East Berlin in 1951. In *Winter's Crown for Nâzım Hikmet* he fondly addresses him as "brother poet" (Neruda 1977: 195) and laments his untimely death:

> Why have you died Nâzım? And how?
> What will we do without your songs?
> Where will we find the source?
> Where will your great smile be waiting for us?
> What will we do without your stance?
>
> (Translated by Susan Drucker-Brown, Turgut 2002: 203)

Neruda's poem is an elegy on the death of the poet. In his *Memoirs* (1974) Neruda reminisces about Hikmet's unjust destiny:

> a legendary writer kept in prison for eighteen years [. . .] condemned to the punishment of hell. The trial was held on a warship. [. . .] My brother poet felt his strength failing him. [. . .] He began to sing [. . .] sang all the songs, all the love poems he could remember, his own poems, the ballads of the peasants, the people's battle hymns. (Neruda 1977: 196)

Neruda's artistic and humane appreciation of Nâzım Hikmet continues: "You sang for all of us, my brother. We need have no doubts any longer or wonder what to do. We know now that we must begin to sing" (196). Singing, therefore, as also pointed out by Roy, becomes a way out of torture, a means of resistance and protest, a metaphor for struggle, and Nâzım Hikmet became its master, "a master of song" (Roy 2002: 205).

# I

As a committed Marxist, Nâzım Hikmet was widely known in Eastern European countries and the Soviet Union. As a student of KUTV in the 1920s, he met Vladimir Mayakovsky and Sergey Jessen, the avant-garde poets of futurism, while with Meyerhold he was active in agitprop theatre (Sverçevskaya 2002: 29–30). In the 1950s, he was translated in the former DDR (German Democratic Republic). Most significantly, with Brecht's support, the first Nâzım Hikmet publication was realized in East Berlin (Hamm 1982 [1964]: 184). It was entitled *Turkish Telegrams* (1956), and was followed by *Gedichte* (1959), a more comprehensive edition of his poetry (Hamm 1982: 184); six of his plays were staged in the DDR alone (Kraft 2008: 10). Nâzım Hikmet enjoyed contrasting receptions in East and West Germany. While in East Germany, mostly, but not only, because of his communist sympathies, he was acknowledged as a literary hero relatively early; in West Germany the recognition came belatedly.

Nâzım Hikmet spent half of his most productive years in prison (the longest term being between 1938 and 1950). His poems were smuggled out of prison and published in France, the country where his wife Münevver and his son Memed had been living since 1961. Their intense efforts to publicize his works were joined by those of other Turkish exiles such as Abidin and Güzin Dino. From France, Nâzım Hikmet's poems were circulated in Italy, Spain, Latin America, the United States, and the Soviet Union (Fish 1969: 419). According to Rady Fish, his poetry triggered a worldwide, long-lasting echo (Fish ibid.).

In 1949, an international campaign began for his release and a petition was signed by illustrious contemporaries such as Tristan Tzara, Brecht, Louis Aragon, Jean-Paul Sartre, Neruda, Georg Lukács, and Pablo Picasso, immediately followed by a hunger strike by the poet himself. In the United States, it was Paul Robeson who supported the petition and published an international call for Nâzım Hikmet's release. In 1950, Nâzım Hikmet shared the Nobel Peace Prize with Robeson and Neruda. Neruda accepted the prize on Nâzım Hikmet's behalf and gave a speech praising his poetry as world poetry (Fish 1969: 446). Nevertheless, according to Gisela Kraft—one of Nâzım Hikmet's translators in German—Hikmet's identity as a poet was overshadowed by his identity as a cult figure of "world communism." This inevitably resulted in the diminished perception of the artistic value of his poems, though they were "poems which touched the reader's heart" (Kraft 2008: 12).

# II

In 1932, Nâzım Hikmet was introduced to the English-speaking public: some selected poems were translated by Nermine Mouvafac in the

American literary magazine *Bookman*, under the title "A Poet of the New Turkey" (Gronau 1998: 7; Blasing and Mizanoğlu-Reddy 2002: 267; Ergil 2008: 29). He was introduced as "Turkey's Communist Poet" with a prophetic vision: "He is Nâzım Hikmet, communist poet, perhaps the only poet of the new generation who will leave a lasting mark" (Mouvafac 1932: 509). Mouvafac praised Hikmet as a world poet "poised between East and West" (514). While quoting lines from Nâzım Hikmet, she remembered Whitman's poetry and pondered on their main similarity, which is the appeal for brotherhood (515). In the following years, many American authors and poets who referred to the Turkish poet compared him to Whitman. A famous case in point is the poet and critic Edward Hirsch and his foreword to Hikmet's *Human Landscape from My Country* (2001):

> Hikmet is one of the great poets of social consciousness. He is a figure comparable, say, to Frederico Garcia Lorca and Miguel Hernandez, to César Vallejo and Pablo Neruda, which is to say that he was a Whitmanesque poet of the empathic imagination who felt his way into the lives of other people, who put his wild creative energies at the service of a human vision. (Hirsch 2002: vii)

Nâzım Hikmet's international dimension is put forward by Hirsch in depicting his poems as "human poems" (*poemas humanos*), comparable to the poetry written by Federico Garcia Lorca, Miguel Hernandez, César Vallejo, and Pablo Neruda. According to Hirsch, Nâzım Hikmet's translation of *Human Landscapes* "is a noteworthy event in world literature [. . .] to put beside Ezra Pound's *Cantos* as a heroic achievement. [. . .] Hikmet shared Pound's concept of the epic as 'a poem including history'" (viii). Hirsch draws another interesting similarity and compares Nâzım Hikmet to James Joyce, for choosing "ordinary characters" and being "inspired by the local, instigated by his native realm to try to create a universal pageant" (ibid.). In his article "Beyond Desolation" Hirsch again compares Hikmet's poems with Whitman's, stating that "like Whitman, he can speak with an overpowering directness" (Hirsch 1997: 37).

The second article in English entitled "The Case of Nâzım Hikmet," published under the initials M. N., appeared in 1950 in *Masses and Mainstream*, an American monthly Marxist review. Nâzım Hikmet is depicted as a unique poet and "great anti-fascist fighter" whose immediate release should be enacted. In this article, the US government "as an accomplice of the police terror in Turkey" (M.N. 1950: 5) was made responsible for Nâzım Hikmet's imprisonment through the Truman Doctrine and the Marshall Plan.

The publication of the first book of Nâzım Hikmet's poems in English had to wait until 1952. *Nâzım Hikmet, Selected Poems* appeared in

Calcutta, India, which had gained its independence from Britain in 1947. The translators were two Turkish women, Nilüfer Mizanoğlu-Reddy and Rosette Avigdor-Coryell who decided on the use of a pseudonym (Ali Yunus) due to political restrictions of the McCarthy period in America (Blasing and Mizanoğlu-Reddy 2002: 267; Baybars 2002: 259). Thanks to "The Union of Progressive Young Turks"[4] who started the campaign for Nâzım Hikmet's release from prison, "these students contacted their friends Nilüfer Mizanoğlu-Reddy and Rosette Avigdor-Coryell, who were then studying at Columbus University in New York," to translate Hikmet's poems into English (Blasing and Mizanoğlu-Reddy 2002: 267).

In January 1954, two years later, a collection entitled *Poems by Nâzım Hikmet* was published by the publishing house *Masses and Mainstream* in New York, with an introduction by Samuel Sillen, the chief editor of the publishing house, who introduced Nâzım Hikmet as "unmistakably, [. . .] an artist who belonged with Neruda and Aragon among the great poets of our age" (Sillen 1954: 5). Sillen's introduction is credited to be the first and therefore image-forming introduction on Nâzım Hikmet's poetry in the United States (Ergil 2008: 54). In this text, the poet is honored as a Marxist and anti-fascist, and a politically engaged poet. Sillen refers to Nâzım Hikmet's poetry as part of "prison literature" and names, and compares Nâzım Hikmet to, political prisoners' literature such as Julius Fuchik's *Notes from the Gallows*, Danielle Casanova's letters, Gabriel Pen's last testament, and the letters and poems of American political prisoners. He concludes that "there is no division between Hikmet the political poet and Hikmet the lyrical poet" (Sillen 1954: 7).

As previously mentioned, the period of the Cold War in the United States was the period of "red-scare" when Marxist and communists were accused of being agents of the Soviet Union, a period of polarization between ideologies, not only in the United States, but more particularly in the Western Bloc of Europe; this context is visible in Nâzım Hikmet's reception, especially in West Germany. Nevertheless, the Cold War period also coincided with a period of peace movement against nuclear weapons, whereby Nâzım Hikmet became the advocate and "a poet laureate of the peace movement" (Göksu and Timms 2006: 268) through his poems "The Little Girl," "The Japanese Fisherman," "Don't Let the Clouds Kill," distributed worldwide by the World Council of Peace. Peter Seeger composed a song of "The Little Girl" as "I Come and Stand at Every Door" in the early 1960s (Blasing and Mizanoğlu-Reddy 2002: 271).

As an official member of the World Council of Peace, Nâzım Hikmet traveled widely. He was actively against the Korean War and the proliferation of nuclear weapons. The World Council of Peace constituted for Nâzım Hikmet a platform to meet intellectuals and writers representing different languages and cultures. Thus, he made the acquaintance of the partisan and writer Joyce Lussu, the Italian delegate at the Stockholm peace conference in June 1958.⁵ The Italian writer Giancarlo Vigorelli described his poems as unique and enthusiastic pieces which introduced the spoken language into poetry: "his language is the language of a modern citizen-poet" (Nesin 2018: 256). According to Vigorelli, the Italian readers were the luckiest readers in Europe, because Nâzım Hikmet's poems were accessible in the 1950s, and his poetry collection was published in 1958 (Nesin 2018: 252–4).

In the English-speaking world since the 1960s, the immense efforts of the translators Mutlu Konuk and Randy Blasing aimed to make him available to American readers. In 1965, Konuk and Blasing realized that Hikmet was not only Turkey's poet but "a world-class poet with an international reputation" (Konuk 2002: 271), "ironically [...] in French, in the heartland of America" (ibid.). Later in 2013 Mutlu Konuk and Blasing would write a comprehensive biography entitled *Nâzım Hikmet, The Life and Times of Turkey's World Poet*.

In Britain, the first publication of Nâzım Hikmet's poetry was Taner Baybars' translation *Selected Poems by Nâzım Hikmet* (1967). Baybars recalls the reception of the book as "encouraging" with "plenty of reviews that qualified Nâzım as a 'discovery,' 'unusual,' 'refreshing'" (Baybars 2002: 261). In 1970, Baybars translated another book, *The Moscow Symphony*, introducing Nâzım Hikmet as a "poet of great humanity and originality of mind, whatever his political commitment" (Baybars 2002: 5). The publication of *Modern Turkish Poetry* followed in 1971 with the support of Daniel Weissbrot and Ted Hughes who were editors of *Modern Poetry in Translation*, and in 1972 with *The Day Before Tomorrow* (Baybars 2002: 263). Baybars confesses his enthrallment with Hikmet's poetry in the following terms: "What fascinated me about Nâzım Hikmet's poetry was its vitality, its originality, the subtle and intriguing use of Turkish. And it was deeply moving" (Baybars 2002: 259).

## III

In France, the first translation of Nâzım Hikmet's poetry was in March 1936, in the journal *Commune* which was edited by Louis Aragon (Basutçu 2002: 285; Göksu and Timms in Turgut 2002: 51). Further poems followed in 1948, published again by Aragon in *Europe* and in *Les Lettres françaises* (Basutçu 2002: 285). In 1958 Nâzım Hikmet visited Paris for the first time and was greeted by a delegation consisting of Tristan Tzara, Charles Dobzynski, the composer Philippe-Gérard, the painter Abidin Dino, and Güzin Dino (Basutçu 2002: 289; Göksu and Timms 2002: 85). The French philosopher Simone de Beauvoir honored Hikmet in her autobiography through recalling Nâzım Hikmet's report during a lunch in Paris in 1958 (de Beauvoir 1965: 390–1).

## IV

In 1960, in West Germany, Hikmet appeared for the first time as the only poet from Turkey in an anthology of modern poetry *Museum der modernen Poesie* (Museum of Modern Poetry), edited by Hans Magnus Enzensberger (Enzensberger 1963). Enzensberger's anthology contained selected works of ninety-six poets from twenty different countries such as Rafael Alberti, Paul Eluard, Konstantinos Kavafis, Vladimir Mayakovski, and Octavio Paz. Suggestively, they were introduced as "poetry of the modernity," part and parcel of the museum of world literature. The representatives of modern poetry were described as cosmopolitan, as "literary engineers" (Enzensberger 1963: 15) who would use the same "poetic world language" (Enzensberger 1963: 13). Enzensberger's anthology was praised by the German literary critics and to this day it remains unsurpassed, unique in its scope and content as canon-forming.

In 1963, in West Germany, Brands translated the third book of *Human Landscapes In Jenem Jahr 1941*. The remaining others were published in a complete edition of *Human Landscapes* in 1979 and 1980, respectively. In 1972 Yüksel Pazarkaya published eleven poems by Nâzım Hikmet in an anthology entitled *Moderne türkische Lyrik*. In the 1980s, sixteen books by Nâzım Hikmet (besides his poetry, his novels, and his plays) were published in West Germany (connected with the development of Turkish Migration Literature).[6] The 1980s thus became the years of Nâzım Hikmet's reception (Dikici 2015: 71).

Aras Ören, a name among the first generation of Turkish migrants' literature, was one of the authors who confessed to the influence of Nâzım Hikmet—along with Brecht's—on his writing (Gezen 2012: 371). In West Germany, Nâzım Hikmet had already been prominent among members of the German Left since the end of 1950. Peter-Paul Zahl, imprisoned in the 1970s for ten years, wrote the preface to *Human Landscapes* (Hamburg, 1978, reprinted in 2001) from prison, comparing his own prison conditions in the Federal Republic and Nâzım Hikmet's in Turkey (Zahl 1981). In Zahl's novel *Die Glücklichen*[7] (The Happy Humans 1979/2001), Hikmet's poem appears as the motto of the twelfth chapter: "Lasst uns die Erde den Kindern übergeben, wie einen riesigen Apfel, wie ein warmes Brot" (Zahl 2001: 285).

In West Germany, it was only in 1977 that the Turkish Academic and Artists' Union's first comprehensive biography and a collection of poetry were published, comprising homages from writers of various countries, such as Anna Seghers, Aragon, Neruda, Sartre, Tzara, Peter Hamm, Ilya Ehrenburg, Konstantin Simonov, Alfred Kurella, Angel Miguel Asturias, Viktor Komissarjevski, and Jean Marcenac, entitled *Nâzım Hikmet: Sie haben Angst vor unseren Liedern* (Nâzım Hikmet: They are Afraid of

Our Songs), published in both Turkish and German. It was republished in 1982 on the occasion of the eightieth anniversary of Hikmet's birth, edited by the *Türkenzentrum Berlin* under the initiative of Mehmet Aksoy. The collection also contains excerpts from biographies by Rady Fish, writings about, and analysis of, his poetry by Ekber Babaev and Asım Bezirci, and an interview by Charles Dobzynski (Aksoy 1982).

Max Leon remembers Nâzım Hikmet's funeral in 1963 and recalls the oratory by Konstantin Simonov: "Hikmet was more than a talented poet, he was truly a great poet. The history may prove such an evaluation. And I am sure that the history will approve this" (Leon 1982: 26). Madeleine Riffaud who met Nâzım Hikmet at the Youth Festival in Berlin in 1951 wrote: "each reader of Nâzım Hikmet, if in France or in Turkey, in Vietnam or in Angola, everywhere where his work is translated, everybody feels him/herself as friend, as brother of Nâzım" (Rifaud 1982: 72). Peter Hamm wrote in 1964 in the weekly newspaper *Zeit* under the heading "Schickt mir Bücher, die glücklich enden!" (Send me books that have happy endings!) that Nâzım Hikmet "was ignored for a long time" (Hamm 1964). This article was reprinted later in 1982 in *Nâzım Hikmet*, Türkenzentrum Berlin. According to Peter Hamm, the "imprisoned" poet Nâzım Hikmet, became a "poet of the people, not only of his own: Japanese[8] fisherwomen printed his poems as leaflets against armament; black Americans carried at demonstrations his larger than life-sized portrait; French workers sent him letters of appreciation; in many countries young people sent his poems as love letters" (Hamm 1982: 182).

Despite the fact that Nâzım Hikmet's poems were translated or rewritten by prominent writers such as Ernst Fischer, Heinar Kipphardt, Stephan Hermlin, and Paul Wiens for their first publication in East Berlin in 1956 and 1959 (Hamm 1982: 184), in West Germany the interest was not very great. The Cold War period is clearly revealed as responsible for the poor reception of Nâzım Hikmet's poetry in West Germany.

In 1964 Hamm called on publishing houses, theatres, and audiences "to take care of Nâzım Hikmet," to initiate translations of his works. An explanation for the late translation of Nâzım Hikmet was delivered by Dietrich Gronau, who in 1991 published a short monograph introducing Nâzım Hikmet's work as "documentation of the 20$^{th}$ century" (Gronau 1998: 7). Gronau indicated that Nâzım Hikmet's "ambivalent appreciation"— "insofar questionable if as communist martyr or as original artist" (8) —as a communist poet in the Soviet Union influenced his literary image in Western countries, although "Hikmet's language, images, metaphors, references, dreams, comparisons and phantasies are of a world citizen and of an unrooted citizen of the modern times" (Gronau 2002: 174).

In this context, Gronau quotes Gisela Kraft: "What Hikmet said, his humanist message, is gradually being heard by the world. How poetic he said it, is realized little by little, and sets standards for the progress of world poetry" (Gronau 1998: 139). Gronau's early political assessment of Nâzım Hikmet's poetry presents him as "a persistent communist [...] a real romantic" (Gronau 1998: 9). Nevertheless, Gronau called the exile period between 1951 and 1963 "Die tödliche Leere" ("the lethal emptiness," p. 122), although Nâzım Hikmet was productive in a literary and political sense for the peace movement. Gronau also claimed that the West German publishing houses were uninterested in publishing and distributing Nâzım Hikmet's work (128). In 2002, Gronau recalled the historical and political conditions in the Federal Republic of Germany to grasp the reasons why Nâzım Hikmet was overlooked and remained unnoticed. Thus, he claimed that the stereotypical objection to Nâzım Hikmet was his devotion to "ideal socialism" (Gronau 2002: 170). Gronau acknowledged the censorship by the governments in Bonn and Washington led by the anti-communism movement, similar to that in Turkey.

In 2002, on the occasion of the hundredth anniversary of Nâzım Hikmet's birth, a collection was published in Germany as *Hundert Jahre Nâzım Hikmet 1902-1963* (One Hundred Years [of] Nâzım Hikmet), edited by Monika Carbe and Wolfgang Riemann (Carbe and Riemann 2002). Interesting and outstanding in this collection are the contributions of contemporary writers Zafer Şenocak and Karin Yeşilada. Şenocak's article is an account of how he was introduced to Nâzım Hikmet's poetry, and how that became a "cult book" (Şenocak 2002: 84) for him, due to its vividness, emotions, and passions (85). Şenocak argues that "Nâzım's political ideology appears only as a coat, with that he covered his passionate poetry, to protect it against the cold and the outer world" (85).

In the last chapter of *Hundert Jahre Nâzım Hikmet*, Karin Yeşilada's "Nâzım's Enkel schreiben weiter" ("Nâzım's grandchildren go on writing") expresses her bewilderment at the unavailability of Hikmet's books in German bookstores, since the previous publications by Dağyeli publishing house had sold out but a reprint was not issued. Nevertheless, she claims, he has become a part of world literature, and "Poems of Nâzım Hikmet in Anglo-American space are standard work, always achievable" (Yeşilada 2002: 181). According to Yeşilada, Nâzım Hikmet's poetry is a means for creative debate and a source of inspiration for "new lyric" (2002: 182). She concludes her essay by underlining that "Nâzım Hikmet's grandchildren write, and they write in German" (182). Nâzım Hikmet's grandchildren[9] were established within the migration literature in Germany, starting from the first generation, such as Aras Ören, Yusuf Ziya Bahadınlı, Saliha Scheinhardt, and Yüksel Pazarkaya, and the second generation with Emine Sevgi Özdamar, Zafer Şenocak, and Habib Bektaş.[10]

Inspired by Nâzım Hikmet's poetry, Berkan Karpat and Şenocak wrote *nâzım hikmet: on the ship to mars* (1998), a poem in twelve segments, and a creative and poetic production with references to mystic elements, using metaphors such as "burning," "singing," and "longing." Thus the symbol of the ship recalls in readers the warship on the Bosphorus, on which the poet was tortured for two days and nights in 1938 (Neruda 1977: 196). "[I] shout my song / towards the walls of the ship cell / I shout towards the walls: you shall burn like Kerem / [. . .] I Nâzım want to burn / so that I become light" (Karpat and Şenocak 1998: 4).

In Emine Sevgi Özdamar's semi-autobiographical novel *The Bridge of the Golden Horn* (Özdamar 2007), the protagonist Emine encounters Hikmet's poems for the first time in Paris through her Spanish boyfriend who reads to her Hikmet's poems aloud in French, calling him a "great socialist poet" and listening to a record by Yves Montand who "sings a poem of Nâzım Hikmet" (2007: 96). Writers and poets such as Nâzım Hikmet encourage and direct her life by raising her consciousness. By the end of the novel, students are demonstrating on the Bridge of the Golden Horn for their friend Vedat Demircioğlu who was killed during a demonstration, and shouting Hikmet's poem in chorus: "My boy, take a good look at the stars" (202).[11]

## V

In 2002, the UNESCO year dedicated to Nâzım Hikmet, many activities were carried out in different countries, and commemoration books were published in Russia, France, and Germany. One of them, *Kardeşim Nâzım* (My Brother Nâzım) edited by Antonina Sverçevkaya and Svetlana Uturgauri, is a collection of the memories of Hikmet's Russian contemporaries such as Yevgeny Yevtushenko, Konstantin Raykin, Konstantin Simonov, and Ilya Ehrenburg. In the preface, Uturgauri introduces him as "a romantic communist" (Uturgauri 2002: 8) and mentions that the idea to publish such a collection rests upon his last wife Vera Tulyakova-Hikmet, who collected writings on Nâzım Hikmet from newspapers and asked Hikmet's contemporaries of writers, theatre directors, and others for their anecdotes and memories (Uturgauri 2002: 9).

Another book of commemoration is *Nâzım Hikmet*, edited by Erhan Turgut, and written in three languages (French, Turkish, and English) with an impressive preface penned through the technique of inner monologue by John Berger. The excerpt by the Guatemalan author Miguel Angel Asturias provides an idea about the reception of Hikmet in Latin America as a poet of "struggle and protest." Asturias highlights Nâzım Hikmet as a poet who provoked great enthusiasm in Latin America because he "fought against the age-old barbarians" (Asturias 2002: 201).

Göksu and Timms wrote the "first comprehensive biography" (Yevtushenko 2006: xiii) of Nâzım Hikmet in English called *Romantic Communist, The Life and Work of Nâzım Hikmet* (1999), approaching his life and work as a combination of "political courage with artistic creativity," "not only a communist committed to revolution, but a romantic," and tracing the time of his exile as "creative, becoming involved in the theatre and broadcasting and entering into further relationships which find their echo in poignant lyrics and love letters, as well as political poetry of great imaginative power" (Göksu and Timms 2006: ix). No doubt, this biography is outstanding in a time in which Nâzım Hikmet's poetry is separated from his politics, or his period of exile viewed as "the lethal emptiness" (Gronau 1998: 121).

Besides the biographies, book reviews, and anthology references, many contemporary authors and poets refer to Nâzım Hikmet's poetry as a source of inspiration. In an interview, the American poet David Wojahn talks about Nâzım Hikmet's influence in his work, especially in *Mystery Train* (Wojahn 1994: 52). Among younger generations of authors and poets who name Nâzım Hikmet as a source of inspiration, Tina Chang (Brooklyn's poet laureate in 2016, the first woman appointed to the position) lists him along with Federico Garcia Lorca, Jack Gilbert, and Carolyn Forché as a poet "whose life and poetry I love":

> I return to these poets time and time again not only for their poetry, but also for their path of experience that has made their lives so memorable to me. [. . .] Their lives have led me in my role as poet laureate. (Chang 2013: 3)

Carolyn Forché is another poet who lists Nâzım Hikmet along with Bertolt Brecht, César Vallejo, Pablo Neruda, Rafael Alberti, Yannis Ritsos, Atilla Jozsef, George Oppen, and Mahmoud Darwish among those whose work is "marked by the impress of extremity and a faith in the salvific possibility of global fraternity and social justice" (Forché 2002: 1). Forché wrote the foreword for *Poems of Nâzım Hikmet* (Blasing and Konuk 2001) emphasizing that "Hikmet's poetry became for me a species of guidebook, a manual for living, advising one to embrace what came to pass, to say *yes*, to live fully, and, most daunting to be able to *die for people—even for people whose faces you've never seen*" (Forché 2001: 1).

## Conclusion

The present chapter on Hikmet's reception concludes with the argument that without doubt Nâzım Hikmet was a world poet and thus part of world literature. As the "greatness of poetry lies in its universality" (Tzara 2002: 201), he was a "universal poet" (Juin 2002: 201). Nâzım Hikmet is generally revered as "myth" (Konuk Blasing 2013: 7), "mythos," "martyr" (Lüdke 2008), as a poetic voice of the Turkish Left, a poet of hope, peace, social justice, and liberty, who could combine and unite poetry and politics. Most tellingly, his poetry is described as a "lyric, directed to the receptive world citizen" (Kraft 2008: 2). According to Aijaz Ahmad, Nâzım Hikmet belongs along with Mayakovsky, Aime-Fernand Cesaire, Bertolt Brecht, Pablo Neruda, Cesar Vallejo, Ernesto Cardenal, and Faiz Ahmet Faiz to "the great decisive poets of the 20$^{th}$ century" who are defined as "the great figures in [. . .] 'Poetry International'" (Ahmad 2000). Thus Hikmet's poetry reunites people on all continents. In Simonov's words, Nâzım Hikmet's quality as a world poet is acknowledged by history itself (Leon 1982: 26). Last but not least, Nâzım Hikmet's poetry still stands for a longing of freedom and peace all over the world.

## Notes

1. Dedicated to my dearest mother Tami Göbenli (1949–2014) and my dearest academic mother Prof. Süheyla Artemel (1930–2018).
2. I gratefully thank Cevat Çapan, Hülya Arslan, Martin Vialon, Adriana Raducanu, Bahriye Çeri, and Jonathan Kim Laykin for their critical insights, careful readings, and recommendations.
3. Regarding his influence on Turkish poetry, social critical poets such as Atillâ İlhan, Ahmet Arif, Enver Gökçe, and A. Kadir have been among the poets who were influenced by Nâzım Hikmet's poetry. The influence of Nâzım Hikmet on Turkish poetry is a research topic for another study, which has been discussed only in a few articles, for example, Mehmet Doğan "A poet of his era" in *Nâzım Hikmet: To Live, Free and Single Like a Tree/But in Brotherhood Like a Forest* (2002).
4. "The Union of Progressive Young Turks" (İleri Jön Türkler Birliği) was founded in Paris (in March 1949) by Turkish students and intellectuals such as Atillâ İlhan, Abidin Dino, Tacettin Karan, Sevim Belli, Zekeriya Sertel, and Yıldız Sertel, and was active between 1949 and 1954 (Yuca 2017: 79–81; Karan 2003: 14–15).
5. Especially his love poems published in 1963 as *Poesie d'Amore* were "bestsellers for years on Valentine's Day in Italy" (Berk Albachten 2012: 98).
6. Azade Seyhan calls Nâzım Hikmet's poetry "the single most powerful source of inspiration for Turkish writers of Germany" (Seyhan 2003: 168).
7. The influence of Nâzım Hikmet's poetry on Zahl's picaresque novel *Die Glücklichen* (The Happy Humans) (1979) constituted Martin Vialon's research topic for a talk in Dortmund, in 2019.
8. Nâzım Hikmet is the first Turkish author to be translated into Japanese, with seven publications between 1955 and 2002 (Baykara 2012: 106).
9. Karpat and Şenocak address Nâzım Hikmet as "Poet Father," and themselves as "Nâzım's grandchildren" (Stockwell 2017: 137–8).

10 The legacy of Nâzım Hikmet's poetry on Turkish and Turkish-German literature was the research topic for Stockwell's doctoral thesis (2017) titled *A Shared Longing: Rewriting Nâzım Hikmet in Turkish and Turkish-German Literature 1963-2017* as well.
11 Later that poem would become a poem of recitation, to mourn revolutionary student leaders of 1970s such as Deniz Gezmiş.

# References

Ahmad, Aijaz. (2000), "Balance Sheet of the Left: A Reflection on Our Times II," Frontline India's *National Magazine*, February 19–March 3, 2000. Available online: https://frontline.thehindu.com/static/html/fl1704/17040850.htm (accessed June 29, 2019).

Akbatur, Arzu and Duygu Tekgül. (2013), *Literary Translation from Turkish into English in the United Kingdom and Ireland, 1920-2012*, Wales: Aberystwyth University.

Aksoy, Mehmet. (ed.) (1982), *Nâzım Hikmet*, Berlin (West): Elefanten Press.

Asturias, Miguel Angel. (2002), "A Fighter for Freedom," in E. Turgut (ed.), *Nâzım Hikmet: To Live, Free and Single Like a Tree/But in Brotherhood Like a Forest*, 199, Paris: Turquoise.

Basutçu, Mehmet. (2002), "Nâzım Hikmet in Pari," in E. Turgut (ed.), *Nâzım Hikmet: To Live, Free and Single Like a Tree/But in Brotherhood Like a Forest*, 277–307, Paris: Turquoise.

Baybars, Taner. (2002), "Translating Nâzım Hikmet's Poetry in Britain," in E. Turgut (ed.), *Nâzım Hikmet: To Live, Free and Single Like a Tree/But in Brotherhood Like a Forest*, 259–65, Paris: Turquoise.

Baykara, Oğuz. (2012), "Turkish Literature in Japanese," *I.U. Journal of Translation Studies* (6): 103–33.

Berk Albachten, Özlem. (2012), "Turkish Literature in Italian: 1923-1912," *I.U. Journal of Translation Studies* (5): 89–120. (Available online: https://dergipark.org.tr/tr/download/article-file/13506 (assessed May 2, 2019).

Blasing, Randy and Nilüfer Mizanoğlu-Reddy. (2002), "A 'Mightily Unknown' Poet in America," in E. Turgut (ed.), *Nâzım Hikmet: To Live, Free and Single Like a Tree/But in Brotherhood Like a Forest*, 267–75, Paris: Turquoise.

Carbe, Monika and Wolfgang Riemann, (ed.) (2002), *Hundert Jahre Nâzım Hikmet 1902-1963*, Hildesheim: Olms.

Chang, Tina. (2013), "Brooklyn's Poet Laureate: An Interview with Tina Chang," Interview by John Gibbs. Available online: http://www.swback.com/interviews/brooklyns-poet-laureate-tina-chang.html (accessed June 10, 2019).

de Beauvoir, Simone. (1965), *Force of Circumstance*. Tr. Richard Howard, New York: G.P. Putnam's Sons.

Dikici, Christine. (2015), "Die Rezeption der türkischen Literatur im deutschen Sprachraum unter besonderer Berücksichtigung aktueller Übersetzungsvorhaben," PhD diss., Sakarya University.

Ehrenburg, Ilya. (1968), *Ilya Ehrenburg'un Hatıraları (Memoirs)*. Tr. Hasan Ali Ediz, Istanbul: As.

Enzensberger, Hans Magnus, (ed.) (1963), *Museum der modernen Poesie*, Frankfurt am Main: Suhrkamp.
Ergil, Başak. (2008), *The Image of Nâzım Hikmet and His Poetry in Anglo-American Literary Systems*, Istanbul: Nâzım Hikmet Culture and Art Foundation.
Fast, Howard. (1950), "To Nazım Hikmet," *Masses & Mainstream*, October 1950. Available online: http://www.trussel.com/hf/nazim/htm (accessed June 10, 2019).
Fast, Howard. (2002), "We Are Many, They Are Few," in E. Turgut (ed.), *Nâzım Hikmet: To Live, Free and Single Like a Tree/But in Brotherhood Like a Forest*, 247, Paris: Turquoise.
Fish, Rady. (1969), *Nâzım'ın Çilesi*. Tr. Güneş Bozkaya-Kolontay, Istanbul: Ararat.
Forché, Carolyn. (2002), "Foreword," Poems of Nâzım Hikmet. Tr. Randy Basing and Mutlu Konuk, ix–xii, New York: Persea Books.
Gezen, Ela. (2012), "Convergent Realisms: Aras Ören, Nazim Hikmet, and Bertolt Brecht," *Colloquia Germanica* 45 (3/4): 369–85.
Göksu, Saime and Edward Timms. (2002), "Biography," in E. Turgut (ed.), *Nâzım Hikmet: To Live, Free and Single Like a Tree/But in Brotherhood Like a Forest*, 29–89, Paris: Turquoise.
Göksu, Saime and Edward Timms. (2006), *Romantic Communist: The Life and Work of Nâzım Hikmet*, London: Hurst & Company.
Gronau, Dietrich. ([1991] 1998), *Nâzım Hikmet*, Hamburg: Roro.
Gronau, Dietrich, (2002), "Hat es Nâzım Hikmet überhaupt gegeben?" in M. Carbe and W. Riemann (eds.), *Hundert Jahre Nâzım Hikmet 1902-1963*, 169–79, Hildesheim: Georg Olms.
Hamm, Peter. (1964), "Schickt mir Bücher, die glücklich enden!" *Die Zeit*, June 12, 1964. Available online: https://www.zeit.de/1964/24/schickt-mir-buecher-die-gluecklich-enden (accessed June 15, 2019).
Hamm, Peter. (1982), "Über Nâzım Hikmet," in M. Aksoy (ed.), *Nâzım Hikmet*, 182–3, Berlin (West): Elefanten Press.
Hirsch, Edward. (1997), "Beyond Desolation," *American Poetry Review* (May–June): 33–39.
Hirsch, Edward. (2002), "Foreword" in *Human Landscapes from My Country: An Epic Novel in Verse*. Tr. Randy Blasing and Mutlu Konuk, vii–xiv, New York: Persea Books. Available online: https://istanbulmemoirs.files.wordpress.com/2015/05/human-landscapes.pdf (accessed May 2, 2019).
Juin, Hubert. (2002), "Nâzım Hikmet, a Universal Poet," in E. Turgut (ed.), *Nâzım Hikmet: To Live, Free and Single Like a Tree/But in Brotherhood Like a Forest*, 201, Paris: Turquoise.
Karan, Taci. (2003), "Paris'in 'jön' delikanlıları (Young Men of Paris)," *Cumhuriyet Dergi* (877): 14-6.
Karpat, Berkan and Zafer Şenocak. (1998), *nâzım hikmet auf dem shiff zum mars*, München: Babel.
Konuk, Mutlu. (2002), "Introduction," in *Human Landscapes from My Country: An Epic Novel in Verse*. Tr. Randy Blasing and Mutlu Konuk, New York: Persea Books.
Konuk Blasing, Mutlu. (2013), *Nâzım Hikmet: The Life and Times of Turkey's World Poet*, New York: Persea Books.
Kraft, Gisela. (2008), "Nachwort (Epilogue)," in *Nâzım Hikmet: Die Namen der Sehnsucht*. Tr. Gisela Kraft, Bern: Amman Verlag. Available online: http://www

.planetlyrik.de/nazim-hikmet-die-namen-der-sehnsucht/2016/08/ (accessed April 10, 2019).
Leon, Max. (1982), "Elveda Nâzım (Goodbye Nâzım)," in M. Aksoy (ed.), *Nâzım Hikmet*, 29, Berlin (West): Elefanten Press.
Lüdke, Martin. (2008), "Der Mythos des Märtyrers," book review *Die Romantiker* (Life Is Good, Brother). Available online: https://www.deutschlandfunk.de/der-mythos-des-maertyrers.700.de.html?dram:article_id=83803 (accessed June 18, 2018).
Mignon, Laurent Jean Nicolas. (2017), "The Beloved Unveiled: Continuity and Change in Modern Turkish Love Poetry (1923-1980)," PhD diss., University of London.
Mouvafac, Nermine. (1932), "A Poet of the New Turkey," *The Bookman* (5): 508-15.
Neruda, Pablo. (1977), *Pablo Neruda Memoirs*. Tr. Hardie St. Martin, New York: Farar, Straus and Giroux.
Nesin, Aziz. (2018), *Türkiye Şarkısı Nâzım*, Istanbul: Nesin.
Özdamar, Emine Sevgi. (2007), *The Bridge of the Golden Horn*. Tr. Martin Chalmers, London: Serpent's Tail.
Riffaud, Madeleine. (1982), "Am Anfang war die Tat (In the beginning was the action)," in M. Aksoy (ed.), *Nâzım Hikmet*, 72-4, Berlin (West): Elefanten Press.
Roy, Claude. (2002), "A Just Man, a Master of Song," in E. Turgut (ed.), *Nâzım Hikmet: To Live, Free and Single Like a Tree/But in Brotherhood Like a Forest*, 205, Paris: Turquoise.
Saunders, Stonor Frances. (2000), *The Cultural Cold War: The CIA and the World of Arts and Letters*, New York: The New Press.
Şenocak, Zafer. (2002), "Meine drei Begegnungen mit Nâzım Hikmet," in M. Carbe and W. Riemann (eds.), *Hundert Jahre Nâzım Hikmet 1902-1963*, 84-9, Hildesheim: Georg Olms.
Seyhan, Azade. (2003), "Enduring Grief: Autobiography as 'Poetry of Witness' in the Work of Assia Djebar and Nâzım Hikmet," *Comparative Literature Studies* 40 (2003): 159-72.
Sillen, Samuel. (1954), "A Note on Nâzım Hikmet," in *Poems by Nâzım Hikmet, Selected Poems*. Tr. Ali Yunus, 5-8, New York: Masses & Mainstream.
Stockwell, Jill Farrington. (2017), "A Shared Longing: Rewriting Nâzım Hikmet in Turkish and Turkish-German Literature (1963-2017)," PhD. diss., Princeton University.
Sverçevskaya, Antonina. (2002), *Nâzım Hikmet ve Tiyatrosu*. Tr. Hülya Arslan, Istanbul: Cem.
Turgut, Erhan, (ed.) (2002), *Nâzım Hikmet: To Live, Free and Single Like a Tree/ But in Brotherhood Like a Forest*, Paris: Turquoise.
Tzara, Tristan. (2002), "The Greatness of Poetry Lies in Its Universality," in E. Turgut (ed.), *Nâzım Hikmet: To Live, Free and Single Like a Tree/But in Brotherhood Like a Forest*, 203, Paris: Turquoise.
Uturgauri, Svetlana and Antonina Sverçevskaya. (2002), *Kardeşim Nâzım*. Tr. Mehmet Özgül, Istanbul: Cem.
Wojahn, David. (1994), "Riding the 'Mystery Train': An Interview with David Wojahn," Interview by David Shirley. *Chicago Review* 40 (2/3): 49-62.

Available online: https://www.jstor.org/stable/25305839 (accessed June 12, 2019).

Yeşilada, Karin. (2002), "Nâzıms Enkel schreiben weiter," in M. Carbe and W. Riemann (eds.), *Hundert Jahre Nâzım Hikmet 1902-1963*, 180-211, Hildesheim: Georg Olms.

Yevtushenko, Yevgeny. (2006), "Preface," in Göksu/Timms, *Romantic Communist: The Life and Work of Nâzım Hikmet*, xiii-xxiii, London: Hurst & Company.

Yuca, İrşad Sami. (2017), "Demokrat Parti Döneminde Sivil Bir Muhalif Örgüt Örneği: İleri Jön Türkler Birliği (An Example of Civilian Opposition Organization During the Democratic Party Era: The Union of Progressive Young Turks)," *Academic Journal of History and Idea* 4 (12): 73-94. Available online: https://dergipark.org.tr/tr/download/article-file/450685 (accessed September 2, 2019).

Zahl, Peter-Paul. (1981), "Es geht darum, dass man sich nicht ergibt." in Peter-Paul Zahl, *Die Stille und das Grelle: Essays*, 227-36, Frankfurt: Verlag Freie Gesellschaft.

Zahl, Peter-Paul. ([1979] 2001), *Die Glücklichen*, München: DTV.

Zahl, Peter-Paul. (2001 [1978]), "Angina Pectoris," in Ümit Güney and Norbert Ney (trans.), *Nâzım Hikmet. Menschenlandschaften*, 3-7, Hamburg: Verlag J. Reents.

# 7

# The Internationalist Left and World Literature

# The Case of Nâzım Hikmet in Greece

*Kenan Behzat Sharpe*

When Alexis Tsipras stepped down from his post as prime minister of Greece in August 2015, he marked the occasion with a poem by the Turkish poet Nâzım Hikmet Ran (1902–63). In his resignation speech, Tsipras announced his hope for the future with the words "Our most beautiful days we haven't lived yet." This was an allusion to Nâzım Hikmet's poem "24 Nisan 1945" (24 April 1945), written from prison to his wife Piraye as part of the series "Saat 21-22 Şiirleri" (Poems from 9 to 10 o'clock). The full poem reads:

> The most beautiful sea:
>                    Hasn't been crossed yet.
> The most beautiful child:
>                    Hasn't grown up yet.
>
> Our most beautiful days:
>                    we haven't seen yet.
> And the most beautiful words I wanted to tell you
>                I haven't said yet
>
>                         (Blasing and Konuk 2002: 100)

Readers of Greek have been familiar with this poem expressing hope within tribulation ever since communist poet Yannis Ritsos (1909–90) included it in his 1966 volume of translations from Nâzım Hikmet as "E Pio Ómorphe Thálassa" (The Most Beautiful Sea) (2002: 83). The poem has also inspired songs. In 1975 Maria Dimitriadi, a renowned singer and member of the Revolutionary Communist Movement of Greece, sang a version of "24 April 1945" arranged by Thanos Mikroutsikos, a composer, politician, and lifelong communist. In 1983, a second musical adaptation of "24 April 1945," this time by left-wing Cypriot composer Manos Loïzos, solidified the poem's place—and Ritsos's translation—in the popular imagination. It was this same version of the poem, written by a Turkish communist and translated by a Greek communist, that Tsipras, former member of the Communist Youth of Greece, used in his speech. In short, with "24 April 1945" as with numerous Nâzım Hikmet poems, the left has been a central mediator in the reception of this Turkish poet, and by extension Turkish literature, in Greece.

Though a Greek head of state can quote a Turkish poet in the twenty-first century, this was not always the case. It would be an understatement to describe the relationship between Turkey and Greece as tortured and complex. A majority of Greeks lived under the Ottomans from the conquest of Constantinople in 1453 until the 1821 Greek War of Independence. After winning independence in 1830 the Kingdom of Greece continued to annex territory from the diminishing Ottoman Empire (including Nâzım Hikmet's birth city of Thessaloniki in 1913), eventually invading Anatolia in 1919. The national forces based in Ankara defeated the Greek army. What came to be seen, by Greece, as the "Asia Minor Catastrophe" was, for the newly established Turkish Republic, a "War of Independence." In this way, the modern nations of Greece and Turkey were both founded through armed conflict with each other. Throughout the twentieth century periods of peace and cooperation were periodically interrupted by traumatic events: a massive exchange of populations, territorial squabbles, pogroms and discrimination against Turkey's remaining Rum (Greek) communities, and conflict over the fate of Cyprus. Today, offshore drilling, the status of refugees from Syria and the Middle East, Turkey's military presence in Northern Cyprus, and irredentist threats all mark the relationship between these two ostensible NATO allies.

It is precisely the turbulent relationship between these two Aegean neighbors that makes the reception of Nâzım Hikmet in Greece a helpful limit case for understanding the position of Turkish literature in world literature. Nâzım[1] remains a widely recognized and beloved figure in Greece. For example, the first book-length Greek translation of Nâzım was published by Yannis Ritsos in 1953. It was then picked up by the left-wing press Kedros in 1966 and remains in print today, having reached its twentieth edition. As of 2019, there have been fourteen other volumes of

Nâzım's poems published in Greece. There are also four books of plays and four prose collections on the market, making a total of twenty-three separate volumes.[2] While Nâzım is far from the only Turkish writer known in Greece (the novels of Orhan Kemal, Zülfü Livaneli, Orhan Pamuk, Elif Şafak, and others have also been translated and continue to be republished), he has been the writer most consistently translated.[3]

Nâzım's vigorous reception in Greece must be squared with the fact that, in many languages around the world, he is also one of the earliest and most widely translated figures from Turkish literature. Long before Orhan Pamuk entered the world stage, Nâzım Hikmet was the Turkish writer that a reader of poetry in Arabic, French, Italian, Spanish or Urdu would be likely to name (Ergil 2008). What then makes Nâzım's place in Greece distinct? In this chapter, I make two interconnected arguments. First, the enabling condition for Nâzım's reception across the world was his explicitly communist and internationalist politics. Second, his enduring popularity in Greece specifically can be explained by long-standing left-wing discourses and rituals that approach the problematic Greek-Turkish relationship through the prism of solidarity and friendship, of which Nâzım Hikmet has become a primary symbol.

I begin this chapter by unpacking Nâzım's global popularity through reference to the internationalist network of left-wing magazines, writers' congresses, and peace meetings that one scholar has dubbed the "People's Republic of Letters" (Djagalov 2017: 26). These cultural networks were supported by the Soviet Union with the participation of figures like Louis Aragon, Langston Hughes, Pablo Neruda, Muriel Rukeyser, Jean-Paul Sartre, and Anna Seghers, among others. These writers and artists composed a generational cohort of politically committed cultural producers with a global reach that Michael Denning has referred to as "radical moderns" (1997: 39). It was precisely because Nâzım was part of this group of closely associated artists, and enjoyed the sponsorship of the world communist movement, that he was the Turkish writer with the greatest global recognition in the early and mid-twentieth century.[4]

After discussing the disproportionately influential place of communists in mid-twentieth-century world poetry, I will turn to the specific example of "radical modern" Yannis Ritsos. The reception of Nâzım in Greece was mediated by Ritsos's well-known translations. Yet Ritsos was also a mediator in a more metaphorical sense: Nâzım has long been domesticated for Greek readers through reference to the many similarities between the lives and work of these two contemporaries. Both spent long periods in prison for their writings and political convictions, and both wrote plainly spoken poetry that reached wide audiences. In the discourse used by leftists on both sides of the Aegean, recognizing parallel forms of suffering opens the door to a shared struggle. Nâzım is often described as a Turkish Ritsos, just as in Turkey Ritsos is described as a Greek Nâzım. The personal friendship between them (they met in the 1950s and 1960s in the Eastern Bloc) is used as a symbol of Greek-Turkish friendship. Finally, I discuss the positive portrayal (rare in the mid-twentieth-century Turkish context) of Greek people in Nâzım's poetry and public statements, exploring how these descriptions are mobilized in Greek assessments of his work.

Throughout the chapter I draw on three of the most influential translations of Nâzım's poetry into Greek—not only Ritsos's 1953/1966 edition of *Poímata* (Poems) but also volumes by Stelios Mayiopoulos (1959) and Aris Diktaios (1976). I analyze which poems are most frequently selected and why. Ritsos produced his Greek versions based on the French edition of Nâzım's poetry by Hasan Gureh (1951). Limited by the poems available in French and further filtered through Ritsos's own aesthetic sensibility, Ritsos's anthology is not representative of the major phases in Nâzım's oeuvre. Yet because these translations fit with the direct, communicative, and intimate quality of Ritsos's own verse, this volume has been the most widely influential.

Stelios Mayiopoulos's expansive, two-volume anthology *Nazím Hikmét: Ta Érga Tou* (Nâzım Hikmet: His Works) for the communist publisher Sýnchrone Epoché contains separate sections for lyric poems, epics, drama, and prose. A scholar of Turkish, Mayiopoulos includes a 120-page essay outlining the life of Nâzım Hikmet and the political and literary context of his writings. Similarly, Aris Diktaois's *122 Poímata* (122 Poems) includes selections from all of Nâzım's most famous lyric and epic/narrative poems plus contextualizing introductory and explanatory notes for terms, places, and people unfamiliar to the average Greek reader. Diktaois is an important postwar Greek poet who was inspired by existentialism. He began writing about and translating Nâzım as early as 1950.

Another central source for tracing the political discourses that shape the understanding of Nâzım's poetry and Turkish literature in Greece is statements by left-wing parties, most significantly the Communist Party of Greece (KKE), and civil society groups promoting Greek-Turkish friendship through publications and commemorative events. Literary exchange has played a crucial role in overcoming hostility and providing common ground for activists in Turkey and Greece. As Leonidas Karakatsanis writes, contact between the left in both countries has been "cultivated through exchanges located in the affective realm of music and art. After all music, songwriting, and poetry both in Greece and in Turkey had been a terrain of struggle [. . .] and the Left had played a definitely hegemonic role" (2014: 53). The shared "political grammars of the Left"—based in a proclivity for radical poetry and song, the experience of exile and imprisonment, and the struggle for basic democracy in the face of military intervention and dictatorship— have made it possible for citizens to forge connections and imagine "another Greece" and "another Turkey" outside of nationalist paradigms.

Just as Greeks and Turks have used world literature for political purposes, studying Nâzım's politicized reception in Greece can point to new avenues for the study of world literature. Pascale Casanova's work on "world literary space" (2004: 3) has been powerful in "rediscovering a lost transnational dimension of literature that for two hundred years ha[d] been reduced to the political and linguistic boundaries of nations" (xi). Similarly, analyses of the "one but unequal" (Moretti 2000: 150) character of world literary space has added nuance to earlier scholarship by ascribing agency to "small literatures." Even so, both models still subscribe to a paradigm in which the recognition of competing cores as well as relations among peripheral or semi-peripheral literatures are difficult to register.

The example of interchange between Greece and Turkey, two semi-peripheral countries on the edge of Europe, complicates the specific core-periphery model that still determines much of the influential scholarship on world literary space. Following Casanova, this chapter will show moments where the reception of Turkish literature in Greece is routed through the canonical "Greenwich meridian" of literature, Paris, as revealed by the fact that Ritsos's Greek translations of Nâzım came through French. Yet Moscow was equally if not more important as a standard-setter for these poets. It was through the publication/translation efforts, international meetings, and literary prizes of the Soviet Union that these poets came into direct contact and it was through shared commitment to the communist project that their poetry was legible to each other. Moscow has too often been overlooked as an alternative "Greenwich meridian," one with its own standards of literariness which throughout the Cold War vied with the autonomous and non-political ideal that Casanova unpacks in the cosmopolitan capitals of Western Europe and North America.

At the same time, this chapter also uncovers more lateral forms of literary exchange. My approach builds on scholarship uncovering south-south literary connections, minor transnationalism, cultural manifestations of the non-aligned movement, and anti-racist or anti-colonial solidarity.[5] Beleaguered left-wing movements in Greece and Turkey, "the only non-Socialist constituents of south-eastern Europe after the Second World War" (Karakatsanis and Papadogiannis 2017: 2), faced periods of military rule, anti-communist repression, and social ostracism. Out of this shared regional situation and history, activists and artists in the two countries developed symbols, discourses, and practices of friendship and solidarity that linked Greece and Turkey in their specificity while also pointing out to wider literary networks.

Just as Marx and Engels were early theorists of world literature, noting in *The Communist Manifesto* that "a world literature" was developing from the "numerous national and local literatures," the argument here is that Marxists have been and remain important practitioners and proponents of world literature. For example, on June 13–14, 2015, the KKE (The Communist Party of Greece) hosted a massive, two-day conference in Athens dedicated to Nâzım's life and work. The event included poetry readings, literary and historical lectures, film screenings, performances by dancers and choirs, and workshops. In his opening statement, Secretary-General Dimitris Koutsoumpas described Nâzım as "a great poet for his country, for humanity. A consistent militant, one of those unbowed by the class struggle" (2016: 22).

Koutsoumpas then connected the poet's significance in Greece and the world to his militancy:

> Turkish literature, in the presence of Hikmet, crosses its borders and becomes global [kseperná ta sýnorá tes kai yínetai pankósmia]. It is read by the workers and laborers of Europe, Asia, America and its verses imagine a more beautiful world. (Koutsoumbas 2016: 22)

Nâzım's poetry, Koutsoumpas suggests, is a truly *pankósmia* (worldwide, global, universal) phenomenon precisely because the Turkish poet was a "true internationalist," concerned with the fate of not merely his own country but also the world. The secretary-general goes on to quote Nâzım's own statements on the question of world literature from a 1958 Paris interview. There Nâzım begins by describing the forms taken by national literatures as a "crucial issue" (Koutsoumbas 2016: 22; Nâzım Hikmet 1992: 131). The poet admits that literature evolves differently in each national situation. "However," he adds, "influences arising from different cultures cause changes [. . .] and this is what gives national culture (*ulusal kültür*) its universal dimension (*evrensellik niteliği*)." He goes on to describe himself as an "heir" not only of Turkish literature but also of world literature, confirming the assessment of Greek communists.

Nâzım's discussion of art as the universal inheritance of all peoples also echoes what Ritsos wrote about him in the preface to his translations:

> Hikmet lived within the unity of world culture [*pankósmias koultoúras*], and despite his particular social and ideological preferences he did not accept firm segregation of intellectual culture into "east" and "west" or typically "progressive" or typically "decadent." And his art, despite its purely national elements, remains, like any true art, transnational—that is, human, or as we say more commonly: pan-human (*pananthropiné*). And his clear politics undoubtedly reflect his human face, the feeling of a citizen of the world. (2016: 21)

As distant as this language of universal humanity might sound to readers today, communist internationalism laid the groundwork for the welcoming of Turkish literature in Greece, and vice versa. Today, in a historical moment when Marx and Engels's prediction that capitalism would undo all "national one-sidedness and narrow-mindedness" could not seem further from the truth—particularly in southern Europe and the Mediterranean—it is illuminating to look back at this mostly forgotten dimension of world literature and culture.

## The (People's) Republic of Letters

If Nâzım is among the most translated Turkish writers in Greece and the world, this widespread reception is directly connected to the left and internationalist commitments expressed in his poems. For example, Nâzım's first work to receive an international reception was *Taranta-Babu'ya Mektuplar* (Letters to Taranta-Babu), a narrative poem decrying Benito Mussolini's invasion of Ethiopia. Upon publication in 1935 the epistolary poem was immediately published in French translation by Louis Aragon in *Commune* (Göksu and Timms 1999: 126). This was followed by translations into Italian, Spanish, and Russian. The poem was also included in Diktaios's Greek translation (1985). Encouraged by the urgency of the fascist threat, the international afterlife of *Letters to Taranta-Babu* was as global as the fictional letters to Taranta-Babu, the wife of the poem's unnamed Ethiopian narrator, that crisscross the world from Rome to Ethiopia to Istanbul in the poem's frame tale.

International readers similarly responded to the global imaginary present in the 1932 narrative poem *Benerci Kendini Niçin Öldürdü?* (Why Did Banerjee Kill Himself?). The poem explores the thoughts of protagonist Banerjee as he struggles against the British in Kolkata and hides from the police. The poem makes stopovers in Manchester, Chicago, Istanbul, Senegal, and the Congo in order to portray the global forces of capitalism and colonialism.

Nâzım's interest in India was not unrequited. Leftists in Kolkata published the first book-length English translation of Nâzım's work (Ghosh: 1952). The opening section of the poem was also included in Ritsos's translation and made famous by composer Mikroutsikos and singer Dimitriadi as "Mikrókosmos" [Microcosm] on their 1975 album *Politiká Tragoúdia* (Political Songs). Longer selections were included in the translations of Diktaios and Mayiopoulos. Overall, the popularity of poems like *Taranta-Babu* and *Benerci* reveals that long before Nâzım could physically begin traveling the three continents of Asia, Africa, and Latin America himself, he was engaged in what Gül Bilge Han calls a "tricontinental poetics of solidarity" (2018: 287) which made his work legible to readers in other contexts.

In the 1950s, Nâzım's own travel itinerary began to keep pace with the internationalism of his poems. After a decade and a half of imprisonment in Turkey, Nâzım's 1950 hunger strike made him a global cause célèbre. Pablo Neruda, Simone de Beauvoir, Jean-Paul Sartre, Paul Éluard, Paul Robeson, and Pablo Picasso all became involved in a campaign to free the poet. He was released in an amnesty later that year, but quickly fled Turkey to avoid further prosecution. Nâzım sought sanctuary in the Soviet Union. Having spent time in Moscow throughout the 1920s and early 1930s, when he visited other artists and studied at the Communist University for the Toilers of the East (KUTV), Nâzım knew that he could find a secure—if precarious—home there (Meyer 2018).

In 1950, he was awarded the Soviet-sponsored World Council of Peace prize alongside Neruda and began traveling across the Eastern Bloc (Romania, Poland, East Germany, Bulgaria, Uzbekistan) as well as Cuba, France, Italy, and Tanganyika. Nâzım was also involved with the Afro-Asian Writers' Bureau, working alongside Mario de Andrade, Faiz Ahmad Faiz, W.E.B. Du Bois, and Ousmane Sembène (Han 2018: 288). And it was these networks that introduced Ritsos to Nâzım, first in East Berlin (1951) and again in Prague and Bucharest (1962).

The investment in global struggles expressed through his poetry, the worldwide recognition he enjoyed, and his globetrotting itinerary as a spokesman of the revolution—these aspects of Nâzım's life and work are connected to his identity as a communist. Nâzım was a key participant in what Katerina Clark calls the "pan-European cosmopolitanism" (2011: 11) of the communist movement, which aimed to create a "transnational cultural space, an intellectual fraternity or a transnational confederation of leftists [. . .] comparable with the 'Republic of Letters' promoted during the Enlightenment by figures like Voltaire" (31). This cosmopolitan transnationalism was made possible by the Soviet Union's sponsorship of dissident intellectuals and other darlings of the global left.

According to Rossen Djagalov, these writers "served as the liaisons between their national literatures and the Moscow centre" (2017: 26). Building on Casanova and Clark, Djagalov dubs this Soviet-sponsored form of world literature a "People's Republic of Letters" (2017: 26). Casanova has little to say about Moscow, but for much of the twentieth century it competed with the publishing centers of Paris or New York while occasionally moving through them, connecting far-flung movements. This cultural infrastructure opened up new possibilities for writers from peripheral countries and marginalized communities. For example, African American novelist Richard Wright recalls of his communist-aligned period that writers like himself "had only to speak and millions listened. Our writing was translated into French, German, Russian, Chinese, Spanish, Japanese. Who had ever, in all human history, offered to young writers an audience so vast?" (Denning 2004: 52). Writing in a language like Turkish, Nâzım could not have enjoyed the same global reach without Soviet sponsorship.[6]

Yet Nâzım's works were not simply foisted upon uninterested readers. The communist internationalism present in his poems made him compelling to people across the world. As Robert J. C. Young remarks, throughout the twentieth century Marxism was central to a variety of political and cultural movements (not just in Europe but across the Global South) because it articulated the links between national and international struggles (2011: 169). As a kind of revolutionary lingua franca, Marxism facilitated "the translation of the universal into the idiom of the local." Neruda once stated, for example, that Nâzım's work "provoked great enthusiasm in Latin America. His struggle for the liberation of Turkey was the same as the struggle waged by our poets and our writers" (Göksu and Timms 1999: 173). Nâzım's poetry was legible across the three continents because it described foreign struggles in recognizable terms. Similarly, Nâzım's friend and translator in Italian, the former anti-fascist partisan Joyce Lussu, remarked that she could comprehend Nâzım precisely because they were both Marxists:

> I don't speak a word of Turkish and know hardly anything about Turkish literature, but I can honestly say that I know Hikmet very well, his entire poetic work, his ideological, ethical, aesthetic and psychological world, the experiences that shaped him, the authors he was interested in, [. . .] his friends and enemies. (Larkosh 2010: 207)

It was fluency in this politicized lingua franca that made Nâzım's poetry eminently translatable.

These examples reveal that the "People's Republic of Letters" in which Nâzım participated did not merely rival the Greenwich meridian of literature as described by Casanova: it operated through an alternative set of rules. If Paris could impress "the stamp of *littérarité* upon texts that came from far-flung lands, thereby denationalizing and departicularizing them, declaring them to be acceptable as legal tender in all the countries under its literary jurisdiction" (87), Moscow similarly impressed its own stamp upon certain works from China, Chile, Japan, Greece, Turkey, and beyond. Yet it did not require denationalization and departicularization in the sense of removing political content and context: instead, it worked by drawing direct political analogies between, say, the situation of an African American writer and a Vietnamese one. Certainly, these comparisons can do damage to particularities, but this is not only a feature of the People's Republic of Letters. In discussing postcolonial literature, Casanova describes how the reception of peripheral writers in the Greenwich meridian is based in homologies that affirm a "structural similarity between the literature and politics of small countries" (250). Yet the ultimate goal for a postcolonial writer seeking success in Paris, London, or New York was to transcend these details and enter the universal. This is why Casanova describes a split in world literary space between a "literary and cosmopolitan pole" and a "political and national pole." In contrast, the specific ideal of *littérarité* supported by Moscow was based on writers being simultaneously cosmopolitan (more accurately, international) and deeply national, literary as well as political.

## Maverick Communists and Turkish-Greek Friendship

And so Moscow had its own standards for establishing literariness. Yet we must also grapple with the fact that Nâzım also appealed to writers outside of socialist countries or movements. How exactly did he understand the relationship between literature and politics, and how does this provide a model for being both national and international? Despite the bombastic and sometimes propagandistic excesses of his early works and the communist networks that sustained his career, Nâzım was not a party hack. As Stathis Gourgouris writes, poets like Nâzım, Ritsos, Mayakovsky, Brecht, Neruda, and Éluard should be understood as "maverick communists" (2000: 73). That is, while being thoroughly committed writers they were heterodox in their doctrine and impatient with "prescriptive aesthetics" of any kind. For instance, Nâzım—dubbed by Stalin's daughter Svetlana Alliluyeva a "romantic communist"—was at one time expelled from the Turkish Communist Party (TKP) and even after he moved to the Soviet Union continued to rock the boat with aesthetic experiments that ventured far beyond official socialist realism (Göksu and Timms 1999: x). Similarly, Turkish writer Şevket Süreyya Aydemir described Nâzım as "uninterested in the rigors of theory or the practical problems of changing the social structure. For him, communism was one perpetual revolutionary excitement, like the seas or roar like the tempests" (Blasing 2013: 14). In the eyes of maverick communists, politics was an extension of aesthetics. They sought to unite mind and heart, communism and poetry, politics and art. This fundamentally aesthetic approach to the question of communism made their work portable and adaptable in ways the output of more doctrinaire literary figures was not.

Nâzım's association with other maverick communist poets has been central in establishing his reception in Greece. For example, in the liner notes to Loïzos's album of songs by Nâzım, music critic Giorgos Tsambras writes: "Across the world and in Greece as well the Turkish poet Nâzım Hikmet is—along with Brecht, Mayakovsky and Neruda—a spokesman of revolutionary poetry" (1983). Most often, Nâzım is compared to Ritsos. The comparison is so well established that a relationship of equivalence has emerged. For instance, as recently as 2018 Nâzım was still described in Greece as "Turkey's Yannis Ritsos" (Gionis 2018). Özdemir İnce, the literary figure most responsible for establishing Ritsos's reputation in Turkey, recalls that in times of censorship the two poets stood in for each other (2016: 84). When the work of one poet is banned, simply use the other.

Ritsos clarifies his thoughts on the role of maverick communists in overcoming national divisions in a July 1962 interview with Nâzım. In a revealing example of the complex networks of affiliation sponsored by the

"People's Republic of Letters," this interview took place in Prague and was conducted in French (Ritsos's and Nâzım's common language). It was then published in Czechoslovakia, republished in the Russian magazine *Den Poezii*, and finally translated from Russian into Turkish in 1978 by leftist poet Ataol Behramoğlu for the magazine *Devrimci Savaşımda Sanat Emeği: Aylık Sanat Kültür Dergisi* (Artistic Labor in the Revolutionary Struggle: A Monthly Arts and Culture Journal). In the interview, Ritsos describes the kind of "contemporary poetry" produced by Nâzım and himself as a "vehicle for mutual understanding between people and brotherhood" (Nâzım Hikmet and Ritsos 1978: 46). Their poetry's "task for humanity" allows its "poetic language to be translated from language to language without overly harming its beauty." Whereas poetry focused mainly on pleasing sounds and formal tricks are trapped within the borders of a single country, Ritsos argues, "poetry worthy of the name carries, above all else, an intellectual and emotional weight, which is international" (47). Ritsos draws a direct line between the "direct and concrete" quality of his generation's poetry and this work's ability to become world literature, the responsibility of which is to support international bonds of friendship.

Ritsos made similar arguments about the power of poetry long after his friend Nâzım's death. In a 1989 interview with writer and translator Herkül Millas, Ritsos asserted that translating and reading Nâzım in Greek made it possible to overcome national hostilities:

> How and where did we in Greece get to know Turks? From reading Nâzım Hikmet. We got to know the Turks that he portrayed. Later we encountered the Turks of Yaşar Kemal's [novels]. We got to know Aziz Nesin's characters. This is how we'll learn about and love one another. (Ritsos 2018: xx).

Nâzım, like the other left-wing Turkish writers Ritsos names, becomes a metonymic stand-in for the Turkish people. World literature is, for Ritsos, a project for instilling internationalism; getting to know another "people" teaches one to love them.[7] In this specific case of Greece and Turkey, literature is a project of friendship, both literal and metaphorical.[8] Throughout the twentieth century, Karakatanis notes, the language of "Greek-Turkish friendship" has been a "discursive medium [for] struggle against the widespread ideology of nationalism, isolation and rigid borders" (2014: 15). Friendship, in this context, contains both a personal and a geopolitical valence. First, there is the face-to-face friendship of the two men, based in mutual admiration. For example, in Ritsos's statements about his late friend Nâzım, he consistently emphasized the latter's remarkable qualities, calling him "one of the best examples of beauty, goodness, and humility in the human race" (İnce 2016: 83). Statements like these stimulate a "feeling of a shared political intimacy" (Karakatsanis 2014: 38) cultivated between Turkish and Greek leftists. In this way, intimate friendship becomes a figure for the possibility of shared struggle between the people of Greece and Turkey.

## Suffering and Solidarity: Greeks in Nâzım's Poetry

Nâzım's most famous poems in Greece are those that explicitly discuss Greek people and the hardships they face. In the early and mid-twentieth century, positive depictions of Greeks were rare in Turkish literature. According to Millas's analysis of mainly canonical Turkish novels and memoirs, the list of the most common words used to describe Greek people included "dirty, disgusting, bloodthirsty, contemptuous, pedant, violent, savage, spoiled, enemy, shameless, ungrateful, cunning, barbarous, appalling," and so on (1996: 80). The main exception to these derogatory literary stereotypes occurs in the works of Marxists like Sabahattin Ali, Suat Derviş, and others who show that hostility between Greeks and Turks is not inevitable but stoked by the ruling classes of both countries (Millas 2009: 82). In Nâzım's case, this political orientation gives a surprisingly intimate emotional charge to his poems describing political hopes and tribulations of comrades across the Aegean. This positive approach did not go unappreciated by Greek readers.

The most famous Nâzım poem in Greece is "Angina Pektoris" (Angina Pectoris). The Ritsos translation (1966: 95) provided lyrics for songs performed by both Dimitriadi and Loïzos. Diktaios has also translated it (1984: 156). The April 1948 poem, written from prison, begins with two contemporaneous events:

> If half my heart is here, doctor,
>     the other half is in China
> with the army flowing
>     toward the Yellow River.
> And every morning, doctor,
>     every morning at sunrise my heart
>         is shot in Greece.
>
> (Blasing and Konuk 2002: 136)

Just a year away from its 1949 victory, Nâzım followed the progress of Mao's Red Army as it crossed the Yangtze to capture Nanjing. While this gives him hope, thoughts of Greece bring him despair. It was Greek partisans, dominated by communists, who successfully routed Mussolini and Hitler's armies from Greece during the Second World War. However, a civil war broke out when the partisans were subsequently targeted by the Greek right-wing and pro-monarchists were given support by Great Britain and the United States (Panourgiá 2009: 117).

The Greek Civil War of 1946–9, one of the first conflicts of the Cold War, ended with the Greek left defeated and the very partisans who fought the Italian and German invaders executed, exiled, or in reeducation camps. In the poem, Nâzım is so caught up in the ordeal of the partisans that his heart, too, is shot "every morning at sunrise." Fulfilling the poetic conceit that describes the poet's internationalist identifications as the source of his coronary disease, Nâzım ends the poem with his heart "beat[ing] with the most distant stars." Though his body is trapped in jail, his heart is worn down, traversing not only the Aegean but the very cosmos.[9]

One reason the Greek left has been open to expressions of affiliation with its counterparts in Turkey is the sense of a shared legacy of suffering and defeat. With few exceptions, Greece has been ruled by the right and leftists have been treated as "dangerous citizens" that must be contained (Panourgiá 2009: 9). After the defeat of the partisans, Greece became, along with Turkey, a NATO member. The country experienced periods of military dictatorship, such as the fiercely repressive Regime of the Colonels (1967–74). The Turkish left also has a long and tragic past. The TKP was founded in Baku in 1920. Mustafa Suphi and the other fourteen founders of the party were murdered off the coast of Trabzon in 1921 (Blasing 2013: 65–6). For most of the subsequent half-century, the TKP was illegal and its cadres faced intense state repression. The Turkish left experienced a period of new possibility in the 1960s, though clandestine TKP members and activists from other organizations underwent torture, imprisonment, and exile during the 1971 and 1980 coups.

Shared suffering became a basis for solidarity among Greek and Turkish leftists. As Karakatsanis and Papadogiannis write, the experiences of repression, coups, and foreign intervention have "moulded similar affective traces or stains of memory in their bodies and minds" (2017: 3). This helps explain why the image used to express solidarity in Nâzım's poem, the battered heart, is so corporeal. Even after Nâzım began to experience a short period of relief, his poetry continued to use images of suffering when expressing solidarity. The 1951 poem "Hapisten Çıktıktan Sonra" (After Getting out of Prison) refers to Greek leftists in a section titled "Doğum" (Birth):

When my son
    came into the world,
children were born in Greek prisons,
their fathers shot by firing squads.
The first thing they saw in this world
        were iron bars.

(Blasing and Konuk 2002: 153)

Even the joyful birth of a son causes the poet to reflect on the experiences of his Greek counterparts. While his son grows up free, he thinks of the orphaned children of executed Greek partisans. The poet's feelings of rage and injustice permeate the most intimate moments of his life.

Another important poem for Nâzım's reputation in Greece is "Karanfilli Adam" (The Man with the Carnation), dedicated to resistance leader Nikos Beloyannis (1915–52). After fighting against the Axis occupation, Beloyannis fled Greece, returning in 1950 to help re-establish the illegal KKE. Beloyannis and ninety-four others were arrested. In March 1952, he was sentenced to death. Despite thousands of telegrams to the Greek government from the likes of Charlie Chaplin, Jean-Paul Sartre, Paul Éluard, and even Charles de Gaulle, Greece's government refused clemency. While Beloyannis was on trial, a photograph of him holding a red carnation in court, and a sketch of it by Pablo Picasso, transformed Beloyannis into a cause célèbre.

It also inspired Nâzım's poem, published in Moscow in April 1952 and translated into Greek by both Ritsos and Diktaios:

> In the darkness of dawn
>    in the light of the projector,
>    the photograph
>    of the man with the white carnation
>       shot up against the wall
>    sits on my table.
>
>    His right hand
>       holds the carnation
>       like a fragment of light from the Greek sea.
>    The man with the carnation
>    looks out from under his heavy black eyebrows
>       he looks out like an innocent child,
>          guilelessly.
>
>    Only folk songs can be this guileless
>    and only communists
>    can take oaths perfectly without guile.
>    His teeth are bright white:
>    Beloyannis smiles.
>
>       (translation by Kenan Sharpe; Nâzım Hikmet 2015: 1507)

The poem begins by linking the speaker sitting at his table gazing at the photograph with Beloyannis holding the carnation in his hand. Beloyannis symbolizes both national identity (his carnation is linked to the geography of the "Greek sea") and what it means to be a communist. Just as the Aegean links Greece and Turkey, it is, Karakatsanis writes, the "shared spectre of a 'leftist' identity [that] connect[s] the political trajectories" of the two countries (2014: 48).

The "folk songs" the poem associates with Beloyannis are, like his smile, "guileless"—precisely because they refuse obfuscation and transcend borders. Nâzım clarified the importance of Beloyannis's life as a symbol of political bonds in a message to the Greek people given over Bucharest Radio in 1952:

> There are two Turkeys and two Greeces. The real one and the fake one. The independent one and the enslaved one. One is the Greece of Beloyannis and the thousands of Greek patriots who languish in prisons [. . .]. This is the genuine Greece. One is Turkey with the thousands of Turkish patriots who are rotting in dungeons [. . .]. This is the genuine Turkey. (Koutsoumbas 2016: 24)

Still quoted by leading communist politicians in Greece in the twenty-first century, Nâzım's urgent speech to save Beloyannis, like the poem "Karanfilli Adam," continues to link suffering, sacrifice, and solidarity.

Another poem that has determined Nâzım's reception in Greece by linking shared experiences to potential collaboration is his 1936 work "Simavne Kadısı Oğlu Şeyh Bedreddin Destanı" (The Epic of Sheik Bedreddin), which focuses on a fifteenth-century proto-communist peasant uprising led by the followers of a heterodox Islamic scholar. At the poem's climax, the ragtag group of militants fights with the sultan's forces. Nâzım portrays the coalitional character of this uprising of the poor and downtrodden:

> A great battle took place.
>     Turkish peasants from Aydın,
>         Greek sailors from Chios,
>             Jewish tradesmen
>     [. . .]
>     plunged into the forest of enemies like ten thousand axes.
>                             (Blasing and Konuk 2002: 58)

In the context of the rise of fascism and the international Popular Front, Nâzım stressed the multiethnic, multiconfessional character of this historical struggle. In a postscript to the poem, Nâzım expresses pride that Anatolia "gave rise to a movement that considered the Greek sailors of Rhodes and Jewish merchants as brothers" (Ertürk 2011: 30). The poet builds from an event ostensibly within national history, but he interprets it internationally. In this way, he articulates an inclusive vision of who "the people" are and who they could become.

Both Diktaios and Mayiopoulos include selections from "To Épos Tou Seíchi Bedrettín" in their translations, including the passage describing Turks, Greeks, and Jews fighting under the same banners. Like Nâzım's participation in what Djagalov calls the "People's Republic of Letters" and his status as a "maverick communist," poems like this continue to structure how the Turkish poet is understood in Greece and reveal the stamp of a Marxist and cosmopolitan conception of *littérarité*. An official write-up on the June 2015 conference on Nâzım's life and work hosted by the KKE again mobilized this passage while describing a musical event that featured songs by Nâzım performed in Greek:

> Saturday's concert provided incentive to read Hikmet again, to get to know him, and to make it possible for the young generation, in particular, to discover him. That is the purpose of all these events: to get to know the poet who sang equally "for the Turkish villagers of Aydın" and "the fishermen of Samos." (*Rizospastis* 2015)

More than eight decades since the poem was written, the same expressions of solidarity continue to resonate. Nâzım's powerful reputation in Greece remains linked to commemorative rituals, the affective ties of poetry and music, and the politics of friendship. Shared suffering in the past is seen as a crucible for a shared future. In this way, left-wing activists and literati in Greece have been instrumental in naturalizing a body of foreign poetry that could otherwise be seen as the product of an enemy nation. Yet left-wing literary-political mediators follow Nâzım's example in describing the poet's work as belonging equally to Turkey and the world.

# Notes

1. I follow the Turkish usage in referring to the poet simply as Nâzım. Ran, his official surname, was chosen in jest and rarely used.
2. See (Çokona 2002) for a list of volumes of Nâzım's poetry, plays, and prose in Greek.
3. See (Eker-Roditakis 2018) for more on Turkish-to-Greek literary translation.
4. The only Turkish literary figure who could boast a similar level of international success was Halide Edip Adıvar (1884–1964). Like Nâzım, her global reputation was connected to political commitments—she became a spokesperson (though not an uncritical one) for the Turkish War of Independence and partially for the Turkish Republic. Unlike Nâzım, however, her reputation rests partly on her ability to compose in English and her association with mainstream literary figures such as those associated with the Bloomsbury Set. One interesting point of overlap to be pursued in further research is the shared recognition both writers had in India. See (Hasan 2010) as well as the chapter by İmşir and Dhanawade in this volume.
5. See works by (Balthaser 2015), (Han 2018), and (Lionnet and Shih 2005).

6 This "extensive cultural diplomacy program" of the Soviet Union was designed in part to counter the equally vigorous activities of the Congress for Cultural Freedom (a CIA-front organization), the Ford Foundation, and other US soft power organizations seeking to demonstrate the cultural superiority of the "Free World" and woo intellectuals away from communism (Spahr 2018: 81). In the Cold War context, the question of world literature was inevitably a political one, and not just when the content of works was specifically *engagé*. For more on Turkish literature during the Cold War see (Günay-Erkol 2013).

7 See Badiou for a description of the internationalist poetry of Nâzım Hikmet, Ritsos and Pablo Neruda, as effecting a "changing of subjectivity" (2014: 101) based in the ability to identify with the struggles of foreigners and strangers. See Dufft's anthology (2009) for other attempts within Turkish literature to forge imaginative connections to social "Others."

8 Ritsos became personal friends with Yaşar Kemal and Aziz Nesin when they met at the Congress of World Writers in Sofia, Bulgaria, in 1978 (İnce 2010: 11).

9 It must be added that support for the Greek anti-fascists in Turkey also went beyond expressions of solidarity. Turkish communist Mihri Belli famously journeyed to Greece to fight alongside the partisans (Karakatsanis 2014: 59). Belli's adventures have inspired a 2008 documentary film in Greece, *Kapetán Kemál* (Captain Kemal).

# References

Badiou, Alain. (2014), *The Age of the Poets: And Other Writings on Twentieth-Century Poetry and Prose*, London and New York: Verso.

Balthaser, Benjamin. (2015), *Anti-Imperialist Modernism: Race and Transnational Radical Culture from the Great Depression to the Cold War*, Ann Arbor: University of Michigan Press.

Blasing, Mutlu Konuk. (2013), *Nâzım Hikmet: The Life and Times of Turkey's World Poet*, New York: Persea Books.

Casanova, Pascale. (2004), *The World Republic of Letters*. Tr. M. B. DeBoise, Cambridge: Harvard University Press.

Clark, Katerina. (2011), *Moscow, the Fourth Rome: Stalinism, Cosmopolitanism, and the Evolution of Soviet Culture, 1931–1941*, Cambridge: Harvard University Press.

Çokona, Ari. (2002), "Yunancaya Çevrilmiş Türk Edebiyatı: Bir Bibliyografya Denemesi," *Çeviribilim Dergisi* 5 (1): 69–87.

Denning, Michael. (1997), *The Cultural Front*, London and New York: Verso.

Denning, Michael. (2004), *Culture in the Age of Three Worlds*, London and New York: Verso.

Djagalov, Rossen. (2017), "Literary Monopolists and the Forging of the Post-WWII People's Republic of Letters," in N. Skradol and E. Dobrenko (eds.), *Socialist Realism in Central and Eastern European Literatures*, 25–37, London: Anthem Press.

Dufft, Catharina (ed.) (2009), *Turkish Literature and Cultural Memory: "Multiculturalism" as a Literary Theme after 1980*, Wiesbaden: Harrassowitz.
Eker-Roditakis, Arzu. (2018), "Repackaging, Retranslation, and Intersemiotic Translation: A Turkish Novel in Greece," in Ö. Berk Albachten and Ş. Tahir Gürçağlar (eds.), *Perspectives on Retranslation: Ideology, Paratexts, Methods*, 67–86, Abingdon: Routledge.
Ergil, Başak. (2008), *The Image of Nazım Hikmet and His Poetry in Anglo-American Literary Systems*, Istanbul: Nazım Hikmet Kültür ve Sanat Vakfı.
Ertürk, Nergis. (2011), *Grammatology and Literary Modernity in Turkey*, Oxford: Oxford University Press.
Ghosh, Asoke. (1952), *Selected Poems by Nazim Hikmet*, Calcutta: Parichaya Prakashani.
Gionis, Dimitris. (2018), "Me Ten Elláda Sten Kardiá Tou," June 10, 2018, *EfSyn*. Available online: https://www.efsyn.gr/themata/peridiabainontas/153257_me-tin-ellada-stin-kardia-toy (accessed June 10, 2019).
Göksu, Saime and Edward Timms. (1999), *Romantic Communist: The Life and Work of Nâzım Hikmet*, London: C. Hurst & Co.
Gourgouris, Stathis. (2000), "The Ark's Void – Communism and Poetry, circa 2nd Millenium," in Mehmet Yashin (ed.), *Step-Mothertongue: From Nationalism to Multiculturalism: Literatures of Cyprus, Greece, and Turkey*, 71–81, London: Middlesex University Press.
Günay-Erkol, Çimen. (2013), "Issues of Ideology and Identity in Turkish Literature during the Cold War," in C. Örnek and Ç. Üngör (eds.), *Turkey in the Cold War: Ideology and Culture*, 109–29, London: Palgrave Macmillan.
Han, Gül Bilge. (2018), "Nazım Hikmet's Afro-Asian Solidarities," *Safundi: The Journal of South African and American Studies* 19 (3): 284–305.
Hasan, Mushirul. (2010), *Between Modernity and Nationalism: Halide Edip's Encounter with Gandhi's India*, Oxford: Oxford University Press.
İnce, Özdemir. (2016), *Agios Ritsos*, Istanbul: Ve Yayınevi.
Karakatsanis, Leonidas. (2014), *Turkish-Greek Relations: Rapprochement, Civil Society and the Politics of Friendship*, Abingdon: Routledge.
Karakatsanis, Leonidas and Nikolaos Papadogiannis (eds.) (2017), *The Politics of Culture in Turkey, Greece and Cyprus: Performing the Left Since the Sixties*, Abingdon: Routledge.
Koutsoumbas, Dimitris. (2016), "Chaireretismoí tou Dimítri Koutsoúmba," in *Nazím Hikmét: Yia Na Yenoúne Ta Sokátadia Lámpsi: Epistemonikó Synédrio, Athens, 13-14 June 2015*, 19–27, Athens: Sýnchrone Epoché.
Larkosh, Christopher. (2010), "Impossible Optimisms? Translating Turkish Modernities into the Metaterranean," *Translation Studies* 3 (2): 201–15.
Lionnet, Françoise and Shu-mei Shih (eds.) (2005), *Minor Transnationalism*, Durham: Duke University Press.
Meyer, James H. (2018), "Children of Trans-Empire: Nâzım Hikmet and the First Generation of Turkish Students at Moscow's Communist University of the East," *Journal of the Ottoman and Turkish Studies Association* 5 (2): 195–218.
Millas, Hercules. (1996), "The Image of Greeks in Turkish Literature: Fiction and Memoirs," in W. Höpken (ed.), *Oil on Fire?*, 79–87, Hanover: Verlag Hansche Buchhandlung.

Millas, Hercules. (2009), "Constructing Memories of 'Multiculturalism' and Identities in Turkish Novels," in Catharina Dufft (ed.), *Turkish Literature and Cultural Memory*, 76-106, Wiesbaden: Harrassowitz.
Moretti, Franco. (2000), "Conjectures on World Literature," *New Left Review* (1): 54-68.
Nâzım Hikmet. (1951), *Poemes de Nazim Hikmet, traduits du Turc*. Tr. Hasan Gureh, introduced by Tristan Tzara, Paris: Les Éditeurs français réunis.
Nâzım Hikmet. (1985), *122 Poímata*. Tr. Aris Diktaois, Athens: S.I. Zacharópoulos.
Nâzım Hikmet. (1992), *Konuşmalar: Yazılar 6*, Istanbul: Adam Yayınları.
Nâzım Hikmet. (2002), *Poems of Nazım Hikmet*. Tr. Randy Blasing and Mutlu Konuk, New York: Persea.
Nâzım Hikmet. (2015), *Bütün Şiirleri*, Istanbul: Yapı Kredi Yayınları.
Nâzım Hikmet. ([1953] 2016), *Poímata*. Tr. Yannis Ritsos, Athens: Kedros.
Nâzım Hikmet. ([1959] 2017), *Nazím Hikmét: Ta Érga Tou*. Tr. Stelios Mayiopoulos, Athens: Sýnchrone Epoché.
Nâzım Hikmet and Yannis Ritsos. (1978), "Nâzım ve Ritsos'la Bir Söyleşi," *Devrimci Savaşımda Sanat Emeği: Aylık Sanat Kültür Dergisi* (3): 44-8.
"Nâzım Hikmet: Yia Na Yenoúne Ta Sokátadia Lámpsi," May 19, 2015. *Rizospastis*. Available online: https://www.rizospastis.gr/story.do?id=8443509 (accessed August 1, 2019).
Panourgiá, Neni. (2009), *Dangerous Citizens: The Greek Left and the Terror of the State*, New York: Fordham University Press.
Ritsos, Yannis. (2010), *Her Zaman En Başta Özgürlük*. Tr. Özdemir İnce, Herkül Millas, and İoanna Kuçuradi, Istanbul: Kırmızı Yayınları.
Ritsos, Yannis. ([1966] 2016), "Paratiréseis Sto Ergo Tou Nazím Hikmét," in *Poímata*, 9-26, Athens: Kedros.
Ritsos, Yannis. (2018), *Bir Mayıs Günü Bırakıp Gittin Beni: Seçme Şiirler*. Tr. Cevat Çapan, Istanbul: Kırmızı Kedi.
Spahr, Juliana. (2018), *Du Bois's Telegram: Literary Resistance and State Containment*, Cambridge: Harvard University Press.
Tsambras, Giorgos. (1983), Liner notes, *Grámmata sten Agapeméne*, Music by Manos Loïzos. Minos. CD.

# 8

# The Influence of Nâzım Hikmet on Arab Poetry

*Mehmet Hakkı Suçin*

Nâzım Hikmet (1902–63) is a representative of a key breaking point in form and content in Turkish poetry. He is also one of the most translated Turkish poets in the world, and he is probably the first name that comes to mind in the Arab literary spheres when Turkish poetry is considered. His poems, plays, and novels were translated early on into Arabic either straight from Turkish or via an interim language. The interest in Nâzım Hikmet in the Arab world is not limited to translations either. Many poets in different Arab countries were influenced by his life story as much as his poetry and elegies were penned after him. In this chapter I will examine the influence of Nâzım Hikmet on several Arab poets such as the Palestinians Tawfīq Zayyād (1929–94), Mahmoud Darwish (1941–2008), Samīh al-Qāsim (1939–2014), and Mu'īn Bseiso (1926–84), in addition to the Egyptian Salāh Abdel Sabour (1931–81) and the Iraqi Abd al-Wahhāb al-Bayātī (1926–99). I will also discuss briefly the Arabic translations of his works in terms of quality and quantity.

Tawfīq Zayyād, Mahmoud Darwish, and Samīh al-Qāsim are considered poets of resistance who helped advance the Palestinian cause. Mahmoud Darwish was among the figures who assisted the preparation of the Palestinian Declaration of Independence in 1988. Mu'īn Bseiso had to leave the Gaza Strip and live the rest of his life in exile after the Israeli conquest in the Six-Day War in 1967. Salāh Abdel Sabour in Egypt and Abd al-Wahhāb al-Bayātī in Iraq were pioneers of the free-verse movement in Arabic poetry. Salāh Abdel Sabour was an intellectual with a sharp political pen and Abd al-Wahhāb al-Bayātī was likewise a critical man of letters who was not afraid of speaking out. He was stripped of his citizenship in 1995.

The literature on Nâzım Hikmet's influence on Arab poetry is limited mainly to pieces in newspaper columns and academic studies on the subject are scarce.[1] In the relatively limited number of articles and essays written by various Arab writers, three points of influence are emphasized. The first point is his plain, clear, and fluid language that maintains its aesthetic qualities without becoming artificial. Most Arab poets who advocated Arab free verse took courage from this plain but deep language of Nâzım Hikmet in their desire to "liberate" Arab poetry in both form and content. The second one is Nâzım Hikmet's not disregarding the Turkish poetic tradition and his drawing on Divan poetry and folk culture, as well as *tasavvuf* heritage. Some critics relate the return to classical Arab literature of many Arab poets, such as the Iraqi Abd al-Wahhāb al-Bayātī, Egyptians Amal Dunqul and Ahmad Abd al-Muʿtī Hijazi, and Syrian Adonis (Ali Ahmad Said Esber), among many others, to the influence of Nâzım Hikmet as such. The third point is how Nâzım Hikmet writes about the pains, worries, and sorrows of the poor, the ordinary people, and those who are oppressed and how he is a revolutionary and libertarian poet who has combined his fight with his poetry. These qualities make Nâzım Hikmet a significant figure for the Arab literary sphere.

Nâzım Hikmet crosses borders with his poems. The Egyptian poet Hilmī Sālim "bears witness" to how, in the first half of the 1970s, they produced works in direct or indirect reference to Nâzım Hikmet's 1948 poem "Angina Pektoris," a poem which was written after the poet was diagnosed with cardiac arrhythmia in prison. The published English translation of Nâzım Hikmet's poem reads:

all I have to offer my poor people
is this apple in my hand, doctor,
one red apple:
           my heart.
And that, doctor, that is the reason
For this angina pectoris
not nicotine, prison, or arteriosclerosis.
I look at the night through the bars,
and despite the weight on my chest
my heart still beats with the most distant stars.

(Nâzım Hikmet 2002b: 136)

Sālim cites from the poem's Arabic translation:

Ana lā amliku mā uʿṭīhi li shaʿbī al-miskīni siwā tuffāḥatan hiya qalbī
Wa al-dhubḥatu lā taftuku bī li taṣallubi shiryānin aw qaswatu sijnin
Fa ana anẓuru ʿabra al-quḍbāni ilā al-layli

Wa raġma al-judrāni al-qā'imati 'alā ṣadrī
Yakhfiqu qalbī ma'a ab'adi najmin.

(2002c: 19)

The verbatim English back-translation of his version is as follows:

> There's nothing else besides an apple that I can give to my people, and that is my heart
> Angina, resulting from arteriosclerosis or the gloom of the gaol, cannot destroy me
> For I gaze at the night from behind the bars
> My heart beats with the most distant stars

There are clearly many formalistic losses as well as those of meaning in the Arabic translation. First of all, the formalistic style, which was kept in the English translation, is not taken into account at all. The melodic repetition of words such as "apple" and "doctor" and phrases in the poem are not replicated in the Arabic translation either. The adjective "red" before the "apple" is dropped in the Arabic translation most probably due to the prosodic obligations in classical Arabic poetry. In a similar vein, although Nâzım Hikmet originally writes "despite the pressure on my breast [figurative plank of faith]" (iman tahtamın üstündeki baskıya rağmen), the loss of this nuance is allowed in the translation of the poem to Arabic, which continues to delineate the pain as "despite the walls over my chest."

Naturally, it is very hard for any poem in translation to reproduce the original text in every respect in the target language. In the case of Nâzım Hikmet, it can be said that his popularity among the Arab writers due to the sociopsychological and ideological atmosphere of the period caused his poems to be endorsed, quoted at large, and adoptively translated. Several writers of Arab poetry were inspired aesthetically and politically by Nâzım Hikmet and they turned to his verses when they took on themes such as the validity of revolt, glories of resistance, and a deep sense of commitment, all of which have an appealing presence in Nâzım Hikmet's *oeuvre*.

## Nâzım Hikmet and Contemporary Arab Poetry

Nâzım Hikmet has made a great impression on contemporary Arab poets with both his poetry and personality. The moment his works were attracting attention was also the moment when the world was witnessing major changes. The star of the USSR was shining, and revolutionary socialism was at its peak. Social realism and surrealism in literature and arts had been gaining momentum and cult names such as Pablo Neruda, Federico

García Lorca, Paul Éluard, Louis Aragon, Vladimir Mayakovsky, Jean-Paul Sartre, Albert Camus, André Malraux, Pablo Picasso, André Breton, and many others were producing some of their best works. In the Arab countries national independence movements were heating up. Some of the Arab countries were liberated from colonialism and "Arab socialism" was growing popular. It is in such a context that the impact of Nâzım Hikmet on Arab poetry gained a greater footing.

Arab poets who have been influenced by Nâzım Hikmet are plentiful, and it is not possible to mention all of them within the limitations of this chapter. Instead, I will examine some of those in whose works his influence is more readily observable and who share a political and literary vision with him. Palestinian poets who have been definitively inspired by Nâzım Hikmet are Tawfīq Zayyād, Mahmoud Darwish, Samīh al-Qāsim, and Mu'īn Bseiso. Among these poets, Tawfīq Zayyād has translated Nâzım Hikmet's poems from Russian to Arabic and the Turkish poet's contribution to Zayyād's intellectual and literary development is great. Zayyād, in a work dedicated to him, writes:[2]

> Neither these journeys will be wasted
> Nor the revolutionary tune that blows like the hurricane
> Burned so that the Anatolian flowers came to light
> That flaming torch of a decade.

(2000: 150)

The influence of Nâzım Hikmet is traceable in Zayyād's prison poems as well. For instance, in his 1959 poems titled "More Impossible than Impossible," some of Nâzım Hikmet's common themes are prevalent. Tawfīq Zayyād addresses his imprisoned comrades:

> Oh my brothers in hunger
> Oh those with whom I share the same calamity
> Oh my handcuffed imprisoned brother
> My comrades whose songs sing of liberty
> Oh my brothers in whose veins red revolution crawls
> Oh my brothers who are at their return's dawn
> Prepare to be born!

(2000: 75)

Just like Nâzım Hikmet, Tawfīq Zayyād also sympathized with the oppressed peoples and as a poet acted as their spokesperson. For him, class struggle was also inseparable from other forms of emancipatory movements and he handled the Palestinian independence alongside a broader class struggle. In one of his poems, he writes:

Oh my brother workers
I love you all
I love those fists of yours
That wave against the scoundrels
Your upright foreheads
At the resistance square
And your roaring courageous words.

(2000: 140–1)

Tawfīq Zayyād's approach to freedom and resistance is not different from that of Nâzım Hikmet. Just like him, Zayyād frames what he wishes to tell through the social realist aesthetic. However, he is unable to match Nâzım Hikmet's dynamic style that masterfully interlaces form and content.

Another Palestinian poet who was inspired by Nâzım Hikmet is the renowned Mahmoud Darwish. The influence of Nâzım Hikmet on Mahmoud Darwish is not as directly observable as his influence on Tawfīq Zayyād. Instead, it is more of a symbolic and implied kind. Darwish is one of the most important names in modern Palestinian poetry and he also has a significant readership in Turkey. His poetics developed, alongside those of Tawfīq Zayyād, Samīh al-Qāsim, and Sālim Jubrān, in the 1960s in occupied Palestine and achieved its zenith in 1967 as a part of "resistance poetry" following the Arabs' defeat against Israel. With the awareness of his mission representing a people's conscience, he published one collection after another and attracted much attention. He created a politically engaged poetry, which as a mode of resistance, recorded Palestinian history. Consequently, he achieved something that very few Arab poets managed to do and created a poetics that attracted the attention of both popular and intellectual readership.

Similarities between Nâzım Hikmet and Mahmoud Darwish are plenty. Poetry for both of these names is a plea from the local to the global scene. Similar to Nâzım Hikmet's works, the tone in Mahmoud Darwish's poetry is revolutionary and insurgent. Yet, at the same time, it is fully in command of the intellectual, cultural, and mythological heritage of its geography. He does not neglect the humanist, literary, and aesthetic mechanisms of poetry and he makes use of Middle Eastern and Greek mythology and religious and mythical symbols skillfully. As such, the works of both Hikmet and Darwish are historical repositories and reflect the sociopolitical transitions in their countries, by giving voice, first and foremost, to the oppressed and traumatized people.

From a formalistic point of view, the works of both poets are generally highly rhythmical and are thus suitable to be read out loud to the public. Hence both poets read their poetry to the masses and had a great impact on the crowds. In fact, sometimes poetry readings of Mahmoud Darwish were held in stadiums when auditoriums were not enough. Likewise, Nâzım

Hikmet is known to have read his poems out loud to large audiences. In that sense, the revolutionary stylistics and practices of both poets become manifest in their engagement with the masses through their passionate and moving poetics.

Thematic overlaps can also be observed in the works of both poets. For instance, they both utilize themes such as "home" and "exile" in a similar fashion, with dramatic tones. Nâzım Hikmet's "On my Country Again," for example, goes as follows:

> My country, my home, my homeland,
> nothing you made remains in my possession,
> not a cloth cap
> or a pair of shoes that once trod your roads.
> Your last shirt wore down long ago to bare threads on my back;
>                       it was homespun cotton.
> Now you live only in the white of my hair,
>                 the failing of my heart,
>                       the lines on my forehead,
> my country,
> my home,
> my homeland.
>
> (Nâzım Hikmet 2002b: 224)

In his "'Ābir Sabīl" (Traveler) Mahmoud Darwish also writes about the traumatic experience of exile and the alienation it brings:

> My homeland is far far away
> Her earth has left me
> Evaporated towards inside me
> But I cannot see her.
> And you're also far far away
> But I can see you
> Like the brilliance of a rose in surprise bloom
> And in my body is the desire to sing songs
> To all the ports.
> . . . I love you.
>
> (2014: 460–1)

He concludes the poem as follows:

> But why?
> Why did the music stop?
> Who broke the record

> Why is it revolving around itself:
> My homeland is far far away
> My homeland
>       My homeland
>            My homeland.
>
> (2014: 462)

In an interview with the Lebanese writer Muhammed Dukrūb in 1968, Darwish mentions how much he is influenced by Nâzım Hikmet and other emancipation and resistance poets. He says, "I see myself as a feeble extension in the Palestinian character of poets such as 'Ṣa ʿālīk' [The Flâneurs] and Nâzım Hikmet, Lorca, Aragon. I have absorbed the poetry and life experiences of these poets. They are the ones who give me an enormous strength" (Dukrūb 2008). In a later interview with poet and translator Samir Abu Hawwash (2002), Darwish mentions how he started to have reservations against the background of Nâzım Hikmet's sweeping popularity:

> First it was Nâzım Hikmet's humanism that allured me. Yet, once he became fashionable I lost my interest in him. However, now when I return to his poetry, I realize that I am discovering him anew. In truth, I discovered that Nâzım Hikmet's poetry is a lot more important than his image in Arab poetry. (Abu Hawwash 2002)

In his 1973 book *Muhāwalat Raqm 7* (Attempt Number 7), in which he combines Palestine-Canaan mythology and lyrical themes, Mahmoud Darwish openly talks about Nâzım Hikmet. For example, in his poem "al-Nuzūl min Karmal" (Descent from Mount Carmel) the Turkish poet appears with both his name and his outcry. In this poem, Mahmoud Darwish talks about his feelings after having been forced out of Haifa and Mount Carmel at gunpoint and the difficulties he encountered on the way home. He ends this long poem as follows:

> I love the lands that I will love
> I love all the women that I love
> Yet the single branch of a cypress in burning Carmel
> Equals the waists of all the women
> And all the capitals
> I love the seas that I will love
> I love the fields that I will love
> Yet         a single drop of water
> On the feather of a lark, perched on the Haifa rock
> Equals all the seas
> And can wash away all my sins

Put me in that lost paradise
So I can cry out like Nâzım Hikmet does:
Ah, but my country!

(2014: 497)

In this poem, Haifa becomes a symbol for the whole of Palestine and this ending is a direct allusion to Nâzım Hikmet's "Elegy for Satan," which ends with a nostalgic cry due homesickness:

We used to miss each other.
He would speak of the gravest matters:
of hunger, of being full, of love.
But he didn't know longing for home.
That's on my head.
When the poet went to heaven,
    he said: "Ah, but my country"

(Nâzım Hikmet 2002b: 180)

The influence of the dramatic image of a poet who is put in heaven but does not give up longing for home is not limited to Darwish in Arab poetry. Another Arab poet Mu'īn Bseiso, when asked at an interview "Where is Mu'īn Bseiso going?" quotes the poem "Elegy for Satan" and answers: "Where the great Turkish poet Nâzım Hikmet referred to in his lines 'When the poet went to heaven, / he said: 'Ah, but my country . . .'" When Israel occupied Lebanon in 1982, Mu'īn Bseiso was away from his homeland in Beirut and crying out:

Here they come, no deals, none at all
Long live resistance!

Bseiso died in exile in London in 1984 and fearing that his tomb might become a symbol of freedom and resistance, the Israeli government did not allow him to be buried in Gaza. Instead, he was interred in Cairo. Exiled even in death, Mu'īn Bseiso and Nâzım Hikmet shared a similar fate. After having spent a long time imprisoned in Turkey, Nâzım Hikmet lived his final days in exile in Moscow and died there in 1963. He had never returned to his homeland after having been accused of treason and expatriated in 1951. In 2009, the Turkish state annulled the 1951 decree that had stripped Nâzım Hikmet of his Turkish citizenship.

    In his collection of prose *Dafātir Filisṭīniyye* (Palestine Notebooks), Mu'īn Bseiso talks about how he went to Baghdad to teach and how he met Nâzım Hikmet there: "With the one dinar that I had on me I bought wine, apple and Nâzım Hikmet's collection of poetry. In the morning Nâzım Hikmet and I first went to al-Diwāniyya and then to the village of al-Shāmiyya.

We wandered around these places together" (1978: 34). In another book, he mentions taking a handful of soil on a visit to Turkey and scattering it around the grave of Nâzım Hikmet in Moscow.

Nâzım Hikmet's influence can be clearly traced in the works of Palestinian poet Samīh al-Qāsim as well. Compared to the previously discussed Palestinian poets, Samīh al-Qāsim's poetry is more straightforward. In his poem "A Conversation at the Marketplace of the Unemployed," he writes:

> Maybe—if you wish—I will lose my bread
> Maybe I will put on sale my garments, my bed
> Maybe I will become a stone worker, a porter or a trash collector
> Maybe I will seek grains in animal dung
> Maybe I will be left starving and ill-clad
> Yet, o the enemy of the sun I will not bargain with you.
> And I will resist until the last throb of my blood.
>
> (1987: 447)

Like the other Palestinian poets, Samīh al-Qāsim cannot ignore Nâzım Hikmet's outcry, "Ah, but my country...." and he ends his poem, "Eid Cards towards Six Directions" as follows:

> I don my shroud
> I cry out: Ah, o my bent mount!
> Ah my country
> Ah my country
> Ah my country!
>
> (al-Qasim 1987)

Such examples indicate that the impact of Nâzım Hikmet on Palestinian poetry, particularly upon resistance literature is quite powerful. In fact, it is such a strong impression that the Palestinian writer Faysal Kurkūtī notes (Hībī 2017): "If Nâzım Hikmet was not Turkish, he would probably be Palestinian due to his life-long struggle. Like every Palestinian he would go straight back to another prison as soon as he was released from one."

Nâzım Hikmet has inspired Arab poets outside Palestine as well. Two of them are of particular importance to show Nâzım Hikmet's ability to cross borders: Egyptian Salāh Abdel Sabour and Iraqi Abd al-Wahhāb al-Bayātī. Some researchers maintain that the poetry of Salāh Abdel Sabour is born out of the combined influences of T.S. Eliot and Nâzım Hikmet (Haridi 2002). The impact of the latter can be observed clearly in the title that he has chosen for his first poetry collection published in 1957: *al-Nās fī Bilādī* (People in My Land). It is not only the title that is strongly reminiscent of the Turkish poet's *Human Landscapes from My Country*, but there are also many parallels in these two works in terms of both technique and content. Subjects such as the peasants, poverty, religion, heroes of the independence war and the like are shared themes. In Nâzım Hikmet's book, Anatolia is the backdrop of these topics and Salāh Abdel Sabour's book is populated by the ordinary people of Egypt, particularly the laborers and the poor.

Nâzım Hikmet's influence on Abdel Sabour's poetry is easily discernible also in terms of poetic techniques. A cinematographic language similar to the one in *Human Landscapes from My Country* also commands Abdel Sabour's *al-Nās fī Bilādī*. Just like the Turkish poet, Abdel Sabour focuses on characters from Egyptian society as if he is carrying a camera. In the background lies the sociocultural life. For instance, Abdel Sabour depicts an Egyptian farmer as follows:

> At the gates of my village sits Uncle Mustafa
> An admirer of Muhammed Mustafa
> Exactly one hour before sundown
> He is surrounded by men, their heads hanging low
> He tells them a story . . . life's lesson
> Hammers in them the sorrow of oblivion
> The men cry their heart out
> Their heads hang low
> Their gazes upon silence.
>
> (Abdel Sabour 1972: 29–30)

The parallels between these lines and the following first few lines from Nâzım Hikmet's *Human Landscapes from My Country* are visible:

> A man
>    stops on the steps,
>       thinking about something.
> Thin.
> Scared.
> His nose is long and pointed,
> and his cheeks are pockmarked.
> The man on the steps,
>    Master Galip,
>       is famous for thinking strange thoughts.
>
> (Nâzım Hikmet 2002a: 5)

The formalistic developments in the early poems which Nâzım Hikmet wrote under the influence of Mayakovsky can be traced in Abdel Sabour as well. Abdel Sabour strives to create a rhythmic and dynamic poetics like that of Nâzım Hikmet through repetitions of words and sounds and through alliterations and other stylistic devices. For example, in his poem "al-Mulku Lak" (The Property is Yours) the repetitions established through the sounds of "l," "m," and "k" create an effect akin to those employed by Nâzım Hikmet:

Qālet liya al-arḍu: "al-mulku lak"
Tamūta al-ẓilālu wa yaḥyā al-wahaj
al-mulku lak
al-mulku lak
al-mulku lak

(Abdel Sabour 1972: 62)

The earth said to me: "the property is yours"
Down with darkness, long live the light
The property is yours
The property is yours
The property is yours

As Muhammad Harīdī (2002) also pointed out, the similarities between the independence struggles of the Turkish and Egyptian societies, the ideological stances of the poets and their societal and socialist priorities, and their shared affinity with the poetry of Mayakovsky and Lorca bring Nâzım Hikmet and Abdel Sabour, and their poetics, close to one another. Moreover, the increasing availability of Nâzım Hikmet's poetry in English and his visit to Egypt in 1962 rendered the Turkish poet a cult personality in the eyes of many people, particularly Abdel Sabour.

The Iraqi poet Abd al-Wahhāb al-Bayātī is another important pen of Arabic literature in whose works the influence of Nâzım Hikmet can be observed. Similar to him, al-Bayātī also spent his life in exile. In 1953, while he was teaching Arabic literature in various high schools, he was arrested due to some of his writings. He was dismissed from his teaching positions and exiled. When the monarchy in Iraq was overthrown after a military coup in 1958, he returned to his country. The next year he was appointed as an educational consultant to Moscow. After two years in this position, he resigned and began teaching at Moscow State University and Asian People's Institute. During his stay in the USSR (1959–64), al-Bayātī met Nâzım Hikmet and was impressed by his revolutionary and libertarian ideas, as well as his poetry.

The two developed a unique and special friendship shaped by their shared artistic and ideological sympathies. At the time, Nâzım Hikmet was influenced by the futurism and structuralism that was prevalent in the artistic sphere. The free verse form that he created under these influences brought a unique vigor and a dynamic rhythm to his works. While in the earlier periods of their poetic lives both Hikmet and al-Bayātī wrote romantic/lyric works combined with mystical/*tasavvuf* tendencies, in time Nâzım Hikmet's socialist ideas shaped al-Bayātī's left-aligned orientation. While his initial poems were written under the influence of romanticism, and at times, symbolism, after the publication of his second collection *Abārīq Muhashshama* (Broken Jugs) in 1954, al-Bayātī began to address a broader public readership by utilizing a more direct language and a social critical perspective. In these later poems, he focused on themes of exile and being far away from home. He borrowed from both the *tasavvuf* tradition and folkloric and mythological narratives. However, he created new imagery out of them by masking his socially defined ideas in them.

Nâzım Hikmet's method of breathing new life into old imagery as such is easily traceable in al-Bayātī's works. For instance, he opens his book *Qamar Shīrāz* (The Beauty of Shiraz), which was published for the first time in 1978, with the following poem that references Nâzım Hikmet's "Like Kerem":

> I breathe in the sweet air that comes out of your mouth
> And I muse on your beauty every day
> My desire is to hear your fine voice
> That is reminiscent of the northern wind that blows
> Love shall restore youth to my body
> Give me your hand that holds your soul
> Let me embrace it, making it my raison d'être
> Call me by my name once more and until eternity
> Your call shall not go unrequited
> "Prayers are discovered, written on a golden plate
> On the soles of a mummy, the writer's name effaced."
> "And he says to me:
> —O you will turn to ash through your own voice!
>      Like
>       Kerem
>        burning
>         in flames
>
> (al-Bayātī 1984: 5)

In *Simavne Kadısı Oğlu Şeyh Bedrettin Destanı* ([The Epic of Sheik Bedreddin, the Son of the Simavne Qadi], translated under the title *The Epic of Sheik Bedreddin and Other Poems*), first published in 1936, Nâzım Hikmet interprets the revolt of Sheik Bedreddin, a famous Muslim Sufi theologian and preacher who with his companions challenged the authority of the Ottoman State in 1416, from a socialist perspective. Similarly, Abd al-Wahhāb al-Bayātī, in his 1964 work "Adhāb Ḥallāj" (The Torment of Hallaj) interpreted the narrative of Mansur al-Hallaj, a Persian mystic and teacher of Sufism, who was executed on religious and political charges, from a socialist perspective. However, while Nâzım Hikmet created a multivocal narrative by combining novelistic and poetic techniques in his work, al-Bayātī formulated his text through poetic form only. Nâzım Hikmet's Sheik Bedreddin says the following in his interrogation:

> Since we have lost this time
> words avail not
> Don't draw it out.
> Since the sentence is mine
> give it—that I may seal it.
>
> (Nâzım Hikmet 1977: 55)

And al-Bayātī's al-Hallaj says:

> A millennia ago you sentenced me to death
> So be it, there I sleep
> Awaiting for the dawn of my salvation
> At the moment of my execution.
>
> (al-Bayātī II 1995a: 16)

Still, despite the similarities, which add up and form an extensive overlap between the works of al-Bayātī and Nâzım Hikmet, it is hard to say that al-Bayātī matches the power of Nâzım Hikmet's narrative dynamism and language that gives life to the *tasavvuf* motifs and folkloric elements.

## Requiems for Nâzım Hikmet

In his poetry collection *Kalimāt Lâ Tamūt* (Immortal Words), published in 1960, Abd al-Wahhāb al-Bayātī reaches out to Nâzım Hikmet by mentioning his son Memet's name in a poem written on June 20, 1958, and collected under the title "Poems from Vienna." The title of the poem is "Farewell Istanbul" and it goes as follows:

> I stopped in Istanbul, I can't say
> I stayed
> Because I was in a hurry
> Because I was ashamed to face Memet
> Ashamed to meet his little face
> He mustn't see me with my empty hands.
> With sleep deprived eyes
> I wander about the streets of Istanbul
> In the loneliness of the faded stars

And in my heart . . .
Ah my beloved
I cannot say
I stopped by.

(al-Bayātī 1995b: 375)

Following the death of Nâzım Hikmet in 1963, al-Bayātī wrote an elegy to him and continued to write more of them later, producing one almost every decade. The first one, which was penned in 1964, that is, one year after the Turkish poet's death, appeared in his collection *al-Nār wa al-Kalimāt* (Fire and Words). It comprises five poems, titled "The Maiden Wave," "Itinerant Singer," "Love in Autumn," "Mevlana Jalaluddin Rumi," and "The End," collected under the main title "Requiem for Nâzım Hikmet." In "The End" al-Bayātī writes:

In Greece, I was executed by a firing squad
The night bloomed two roses
My blood streamed down the sleepy moon's forehead
And two lovers
Returned from the journey of sorrows and of having been lost
My heart beat with the children in the garden of time
And the clock of the square ticked
So here ends our journey
Farewell brothers!
Captain
Striding through the seas, the virgin wave returned
The human-poet returned
To the homeland of the homelands
Shirin, oh my beloved
The bells are ringing in the cities of smoke
World's most beautiful person is dying
The most beautiful of the songs
So here ends our journey
Farewell oh brother!

(al-Bayātī 1995b: 470)

Setting this poem in Greece, al-Bayātī emphasizes that Nâzım Hikmet was not limited to prescribed national borders and his commitments were of an international kind, which contributed to his figure in the world literature scene.[3]

The second elegy is also in the same collection and bears the title "Another Elegy for Nâzım Hikmet" (al-Bayātī 1995b: 471–4). It opens with a note that says "the legendary hero returns from his final journey with glory and embraces his end" and it comprises four poems titled "Cloud, the Bard,"

"Sleeping Prince," "Winter in Paris," and "Return from Exile." Another, much longer elegy followed ten years after Nâzım Hikmet's death in 1973 that consists of three parts and is titled "Death in the Bosphorus." The poem gives the sense of historical continuity of comradeship and it is published in his collection titled *Sīra Dhātiyya li Sāriq al-Nār* (The Life Story of the Fire Thief). Finally, al-Bayātī laments the death of Nâzım Hikmet in a short 1985 poem that ends with a note that marks the date and place as "Aseelah/Morocco, 6 September 1985" and carries the title "Nâzım Hikmet was there":

> Nâzım Hikmet was not happy
> in Aleppo. Here his childhood was the honey
> But the bee arrived fifty years late
>
> Nâzım Hikmet
> Was not happy anywhere; now he
> Is lonesome and exiled underneath the skies of other lands
> In a tomb covered in the snows from the ages of Creation
> Like in the dream ...
> He was with me; when he mused over the face and the mask
> Of a twenty-year-old girl
> He flew like a bee and went up in flames
> In the autumn fire of the mortal human
> I remember him saying these words with the sorrow of the seeing eyes:
> The sultan of my heart,
> Fill the wine
> Of a guest
> Who can be happy
> Neither in Aleppo nor in Berlin.
>
> (al-Bayātī 1995c: 551–2)

While al-Bayātī wrote many such noteworthy elegies after Nâzım Hikmet's death, he is not the only Arab poet who has done so. The Egyptian poets Salāh Jaheen, Naguib Surūr, Hasan Fath al-Bāb, and many other names from the Arab world penned similar works after him. This is very much a result of Nâzım Hikmet's visit to Egypt in 1962 and his involvement with the political, social, and class-related problems of the region. The Egyptian poets who have written elegies for Nâzım Hikmet frequently allude to his poem "Ya Ayni, Ya Habibi!" in which he has told the story of Mansour from Port Said. For example, in Salāh Jaheen's poem "Elegy for Nâzım Hikmet," the following lines appear:

> Has it been a year since you were here last
> In search of the child in your Port-Said poem
> [...]

> Still human landscapes in Anatolia
> Still hopes are in agony
> The walnut tree in Gallipoli drying in thirst
> The branches withered, turned into daggers
> And you are a poet
> Your nightingale heart gave life to them in embrace, migrant
> O the great Nâzım
> That wound that killed you is not the old wound!
>
> (Jaheen n.d.:118–20)

Another Egyptian Naguib Surūr, in the long elegy he wrote in 1963–4 titled "Dialogue with Nâzım Hikmet" employs a multivocal perspective. First, a mourner invites everyone and everything to silence, because Nâzım Hikmet has died. Then a passerby invites him to rest in peace. He is followed by a Turkish man who says, "Sleep friend / It's your heart's right / How sleepless they caused you to be . . ." After them, someone from Madrid and another person from Africa take their turn, and they are finally followed by the poet persona. He sets up a dialogue between himself and Nâzım Hikmet:

> — The name of your excellency?
> — My name is Naguib.
>  I'm one of the thousands of sons of Nâzım
> — There's sadness in your eyes Naguib.
>  This is not the sorrow of homesickness
> He is at arm's length, I'm almost going to touch him
> It's the sorrow of exiles . . . Unconcealed in the eyes.
>
> (Surūr 2009: 185–6)

Requiems by Arab poets for Nâzım Hikmet show that they not only mourn for the loss of a great poet but also feel a deep sorrow for the loss of a close friend who reached their hearts and speak in familiar voices. These poems nostalgically project Nâzım Hikmet's struggles onto different contexts, some with Arabic and others with international settings. That Nâzım Hikmet was a voice of the people who are unable to speak for themselves is underlined in the poems and embraced as a role shared by them in their respective cultures.

# The Difficulty of Translating Nâzım Hikmet

Nâzım Hikmet's poetry began to be translated into Arabic in the 1950s, which, combined with its increasing availability in English and the Turkish poet's visit to Egypt in 1962, rendered Nâzım Hikmet a cult personality in the eyes of many people. The first book of Nâzım Hikmet's poetry in Arabic translation is a selection of his poems titled *Min Shi'r Nāzım Ḥikmet* (From Nâzım Hikmet Poetry), which is translated from French by Ali Sa'ad. It was published in 1952 in Beirut and included forty-four of Nâzım's poems that were printed by then. Four years after this translation, in 1956 a selection of poems from around the world, including those of Nâzım Hikmet was published in Beirut by Abd al-Wahhāb al-Bayātī, titled *Risāla ilā Nāzım Hikmet wa Qaṣā'ida Ukhrā* (Letter to Nâzım Hikmet and Other Poems).

In 1971 another collection of selected works was translated from French by Muhammad al-Bukhārī and published under the title *Ughniyāt al-Manfā* (Exile Songs). A collection of all of his poems translated by Fāḍil Luqmān, *Nāzım Ḥikmet: al-A'māl al-Shi'riyye al-Kāmila* (Nâzım Hikmet: Complete Poems) was published between 1980 and 1987 in six volumes, also in Beirut. These were translated directly from Turkish into Arabic and they were sold out in a short time due to the popularity of the poet. Also, certain parts (from IV to almost the end of VI) of *Human Landscapes from my Country* were translated by Muhammad Harb and published under the title *Malḥamat Ḥarb al-Istiqlāl* (The Epic of the War of Independence) by the Egyptian Ministry of Culture in 2005.

Nâzım Hikmet's semi-autobiographical novel, *Yaşamak Güzel Şey Be Kardeşim* (*Life's Good, Brother*) was translated from English and published in Damascus for the first time in 1983. The translator of the book, Nazīh al Shoufī, notes at the end of the work that its translation was completed in 1977. In the preface to the translation, he also notes that they have checked the book's English translation with the Turkish translator who has done its Serbo-Croatian translation. The same work was translated again, this time from Russian, in 1990 and was published in Beirut. Its translation directly from its original Turkish came much later in 2016 in Cairo. After the translation of *Bir Aşk Masalı* (A Love Story) into Arabic in 1955, there has been a significant increase in the translation of his plays and most of these works have been translated directly from Turkish.

As can be seen, most of the works of Nâzım Hikmet in different genres such as poems and plays as well as nonfiction were translated into Arabic. Some of them were retranslated by different translators and many readers who have been unable to follow the Turkish poet's works in other languages gained access to them directly through Arabic. As these readers included Arab-speaking writers, the translations expanded the influence of Nâzım Hikmet on Arab poetry considerably.

Before concluding this chapter on Nâzım Hikmet's voice in Arabic and how it contributed to his image as an internationalist poet on the world literature stage, I would like to comment on the quality of his texts in translation. A comparative discussion of one of his poems by two different translators might prove helpful to show that not only the texture but also the content of Nâzım Hikmet's poems change while being translated into Arabic. I would like to use the example of a popular poem "Ya Ayni, Ya

Habibi," which was translated by Muhammad al-Bukhārī and Fāḍil Luqmān separately. In this poem, Nâzım Hikmet depicts a character named Mansour and through his story presents the crisis resulting from the decision of the then-president of Egypt, Gamal Abdel Nasser, to nationalize the Suez Canal, which led to the occupation of the country by France and Britain in 1956.

(Mansour), who is in his teens, contributes to his family's income by shining shoes. He is a weak, frail, and malnourished child. In the poem, Mansour's polishing of shoes represents the labor of the worker, that is, Mansour stands for the Egyptian people. The boy keeps singing the same song, representing the unison of the people's joy, "ya ayni ya habibi." However, he is still unable to prevent being trampled under the cruel feet of imperialism and ends up "a tiny dead body":

> My Mansur of Port Said, aged thirteen or fourteen years,
> barefoot, head close-cropped, sits shining shoes
> by his box with its mirrors and bells.
> High heels, soft shoes, army boots, walking shoes,
> dusty, muddy, hopeless,
> worn out, old,
> mount the box with its mirrors.
> Brushes take wing, red velvet glows,
> high heels, soft shoes, army boots, walking shoes,
> joyous, lively, young,
> hopeful, shining,
> step off the box with its mirrors.
>
> My Mansur, dark and skinny
> like a date-stone,
> my sweet Mansur
> always sings the same song:
> "light of my eye, my darling!"...
>
> They set fire to Port Said, they killed Mansur:
> I saw his photograph this morning in the paper;
> a little corpse among corpses.
> "Light of my eye, my darling!"
> like a date-stone.
>
> (Nâzım Hikmet 2002c: 194)

As can be seen, the many adjectives multiply and thus deepen the meanings in the poem. An aesthetic dimension is added to human labor through colloquialisms and repetitions. The poem is formalistically rich with differing forms of rhymes (e.g., yaşında/başında; yalnayak/başıkabak; papuçlar/postallar; kunduralar/boya boyar/ihtiyar/çıkar/fırçalar/parlar;

tozlu/çamurlu; aynalı/çıngıraklı; sevinçli/dipdiri/çekirdeği/gibi/ayni/habibi) and a rhythm that is established via alliterations (e.g., yalnayak, başıkabak; iskarpinler, papuçlar, postallar) and repetitions (e.g., yorgun argın; kara kuru; ya ayni, ya habibi [three times], iskarpinler, papuçlar, postallar, kunduralar [two times]; Mansur [five times]; aynalı sandık [two times]; hurma çekirdeği gibi [two times], Port Said [two times]; gibi [two times]).

The first translation of the poem was by Muhammad al-Bukhārī in his *Ughniyyāt al-Manfā* (Exile Songs) in 1971 (Nâzım Hikmet 1971: 212–14). The poems in this collection were translated from French into Arabic. I will refer to this text as *Target Text 1* (TT1). The second translation of the poem is by Fāḍil Luqmān (Nâzım Hikmet 1987: 264–6) in *Nāzım Ḥikmet: al-Aʿmāl al-Shiʿriyye al-Kāmila* (Nâzım Hikmet: Complete Poems), which appeared in 1980 as a part of the six-volume set published in Beirut. This version was translated directly from Turkish into Arabic. I will refer to it as *Target Text 2* (TT2).

The choice of titles stands out first when the formalistic qualities of the translations are examined. In TT1, Nâzım Hikmet's title "Ya Ayni, Ya Habibi" is changed into "Būr Saʿīd" (Port Said) but it is kept as is in TT2 with the addition of an exclamation mark at the end. In the latter case, the translator has included a note that explains his choice by pointing out that the title of the original text is already in Arabic. Moreover, in TT1 there are twenty-three lines to the poem, which is closer to the original in twenty-two lines. In TT2 the number of lines is twenty-eight. There are also differences in the translations in terms of where the stanza breaks are. While TT1 comprises a short and a long section, TT2—like the target text—consists of one long and two short sections. TT2 is closer to the original text, in regard to punctuation as well. TT1, on the other hand, mainly lacks punctuation except for a couple of cases of quotation marks and one case of two dots.

There are quite a few rhymes in the source text, rendering the poem rich in rhythm. Accordingly, TT1 is translated with the classical Arab poetry's traditional element of measure, that is, the *tafʿīla* meter. However, despite the fact that TT1 is highly rhythmic as a result, much of the content has been sacrificed to achieve that end. In TT2, on the other hand, there is not much effort to create a rhythm and the rich sound and meter in the Turkish original is not replicated. In that sense, in TT2 the content appears to be prioritized at the expense of form.

The content, likewise, changes in translation. In the original text, Mansur is "13–14 years of age." In TT1, he is just "10" years old. In the original text and also in TT2, Mansour "sings the same song"; however, in TT1, what he chants is turned into a "prayer." TT1 also includes extra verses such as the verse "Port Said'de gemilerin haddi hesabı yok" (the ships at Port Said are innumerable) which does not appear in the original poem. Several descriptions, which contribute to the rhythm of the original poem, are lost in translation, most probably because of the efforts of the translator to meet metric obligations in TT1. Losses are minimal in TT2, but it is hard to say that TT2 catches the dynamic rhythm of the original text.

As can be seen in the comparative analysis of the two different translations of the poem "Ya Ayni, Ya Habibi," the form-content balance was not achieved in translation. Translators had to allow for losses in content while trying to keep the form of the poems, or while trying to keep the content as is, they failed to create the artistic form of the original text in Arabic. There has not been a comprehensive study on the translations of Nâzım Hikmet made directly from Turkish to Arabic. Therefore, "Nâzım Hikmet in Arabic" is a field open for further research, while many such poems await new efforts at translation that might achieve a better form-content balance.

In conclusion, translated either straight from Turkish or via an interim language, the inspirational impact of Nâzım Hikmet on Arab poetry has been strong, and it continues to be so today. Nâzım Hikmet and his poetry provide a means of crossing national boundaries and voicing the plight of the common people. His poems have inspired a passionate dialogue in Arab literature, in which several poets have reflected on themes and symbols often used by him. They have also referred to him in person and to the autobiographical details of his life so as to make him a witness, an overseer of their particular experiences in their Palestinian or broader Arab contexts. This dialogue shows not only the worldwide use of poetry as an instrument of remembering and resistance but also how poetry propagates in the greater world literature scene, despite barriers of language and political pressures.

Translated by Burcu Alkan

## Notes

1 The works of Muhammad Harīdī (2002), Abd al-Razzaq Barakāt (2006), Nurullah Yılmaz (2013), Salih Tur (2014), and Muhammad Hībī (2017) form the backbone of the said literature.
2 The excerpts from Arabic works in this chapter are translated from Arabic to Turkish by Mehmet Hakkı Suçin and from Turkish to English by Burcu Alkan, unless otherwise stated.
3 For a detailed discussion of Nâzım Hikmet in Greece, see Kenan Sharpe's chapter in this volume.

## References

Abdel Sabour, Salāh. (1972), *Dīwān Ṣalāh Abd al-Ṣabbūr*, Beirut: Dār al-'Awda.
Abu Hawwāsh, Samir. (2002), "Ḥiwār ma'a Mahmûd Darwish," *Nizwa*, January 2002.
al-Bayātī, Abd al-Wahhāb. (1995a), *Abārīq Muhashshama*, Beirut: al-Mu'assasa al-'Arabiyya li al-Dirāsāt wa al-Nashr.

al-Bayātī, Abd al-Wahhāb. (1995b), *al-A'māl al-Kāmila I*, Beirut: al-Mu'assasa al-'Arabiyya li al-Dirāsāt wa al-Nashr.
al-Bayātī, Abd al-Wahhāb. (1995c), *al-A'māl al-Kāmila II*, Beirut: al-Mu'assasa al-'Arabiyya li al-Dirāsāt wa al-Nashr.
al-Bayātī, Abd al-Wahhāb. (1984), *Qamar Shīrāz*, Cairo: al-Hay'a al-Miṣriyya al-'Āmma li al-Kitāb.
al-Qāsim, Samīh. (1987), *Dīwān Samīḥ al-Qāsim*, Beirut: Dār al-'Awda.
Barakāt, Abd al-Razzāq. (2006), *Dirāsāt Muqārina fī al-Adab al-'Arabī wa al-Turkī al-Mu'āṣir*, Cairo: 'Ayn li al-Dirāsāt.
Bseiso, Mu'īn. (1978), *Dafātir Filisṭīniyye*, Beirut. Dār al-Fārābī.
Darwish, Mahmoud. (2014), *al-A'māl al-Shi'riyya al-Kāmila I*, Ramallah: Mahmoud Darwish Foundation.
Dukrūb, Muhammad. (2008), "Bayna Shi'r al-Qaḍiyya wa Qaḍiyya al-Shi'r," *al-Akhbâr*, August 11, 2008.
Harīdī, Muhammad. (2002), "Ṣūrat al-Nās fī Bilād Nâzım Hikmet wa al-Nās fī Bilād Ṣalāh Abd al-Ṣabbūr," Nâzım Hikmet Symposium, 1–20, Cairo: al-Majlis al-A'lâ li al-Thaqāfa.
Hībī, Muhammad. (2017), "Nāzım Ḥikmet wa Atharuhu fī al-Shi'r al-Filisṭīnī al-Ḥadīth." Available online: http://www.diwanalarab.com/spip.php?page=article&id_article=46485 (accessed March 18, 2019).
Nâzım Hikmet. (1971), *Ughniyyāt al-Manfā*. Tr. Muḥammad al-Bukhārī, Cairo: Egyptian Book Organisation.
Nâzım Hikmet. (1977), *The Epic of Sheik Bedreddin and Other Poems*. Tr. Randy Blasing and Mutlu Konuk, New York: Persea Books.
Nâzım Hikmet. (1987), *Nāzım Hikmet: al-A'māl al-Shi'riyya al-Kāmila*. Tr. Fādil Luqmān, 6 volumes, Beirut: Dār al-Fārābī.
Nâzım Hikmet. (2002a), *Human Landscapes from My Country – An Epic Novel in Verse*. Tr. Randy Blasing and Mutlu Konuk, New York: Persea Books.
Nâzım Hikmet. (2002b), *Poems of Nazim Hikmet – Revised and Expended*. Tr. Randy Blasing and Mutlu Konuk, New York: Persea Books.
Nâzım Hikmet. (2002c), *Beyond the Walls: Selected Poems*. Tr. Ruth Christie, Richard McKane and Talât Sait Halman, London: Anvil Press Poetry.
Jaheen, Salāh. n.d. *al-A'māl al-Kāmila*, Beyrut: Dar al-Safwa.
Sālim, Hilmī. (2002), "Ayya Athar Taraka Nāzım Ḥikmet 'alā al-Shi'r al-'Arabī," *al-Ḥayāt*, May 2, 2002.
Surūr, Naguib. (2009), *Luzūm mā Yalzam*, Cairo: Dār al-Shurouq.
Tur, Salih. (2014), "Abdulvahhâb el-Beyyâtî ve Nâzım Hikmet Ile İlgili Şiirleri," *İstanbul Üniversitesi Şarkiyat Mecmuası* 24, (1): 147–69.
Yılmaz, Nurullah. (2013), "Nâzım Hikmet ve Mahmûd Dervîş'in Şiirlerinde Ortak Temalar: Sürgün, Hapishane ve Vatan Özlemi," *İstanbul Üniversitesi Şarkiyat Mecmuası* 22, (1): 175–95.
Zayyād, Tawfīq. (2000), *Dīwān Tawfīq Zayyād*, Beirut: Dār al-Awda.

# PART III

# Contemporary Forms and Cosmopolitanism

# 9

# World Literary Refractions

# Orhan Pamuk and Juan Goytisolo

## *Başak Çandar*

In a rare instance of interaction between Spanish and Turkish literary contexts, in 1995 the late Juan Goytisolo (1931–2017) wrote a review of Orhan Pamuk's (1952–) fourth novel from 1990, *Kara Kitap* (*The Black Book*), based on the French translation of the work, *La livre noir*.[1] Titled "El libro negro de Orhan Pamuk: Constantinopla Constantinopolizada," the review ends with a Spanish tongue twister:

Cons-tan-ti-no-pla está cons-tan-ti-no-po-li-zada
¿Quién la des-cons-tan-ti-no-po-li-za-rá?
El des-cons-tan-ti-no-po-li-za-dor que la
des-cons-tan-ti-no-po-li-ce,
buen des-cons-tan-ti-no-po-li-za-dor será (Goytisolo 2001:200)

("Constantinople is constantinopolized.
Who will deconstantinopolize it?
The de-cons-tan-ti-no-po-li-zer that
De-cons-tan-ti-no-po-li-zes it
Will be a good de-cons-tan-ti-no-po-li-zer.")[2]

"*The Black Book* seems like an embodiment of the tongue-twister," Goytisolo writes. "Its complexity, richness, hieroglyphics are the best encouragement for the reader, who actively participates in the novel's creative adventure, turning it into his own. The work de-cons-tan-ti-no-po-li-zes the palimpsestic city, and the author of such an audacious labyrinth of layers, composed and undone, a 'good de-cons-tan-ti-no-po-li-zer' will be" (Goytisolo 2001: 200). As these words conclude the review, there is no clear explanation for Goytisolo's decision to call Pamuk, who had spent the majority of his life in Istanbul, a "buen des-cons-tan-ti-no-po-li-za-dor"—a good de-constantinopolizer. What does it mean to de-constantinopolize Constantinople and how does one do it well, especially when the de-constaninopolizer in question has built their literary career through their relationship with Cons-tan-ti-nop-la?

The Turkish translation of the review was published in the journal *Defter* a year later, under the title "Orhan Pamuk'un Kara Kitabı" ("Orhan Pamuk's *Black Book*"), which left out what comes after the colon in Goytisolo's title: "Constantinopla Constantinopolizada." There is, however, a translation for the tongue twister: "Kons-tan-ti-nopl-u kons-tan-ti-nopl-laş-tır-mış-lar/ Kim onu *des-kons-tan-ti-nopl-laş-tı-ra-cak*?/ Des-kons-tan-ti-nopl-laş-tı-ra-cak her kim olursa,/iyi bir des-kons-tan-ti-nopl-laş-tı-rı-cı olacak" (Goytisolo 1996: 94, emphasis mine). The verb *constantinopolizar* (to Constantinopolize) is translated into Turkish, but the translation curiously keeps the "des" prefix in its translation of *desconstantinopolizará,* turning it into "*des-kons-tan-ti-nopl-laş-tı-ra-cak.*" A footnote explains that the word has not been translated because it is nonsensical, used simply to create a rhyme ("Yalnızca tekerlemeyi gerçekleştirme amacıyla uydurulmuş bir eylem kalıbı olduğundan çevrilmedi"), but, of course, "*des-kons-tan-ti-nopl-laş-tı-ra-cak*" is a translation, to the extent that it is not the original Spanish word Goytisolo uses (94). What is left untranslated is the prefix "des." When the word appears again in the paragraph following the tongue twister, the translation provides a parenthetical explanation that when Goytisolo claims *Kara Kitap* "de-cons-tan-ti-no-po-li-zes the palimpsestic city," he means "[it] analyzes Constantinople by separating it into its parts."[3] The parenthetical insert thus effectively translates the word and contradicts the footnote that appeared a mere couple of sentences before.

I highlight these curious and difficult translation choices because the critical impetus of the review (and according to Goytisolo, *Kara Kitap*'s genius) resides in the mysterious action of deconstantinopolization. But the "des" prefix inadvertently muddles this point when it appears untranslated in Turkish. The equivalent of the "de" prefix in English, in Spanish the prefix suggests an undoing, but in Turkish the prefix has no such function and appears truly meaningless. In the original review, on the other hand, the prefix captures the ability of language and literature to estrange and confuse, and (by implicit extension), to move away from homogenizing, repressive national legacies. As Goytisolo well knows, Constantinopla, the Spanish word for Constantinople, is a politically charged word. Although Istanbul was called Constantinopolis for centuries—the city of Constantine—during its history as the capital of both the Byzantine Empire and the Ottoman

Empire, following the founding of the Turkish nation-state the city's name officially changed to Istanbul in 1930, the old title gradually becoming anathema. Today one cannot hope to call the city Constantinople in Turkey and claim neutrality: non-academic uses of the word are considered attempts to undermine the city's "Turkishness" by championing its Greek past. Of course, the city has been neither Turkish nor Greek but multicultural for centuries, and it went by many names that traveled between different languages: Konstantinoúpolis, Konstantiniyye, Stamboul, and Islambol, to name a few.[4] In an ironic demonstration of the artificiality of national histories claiming pure lineages, "İstanbul" itself derives from the Greek (Georgacas 1947: 366–7). Who will de-constantinopolize Constantinople, asks the tongue twister. For Goytisolo, it will be someone who can de-nationalize it and undo the nationalist myths that construct it as singular, in order to reclaim its diverse history. Goytisolo suggests that Pamuk is a "buen deconstantinopolizador" because, like the tongue twister itself, Pamuk can take the city and reconceptualize it through a non-nationalist framework.

Writing from the other end of Europe, Goytisolo too devoted his prolific literary career to undoing nationalist myths, consistently undermining the idea of a singular, monolithic Spain. As Jorge Carrión has argued, Goytisolo's literary ethics can be defined as a "writing against," aggressively attacking Spain and Spanish historical and cultural tropes (Carrión 2009: 36). In a 1984 *El País* article Goytisolo argues, "No hay así en los grandes autores ni en los periodos más fructuosos y ricos de una literatura influjos unívocos, ni esencias nacionales, ni tradiciones exclusivas: sólo poligénesis, bastardeo, mescolanza, promiscuidad" ("neither in great writers nor in the most fruitful and rich periods of a literature are there univocal influences or nationalist essences or exclusive traditions: there is only polygenesis, bastardization, mingling, promiscuity") (Goytisolo 1984). In Goytisolo's writings, struggling against forgetting takes the form of recreating this "polygenesis, bastardization, mingling, [and] promiscuity." The difficulty of many of Goytisolo's works arises from this desire, as he builds literary worlds that attest to a chaotic multiplicity, refusing any pure lineages or cultural attachments. His literature puts forth a deliberate and continuous attack on "Spain" as a singular national category. Ever the dissident, Goytisolo understands his present and his culture always against and in spite of official national narratives.

Given these sensibilities, it is not surprising that Goytisolo commends Pamuk as a good deconstantinapolizer, for managing to create and recover a non-national version of Istanbul.[5] This is high praise coming from Goytisolo, but it might also be a surprising claim for readers familiar with Pamuk's current reputation within what Pascale Casanova has famously termed the world republic of letters (Casanova 2007). In 2006, a decade after Goytisolo's review, Pamuk won the Nobel Prize for Literature, which not only turned him into a global author but also cemented his position as *the* Turkish writer—one only needs to look at Margaret Atwood's review of *Kar* (*Snow*), in which she lauds Pamuk for "[narrating] his nation into being" (Atwood 2004). Within Turkey, however, Pamuk has been repeatedly vilified for doing exactly the opposite and supposedly writing for the West at the expense of his nation. In this sense, Pamuk is perhaps Turkey's most and least national writer.

Interestingly, these seemingly contradictory positions are complementary: Pamuk's global fame is in part about his ability to write compellingly of Turkey, while complaints about Pamuk in the popular Turkish press revolve around the sense that he *exposes* Turkey too much for too large a Western audience, to be judged and humiliated. In other words, Pamuk angers certain parts of Turkish society *because of* his position as a global author who writes about Turkey and whose representations of Turkey circulate through global literary markets. It is worth considering whether Pamuk would be as vilified in Turkey had he not been as successful in garnering international attention, or whether he would have become as successful internationally if his fiction were less specific, less focused on Turkish culture and history.

As these questions begin to demonstrate, world literariness—the quality that allows works to circulate as world literature—constructs itself in part through this contradiction between being simultaneously global and national. In what follows I offer a comparative analysis of Pamuk and Goytisolo that allows for a more nuanced consideration of this two-way dynamic, a dynamic that has significant implications for Turkish literature's position within world literature. As I argue, Pamuk's conflicting position as a *global* and *national* author, who is both so equated with Turkey as to be assumed to narrate it into being and vilified at home for being too concerned with his readers in "the West," is defined by acts of refraction. Pamuk becomes vilified in Turkey not just because he is perceived as a dissident voice, but because he is perceived to represent Turkey *for* the judgmental gaze of a global public. One part of this criticism assumes a dishonest refraction in Pamuk's literary representations that "distorts" Turkey's image. These criticisms themselves rely on a refracted image of a supposedly homogenous Western readership, reading Pamuk to censure the shortcomings of the Turkey he presents. In Pamuk's circulation as a global author, on the other hand, both his position within Turkey and his representations of Turkey become refracted to enable an equivalence between the author and his nation, even as his works show that nation to be plural, cacophonous, and impossible to capture as a fixed reality. When Goytisolo calls Pamuk a *buen deconstantinopolizador*, he commends Pamuk for being able to expose "the nation" as a refraction, a mythical unity that does not correspond to or capture the multiplicities and impurities of the cultures and histories within it.

In her recent book *Orhan Pamuk and the Good of World Literature*, Gloria Fisk makes a similar argument, analyzing Orhan Pamuk's position within world literature through an examination of the uneven dynamics of literary globality and world literary canonization. According to Fisk, these dynamics push Pamuk into the position of a dissident ambassador of Turkey. Alongside Casanova, Fisk argues that "writers in less culturally endowed nations become obligated to do extra-literary work for their states and their people" (Fisk 2018: 8) and suggests that the standards imposed on these authors to "deliver the good of world literature" require them "to speak in ways that are foreign, if not offensive, to [their] domestic public." For Fisk, the problem here is the imposition of a definition of good citizenship that "obtains in participatory democracy, which is to say, in the West" (129).

While I find Fisk's premise insightful, what I identify as the power of Pamuk's works, encapsulated by Goytisolo's description *buen deconstantinopolizador*, cannot be explained by a status of "non-Westernness." Fisk's argument relies on the distinction between Western and non-Western authors, which I find to be an unconvincing distinction, even as it is offered as a means to describe the uneven dynamics of literary globality. In fact, my argument is that the works of Pamuk and Goytisolo deliberately play with the descriptive powers of East and West to ultimately show these categories as anything but fixed. In Fisk's argument, however, there are distinct camps of Western and non-Western authors, even as these categories reveal themselves to be impossible to delimit or define. In Fisk's argument, not only Orhan Pamuk but also J. M. Coetzee and Imre Kertész appear as "non-Western" authors (21, 136), tellingly raising questions about who exactly counts as Western and who as non-Western. The appearance of this East/West binary in a text that otherwise champions Turkish literature and adds nuance to Pamuk scholarship is especially revealing, I think, of the persistence of East/West binaries within world literature scholarship, especially when dealing with more peripheral literary contexts, even as world literature sets out to transcend the binary. As I argue, this reliance on East/West binaries and the resulting tendency to exoticize smaller literary contexts derive in part from the notion of world literature as elliptical refraction between two points.

## World Literature as Elliptical Refraction

In *What Is World Literature?* David Damrosch ventures a threefold definition for world literature as "an elliptical refraction of national literatures," "writing that gains in translation," and "not a set canon of texts but a mode of reading: a form of detached engagement with worlds beyond our own place and time" (Damrosch 2003: 281). Thought of as a mode of reading and circulation, world literature reveals how works from particular national or cultural contexts change and become refracted through circulation—hence Damrosch's notion of "elliptical refraction," whereby a text bears the traces of its national origin but "these traces are increasingly diffused and become ever more sharply refracted as a work travels farther from home" (283). This ability to circulate and enter into different temporal, linguistic, and cultural contexts brings Damrosch to his second definition of world literature "as writing that gains in translation." Postulated against the traditional view of translation as always resulting in a loss, Damrosch argues for a perspective that highlights what texts gain as they enter into new linguistic and cultural contexts. He suggests that texts that are too locally specific or pose too many challenges to translation simply lose too much in circulation and cannot remain relevant or literary in contexts beyond their own immediate origins. For texts that do travel and translate well, however, world literature functions as "a mode of reading" that allows readers to see how these works have changed through their circulation.[6]

The central premise of Damrosch's argument is that "a literary work *manifests* differently abroad than it does at home" (6), which prompts his emphasis on circulation as a defining aspect of world literature. The word circulation suggests forming or moving around in a circle, but since works change as they travel and experience a "double refraction ... with the source and host cultures providing the two foci," Damrosch offers the compelling image of an ellipse to describe this trajectory. *Elliptical* refraction attends to both the inequalities that govern world literary circulation and the distortions a text experiences as it travels away from its national origin. Thought of as a mode of reading and a mode of circulation, Damrosch's world literature analyzes the different temporal and transcultural layers any text of world literature carries, as well as the inequalities and hierarchies that govern the circulation of texts, since "works rarely cross borders on a basis of equality" (24).

A comparison of Pamuk and Goytisolo nuances this model of circulation. Pamuk and Goytisolo's commitment to a process of "deconstantinopolization," an attempt to denationalize history and culture, complicates the notion of world literature as "a negotiation between two different cultures" (Damrosch 2003: 283). In their works, both authors challenge singular national(ist) discourses by revealing the multiplicities and contradictions found in all national contexts, which threaten such discourses by exposing their myths of homogeneity. Both authors reject nationalist genealogies of purity and, instead, demonstrate the syncretism and impurity that are fundamental to any culture. Damrosch's understanding of elliptical refraction becomes complicated against this attack on the "national context," precisely because the works of these authors reject the premise that the "national origin" can be taken as *a point*. While Damrosch's notion of world literature as "elliptical refraction" suggests an interaction between *two points*, where "a single work of world literature is the locus of a negotiation between *two different cultures*" (283, emphasis mine), in the works of Pamuk and Goytisolo, there is no self-identical point that can be taken as *a* national context or *a* culture. Instead, the points of origin deliberately reveal themselves as multiple and as simultaneously Eastern and Western, confounding the East/West binary.

Goytisolo commends Pamuk precisely for this understanding of the multiplicities of the national context. For Goytisolo, "la originalidad es la vuelta al origen" ("originality is the return to the origin") (Goytisolo 2001: 194). In this conception, there can be no single or fixed original context. The national space itself is multiple and always already an ongoing refraction. Both authors' works can be understood as a challenge to the reduction of the national to *a* point. They embrace "elliptical refraction" to be a reality that conditions all culture. At the same time, Pamuk's and Goytisolo's circulation within and as world literature reveals the hierarchies and exoticizing impulses within world literary circulation. While Pamuk is conceptualized as *the* Turkish writer and forced into an endless metaphor of Turkey (and himself) as the bridge between East and West, Juan Goytisolo's works, which unfold through an insistent East/West syncretism, do not result in similar reductions. It bears thinking about why the former so consistently becomes conflated with an entire nation, while the latter's persona and works are not reduced in the same manner.

The tendency to conflate authors with entire nations is related to world literature's concurrent challenge to and reliance on "the national" as a category. Comparative literature and world literature have long imagined themselves as antithetical to nationally specific approaches to literature, but they have also had to contend with the persistence of nationally specific understandings of literature. Damrosch quotes Albert Guérard, who thought of comparative literature as "the grand corrective for the nationalistic heresy" (Damrosch 2003: 282). Similarly, Franco Moretti has suggested that challenging nationally demarcated approaches to literature is the only justifiable purpose of the study of world literature. "There is no other justification for the study of world literature (and for the existence of departments of comparative literature) but this," Moretti writes, "to be a thorn in the side, a permanent intellectual challenge to national literatures— especially the local literature" (Moretti 2000: 68).[7]

As Damrosch insightfully points out, however, despite these challenges "the nationalistic heresy" is alive and well. He thus proposes the elliptical refraction model to clarify "the vital, yet also indirect, relation" between national literatures and world literature (Damrosch 2003: 283). Damrosch's model emphasizes the national as a significant category, even as it wishes to move beyond nationally specific understandings of literature. It understands the world literary space to be inter-national, a place of interaction between different national contexts—hence the emphasis on circulation and the relationship between original and host contexts. In many ways, this attentiveness to national contexts is a valuable and necessary paradigm through which to study literature.

Instead of postulating an anchorless and equal "global," world literature attends to the specific contexts that produce literary works. The focus on the "national" also enables an analysis of hierarchies within "the world republic of letters," a global literary space driven by market capitalism that has unequal but interrelated dynamics. Recognizing that within this literary space "French" literature occupies a different position than "Turkish" literature is not a bad thing, after all. At the same time, by attending to the circulation between national contexts, world literature makes it possible to study the Turkish and Spanish contexts in tandem, for instance, or to look into the afterlives of Cervantes's *Don Quixote* as it circulates through different national and cultural spaces.

However, the emphasis on the national also exposes world literature's reductionist tendencies, whereby works or authors become conflated with entire nations. This conflation does not affect all literary contexts equally; it disproportionately affects those already considered peripheral—not from Western Europe or North America. Since there are fewer writers represented from those contexts, the few that are included in world literature canons are at a higher risk of such reductions. Thus, Pamuk is much likelier to become *the* Turkish writer, while Goytisolo remains one specific and by no means national voice within a chorus of contemporary Spanish authors.

This unequal dynamic cannot be divorced from world literature's reliance on "the national" as a category. Furthermore, it is related to the model of elliptical refraction understood as happening between two points. Conceived of as originating from self-identical points, works of world literature always run the risk of being conflated with their original national contexts, *especially* given the hierarchies that govern global literary markets and literary history. The deliberate "deconstantinopolization" found in Pamuk's and Goytisolo's works, which exposes the national space as refracted and multiple, disrupts this conflation by showing the origin to be multiple. Even though Pamuk's canonization as a global author magnifies the reductive or exoticizing tendencies of world literature, as Goytisolo reminds us, the image of Turkey and Istanbul that appear in Pamuk's works are insistently complex, neither fully European nor Middle Eastern, belonging neither to the "West" nor to the "East." These ambivalent representations complicate world literature's assumption of the nation as a singular category, even as Pamuk's global image as *the* Turkish writer who narrates Turkey into being reveals the risks of a tokenistic gaze. Comparison of Goytisolo's and Pamuk's works thus complicates elliptical refraction by showing the nation as multiple and cacophonous, while a comparison of their position within world literary circulation reveals the unequal axis governing this refraction, as it traverses the divide between "the East" and "the West." If both authors insistently push back against the East/West binary, why are Pamuk and his country called on to function as bridge metaphors, while Goytisolo and Spain escape this allegorization?

## National Cacophonies

In his review of *Kara Kitap*, Goytisolo likens the novel's mysteries to the unresolved reading games in the works of Cervantes and Borges (Goytisolo 2001: 199). "Desde Cervantes, la novela es el reino de la duda" ("Since Cervantes, the novel has been the kingdom of doubt"), Goytisolo writes, and praises Pamuk for being able to capture a version of Istanbul that is neither Eastern nor Western but, rather, both and neither at once (194). It is, therefore, not Istanbul as "the bridge" that Goytisolo emphasizes as *Kara Kitap*'s vision, but Istanbul as plural and layered, capable of holding contradictions within it. In other words, Goytisolo appreciates *Kara Kitap* because it deconstantinopolizes Constantinople, so that the city ceases to be self-identical with itself. It ceases to be *a point*, emerging as a fluid multiplicity.

This is precisely what Goytisolo tries to do to Spain in his works. His literary project is perhaps best exemplified by his infamous Álvaro Mendiola trilogy, consisting of *Señas de identidad* (*Marks of Identity*), *Don Julián* (*Count Julian*), and *Juan sin tierra* (*Juan the Landless*). In *Señas de identidad*, the protagonist Álvaro has just returned to Spain from self-imposed exile and struggles with his Spanish identity, which he experiences as a burden. *Don Julián,* unfolding through unfinished sentences separated by incessant semicolons, re-imagines the famous traitor Count Julian, who allowed Arabs to invade the Iberian Peninsula in the eighth century, as commendable for his ability to rid himself of his homeland (Frohlich 2003: 58). The final book, *Juan sin tierra*, is an unforgiving attack on Christian morality and Spanish identity. As Goytisolo self-consciously fractures the narrating voice, he builds another history and genealogy for the narrator (and himself), populated by those who refused to be of one place: Anselm Turmeda—a fourteenth-century priest from Mallorca who converted to Islam and lived in Tunis— Alexandrian Greek poet Constantin Cavafy, Lawrence of Arabia. The book ends with a few pages in which Spanish slowly turns into Arabic, definitively shutting out non-Arabic-speaking Spanish readers. The content of the Arabic passage mimics the effects of the performance: "If you don't understand, stop following me. Communication between us is ended. I've gone definitively over to the other side, with the eternal pariahs, sharpening my knife" (Goytisolo 2009: 163).[8] Needless to say, this is an incisive ending to a trilogy written in Spanish about Spain, insisting on Arabic as the only means of communication henceforth.

In these works, the distortion of the line between East and West is a means to challenge Spain's self-image as European and Western, all the while consciously mobilizing Spanish anxieties about the centuries-long presence of Islam on the Iberian Peninsula. By imbuing Spanish culture and personas with Muslim, pagan, or other (often irreverent) histories, Goytisolo undoes what he considers to be the pillars of Francoist Spain in which he grew up: Catholic morality and national purity. *Juan sin tierra* begins with the image of a sugar plantation in Cuba and a desire to undo "[el] pecado de origen con que te han abrumado" (Goytisolo 2013: location 57) ("the sin of your origin with which they have burdened you" [Goytisolo 1991: 5]) before delving into a hilariously shocking scatology. In a scathing mockery of Catholic morality, which condones slavery but remains suspicious of all bodily functions, *Juan sin tierra*'s opening pages offer a religious take on defecation: the toilet bowl, "hijo querido de la puritana ocultación" ("the beloved son of puritan concealment") is a gift since "el demonio se expresa a través de él y por eso os demoráis en la inmundicia de la defecación y os entregáis sin pudor al vicio de la sodomía (Goytisolo 2013: location 156) ("the demon expresses himself through [shit], and that is why you remain mired in the filth of defecation and shamelessly give yourselves over to the vice of sodomy" [Goytisolo 1991: 13]). The point is not simply irreverence: the events take place on a sugar plantation, owned by Catholics who worry about defecation and the purity of souls, but continue to torture the enslaved. Moreover, the autobiographical resonances of this work recognizable to initiated readers (Goytisolo's great-grandfather held a sugar plantation in Cuba) suggest that Goytisolo is trying to undo and atone for his own genealogical burden. By undoing Spain and Spanish history as they exist, he creates a dispersed, irreverent, amoral origin: the return to the origin through originality (Goytisolo 2001: 194).[9]

The distortion between East and West becomes especially clear in *El sitio de los sitios* (*State of Siege*), Goytisolo's 1995 novel based on his experiences in Sarajevo. Like *Kara Kitap*, *El sitio de los sitios* reads like a detective novel that creates reading games it refuses to resolve. In *El sitio de los sitios*, however, the quest is for a cadaver, which mysteriously disappears. The novel opens with the arrival of a man called J.G in a hotel room in Bosnia during the siege, who is then killed by a mortar that hits his room. By the time the International Peacekeeping Force arrives, J.G.'s cadaver has disappeared. Suspecting that J.G. is from Spain, the Spanish Major of the Force begins to investigate the disappearance, mainly following clues from a manuscript and a collection of poems J.G leaves behind. By the end of the quest, the Major loses his mind, the multiple narrators in the novel lose the thread of the textual game they initiated, and various possible identities are attributed to J.G. He might be an old Moroccan who secretly traveled to Bosnia (Goytisolo 2002a: 133), he might be the reincarnation of a Moroccan saint Ben Sidi Abú Al Fadaíl (141) or an alter ego of the Major's Spanish uncle Eusebio, "rojo, poeta y maricón" ("Red, poet and faggot")[10] (170), who was arrested during the Spanish Civil War, interned at a mental asylum, and then escaped. In this self-conscious textual game, East/West distinctions collapse, melding together marginal identities from the Spanish Civil War, Islamic mysticism, and Bosnian society. J.G. might be a queer leftist from Spain, he might be a Moroccan saint, or he might be both at once. In *El sitio de los sitios*, there is no binary, but, rather, a series of identity positions that are repressed and marginalized in the name of official histories and a fraudulent purity.

Goytisolo's literary project is devoted to showing that Spain is not *one* thing or place and has never been so. More importantly, *no* place can be conceptualized purely in national or homogenous terms, since all culture is "polygenesis and bastardization." There is no East and West, because the East is Western and the West is Eastern. In this sense, we can see Goytisolo as adhering to a radical belief in circulation, which Damrosch identifies as a defining element of world literature. Goytisolo's works suggest that all culture and art arise from circulation. In this framework, "elliptical refraction" ceases to be descriptive of world literature and comes to describe all art, in every cultural context. Exposing such refractions within contexts considered singular and homogenous is the essential task of "deconstantinopolization."

Goytisolo sees Pamuk as a kindred spirit because of the ways in which Pamuk plays with such binaries, constructing an image of Turkey that is a plural, if cacophonous, society. In *İstanbul: Hatıralar ve Şehir* (*Istanbul: Memories and the City*), Pamuk represents Istanbul as holding multiple layers of history, a mnemonic site in which the present always bears the traces of the past—hence, the unmistakable *hüzün* of the city, its melancholy (Pamuk 2006a/b: 99–100). Although the book is structured like a memoir, as Pamuk the narrator assumes the role of flâneur, reading the city as he strolls through it, he recounts memories that are not only personal but also frequently attest to a *political* project. Istanbul reminds Pamuk of an unwanted, forcefully forgotten past: the history of the Ottoman Empire, which the Republican era so desperately wanted to forget.

Changes like the disappearance of Istanbul's non-Muslim residents, to which there are repeated references in *Istanbul*, are not spontaneous urban changes, but the direct result of the Turkification policies of the Turkish nation-state.[11] The desire to cut ties with the Ottoman past was not only an attempt to start anew, after all, but also a means to create a new *homogenous* national identity. As a result, the rupture also entailed the destruction of Istanbul's multiplicity, which Pamuk repeatedly underlines in *Istanbul*.[12] Ever the good deconstantinopolizer, Pamuk's ability to narrate this past allows him to recover Istanbul from the Republican purification project. In the end, the Istanbul that emerges is deeply multifaceted, fragmented, and palimpsestic. It is neither of the East nor of the West, not a single point but a constellation of dispersed points. It is Turkish, but never only or purely so.

This particular blurring of the boundaries is more radical in Pamuk's 1985 novel *Beyaz Kale* (*The White Castle*). Like many other Pamuk novels, *Beyaz Kale* is a reading game. An archivist, Faruk Darvınoğlu, claims to have found an Ottoman manuscript titled "The Quiltmaker's Stepson," which he introduces to readers after loosely transliterating it into modern Turkish. The majority of *Beyaz Kale* is this manuscript, but by the end of the novel it is impossible to ascertain who has written it and who has imagined whom.[13] The manuscript begins with the enslavement of a young Venetian scholar, who is captured by the Ottoman navy while traveling from Venice to Naples. Soon, he is handed over to an Ottoman scholar who simply goes by *Hoca*, who also happens to be the stepson of a quiltmaker.[14] The Venetian man, who is never named, is supposed to help *Hoca* in his discoveries. Upon seeing one another, the two men realize that they look eerily alike and they begin to play a devious game to grasp one another's "soul." Not only does *Hoca* want the Venetian man to teach him what he knows, he also insists that the Venetian act as a representative of all Europe and teach him what "they," the Europeans, know. Not satisfied with scientific knowledge, *Hoca* then demands to know what makes the two of them different. Obsessively, *Hoca* asks over and over again: "niye benim ben?" (Pamuk 1994: 64) ("why am I what I am?" [Pamuk 1998: 58]). As they try to answer the question, it becomes harder and harder for the two men to differentiate themselves from each other. By the end of the novel, the "I" of the narrative has become impossible to identify. Readers can no longer definitively tell who the Italian man is and who the Ottoman is.

*Beyaz Kale* is playful, but it does not trivialize the East/West binary. Rather, the terms hold immense descriptive power to the extent that they form the basis of identity formation. Without the image of the other, *Hoca*'s identity all but collapses and he sinks into a deep existential panic when he fails to differentiate himself from his European counterpart. In this sense, the binary is shown to be effective only as a relational category. There is no substance to either definition, simply an opposition. The two men look so alike that when they stare at one another, they have the eerie sense of seeing themselves in the mirror. When they switch places, people suspect them, but no one can tell with any certainty who is who.

This is, of course, a rather heavy-handed take on the terms East and West, but *Beyaz Kale* is striking in its refusal to resolve the question. As the readers realize that the "I" they have been reading and imagining as an Italian man might, in fact, be an Ottoman man, or the Italian man after having lived and passed as *Hoca* for many years, the artificiality and complexity of these categories become evident. If there is, indeed, a civilizational divide, how can the East be so easily mistaken for the West and vice versa? The question might seem too simplistic at first, but when one thinks of the histories of places like Turkey and Spain, full of anxieties of not being fully one or being too much of the other, the emphasis on the ambivalence begins to seem much more appropriate.

## Hierarchies of Circulation

There are many similarities between Pamuk and Goytisolo. Both hail from national spaces marked by persistent state violence and dictatorial regimes.

While Pamuk started his career in the early 1980s in the repressive aftermath of three military coups, Goytisolo's life was indubitably marked by the Spanish Civil War (1936–9) and the 35-year-long Franco dictatorship.[15] In light of this legacy, both authors devote their works to recovering and complicating the past. Both writers use similar postmodernist tropes, often blurring the boundary between fiction and reality.

Despite these similarities, Pamuk and Goytisolo have fared quite differently in circulation. Even though Goytisolo has achieved national and global success, he has not been conflated with Spain as *the* Spanish writer. Neither has he achieved the level of fame Pamuk has garnered since receiving the Nobel Prize in 2006. The difference can be explained in part by the notorious difficulty of Goytisolo's novels, his linguistic and narrative experimentation as well as his demanding intertextuality. His books are difficult to translate and difficult to follow without significant contextual knowledge. The deliberate irreverence and scatology of works like *Juan sin tierra* certainly make Goytisolo a more marginal voice, a position he deliberately cultivated throughout his career, which has limited his circulation.[16]

The degree of recognition Pamuk enjoys internationally cannot be explained only through the Nobel Prize, however, as other laureates like Herta Müller or Patrick Modiano, laureates from 2009 and 2011, respectively, have not experienced the same degree of interest or translation as Pamuk. I would like to suggest that Pamuk's global canonization is intimately tied to Turkey's position, both geopolitically and within the world literature imaginary. Conceptualized incessantly as "the bridge" between East and West, Turkish literature is repeatedly pushed into the role of narrating this in-betweenness that takes the terms of the East/West binary for granted.

In the absence of a global literary market filled with competing Turkish names, Pamuk quickly becomes conflated with Turkey as a whole and codified as the Turkish author who best represents the image of Turkey as a bridge. As Shouleh Vatanabadi has argued, this image caters to the gaze of the global tourist of the neoliberal era, "indicating the passing-through of boundaries, the crossing of a civilizational divide" (Vatanabadi 2013: 299). The Nobel Committee's own reasoning for choosing Pamuk also reflects this premise: they conceptualize Pamuk as an author "who in the quest for the melancholic soul of his native city has discovered new symbols *for the clash and interlacing of cultures*" (Nobel 2006, emphasis mine). Sibel Erol has argued that the wording of this explanation is "a coded, evocative way of simultaneously bringing up the now well-worn phrase 'the clash of civilizations' and disavowing it by replacing 'civilizations' with 'cultures'" (Erol 2007: 403). Indeed, the particular framing of Pamuk's talents fixes him as a mediator, while keeping the notion of the civilizational divide intact.

Pamuk's global image is shaped precisely through this simultaneous acceptance of a civilizational divide and the recognition of Pamuk as capable of overcoming it. As this image becomes more difficult to uphold in the face of Turkey's increasing authoritarianism since the Gezi Protests of 2013, Pamuk's global image has also shifted from mediator to dissident. Rather than being incessantly called on to attest to Turkey's position as "a bridge," since 2013 Pamuk has been more often called on to lament the collapse of this image of Turkey as cultural intermediary. As Vatanabadi judiciously points out, "Pamuk's reception in the print media and scholarly discussion over the past decade as the author positioned between East and the West compels him to contradict himself" (301). In a 2002 interview with Elizabeth Farnsworth from *PBS*, for instance, Pamuk had pointed out that in his novels, he tries to show generalizations about the East and West to be just that: "Don't believe them, don't buy them," he says (Farnsworth 2002). Fifteen years later, in a 2017 interview with *La Stampa*, the distinction between East and West appears much more pronounced for Pamuk. After writing compellingly of Turkey as neither fully Western nor Eastern and therefore capable of disrupting the binary altogether in his novels, Pamuk suddenly claims in the interview that "Turkey's future is in the West" (Silipo 2017).

As Nergis Ertürk cautions, "hierarchical and monolithic comparative categories such as West/East and Europe/Turkey do not simply disappear in the magical moment when we expose them as fictions" (Ertürk 2008: 43). Thus, despite insistent claims about the arbitrariness and inaccuracy of the divide, dramatized and destabilized in the works of Goytisolo and Pamuk, the terms "East" and "West" still hold extraordinary descriptive power. This is especially the case in Turkey, where modernization has been seen as synonymous with Westernization. When Pamuk says that he believes Turkey's future to be in the West and that he was raised with that conviction, he is, indeed, attesting to the experience of many middle- and upper middle-class Turkish citizens. Thus, my aim here is not to pretend that East and West do not have descriptive potential, but to think through their purchase in world literature, a field of study that explicitly wishes to muddle this binary.

Such conflations are part and parcel of a world literature that imagines itself as articulating the circulation of texts as they travel between nations. Taken as self-identical and singular, the punctiform "national context" cannot help but lead to exoticizing reductions, a tendency to conflate the author (also seen as a self-identical point) with his or her nation. Not only does this model contradict world literature's self-conception as against nationally specific studies of literature, but it also reduces authors like Pamuk and Goytisolo to a singularity that their works persistently reject, so much so that Pamuk, "the good deconstantinopolizer," becomes compelled to reify the binaries his own works complicate. In this sense, perhaps Emily Apter's much criticized title *Against World Literature* (2013) is not so misguided after all. Challenging the hierarchies that fix peripheral and semiperipheral literary worlds into monotonous allegories might require being a bit against world literature.

# Notes

1 The Spanish translation of *Kara Kitap* came out in 2001.
2 Translations are mine unless otherwise noted.
3 "Yapıt palimpsest kenti des-kons-tan-ti-nopl-laş-tı-rı-yor [yani Konstantinopl'u parçalarına ayırarak çözümlüyor]; birleştirilmiş ve parçalara ayrılmış katmanlardan oluşan böylesi bir cüretli dehlizin yazarı da kuşkusuz 'iyi bir des-kons-tan-ti-nopl-laş-tı-rı-cı olacak'" (Goytisolo 1996: 94).
4 For more on Istanbul's names, see Demetrius John Georgacas (1947), "The Names of Constantinople." In *Istanbul – Kushta – Constantinople*, Christopher Herzog and Richard Wittmann note that it is possible to count as many as 135 names for Istanbul, which they see as indicative of the city's former cosmopolitan makeup (Herzog and Wittmann 2018: 1).
5 Goytisolo himself has written about Turkey in *Estambul otomano* (Ottoman Istanbul) (1989) and *Aproximaciones a Gaudí en Capadocia* (Approaching Gaudí in Capadocia) (1990), in which Turkey, and especially Istanbul, appears as a site of intriguing hybridity. Neither has been translated into English, but Gül Işık, the translator of Goytisolo's aforementioned review, translated *Estambul Otomano* to Turkish in 2002, while Zerrin Yanıkkaya translated *Aproximaciones a Gaudí* in 2015 (Goytisolo 2002b, 2015).
6 Damrosch's famous example for this type of reading can be seen in his analysis of the *Epic of Gilgamesh*. See (Damrosch 2003), *What Is World Literature?*, Chapter 1, "Gilgamesh's Quest."
7 The phrase "world literature" is often traced to the coinage of the word *Weltliteratur* by Goethe and its use by Marx and Engels in *The Communist Manifesto*. In both cases, the word is evoked as a corrective against "national one-sidedness" (Moretti 2000: 54). This oft-cited genealogy demonstrates an anti-nationalist position to be embedded in the field's own sense of self. For more on world literature genealogies, see David Damrosch (2003), Franco Moretti (2000), John Pizer (2006), *The Idea of World Literature*, and Pheng Cheah (2008), "What Is a World?"
8 Goytisolo provides the Spanish translation of the Arabic in his afterword to the revised edition of *Juan sin tierra*. The English translation is by Peter Bush.
9 *Aproximaciones a Gaudí en Capadocia* similarly highlights idiosyncratic origins. In the narrative, Goytisolo imagines the famous Catalan architect Antoni Gaudí to be living in Capadocia, drawing inspiration from Islam and "Mudejar hybridism." "Su insipiración no fue nunca renacentista ni neoclásica: él buscaba, como Cervantes y Goya, la España profunda y la halló en los estratos ocultos del enjundioso mestizaje mudéjar." ("His inspiration was neither Renaissance nor neoclassical: he searched, like Cervantes and Goya, for the deep Spain and he found it in the hidden parts of a substantial Mudejar hybridism.") (Goytisolo 1990: 19, 20).
10 Translation by Helen Lane.
11 See Chapter 19 in particular, "Fetih mi, Düşüş mü: Constantinople'un Türkleştirilmesi" ("Conquest or Decline? The Turkification of Constantinople").

12  The heavy sanctions placed on minorities, such as the "wealth tax" in the 1940s, the pogroms in the 1950s that targeted Greek communities in Istanbul, and the increasing pressures and expulsion of the Greek communities in the mid-1960s, all took a serious toll on this multiplicity. For more on this history especially as it pertains to the Greek minorities, see Aslı Iğsız (2018), *Humanism in Ruins: Entangled Legacies of the Greek-Turkish Population Exchange.*

13  For more on the novel and Pamuk's relationship with the Ottoman legacy, see Erdağ Göknar (2013), *Orhan Pamuk, Secularism and Blasphemy*, especially Chapters 3 and 4.

14  The translation simply calls him *Hoja*, but in Turkish the word means both "teacher" and "religious scholar."

15  In an obituary for Franco, Goytisolo writes that Franco was "el origen de la cadena de acontecimientos que suscitaron [su] exilio y vocación de escritor" ("the origin of the chain of events that resulted in [his] exile and his vocation as a writer") (Goytisolo 1975: 163).

16  Most of Goytisolo's English translations are currently out of print.

# References

Apter, Emily. (2013), *Against World Literature: On the Politics of Untranslatability*, New York: Verso Books.
Atwood, Margaret. (2004), "Headscarves to Die For," *The New York Times*, August 15, 2004. Available online: https://www.nytimes.com/2004/08/15/books/headscarves-to-die-for.html
Carrión, Jorge. (2009), *Viaje Contra Espacio, Juan Goytisolo Y W.G. Sebald*, Madrid: Iberoamericana.
Casanova, Pascale. (2007), *The World Republic of Letters*. Tr. Malcolm DeBevoise, Cambridge: Harvard University Press.
Damrosch, David. (2003), *What Is World Literature?* Princeton: Princeton University Press.
Erol, Sibel. (2007), "Reading Orhan Pamuk's *Snow* as Parody: Difference as Sameness," *Comparative Critical Studies* 14 (3): 403–32.
Ertürk, Nergis. (2008). "Modernity and Its Fallen Languages: Tanpınar's 'Hasret,' Benjamin's Melancholy," *PMLA* 123 (1): 41–56.
Farnsworth, Elizabeth. (2002), "Orhan Pamuk: Bridging Two Worlds," *PBS*, November 20, 2002. Available online: https://www.pbs.org/newshour/show/orhan-pamuk-bridging-two-worlds
Fisk, Gloria. (2018), *Orhan Pamuk and the Good of World Literature*, New York: Columbia University Press.
Frohlich, Margaret. (2003), "The Violent Narration of 'Pure' Spain: National Identity and Treason in *Reivindicación del conde don Julián* by Juan Goytisolo," *Romance Review* 13 (1): 55–68.
Georgacas, Demetrius John. (1947), "The Names of Constantinople," *American Philological Association* (78): 347–67.
Göknar, Erdağ. (2013), *Orhan Pamuk, Secularism and Blasphemy: The Politics of the Turkish Novel*, New York: Routledge.

Goytisolo, Juan. (1975), "In Memoriam F.FB," *El País*, November 25, 1975.
Goytisolo, Juan. (1984), "Abandonemos de una vez el amoroso, cultivo de nuestras señas de identidad," *El País*, April 10, 1984. Available online: http://elpais.c om/diario/1984/04/10/opinion/450396011_850215.html
Goytisolo, Juan. (1989), *Estambul otomano*, Barcelona: Editorial Planeta.
Goytisolo, Juan. (1990), *Aproximaciones a Gaudí en Capadocia*, Madrid: Mondadori.
Goytisolo, Juan. (1991), *Juan the Landless*. Tr. Helen Lane, London: Serpent's Tail.
Goytisolo, Juan. (1996), "Orhan Pamuk'un Kara Kitap'ı. Tr. Gül Işık," *Defter* 9 (27): 81-94.
Goytisolo, Juan. (1999), *Reivindicación del conde don Julián*, Madrid: Alianza Editorial.
Goytisolo, Juan. (2001), "El libro negro de Orhan Pamuk: Constantinopla Constantinopolizada," *Quimera* (207-208): 192-200.
Goytisolo, Juan. (2002a), *El sitio de los sitios*, Barcelona, Seix Barral.
Goytisolo, Juan. (2002b), *Osmanlı'nın İstanbul'u*. Tr. Gül Işık, İstanbul: Yapı Kredi Yayınları.
Goytisolo, Juan. (2007), *Señas de identidad*, Madrid: Alianza Editorial.
Goytisolo, Juan. (2009), *Juan the Landless*, rev. ed. Tr. Peter Bush, Champaign: Dalkey Archive Press.
Goytisolo, Juan. (2013), *Juan sin tierra*, Pamplona: Leer-e. Kindle.
Goytisolo, Juan. (2015), *Kapadokya'da Gaudi'nin İzinde*. Tr. Zerrin Yanıkkaya. İstanbul: Alef.
Herzog, Christoph and Richard Wittmann (eds.) (2018), *Istanbul - Kushta - Constantinople: Narratives of Identity in the Ottoman Capital, 1830-1930*, New York: Routledge.
Iğsız, Aslı. (2018), *Humanism in Ruins: Entangled Legacies of the Greek-Turkish Population Exchange*, Stanford: Stanford University Press.
Moretti, Franco. (2000), "Conjectures on World Literature," *New Left Review* (1): 54-68.
Pamuk, Orhan. (1994), *Beyaz Kale*, İstanbul: İletişim Yayınları.
Pamuk, Orhan. (1998), *The White Castle*. Tr. Victoria Holbrook, New York: Vintage International.
Pamuk, Orhan. (2006a), *İstanbul: Hatıralar ve Şehir*, İstanbul: İletişim Yayınları.
Pamuk, Orhan. (2006b), *Istanbul: Memories and the City*, Tr. Maureen Freely, New York: Vintage International.
Pizer, John. (2006), *The Idea of World Literature: History and Pedagogical Practice*, Baton Rouge: Louisiana State University Press.
Silipo, Rafaella. (2017), "Hanno distrutto la Istanbul che amavo," *La Stampa*, October 14, 2017. Available online: https://www.lastampa.it/2017/10/14/cultu ra/hanno-distrutto-la-istanbul-che-amavo-mVyhD5FgDU5cYuHl6f0DZO/p remium.html (accessed January 10, 2020).
"The Nobel Prize in Literature 2006," The Nobel Prize. Available online: https://ww w.nobelprize.org/prizes/literature/2006/summary/ (accessed January 10, 2020).
Vatanabadi, Shouleh. (2013), "'The Uneven Bridge of Translation:' Turkey in between East and West," in E. Alsultany and E. Shohat (eds.), *Between the Middle East and the Americas*, 299-318, Ann Arbor: University of Michigan Press.

# 10

# Teaching *The Museum of Innocence* in Arts and Design Context

## *Irmak Ertuna Howison*

Orhan Pamuk's novels have been instrumental in securing the place of Turkish literature in the world literature curriculum. As Pamuk's rise to fame coincided with the "postmodern turn" in literary studies, novels such as *The White Castle* (1985, 1990 in English), *The Black Book* (1990, 1994 in English), and *My Name Is Red* (1998, 2001 in English) became staples of courses that explore postcolonial questions, the nature of reality, representation, and the novel form. While these issues are at the forefront of Pamuk's writing (and to an extent the reason for his fame), their thorough discussion requires that students already be initiated in literary theory. However, as instructors we are often tasked with teaching introductory level courses or electives where students are engaging with world literature for the first time. How, then, can we incorporate Pamuk in the curriculum without assuming students are fluent in discussions of literary postmodernism?

In the spring of 2018, I started preparing an elective world literature course in a small arts and design college in central Ohio. I knew in advance that this would be the first-world literature course the students would be taking, but it quickly became apparent that this also happened to be the first college level literature course for most of the enrolled students. Constrained by the students' limited literature training and the time allocated to the course (16-week semester), I decided to shape my course around a few basic objectives that would have an impact on their future classes and career. In other words, I aimed to offer a selection of diverse themes, texts, and topics that would be relevant to their professional and intellectual development. To this end, I decided to focus on fostering a cosmopolitan understanding of the material reality of the world as a course objective and aimed to explore two key themes, objects and museums in *The Museum of Innocence,* one of the texts covered in the course.

## Rationale for the Course Objective

World literature is a broad term that could define a variety of scholarly approaches, all with their own set of shortcomings. The study of world literature could span an exploration of ancient, classical canon to masterpieces from around the world, and more recently, to the "set of windows on the world" (Damrosch 2009: 503). Whatever the approach, the vastness of the scope, the ideologies underpinning the study of other cultures, and the nature of the literary field as a market, all present problems to tackle. And perhaps more importantly, the suspicion that the "consumption" of world literature as an ineffective and self-gratifying means to deal with pressing global problems lurks at the background of any such endeavor. But at the end of the day, when we, as instructors, sit down to prepare our syllabi, we have more practical concerns in mind: How to entice our students into this vast textual field? How to instill in them a sense of enthusiasm for discovery of literature from around the world? How to make them relate to and appreciate the diversity of texts without reducing their cultural differences? And finally, how to render it all significant in national settings that are becoming more insular as a reaction to globalization?

While the debates around world literature informed my approach to the course as an instructor, I was more focused on the simple and interrelated objectives of fostering a cosmopolitan understanding of world literature and evaluating the relevance and value of literature in addressing the social and ethical issues shared by the global community. This was in part due to current affairs (the rise of Donald Trump's anti-immigrant rhetoric, Brexit, and the looming global consequences of climate change, to name a few) that swarmed the public mind at the time, but also to my own pedagogical commitment to a particular understanding of world literature as openness to diversity and cosmopolitan frame of reference through an engagement with *thematic intersections.* As Longxi Zhang argues, "despite the leveling effect of globalization in the production and distribution of material goods as commodities, the emphasis in the creation and appreciation of literary and artistic works lies precisely on diversity, specificity, and local identities, on the features of a particular tradition that are nonetheless accessible to a global audience or reading public" (2015: 2). In other words, it is through the diversity and specificity offered by texts that we can successfully understand the effects of globalization, which homogenizes the world, and offer counter-narratives to those that assist such homogenization.

Literature offers a unique way to map out intersections between the global and the local to guide the student into a cosmopolitan frame of thought. Vilashini Cooppan, for example, argues that "pedagogical injunction" of globalization lies in reconceptualization of culture as network, intersection, and routes (2004: 20). Many world literature scholars argue that it is "cosmopolitanism" that constitutes the human experience of the networked, intersected, and global culture. Pheng Cheah defines cosmopolitanism as being "about viewing oneself as part of a world, a circle of political belonging that transcends the limited ties of kinship and country to embrace the whole of deterritorialized humanity" (2016: 3). In this sense, it is an "imagined" construction much like world literature itself. Following Kwame Anthony Appiah, the most influential proponent of cosmopolitanism as a basis for contemporary ethics, Kristian Shaw argues that it "fosters a civic responsibility to both global and local frames of reference and concerns" (2016: 176). It is, in this sense, an ethical imperative that challenges the dehumanizing effects of globalization or as Susan Choo quotes Pheng Cheah, it is the "'normative' or 'human' face of globalization" (2011: 59).

These intersections between the local and the universal have the potential to become a fertile yet unsettling ground for a cosmopolitan-minded education (Hansen 2008: 296). This dynamic space does not exclusively create commodities for easy consumption, it also generates uncomfortable differences that nevertheless emerge together to inform a cosmopolitan moral imperative that concerns our ethics as "world citizens." Rather than an erasure of differences or, conversely, a coexistence of different cultures as separate entities, cosmopolitanism can be defined as an attitude with which an individual can construct, deconstruct, and reconstruct a globally oriented set of norms and values. Imagination and fiction hold a pivotal place in the formation of a cosmopolitan worldview since "fiction offers the cosmopolitan imagination means of envisioning alternative configurations by which we can modify our relations with one another, thereby possessing a progressive socio-cultural function" (Shaw 182).

Specifically, cosmopolitanism, as a curricular objective, presents a potential response to different charges leveled against the practice and concept of world literature. On the one hand, contrary to criticism that deems study of the world literature a neoliberal tool of continued cultural imperialism whereby only the "easy" or "consumable" texts gain recognition, or their "foreignness" is domesticated, a cosmopolitanist study of world literature does not seek to create cultural "tourists" out of readers. On the contrary, it is wary of an essentialist view of culture where each national literature is treated as a discrete and pure entity in and of itself. Cosmopolitanism in the curriculum is a practical and creative way to "push toward openness instead of closure and values diversity and ambiguity rather than singularity and purity" (Choo 2014: 72).

As for my own course, I wanted the students to be able to engage with literature as a way to understand global issues and develop an ethics based around cosmopolitanism. I ensured that this elective world literature course avoided the pitfalls of fetishizing cultures or reinstating the neoliberal dynamics of "consuming" another's literature. In fact, with a thematic focus on the objects and their global material flows, the course would explore the ways in which local traditions and identities respond to these same global dynamics. One of the most appropriate texts for such a course was Orhan Pamuk's 2008 novel *The Museum of Innocence* with its creation of a fictional world of objects that have interwoven personal and cultural meanings.[1]

## Pamuk within the World Literature Framework

Pamuk, now among one of the most recognized authors in global literature, has often been criticized for "distorting cultural realities for personal gain in a global marketplace that values difference without discord" (Fisk 2018: 177). This, however, is related to what Adam Kirsch articulates as the most common charge against world literature, namely, that "by making foreignness into a literary commodity, it prevents the possibility of any encounter with difference" (2017: 14). In Pamuk's case, a close textual analysis of his works reveals a complicated reality that would, in fact, enforce "foreignness": Pamuk is immersed in "distortion" quite simply as a creator of fictions, a feat he is not hesitant to disclose within his novels themselves. It is not necessarily the facts of Turkish history that Pamuk is trying to record, although the backdrop of his fiction always addresses particular historical issues within Turkish modernization, such as gender, secularization, and Westernization. His novels always underline their fabricated nature through explicit references to the act of writing and authorship. In other words, even though his critics like to dismiss him as "distorting" (or, even worse, "insulting") Turkish history and experience, he is, in fact, unequivocal in his disloyalty to factual representation of truth.

In that sense, Pamuk is not necessarily an effortless author for any first-time reader of Turkish literature who is seeking an uncomplicated, delightful literary trip to an unknown geography. But that is precisely why his novels are the ideal picks for lower- and upper-level world literature courses that aim to complicate the experience of reading a "foreign" work. For example, Gloria Fisk discusses how both Turkish and non-Turkish visitors to the physical Museum of Innocence in Istanbul are "brought together in a shared experience of remembering the novel, *The Museum of Innocence*, which is recalled by the referents of a past that happened only in fiction. The imagined and the real trade places with the familiar and the foreign, which are contrasted here as constitutive features of its reading experience" (2018: 75). This experience of the fictive world as "real" complicates the "facticity" of the novel but not its "truth" per se.

*The Museum of Innocence* is a love story that spans the 1970s in Istanbul. At its core lie the themes of class and gender difference. Kemal, the protagonist, is a Western-educated heir of a family business. When he falls in love with a poor distant relation, Füsun, and breaks off his engagement with his fiancée Sibel, he upsets the social order he is supposed to maintain. Kemal is unable to pursue his true love because of social constraints, and by the time he gathers his courage to defy familial and social expectations it is too late: Füsun is already married. Following this heartbreak, Kemal develops an obsession with stealing small objects from Füsun's family home and thus accumulates the collection that will later turn into the museum memorializing his love for her. Following the plotline of the 1970s Turkish melodramas,[2] the novel deploys the well-known tropes of poor girl/rich man, premarital sex, and marriage. The persistence of traditional values regarding women's conduct in a country where lifestyles were becoming seemingly modern is the social conflict that drives the plot and, indeed, leads to Füsun's tragic demise. However, unlike the traditionally misogynistic melodramas where women's "honor" is a precarious asset, a critical novelistic approach to social context takes precedence in *The Museum of Innocence*. Pages and pages devoted to the description of milieus and objects, the actual museum and its accompanying nonfiction collection *The Innocence of Objects* (published three years after the novel) indicate that material flows and their cultural significance were very much on Pamuk's mind when writing the novel. Ultimately, the love story reads as a vehicle to explore the "uncomfortable truths" of gender relations in Turkey in the context of the country's integration to the global economy.

The novel's concern with material flows, which I discuss in detail in the following sections, gave me a leeway to carve an interest in arts and design students. After all, their education and future craft involves intensive work with material objects themselves. My students already had a very advanced understanding of how to form, manipulate, and use objects. However, they did not have the chance to discuss the symbolic and cultural significance of the objects themselves in their studio work. Formally and thematically centered on the idea of the "museum," *The Museum of Innocence* provides a fertile ground for discussions on objects and collections. In his study of Pamuk's novels, Erdağ Göknar points out that *The Museum of Innocence* "merges the objects of everyday material culture with mystical redemption in the creation of a novel that is a museum" (2012: 321). Kemal's museum can, in fact, be read as a surrogate for his obsessive love for Füsun. In this context, the novel, and the museum, act as vehicles of "material recuperation for spiritual loss" and in a larger sense become the repository of a national-cultural memory (Göknar 2012: 322). Given the centrality of the material culture in its plot, *The Museum of Innocence* presented an occasion to examine the circulation of objects through different cultural contexts and geographies. Although we discussed the Turkish context of modernization and gender relations, we spent most of our time exploring the themes of objects, collections, and museums through a variety of classroom exercises. Ultimately, thematic and comparative focus on the objects facilitated the formation of a link between arts and design students' own practices and the literary world of Pamuk. In the following sections, I discuss each thematic module in depth and describe class responses.

# First Module on the Cultural Significance of Objects

A comparative method is undoubtedly a staple of any world literature course, especially one that aims to foster a cosmopolitan worldview. *The Museum of Innocence*, when analyzed as a stand-alone text, yields fruitful discussions on character development, gender relations, and the Turkish social setting. However, that kind of textual analysis also runs the double risk of alienating students or reduces the text to its plot elements. The former risk is the name of the game in the study of world literature: the well-intentioned instructor and uninitiated student travel into the fictional world of an exotic locale and get lost (and occasionally bored) in the details of the unique setting. Predicting that such a long novel would intimidate students with its abundance of details, I aimed to stray away from this path. The latter risk, on the other hand, curtails the discussion to simple and universal questions of character development, conflict, and resolution without recognizing the unique nature of the novel as a product of a specific culture. To put it simply, I did not want this novel to be another occasion where we conclude: "Look, even though they lived an ocean away decades ago, they are just like us in their class and gender relations!"

Intertextuality is a handy approach to avoid this reductionist trap and cements multiplicity in literary analysis. Choo argues that intertextuality fosters a sense of cosmopolitanism because it "functions as a form of ethical interruption since the aim is to guide the students to move beyond their interpretive judgments of the other in order to expand their imaginative capacity to perceive multiple value systems in the world" (2014: 81). Given the novel's concern with objects and their values which diverge and converge within a global flow, it was especially fitting to bring *The Museum of Innocence* in conversation with two graphic novels, Özge Samancı's *Dare to Disappoint* and Marjane Satrapi's *Persepolis*. When cast along these two works in the curriculum, Pamuk's novel diversifies the questions on the cultural meaning behind physical objects and how that corresponds to global power dynamics.

Özge Samancı's *Dare to Disappoint* (2015) is a graphic memoir that depicts the protagonist's coming-of-age as she struggles with social demands, questions of religion and secularism, living in a post-coup Turkey, and finding the courage to follow her true passion in art. In many respects, it shares similarities with Marjane Satrapi's now classic *Persepolis* (2000) in its treatment of experience of growing up as a female in a predominantly Muslim country, easing into nonconformity, and asserting individuality even when it is safer to follow the herd. Moreover, when cast alongside *The Museum of Innocence*, these two graphic novels that center on the woman's experience in a traditionally conservative culture can shine light on the unvoiced desires and aspirations of Pamuk's intentionally "silenced" female protagonist.

These three texts also invite a unique comparative exercise in discussion of the diverse values that we attach to the objects across the globe. While reading these novels, American students frequently notice how the meaning of what they take to be simple household items or pieces of clothing changes across cultures. Even if the global economic dynamics dictate an unbalanced flow of material wealth, the cultural value of actual material goods is not necessarily determined by their place of origin but, rather, by the unique social milieu in which they are used. In order to set up the groundwork for this discussion before starting *The Museum of Innocence*, I zoomed in on the memorable objects in both *Dare to Disappoint* and *Persepolis* as we were analyzing these graphic memoirs. I asked students to record objects highlighted in the texts in their discussion board entries and during in-class discussions for each novel. Students first started with objects that had "personal" significance like *Persepolis* protagonist Marjie's confiscated bracelet but as we progressed into the novel they started pinpointing objects that revealed a deeper cultural significance.

Take, for example, "corn flakes" in Samancı's memoir; the ubiquitous breakfast staple of an ordinary American kitchen turns into a mysterious treat to be eaten after breakfast in the 1980s Turkish household. Students not only appreciated the humor of the panel but also grasped how the value of a commodity is not predicated on its utility. Reading this panel alongside the following passage from Pamuk's novel further illustrates the point:

> [W]e remembered how the Istanbul bourgeoisie had trampled over one another to be the first to own an electric shaver, a can opener, a carving knife, and any number of strange and frightening inventions, lacerating their hands and faces as they struggled to learn how to use them. We talked about all those tape recorders brought back from Europe that usually broke on first use, and the hair dryers that blew the fuses. (2009: 125)

FIGURE 10.1 *"Corn flakes" panel from* Dare to Disappoint. *Permission by author (2015: 60).*

In other words, when objects such as corn flakes and can openers with utility find their place in the global market as commodities, an almost mysterious valuation process occurs. It is mysterious insofar as it does not necessarily reflect the "objective" worth of the commodity but, rather, its value within a culture. Similarly, *Persepolis* vividly describes how the regime change in Iran brings about a complete revaluation of the objects originating from the West. Commodities associated with the Western culture are now deemed as "decadent" and people who own or carry them are viewed as suspect. There is a particularly ironic panel in the novel that highlights how meanings we attach to the objects reveal the cultural (and hence arbitrary) nature of value making. When Marjie is caught wearing a Michael Jackson T-shirt, she defends herself by saying it is a Malcolm X T-shirt, hoping to appease the guards with this Muslim icon of American radicalism (Satrapi 2003: 133). Students find this episode ironic since a T-shirt featuring Malcolm X, a political figure who has been under FBI surveillance for most of his life, would have been more suspicious to the law enforcement in the United States than the "pop star" Michael Jackson. This moment, in which separate histories of dissidence intersect, is a perfect occasion for students to contextualize not only the culture of a foreign country but also their own, and thus presents how global and local interact in tangible ways.

The examples of material objects from *Dare to Disappoint* and *Persepolis* led into our analysis of the same themes in *The Museum of Innocence*. As we read, I asked students to note specific objects and jot down their personal and cultural significance (as described in the novel). Students quickly picked up the objects with most symbolic value: the "fake" Jenny Colon bag, Füsun's lost earrings, and cigarette butts. While we visually examined these objects on the website for the Museum of Innocence in Istanbul, we also analyzed their significance in terms of plot. In order to provide a sense of our discussions, I am including some excerpts from students' brainstorming as recorded in the online discussion board in the Appendix to this essay. Our analysis made it clear that one of the underlying themes of the novel is that the quantitative value of an object does not determine its worth. Moreover, considering how the novel takes place in the context of Turkey's integration into the global economy, this particular theme is, in fact, a criticism of the leveling forces of a market that reduce everything to a numeric value and hence render objects interchangeable.

The protagonist of the novel Kemal observes that "the power of things inheres in the memories they gather up inside them, and also in the vicissitudes of our imagination, and our memory—of this there is no doubt" (Pamuk 2009: 324). However, his reach into the "power of things" goes beyond the confines of his personal experience. In this sense, *The Museum of Innocence*, a love story that takes place in 1970s Istanbul, is global in its reach. Upon losing Füsun once and for all, Kemal intensifies his collecting and his quest takes him into home museums all around the world. His travels make him contemplate the relations of people with the objects that surround them as well as the flow of objects through the globe. For example, he notices "that in most of the world's homes there was a china dog sitting on top of the television set" and asks, "Why was it that millions of families all over the world had felt the same need?" (Pamuk 2009: 373). In class discussions, bringing up contemporary common household objects, such as IKEA trays, hugging salt and pepper shakers, or waving lucky cats drove the point home: globalization is not just about iPhones, Nikes, or Visa, it is also about sharing a mundane material world that is invisible in its pervasiveness. Kemal observes another common object found across the globe:

> To contemplate how this saltshaker had spread to the farthest reaches of the globe suggested a great mystery as great as the way migratory birds communicate among themselves, always taking the same routes every year. Another wave of saltshakers would always arrive, the old ones replaced with the new, as surely as the south wind deposits its debris on the shore, and each time people would forget the objects with which they lived so intimately, never even acknowledging their emotional attachment to them. (Pamuk 2009: 510)

The Museum of Innocence thus becomes a novel about the trajectory of objects, from their market origins into the homes of people who acquire them and onward across the globe. It is an indictment against fetishization, whether it is the single-minded idealization of a love interest or the reification of objects. In his analysis of Walter Benjamin's figure of the collector, Ackbar Abbas writes that the collector indulges in "the sex appeal of the inorganic" while also being engaged in "a struggle against universal commodification" (1988: 220). Just as Kemal's idealization turns Füsun into an object of mystery, rather than an actual woman with her own dreams and desires, reification of objects as a rule of the market strips them of their substantive impact on human lives across the globe. As Kemal's obsession with Füsun turns into a futile quest to recreate his memories with her by collecting the objects that once surrounded her, the novel also counteracts this fetishization by looking at the moments where the commodity spell is broken and the fetishized love object gets her final say. It is a moment of revelation for the readers when right before her demise Füsun confronts Kemal and says, "Because of you, I haven't had the chance to live my own life" (Pamuk 2009: 486).

The final step in the trajectory of the objects Kemal collected is their enshrinement in the fictional (and actual museum). In the initial stages of his collecting (in fact, pickpocketing), Kemal confesses his shame: "Actually I had no desire to share my collection with others, nor did anyone know I was hoarding things—I was ashamed of what I was doing" (Pamuk 2009: 374). But once again, the novel takes us in a different direction where Kemal ultimately takes pride in his endeavor and adopts a more global mission than just reanimating his memories of Füsun. He says,

> With my museum I want to teach not just the Turkish people but all the people of the world to take pride in the lives they live. I've traveled all over, and I've seen it with my own eyes: While the West takes pride in itself, most of the rest of the world lives in shame. But if the objects that bring us shame are displayed in a museum, they are immediately transformed into possessions in which to take pride. (Pamuk 2009: 518)

His remorse, obsession with Füsun's objects, and travels around the world lead him to create a museum to share his happiness with strangers. This museum theme is of special interest to arts and design students since their knowledge and expertise involve dealing with objects in sterile settings such as galleries and museums.

# Second Module on Collecting and Museums

As previously noted, one important teaching module for *The Museum of Innocence* revolves around the discussion of the concept of collections and museums. Lucia Serrano remarks that the novel exhibits "concepts of appropriation, display, and objectification, as well as logic and organization of a museum catalog" (2017: 209). The physical museum, which opened in 2014 in Istanbul, displays "actual" objects from the period in which the novel takes place, as well as some objects, such as Meltem soda or the Jenny Colon bag, that exist only in the fictional world created by Pamuk. This blurring of the demarcation between fiction and reality is a trademark of Pamuk's work and in the context of collecting and museums, it highlights the personal and cultural ways in which the objects are imbued with meaning.

In order to analyze how real and fictional objects in the novel are framed within the museum, I introduced a class discussion on the concept of museums and collections. I initiated the discussion with a few questions such as "Is there a museum that really affected you?" and "Why were you affected by this museum?" Most students' responses came from the Midwest region as not many of them had had the chance to travel abroad. Once they had shared their personal experiences with museums, we categorized the types of museums according to their purpose and strategies of display. Some museums created their affect because of the particular histories they displayed (such as the Holocaust) and some because of the unconventional ways in which they displayed it (such as the living history museum at Greenfield Village). Students also mentioned a few art museums famed for either the expanse of their collection or for their use of diverse media in their displays.

After this initial warm-up discussion, I posed the question of whether museums have a right to collect and display objects. At first students were taken aback by this question; for them, museums had such a right especially if it served an educational purpose. But then I reminded them of big museums in the West such as the Metropolitan Museum of Art in New York City and the Pergamon Museum in Berlin where artifacts from different geographies were all displayed under one roof as a mega showcase of human history. Did the Western nations have the right to appropriate the African masks, Egyptian tombs, or Ancient Greek temples? And who, ultimately, should be the sole owner of such historical artifacts? This question resonated with students because of their own artistic practice and cultural background. They had close familiarity with issues of cultural appropriation in the United States and were careful in their own practice to respect and give credit to their source of inspiration if it came from a racial or ethnic group different from their own. At this point, I directed them to this poignant passage in the novel:

> Anyone remotely interested in the politics of civilization will be aware that museums are repositories of those things from which Western Civilization derives its wealth of knowledge, *allowing it to rule the world*, and likewise when the true collector, on whose efforts these museums

depend, gathers together his first objects, he almost never asks himself what will be the ultimate fate of his hoard. When their first pieces passed into their hands, the first true collectors—who would later exhibit, categorize, and catalog their great collections (in the first catalogs, which were the first encyclopedias)—initially never recognized these objects for what they were. (Pamuk 2009: 73, emphasis mine.)

For students who were already critical of Kemal's behavior throughout the novel, only a slight nudge was needed to connect this alliance between collecting and dominance to Kemal's failed personal relationship with Füsun. Just as the collector has power over the collected, Kemal wants to exert his control over Füsun, with tragic consequences. So, then, why would Kemal's museum redeem him in our eyes or be any different from Western displays of power? Actually, for many students it did not redeem Kemal; most agreed that the narrative structure of the novel exposed the shaky

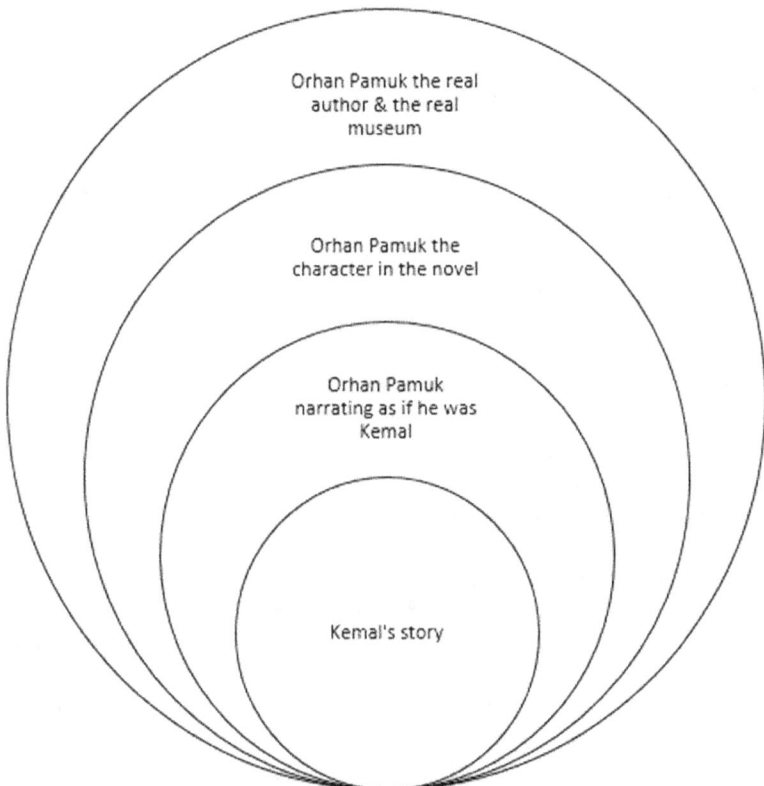

FIGURE 10.2 *Narrative layers of* The Museum of Innocence, *a class diagram.*

foundations on which we create stories about ourselves, others, our nations, and our world at large.

Yin Xing points out how *The Museum of Innocence* interweaves a personal and national story. On the one hand, objects displayed in the museum belong to "the Turkey fascinated by Western commodities for the first time, even as its material world remained immersed in the traditional patriarchy, political repression, and cultural loss that had accelerated with the Kemalist reforms of the 1920s" (Xing 2017: 215) On the other hand, there is a "link between Füsun and the Turkish people, between Kemal the collector and his collected objects, and between the personal history and memory of Pamuk's heroine and those of the nation as a whole" (Xing 2017: 216). This link, in fact, intensifies with the surprising narrative disclosure that ends up objectifying Kemal himself. In the same chapter Kemal discusses different types of collectors, and in a very Pamukesque turn, he also reveals that he, in fact, is not the author of the story:

> This is how I came to seek out the esteemed Orhan Pamuk, who has narrated the story in my name, with my approval [. . .] Coming as he did from an old Nişantaşı family that had lost its fortune, he would, I thought, have an excellent understanding of the background of my story. I had also heard that he was a man lovingly devoted to his work and who took storytelling seriously. (Pamuk 2009: 512)

I have previously argued that Kemal's inability to tell his own story and his minimal freedom as a collector "force [sic] him to inhabit a limbo between objective and subjective world" (Ertuna 2010: 111). Marking how the narrator becomes the object of narration defamiliarizes students and opens up a perspective that seeks stories beyond those created and distributed by structures of power.

We tried to visualize the layers of the story as a class and came up with a version of Figure 10.2. With this graphic visualization in mind, I asked students where Füsun's story was situated. After all, Füsun is at the heart of Kemal's quest. What is deliberately missing from Kemal's story is Füsun's perspective and that gap functions as a reminder of the limits of knowability of the other. Following Martha Nussbaum, Shaw writes that fiction occupies a special place in forming a cosmopolitan sensibility, because narrative imagination puts us in the shoes of someone else (2016: 173). But this is a risky feat because as Marcus Wood claims, "the dirtiest thing the Western imagination ever did, and it does it compulsively still, is to believe in the aesthetically healing powers of emphatic fiction" (qtd. in Fisk 2018: 43). Füsun's poignant silence undermines the possibility of empathy acquired through narratives. Through the fictional layer of Pamuk as the author of the text, the narrative imagination goes a step further and reminds the reader that such an imagination could never be complete or accurate. As

Delanty argues, "The term cosmopolitanism signals a condition of self-confrontation, incompleteness" (2006: 38) and the novel's structure reflects such a definition. Ultimately, the novel, and the museum, are rich exercises in imagination and storytelling because as Kemal points out, "isn't the purpose of the novel, or of a museum, for that matter, to relate our memories with such sincerity as to transform individual happiness into a happiness all can share?" (Pamuk 2009: 337)

## Conclusion

Analyzing *The Museum of Innocence* in an elective world literature course has its challenges. By focusing on the ultimate course goal of enhancing a cosmopolitan understanding of world literature, I centralized the novel's two key themes—objects and museums—through a comparative analysis of *Dare to Disappoint* and *Persepolis*. Rather than getting lost in the particularities of the 1970s, which are admittedly important but not conducive to the engagement of novice world literature students, we sought intersections and insights into the dynamics of the global flow of goods and the stories embedded in them. As Hansen argues, "world inheritance is something other than a sum of the parts [...] it is not concocted by incorporating prefigured inheritances from particular communities" and a cosmopolitan education entails a shift or opening up "of perspective or orientation as it influences people's reception and response to content" (2008: 297). In other words, instead of cataloging stories from around the world as valuable examples of others' experiences, our thematic emphasis focused on altering the way we view the everyday world in its global connections. Our discussions ended up yielding unexpected results when students brought up objects imbued with cultural meaning from their own lives (such as crop tops or durags) and later when they presented their final creative projects. Quite a few of them had taken the lead from our discussion of objects in *The Museum of Innocence* and applied it to other class texts by transforming and revealing the cultural significance of certain fictional objects (sexy lingerie, doors, sneakers, and masks) in photographs, paintings, and 3D animations they made for our class.

## Appendix

(For this discussion board entry, I asked the students to elaborate on the meaning of one of the objects in the novel [and the museum]. The posts are reproduced here without editing and with permission from students.)

Füsun talks about how the bag is indeed a fake but begins a discussion about how the point of the bag is not that it is a fake, but that other people will form opinions on you based on status and money. This reflects the relationship between Füsun and Kemal in the first half of the book, since Kemal and other people in his social class do not see Füsun as "genuine," and while that doesn't matter to Kemal based on how much he loves her, a bag is just a bag, but the problem is that Kemal will care what other people think which is why they could never work (Student A).

In Museum of Innocence, Kemal collects a variety of objects from Füsun throughout the book. Her earrings that went missing at the beginning represent a symbol of trust because he lied to her right from the beginning and they come full circle in the end when he tries to give her new ones. The "Jenny Colon" fake bag shows how he seems fake toward Füsun and Sibel. He lies to them both consistantly and with the bag and the earrings, Kemal sees things as replaceable. On the other had he values things that are literally worthless, like her cigaret butts. He keeps them and labels them to show her feeling each emotion. During the engagement party, Füsun also says something about the authenticity of things and how she feels that it isn't important nor should it be (Student B).

The values of all of these objects are entirely subjective. For example, the fake Jenny Colon bag was very expensive, but Sibel finds it worthless because it is off brand. (Even though her fiancé was the one giving her a gift, she wasn't interested unless it had the value of being a genuine Jenny Colon bag.) An opposing example would be that Kemal takes things such as cigarettes and cheap ceramic decorations from Füsun's house. Although these objects are seemingly worthless, Kemal basically worships them because they remind him of Füsun. There is an emotional value that surpasses any monetary value that there may be (Student C).

## Notes

1  The novel is published in English in 2009.
2  Commonly referred to as *Yeşilçam* films, named after the location of the film studios.

## References

Abbas, Ackbar. (1988), "Walter Benjamin's Collector: The Fate of Modern Experience," *New Literary History* (20): 1, 217–37.
Cheah, Pheng. (2016), *What Is a World?: On Postcolonial Literature as World Literature*, Durham: Duke University Press.
Choo, Suzanne S. (2011), "On Literature's Use(ful/less)ness: Reconceptualizing Literature Curriculum in the Age of Globalization," *Journal of Curriculum Studies* (43): 1, 47–67.

Choo, Suzanne S. (2014), "Cultivating a Hospitable Imagination: Re-envisioning the World Literature Curriculum through a Cosmopolitan Lens," *Curriculum Inquiry* (44):1, 68-89.
Cooppan, Vilashini. (2004), "Ghosts in the Disciplinary Machine: The Uncanny Life of World Literature," *Comparative Literature Studies* (41): 1, 10-36.
Damrosch, David. (2009), *How to Read World Literature*, West Sussex: Wiley-Blackwell.
Delanty, Gerard. (2006), "The Cosmopolitan Imagination: Critical Cosmopolitanism and Social Theory," *The British Journal of Sociology* (57): 1, 25-47.
Ertuna, Irmak. (2010), "The Mystery of the Object and Anthropological Materialism: Orhan Pamuk's Museum of Innocence and Andre Breton's Nadja," *Journal of Modern Literature* (33): 3, 99-111.
Fisk, Gloria. (2018), *Orhan Pamuk and the Good of World Literature*, New York: Columbia University Press.
Göknar, Erdağ. (2012), "Secular Blasphemies: Orhan Pamuk and the Turkish Novel," *NOVEL: A Forum on Fiction* 45 (2): 301-26.
Hansen, David T. (2008), "Curriculum and the Idea of Cosmopolitan Inheritance," *Journal of Curriculum Studies* (40): 3, 289-312.
Kirsch, Adam. (2017), *The Global Novel: Writing the World in the 21st Century*, New York: Columbia Global Reports.
Pamuk, Orhan. (2009), *The Museum of Innocence*. Tr. M. Freely, New York: Vintage International.
Pamuk, Orhan. (2012), *The Innocence of Objects*. Tr. Ekin Oklap, New York: Abrams.
Samancı, Özge. (2015), *Dare to Disappoint: Growing Up in Turkey*, New York: Farrar, Straus and Giroux.
Satrapi, Marjane. (2003), *Persepolis: The Story of a Childhood*, New York: Pantheon.
Serrano, Nehora Lucia. (2017), "Illuminating *My Name Is Red* and *The Museum of Innocence*," in S. Türkkan and D. Damrosch (eds.), *Approaches to Teaching the Works of Orhan Pamuk*, 202-10, New York: The Modern Language Association of America.
Shaw, Kristian. (2016), "Teaching Contemporary Cosmopolitanism," in K. Shaw (ed.), *Teaching 21st Century Genres*, 167-84, London: Palgrave Macmillan.
Xing, Yin. (2017), "The Novel as Museum, the Museum as Novel: Teaching *The Museum of Innocence*," in S. Türkkan and D. Damrosch (eds.), *Approaches to Teaching the Works of Orhan Pamuk*, 211-18, New York: The Modern Language Association of America.
Zhang, Longxi. (2015), *From Comparison to World Literature*, Albany: SUNY Press.

# 11

# Elif Şafak and Her Fiction

# Cultural Commodities of the Global Capital

*Simla Doğangün*

Since her worldwide introduction with her first novel in English *The Saint of Incipient Insanities* (2004), the world literary market has been showing a growing interest in Elif Şafak. Her novels have been translated into forty languages and published by some of the world's leading presses, including Viking, Penguin Random House, Rizzoli, and Phébus. In 2010 she was given the Chevalier of the Order of Arts and Letters honorary award, one of France's most prestigious awards. Her latest novel *10 Minutes 38 Seconds in This Strange World* (2018) was shortlisted for the 2019 Booker Prize from among thirteen authors, including Salman Rushdie, Margaret Atwood, and Jeanette Winterson. Writing in both English and Turkish, she is considered an influential author with her numerous novels and articles, along with the talks she has given.

Elif Şafak was born in Strasbourg as the daughter of a Turkish diplomat and a scholar of social psychology. Having been educated in Madrid and Turkey, she moved to the United States where she held teaching positions. She currently lives in the UK. Şafak situates herself as a world citizen and a storyteller who has combined her thoughts on identity and belonging and worked her concerns into her fiction. In each of her novels she chooses to underscore a theme that would be appealing to readers from all around the world. It is also her childhood and upbringing that resonates in the themes she deploys in her works. Given her "half-nomadic life," it is rather autobiographical that her writing dwells on themes of multiculturalism, cosmopolitanism, and multiple belongings. Elif Şafak's status as a British-Turkish writer in relation to world literature has been vigorously debated in both national and international contexts.[1] Having become national bestsellers in Turkey and abroad, her novels are now considered significant cultural exports.

The thematic appeal of Şafak's fiction on the world literature stage and its dynamics comprise the focus of this chapter. Hybridity and cosmopolitanism are the two popular concepts frequently used by Elif Şafak to articulate both her identity and her works in the discussions on world literature. These concepts are embedded within the theoretical discourse of the politics of resistance against globalization, but there is also criticism directed toward them for being informed by elitist and Eurocentric approaches. Following the use of such themes in Şafak's works critically proves to be an apt response in situating her authorial position within the context of world literature. Within the context of Turkish literature, the aspiration to connect with the world becomes a concern of thematic appeal (other than translation) that culminates in a complicated tension between Şafak's fiction and world literature. The cosmopolitical significance of Şafak's writing needs to be reexamined, if one is to discuss it as a multiply linked and layered vision that resists Eurocentric approaches.

Where cultural hybridity can be employed as a mechanism for resistance against the discourse of globalization, in line with Homi Bhabha's insights, in its unsettling of categorizations, it can also serve as a bridging concept, "extending the parameters of analysis and highlighting a mode of explanation which is alert to the role of difference and contingency in contemporary society" (Papastergiadis 2000: 5). Offering a syncretic cultural flexibility and challenging in-betweenness, cultural hybridity can expand our understanding of identity and culture in societies. Nevertheless, the term is also deeply problematic due to its co-option by global capitalism, which seeks to homogenize differences. These two opposing claims to the term are concerns in Şafak's work and authorial position. Cosmopolitanism, the buzzword for twenty-first-century forms of belonging, is likewise often championed for its ability to imagine social difference within today's multicultural societies. Literature is one site where the processes of constructing cosmopolitan viewpoints might take shape (McCallum 2011: 2); as Kwame Anthony Appiah contends, "the novel [is] a testing ground for a distinction between cosmopolitanism, with its emphasis on a dialogue among differences" (2011: 207).

In all of Elif Şafak's novels, issues relating to cultural diversity, migration, and multiple belongings can be discerned as representing her literary universe. Conceived as a phase in the process of multiculturalism, concerns of cultural conflict are presented to the reader with a touch of

Islamic mysticism in *Pinhan*, her first novel, which won the prestigious *Mevlana Award* in 1998. In *Şehrin Aynaları* (1999), she handles the clash of Eastern and Western cultures and highlights the differences within the East and the West themselves, while situating religion as the basis of this difference. *Mahrem* (2000; translated as *The Gaze*, 2006) is a novel which brings together people from different periods, nations, languages, and religions, emphasizing the importance of coexistence rather than conflict. Bonbon Palas, a ten-story apartment building, constitutes the cultural diversity of *Bit Palas* (2002; translated as *The Flea Palace*, 2004), with the distinctive identity and personality of Agripina and Pavel. *Baba ve Piç* (2006; translated as *The Bastard of Istanbul*, 2007) zooms in on the different cultures living in harmony within the multicultural Ottoman Empire prior to the events of 1915, with the emphasis on the resentment that continues to deepen in each new generation. The parallel narratives of Turkish and Armenian families converge in Istanbul where the stories first began. Şafak's autobiographical novel *Siyah Süt* (2007; translated as *Black Milk*, 2011) is full of fantastic elements and depicts her inner journey in the quest of finding her new identity as a mother. This inner journey reminds her that conflict is necessary to achieve harmony. This time the cultural conflict is based on the struggle of the author with her own self. *İskender* (2011; translated as *Honour*, 2012) begins in a Kurdish village and extends to Istanbul, London, and Abu Dhabi, focusing on displacement, love, and the ability to change. The novel has been subjected to claims of plagiarism: Şafak has been accused of using themes and characters from Zadie Smith's *White Teeth*. In response to these claims Smith later wrote Şafak a letter of support.[2]

What follows focuses on how multiple belongings and hyphenated identities are treated in two of Şafak's works, namely, *Aşk* (2009; *The Forty Rules of Love: A Novel of Rumi*, 2010), and *Araf* (2004; *The Saint of Incipient Insanities*). *The Saint of Incipient Insanities* and *The Forty Rules of Love: A Novel of Rumi* were originally written in English, something unusual for the Turkish literary scene.[3] As a bestseller and a work that was longlisted for the 2012 International IMPAC Dublin Literary Award, *The Forty Rules of Love: A Novel of Rumi* seems to offer a hybrid text showing Şafak's perspective on blending two diverse cultures or traditions as well as the contradictions inherent in her approach. *The Saint of Incipient Insanities* is an unusual way of engaging with belonging, this time through the inclusion of different personalities from many parts of the world.[4] The "global village" Şafak creates in these works weaves together expressions of cosmopolitanism and related discourses of hybridity.

David Damrosch's definition of world literature as encompassing "all literary works that circulate beyond their culture of origin, either in translation or in their original language," and his situating of the world literary work as being encountered "not at the heart of its source culture but in the field of force generated among works that may come from very different cultures and eras" can be rethought by way of Şafak's thematic choices in her two representative works (2003: 300). Reading one novel through the lens of hybridity and the other through cosmopolitanism proves useful in seeing to what extent Şafak's precarious identity politics are at work. Such a reading also exposes her continued exploration of different perspectives and often conflicting arguments and stances, rendering her literary persona characteristic of the current and potential features of world literature as an area of study.

## Hybridity and *The Forty Rules of Love*

In *The Location of Culture* (1994), Bhabha claims that hybridity is a site where transformations occur. As a liminal space between the cultures of the colonizer and (post)colonial subjects, hybridity makes both undergo a process that recasts their identity and renders possible the third space of enunciation. As neither the center nor the periphery, neither the first nor the third world, this third space negates the possibility of such dualisms. Hybridity thus makes it possible to address the contradictions and internal differences in the making of identity. In other words, embracing the hybrid nature of cultures encourages us to move away from the exclusionism inherent in alleged notions of cultural purity and authenticity, and in so doing, allows a reconceiving of the world.

Critiques of hybridity claim that it is mired in two paradoxes (Kraidy 2002: 321). The first is that it is understood as subversive and pervasive, exceptional and ordinary, marginal and mainstream (Werbner 1997: 1). Indeed, it follows that if everything is hybrid, then there is no need for a special category of hybridity unless specific forms of it are historically and structurally distinguishable from others. The second paradox is that hybridity's foggy circumference, its openness, allows for unpredictable, arbitrary, and exclusionary closure (Kraidy 2002: 322). As its nature is based on elasticity and openness, it can be appropriated by anyone to mean practically anything.

Arif Dirlik observes a similar downside to Bhabha's conception of the term, arguing that Bhabha transformed hybridity into an abstraction with no particular location (2002: 105). To him Bhabhaian hybridity and its associated concepts of "thirdspace" and "in-betweenness" have been emptied out in their application "to be rendered into universal standardization" (2002: 105). When abstracted from its sociohistorical context, it blurs, in the name of difference, the distinctions between different differences (2002: 106). In Aijaz Ahmad's terms, this is "speaking with virtually mindless pleasure of transnational cultural hybridity, and of politics of contingency," which "amounts, in effect, to endorsing the cultural claims of transnational capital itself" (1996: 12).

Elif Şafak's experience as an author captures this blurring of identities, as she explained in a 2010 TED Talk:

> There's a fuzzy category called multicultural literature in which all authors from outside the Western world are lumped together. I'll never forget my first multicultural reading, in Harvard Square about ten years ago. We were three writers, one from the Philippines, one Turkish and one Indonesian—like a joke, you know. And the reason why we were brought together was not because we shared an artistic style or a literary taste. It was only because of our passports. (Şafak 2010b)

The idea of multiculturalism that Şafak critiques here is one possible consequence of the obscurity the term hybridity creates. Her experience exemplifies the elusiveness of hybridity that allows for a reduction of complexity to a "statement of mixture" (Dirlik 2002). It also points out that hybridity is hegemonically constructed in the interest of the socially dominant, in this case a literary industry largely motivated by American customer expectations.

Elsewhere, in an interview with Myriam J. A. Chancy, Elif Şafak states that her past and her fiction "have been deeply shaped by the notion of borders and the endeavor to transcend these" and that she embraces her own identity as one under the influence of "a never-ending quest, a perpetual transition" (2003: 82). While she hints at the complications that identity politics poses, she seems to be consonant with its influence on defining her own identity.

On the thematic level, *The Forty Rules of Love* also develops this contradiction. Şafak positions love as instrumental in enabling characters to move beyond their given identities and localities. The interactions of Eastern and Western cultures and the reciprocal relationship between perceptions of the present and the past are integral to the deployment of love as the overarching theme of the novel. Imbricated in the Sufist interpretation of Islam, the novel touches on the transcendental nature and influence of love with respect to issues of belonging. The intersecting lives of the four main characters of the novel, Ella, Aziz, Shams of Tabriz, and Rumi the Master, constitute the backbone of the story: the friendship between Rumi and Shams fosters feelings of companionship between Ella and Aziz. At the start of the novel, the plot centers on Ella's inner transformation after being hired to edit Aziz's "Sweet Blasphemy," a novel about the close friendship between Rumi and Shams, who lived in thirteenth-century Konya in Anatolia. As American Ella reads the novel, she becomes curious about its author Aziz who, at the time, lives in Amsterdam.

Ella is a typical middle-class, middle-aged, and unhappily married white woman whose life revolves around her husband and children. She feels trapped and deeply unsatisfied despite her comfortable suburban life in Northampton, New England, due to her husband's distance and unfaithfulness and her teenage children's growing away from her. Aziz, a man of Scottish origin who later became a Sufi and adopted a new name and destiny, is a photographer and traveler, "a wandering dervish at heart" (Şafak 2010a: 324). He follows the precepts of Sufi philosophy as interpreted by Shams, who claimed that love is a kind of journey in which "east, west, south, or north makes little difference. No matter what your destination, just be sure to make every journey a journey within. If you travel within, you'll travel the whole world and beyond" (86).

The two stories of Ella and Aziz, and of Rumi and Shams, intermingle in accordance with Şafak's desire to move beyond the borders of nations and belief systems. Her intention resonates with Shams's perception of love: "All you need to do is keep in mind how everything and everyone in this universe is interconnected. We are not hundreds and thousands of different beings. We are all One" (Şafak 2010a: 135). Shams's vision of hybridity promotes seeing everyone as ultimately the same even in their individual and historical difference—a stance that risks being perceived and critiqued as assimilationist.

The inner journey that Shams describes is accompanied by a spatial journey which brings him to Anatolia, the place that Aziz writes about in the foreword of "Sweet Blasphemy":

Beset with religious clashes, political disputes, and endless power struggles, the thirteenth century was a turbulent period in Anatolia. In the West, the Crusaders, on their way to Jerusalem, occupied and sacked Constantinople, leading to the partition of the Byzantine Empire. In the East, highly disciplined Mongol armies swiftly expanded under the military genius of Genghis Khan. In between, different Turkish tribes fought among themselves while Byzantines tried to recover their lost land, wealth, and power. It was a time of unprecedented chaos when Christians fought Christians, Christians fought Muslims and Muslims fought Muslims. Everywhere one turned, there was hostility and anguish and an intense fear of what might happen next. (Şafak 2010a: 19)

From a historical point of view, Anatolia has always been a land of diverse tribes and empires, with citizens who endorsed heterogeneous beliefs and lifestyles. In order for the text to be attractive to its contemporary, first-world reader, an exotic place (from a different time) emblematic of the text's message must be inserted; this brief foreword is necessary in order to bridge the temporal and the spatial gaps between the third-world backbone of the story and the perception and expectation of the first-world reader.

That the theme of companionship and love derives its force from Sufism is another platform from which the attempt for unity between cultures of the

East (content) and the West (reader) is performed. In "Sweet Blasphemy," the rules of love that are laid out by Shams are actually the precepts constituting Sufism or Islamic mysticism, which aims to bring the soul into relation with the sanctity of the other world, thus orienting it to divine truth. After a night of drinking, Shams carries Suleiman home. When Suleiman asks whether it is real or metaphorical wine that the Sufis praise, Shams answers:

> What difference does it make, my friend? There is a rule that explains this: When a true lover of God goes into a tavern, the tavern becomes his chamber of prayer, but when a wine bibber goes into the same chamber, it becomes his tavern. In everything we do, it is our hearts that make the difference, not our outer appearances. Sufis do not judge other people on how they look or who they are. When a Sufi stares at someone, he keeps both eyes closed and instead opens a third eye—the eye that sees the inner realm. (Şafak 2010a: 141)

Here Shams promotes the idea of difference among believers of God—and that in order to understand these differences, one should "open a third eye," use intuition, as a means of getting back to and knowing the things themselves in all their uniqueness and their ineffable originality. Paradoxically, on the path to becoming "one" with God, one should notice the dissimilarities among believers.

According to Paul L. Heck, "Sufism is itself a complex form of religiosity but constitutes an integral part of Islam" that is "peace-loving, amiable and convivial" (2007: 13). He proposes, "It is best to speak of the politics of Sufism in terms of engaged distance—engaged with society but in principle distant from worldly power" (2007: 14). In this respect, Şafak's usage of Sufism fails to acquire specific political significance. That is to say, although her employment of Sufism is in tune with her personal commitment to multiple attachments that advocate moving beyond national affiliations, it falls flat in putting this idea in the service of the expectations of the Western literary market. In her article on Şafak's *The Forty Rules of Love*, Elena Furlanetto discusses the deployment of Rumi for an American audience and states, "The Turkish author not only succumbs to the oversimplification and decontextualization of Rumi's work perpetrated by the American initiators of the Rumi phenomenon, but also employs Orientalist strategies in the ways in which she positions the East as being instrumental to the West" (2013: 201). Such coexistence of clashing arguments renders Şafak's position vulnerable and open to criticism on the grounds that the hybrid outlook she constructs in the novel is rather one that reproduces further polarization concerning the logic of globalization.

Taking into account the possibility of a critical hybridity and Şafak's own quest for "political identity" as indicated earlier, the novel thus demonstrates different and potentially contradictory aspects of hybridity:

it presents love as having the power to surpass borders, encourages unification and universalism, and enables a quietist detachment from worldly matters. Sufi mysticism and political border crossings are fused in the text. To the extent that, as Amal Amireh and Lisa Suhair Majaj have argued, "literary decisions come together with market strategies and assessments of audience appeal (ranging from the interest in the 'exotic' to feminist solidarity)," Şafak's book literally travels to other places (2000: 5). Ella, the editor of "Sweet Blasphemy," acquires a charged significance in this regard in that she represents the Western readership of both "Sweet Blasphemy" and *The Forty Rules of Love*. Within the novel, she is the Westerner exploring the exotic Aziz and his equally exotic world, a clear indication of Şafak's critical examination of the desire of the West to learn, explore, and dominate that which belongs to the East. Moreover, in choosing the Western Ella as her protagonist, Şafak upends the idea that Turkish writers will stay within the limits of third-world fiction. While this act does not necessarily prove that the existence of the first-world protagonist makes the text first-world literature, it shows that taxonomy is both inevitable and expected as the relationship between the third-world writer and her text on the one hand, and market forces on the other, shape first-world readers and mediators. A variety of opposing influences such as national culture and world ethics, regional knowledge and global awareness pervade *The Forty Rules of Love*, creating a conflict between the local and the universal.

An analysis of how Şafak's aesthetic and stylistic choices perform the condition of hybridity through the theme of love reveals that they may imply either a celebration of differences or the very confirmation of their existence. This is a shaky ground on which Şafak's identity politics rests. To further this precarious positioning with regard to world literature, using a critical lens on the seemingly global promise of cosmopolitanism in *The Saint of Incipient Insanities* looms large. Although hybridity is mainly used within the context of postcolonial discourses, it reverberates in discussions of world literature as it is a term whose treatment and epistemological consistency depend upon the manner in which contemporary authors link the concept with theories such as globalization.

## Cosmopolitanism and *The Saint of Incipient Insanities*

The changing nature of the pressures of globalization has led to the question of what it means to be a citizen of the world and how to underline the importance of diversity. To be cosmopolitan is usually taken to be a refusal to be defined by one's local origins and group membership but, rather, by one's commitment to humanity as a whole. As articulated by the Enlightenment, cosmopolitanism implies an impulse to be rootless. What should be noted is that the ideals of having no exclusive loyalty to any particular community, being capable of renouncing identity, being motivated by universal values, and the capacity to be mobile are also a function of belonging to an elite class. As Aihwa Ong rightly observes, class stratification is intertwined with global systems of production as well as the differences in the power of mobile and non-mobile subjects. According to Ong, ignoring these circumstances "gives the misleading impression that everyone can take equal advantage of mobility and modern communication and that transnationality has been liberatory, in both a spatial and political sense, for all peoples" (1999: 11).

Another concern with respect to the concept of multiple belongings is related to the way globalization is conceived. Joan Tomlinson defines globalization as "the rapidly developing and ever-densening network of interconnections and interdependencies that characterize material, social, economic and cultural life in the modern world" (2007: 352). In many debates concerning globalization, the United States of America has been at the center, setting and consolidating its global sphere of influence. Some prominent cultural and social theorists of the 1990s claimed that globalization was actually "Americanization" (Latouche 1996) or "McDonaldization" (Ritzer 1993) in a universalist disguise. Adding the issue of America being always at the center of globalization to the critique of cosmopolitanism as elitist and Western brings to the fore the necessity to critically approach cosmopolitanism by asking whether it forecloses a true cosmopolitan outlook or makes possible a new kind of cosmopolitanism.

In *The Saint of Incipient Insanities* (2004), Şafak engages with the question of how the ceaseless homogenization of the world through globalization and/or Americanization makes it necessary to underline the diverse perceptions of the global within the literary domain. According to Timothy Brennan, the new cosmopolitan literature that has emerged with global capitalism is "plebeian": "the cosmopolite in this fiction is not an elitist or jet-setter alone, but also simply the 'people'" (1997: 39). Exemplary of this, Şafak's novel revolves around the social, cultural, and emotional experiences of three international doctoral students who have recently arrived in Boston. The three roommates, Abed from Morocco, Piyu from Spain, and Ömer from Turkey, try to make sense of love and life as they plan to finish their doctoral degrees. The novel focuses mainly on the relationship between Ömer and Gail, the peculiar, manic-depressive Jewish-American girl who becomes Ömer's wife and eventually commits suicide by jumping off the Bosphorus Bridge, "the perfect place of inbetweendom," in her words, when they visit Ömer's family in Istanbul (Şafak 2004: 347).

The "inbetweendom" Gail notes points to both the possibilities and limitations of cosmopolitanism in the different characters of *The Saint of Incipient Insanities.* As can be seen in Ömer's words, "When you are a foreigner, you can't be your humble self anymore. I am my nation, my place of birth. I am everything except me" (Şafak 2004: 110), representation is key to how one defines his or her identity in the face of others and is intertwined with the issue of belonging—which is what cosmopolitanism seeks to discover. A key representative moment of Ömer's struggle is when, while sitting in a bar in Boston, he "put[s] the dots of [his] name back to their place" by making huge holes in the napkin with his pen (Şafak 2004: 5). The narrator notes, "When you leave your homeland behind, they say, you have to renounce at least one part of you. If that was the case, Ömer knew exactly what he had left behind: his dots!" (Şafak 2004: 5) This is no coincidence on Şafak's part: the power of names is linked directly to social agency (Bourdieu 1990: 134) and Ömer's attempt to regain his "dots" can be read as a challenge against the "Americanized" reality he is absorbed in. However, the text also acknowledges the removal of dots as a means for "better" inclusion through assimilation.

This contradiction can be seen as a symptom of the simultaneous cultural homogenization and cultural heterogenization of our world. Through de-naming and renaming, one is supposed to gain the opportunity to regenerate one's identity. However, as there is neither an inside nor an outside to the effects of globalization, the ability to detach one's persona from national or linguistic boundaries falls flat. The compulsion of representation becomes manifest in an unexpected event: while having sex with his ex-girlfriend Tracey, Ömer feels shaken by her question about the condom he fetches from his pocket: "Is that a Turkish condom? Check if there is a slit before putting it on" (Şafak 2004: 110). Although he pretends that he is not offended, his penis is more honest in "shrinking rapidly inside the Turkish condom" (Şafak 2004: 110).

While Ömer is in pursuit of his "dots," his eccentric, young Jewish-American wife Gail keeps changing names. This can be regarded as a necessary detachment from her roots, generating a possible cosmopolitan viewpoint. However, in contrast to Ömer's position, Gail's penchant for multiple attachments invokes Bruce Robbins's insight on "actually existing cosmopolitanisms," which signifies "a reality of re-attachment, multiple attachment, or attachment at a distance" (1998: 3). The idea of "multiple attachments" is hinted at in the passage in which Gail discusses her envy of birds who, living in diverse geographies, are differently named based on location, and who do not settle in any one place. That Gail is especially fascinated by the idea of renaming is linked with her inclination to reinscribe her identity. In the novel, before she adopts the name Gail, she also calls herself Zarpandit, inspired by an Assyro-Babylonian goddess. Behind her manifest will to assert ties with a wider reality, her obsessive act of appropriating exotic otherness resurfaces as an attempt to maintain supremacy over her surroundings.

I read Gail's view of non-belonging as purely elitist and Western, overlooking the historical differences that mark living conditions in the third world. She is a person who does not want to be "anchored in a world that fixes names forever" but who hopes "to fish out new letters to recompose her name and her fate every time she thrusts her spoon into the alphabet soup, a reference to the childhood game she played with her mother" (Şafak 2004: 58):

> They played it because sometime in the past God up there in heaven had cooked himself an alphabet soup and let it cool down in a huge bowl near his kitchen window. But then a strong, insolent gale, or a mischievous, rotten angel, or perhaps the devil himself had either incidentally or intentionally (this specific component of the story was subject to change each time it was retold) dropped the bowl to the floor, that is to say to the skies, and all the letters inside the soup were scattered far and wide across the universe, never to be gathered back again. Letters were everywhere, waiting to be noticed and picked up, wishing to be matched to the words they could have written had they remained inside their Bowl of Eden. (Şafak 2004: 37)

Where Özlem Öğüt Yazıcıoğlu reads the childhood game as representative of "identities that constantly change and crystallize in endless configurations in their ongoing interaction" (2009: 59), I contend that this passage aptly conveys a naïve and bland version of Western cosmopolitanism unaffected by considerations of first- and third-world politics. If the "God" in the quotation is perceived to be a metaphor for globalization or Americanization, then the letters coming out of the soup can be understood as the process that shows the dissolving of nations within "the imperialist global rainbow," which Michael Hardt and Antonio Negri have pinpointed in *Empire*, contending that globalization "manages hybrid identities, flexible hierarchies, and plural exchanges through modulating networks of command. The distinct national colours of the imperialist map of the world have merged and blended in the imperialist global rainbow" (2000: xxii–xxiii). Within the context of globalization, considering the act of stirring the alphabet soup as promoting a constant remaking of her world (in a positive sense) and projecting an open-ended imagining of a world community thriving on recurrent reassemblage prove an obliviousness to the Western-motivated attempts behind this act of reassembling.

Gail's attempts to establish a bond between herself and everything else find expression most explicitly in the variety of chocolate figures she makes, which represent diverse cultures and creatures. While naming her female cat the West and the male cat the Rest is a tongue-in-cheek attempt to undo binary divisions, the issue of representation she hints toward underscores the point that cosmopolitanism has the drawback of referring to a class privilege, belonging to the elite. Indeed, the type of cosmopolitanism that Gail embodies is privileged. During Allegre's (Piyu's girlfriend) birthday party, in the midst of a diverse group of people, Gail suggests that everybody exchange their names, saying:

> Only if we stop identifying ourselves so much with the identities given to us, only if and when we really accomplish this, can we eliminate all sorts of racism, sexism, nationalism, and fundamentalism, and whatever it is that sets barricades among humanity; dividing us into different flocks and sub-flocks. (Şafak 2004: 145–6)

What she fails to recognize is that the idea of non-belonging is a luxury that only few people can enjoy. The Moroccan PhD student Abed objects with fervor to Gail's remark on moving beyond pre-given identities, noting "it is easy for you to say that [. . .] You are not the one who has to fight against discrimination all the time" (Şafak 2004: 146).

Gail's relationship with the idea of belonging is obsessive: she fetishizes, absolutizes, and paradoxically essentializes non-belonging. In contrast to her problematic obsession with non-belonging, Abed's version of world citizenship is based on real-life experience. His critique is directed toward cosmopolitanism as elitist: only certain people can "afford" to be so, usually because they are economically and politically privileged. Moreover, Gail's worshipping of non-belonging and her knack for thriving on multiplicity contrast with Abed's refusal to isolate himself from his specific locality. He resents Gail's attitude because his experience has rendered him responsive toward cultural inequality. By mentioning the historically embedded circumstances that shape his perception of multiple attachments, Abed not only underlines his rootedness but also criticizes the privileged Westerner's supposedly "superior" position. The weight of colonial history still haunts any cosmopolitan outlook.

The passage also implies that the context of Abed's perception is marked by enduring problems of representation. Abed's feeling of uneasiness in relation to Gail's remarks stems from the burden of having to represent his nation as more than "a walking bed sheet," as Moroccans were referred to in the popular film Casablanca (Şafak 2004: 146). However, elsewhere in the novel he makes explicit that the same problem of representation makes him judgmental of other Moroccans in America. When three Muslim girls wearing headscarves enter a chic café, he cannot help observing the relationship one girl has with her child. As the baby slides down from his mother's lap and starts to crawl on the floor, he cannot account for the tension he feels until the Muslim girls leave the café. As he attempts to "see how they were seen in the eyes of Americans," his own stare dwindles "to a judgmental gaze toward the girls, especially toward the mother, getting furious at her for letting the baby crawl like that on the dirty floor" (Şafak 2004: 110). The same representational issues drive the shame he feels.

The problem of representation assumes a different significance in Piyu's situation. As the narrator mentions, "With Latinos it is neither this nor that. They are part of this country, but the less integrated in a way" (Şafak 2004: 111). The narrator hints at the ongoing significance of ethnic binarism for American Latinos as well. For instance, Piyu admits that he feels "incredibly aloof to the Hispanic communities [in America] especially to the Tex-Mex and their ways" (Şafak 2004: 111). He also cannot help but maintain his judgmental gaze toward his own Spanish culture. Especially in his relationship with Allegre, he feels distant from her "big" Spanish family. Piyu's experience with regards to the concept of belonging suggests that there are not only shared commonalities but also different practices between the cosmopolitan citizens of the world.

In contrast to Piyu, Ömer's links with his nation are problematic because of locally specific circumstances as well as class issues. When Ömer lands in America, the simultaneous feelings of belonging and non-belonging strike him. Unlike how "in other parts of the world, to be a newcomer meant you had now arrived at a new place where you didn't know the ways and hows," he says that "in coming to America for the first time" he feels that America is not "that new" since he senses that he already knows most there is to know about this country—he is "an avid fan of Seinfeld, a devoted Sandman reader, addicted to the Simpsons" (Şafak 2004: 73–4). The feeling is rendered possible by the escalation of global-spatial proximity, which I have before referred to as "Americanization" at the center of globalization. This feeling of connection can also be regarded as the privileged perception of the cosmopolitan elite. Well raised thanks to his upper-class family, Ömer is labeled as a "foreigner" (by Şafak) even in his native Turkey because of his modern family. When he travels with Gail to Istanbul to introduce her to his parents, Gail observes that the bellboy of the hotel in which they stay takes Ömer to be a tourist. The narrator notes that Gail sensed "a structural riddle, some sort of a duality that divided Turkish people into two camps" (Şafak 2004: 330): the everyman and the educated elite who could easily be mistaken for a foreigner. Behind the idea of "the citizen of the world," issues of economic inequality endure, and this is one of the most important messages that Şafak incorporates in her narrative.

In contrast to Ömer's explicit discomfort with the idea of national belonging, Abed seems certain that he will go back to Morocco, marry Safiya and live happily ever after. Unlike Ömer's modern, secular, and sophisticated parents, Abed's father has passed away, leaving him only with his undereducated mother, Zahra, who "with all her heart wants [him] to have a PhD in a branch she can't even pronounce" (Şafak 2004: 173). The contrast between the two migrants, Ömer and Abed, is exacerbated by the import of religious issues. When Zahra decides to sacrifice a ram in order to save Abed from the jinni (because she believes they disturb Abed and turn his dreams into nightmares), Abed asks help from Ömer to find a butcher for slaughtering the animal. In desperation, he says, "Ömer, my brother. You should help me. No matter what, you are a Muslim, right? At least you come from a Muslim country. You are the only person in this house who can help me" (Şafak 2004: 198). Ömer helps Abed, but because he is against the slaughtering of animals, he lies when he tells him that the meat on the table is actually from the sacrificed ram. In truth, he has bought it from a butcher. After all, he is "a born Muslim who wanted to have nothing to do with Islam or with any other religion whatsoever" (Şafak 2004: 14). As mentioned earlier, this diversity is what new cosmopolitan writing aims for: including non-elitist and anti-globalist cosmopolites who are, in Brennan's view, the "'they' to the cosmopolitan 'we' in the arena of literature" (1997: 39). Furthermore, the point of the difference between the two third-world characters is that we must assume the presence, as well as the coexistence, of divergent cosmopolitanisms, which should be historically and geographically situated with regards to globalization.

The inevitable interdependence caused by globalization accords with the feeling of loneliness cosmopolitanism brings about. The gap between the reality of Şafak's "global village" and the well-insulated comfort zones of the characters can be discerned in the problems they face when communicating with others. Sibel Erol underscores the lack of communication and the inability to deliberate its reasons when she writes that the characters intentionally refuse to question why they are faced with particular predicaments and that "why" is a question that escapes the novel (2006: 55). For instance, when he discovers his wife's past lesbian relationship, Ömer feels distressed and decides, "not to think about it anymore" (Şafak 2004: 23). Similarly, Gail cannot explain what her problem is before she commits suicide: "there was no apparent reason why" (Şafak 2004: 346). According to Erol, in the novel the characters never have sincere conversations or share secrets with others. They keep each other at bay even in day-to-day encounters, revealing only the bits of themselves that will not alienate others (2006: 55). So, the will to multiple attachments is shadowed by further sharpening of individual boundaries.

Reading cosmopolitan attachments in the novel as suggesting the opposite of parochialism, the negation of ethnocentric tribalism or narrow-minded nationalism is what Şafak proposes to her readers worldwide. Yet, at times, the global town she fabricates in the text gets caught up with questions of agency, namely, regarding class issues surrounding this version of cosmopolitanism that is privileged and elitist. Rather than reading more on the possibilities of agency on the part of Ömer and Abed, one finds the evocation of alternative worlds in a Western character that commits suicide at the end of the novel. Cosmopolitanism calls for a further criticism of globalization. In this sense, the subversive potential of Şafak's fiction is limited to an attempt to appeal to the first-world reader.

Love homogenizes differences in *The Forty Rules of Love*, rendering them invisible. The novel demonstrates a continuum of hybridities, from the unification of all differences to the need to move beyond borders and the enduring presence of singularities. This emphasis on singularities renders the use of hybridity in the novel critical, although the inclusion of Sufi metaphysics suggests a distance between its precepts and the world in its reality. As it becomes evident in the title of the book and the deliberate insertion of the glossary, the anticipation of Western readership, along with the decisions made by market choices ultimately makes the narrative unstable and reifies the existence of boundaries. In *The Saint of Incipient Insanities*, cosmopolitanism calls for a pointed criticism of globalization that entails the awareness of class inequalities and the historical differences that influence modes of belonging to the world.

In my critical analysis of *The Forty Rules of Love* and *The Saint of Incipient Insanities*, and of Şafak's cosmopolitan attachments, I have drawn from the two aspects of cultural hybridity and cosmopolitanism to see how they speak to the major issues in world literature and to analyze to what extent Şafak and her works have themselves become cultural commodities of the global capital. Yet, world literature is, after all, an elusive term: there is no one way to characterize "good" or "correct" world literature. The link between Şafak's fiction and world literature can be seen in her continued re-positioning in the face of global issues, particularly ones related to belonging. Şafak's position is better explained in Zhang Longxi's approach to world literature: "World literature demands a global and cosmopolitan vision that always sees beyond our immediate circles and local concerns" (2018: 178). Offering us a cosmopolitan vision to create fellow world citizens with all those "whose literature and culture we appreciate and love as much as our own," both Şafak and her works are situated at the crossroads of the local and the global.

## Notes

1 See (Elif Öztabek-Avcı 2007), (Laschinger 2019), (Atayurt-Fenge 2017).
2 See the press release: https://m.bianet.org/english/culture/213210-elif-safak-statement-by-publishing-house-there-is-no-plagiarism
3 The novel was originally written in English and then translated into Turkish by Kadir Yiğit Uz. The original version was published later in 2010.
4 As opposed to Orhan Pamuk's non-Western characters in his novels.

## References

Ahmad, Aijaz. (1996), "The Politics of Literary Postcoloniality," *Race Class* 36 (1): 1–20.
Amireh, Amal, and Lisa Suhair Majaj. (2000), "Introduction," in A. Amireh and L. Suhair Majaj (eds.), *Going Global: The Transnational Reception of Third World Women Writers*, 1–25, New York: Garland Publishing Inc.

Atayurt-Fenge, Zeynep Z. (2017), "This Is a World of Spectacles": Cyclical Narratives and Circular Visionary Formations in Elif Shafak's The Gaze," *Critique: Studies in Contemporary Fiction* 58 (3): 287-99.
Bhabha, Homi. K. (1994), *The Location of Culture*, London: Routledge.
Bourdieu, Pierre. (1990), *In Other Words: Essays Toward a Reflexive Sociology*. Tr. Matthew Adamson, Cambridge: Polity Press.
Brennan, Timothy. (1997), *At Home in the World: Cosmopolitanism Now*, Cambridge: Harvard University Press.
Chancy, J.A. Myriam. (2003), "Migrations: A Meridians Interview with Elif Şafak," *Meridians* 4 (1): 55-85.
Damrosch, David. (2003), *What Is World Literature?* Princeton: Princeton University Press.
Dirlik, Arif. (2002), "Bringing History Back In: Of Diasporas, Hybridities, Places, and Histories," in E. Mudimbe-Boyi (ed.), *Beyond Dichotomies: Histories, Identities, Cultures, and the Challenge of Globalization*, 93-128, Albany: State University of New York Press.
Erol, Sibel. (2006), "Review of Elif Shafak's *The Saint of Incipient Insanities*," in *AATT Bulletin*, 20th Anniversary Special Issue (35-36): 53-8.
Furlanetto, Elena. (2013), "The 'Rumi Phenomenon Between Orientalism and Cosmopolitanism: The Case of Elif Şhafak's *The Forty Rules of Love*," *European Journal of English Studies* 17 (2): 201-13.
Hardt, Michael, and Antonio Negri. (2000), *Empire*, Cambridge: Harvard University Press.
Heck, Paul L. (2007), "Sufism – What Is It Exactly?" *Religion Compass* 1 (1): 148-64.
Kraidy, Marwan M. (2002), "Hybridity in Cultural Globalization," *Communication Theory* 12 (3): 316-39.
Laschinger, Veronique. (2019), "Whirls of Faith and Fancy: House Symbolism and Sufism in Elif Shafak's *The Flea Palace*," *Journal of World Literature* (1): 1-24.
Latouche, Serge. (1996), *The Westernization of the World*, Cambridge: Polity Press.
Longxi, Zhang. (2018), "World Literature, Canon, and Literary Criticism," in W. Fang (ed.), *Tensions in World Literature: Between the Local and the Universal*, 171-90, Beijing: Palgrave Macmillan.
McCallum, Pamela. (2011), "The Cosmopolitan Novel: Notes from the Editor," *Ariel* 42 (1): 1-3.
Ong, Aihwa. (1999), *Flexible Citizenship: The Cultural Logics of Transnationality*, Durham: Duke University Press.
Öztabek-Avcı, Elif (2007), "Elif Şafak's *The Saint of Incipient Insanities* as an 'International' Novel," *ARIEL: A Review of International English Literature* 38 (2-3): 83-99.
Papastergiadis, Nikos. (2000), *The Turbulence of Migration: Globalization Deterritorialization and Hybridity*, Cambridge: Polity Press.
Ritzer, George. (1993), *The McDonaldization of Society: An Investigation into the Changing Character of Contemporary Social Life*, Thousand Oaks: Pine Forge Press.
Robbins, Bruce. (1998), "Introduction: Part I," in P. Cheah and B. Robbins (eds.), *Cosmopolitics: Thinking and Feeling Beyond the Nation*, 1-20, Minneapolis: University of Minnesota Press.

Şafak, Elif. (2004), *The Saint of Incipient Insanities*, New York: Farrar, Straus and Giroux.
Şafak, Elif. (2010a), *The Forty Rules of Love: A Novel of Rumi*, London: Viking.
Şafak, Elif. (2010b), "The Politics of Fiction," Filmed July 2010 at TEDGlobal, Oxford, UK. Video: 19:30. Available online: https://www.ted.com/talks/elif_shafak_the_politics_of_fiction?language=en (accessed January 10, 2020)
Şafak, Elif. (2013), "The Religion of Love," *Turkish Daily News*, January 22, 2013. http://www.elifsafak.us/yazilar.asp?islem=yazilar&id=17&kat=Turkish%20Daily%20News (accessed January 10, 2020)
Tomlinson, John. (2007), "Cultural Globalization," in S. Ritzer (ed.), *The Blackwell Companion to Globalization*, 352–67, Oxford: Blackwell Publishing.
Werbner, Pnina. (1997), "Introduction: The Dialectics of Cultural Hybridity," in T. Moddod and P. Werbner (eds.), *Debating Cultural Hybridity: Multi-Cultural Identities and Politics of Anti-Racism*, 1–26, London: Zed Books.
Yazıcıoğlu, Özlem Öğüt. (2009), "Who Is the Other? Melting in the Pot in Elif Şafak's *The Saint of Incipient Insanities* and *The Bastard of Istanbul*," *Litera* 22 (1): 53–70.

# 12

# For/Against the World

# Literary Prizes and Political Culture in the "New Turkey"

## *Kaitlin Staudt*

In an interview for *The New Republic* in the wake of the 2013 Gezi Protests, Pankaj Mishra asks Turkey's Nobel Laureate Orhan Pamuk to consider the connection between secular culture, progressive art forms, and the rise of President Recep Tayyip Erdoğan's Justice and Development Party (AKP):

> **PM:** That question is now asked in different ways: Why has Turkey turned Islamist? There is the assumption that secularization leads to the development of progressive political forces and progressive art forms, but now Turkey seems to be going back and becoming more Muslim.
>
> **OP:** I would say politically and also culturally, that this change is not that deep really. Perhaps the class that I belong to doesn't have political power anymore, but I feel that my generation has the cultural power. And yes, maybe Turkey has an Islamist conservative government, but on the other hand, they are not culturally that powerful. Culture is represented by—I wouldn't say the left, but definitely by the secularists. That's why, until recently, the minister of culture in Erdoğan's government was a secular, leftist guy, who was just fired some six months ago. (Mishra 2013)

This question of Turkish cultural power, who has it, and the ways in which it impacts representations of Turkey in the world, has important ramifications for scholarly understanding of the relationship between national and world literature. This chapter takes the literary prize as a case study to illustrate how rhetorical divisions in Turkey's cultural sphere contain competing visions of the world through which Turkish literature circulates. This requires scholars to rethink the relationship between national and world literary spaces, in which success at the international level is followed by success at the national level, referred to as the "concentric circle" model of world literature (Berman 2009: 27). Turkish literature and its surrounding literary prize culture is a compelling focal point for this re-evaluation because of the ways in which the nation/world relationship is constructed and imagined by different cultural stakeholders: one which imagines the world as an alternative literary space to the national, and the other in which the national is the basis for constructing an alternative world.

As can be seen from Mishra's question and Pamuk's response, there is a dualistic framing of secular versus religious, Kemalist versus AKP that haunts Turkey's cultural discourse. A recent Turkish public opinion survey by Kadir Has University confirms that when asked if respondents see Turkey as secular or religious, Western or Eastern, European or Middle Eastern, the population is split nearly 50/50 between these indicators of core national identity.[1] This divide is largely discussed as symptomatic of a long-standing sociopolitical rift between Turkey's Kemalist old guard and Turkey's new middle class who largely support the current AKP government and the *büyük restorasyon*, or "great restoration," a reorientation of Turkish culture, politics, and identity inward and toward the Islamic Middle East. While scholars have pointed out that these binaries are overly simplistic and do not adequately account for the variety of competing identity claims within Turkey, this dualistic framing continues to dominate public discourse.[2]

These two political ideologies have given rise to two distinct Turkish literary cultures that have competing claims to representing Turkey in the wider world. One of these literary cultures circulates on what scholars would traditionally consider to be the world stage of international literary prizes and human rights–focused literary institutions. The plight of these authors vis-à-vis the Turkish government has been received beyond Turkey's borders as an attack on the foundations of world literature's humanitarian inclinations. The second world of Turkish literature is circumscribed by borders evocative of President Erdoğan's "Ottoman Islamist" policies, which resuscitates the cultural ties between Turkey and ex-Ottoman lands (Hintz 2018: 3). The values of this literary world are newly emerging yet can be understood as a continuation of the AKP's emphasis on social conservatism and piety as foundational Turkish moral values. This world also characterizes literature as a means of gaining political power in former Ottoman lands so that Turkey can resume its place as the moral and political head of the Muslim world and also establish itself as a center which exerts cultural power in the former Ottoman periphery.

In both literary groups, contestations over Turkishness and Turkish cultural values explicitly structure the kinds of world-making engaged in through literary prizes. In the cosmopolitan, secular world of literature, literary prizes have in recent years been increasingly used to codify Turkish fiction as world literature under attack. Exploring this phenomenon in relation to novelist Aslı Erdoğan, this chapter examines the justifications of prizes she has been awarded, alongside interviews with Erdoğan and articles in the non-Turkish press to illuminate how contemporary Turkish authorship is positioned within the global literary sphere of human rights. Beyond her articulation of literary values, Erdoğan emphasizes how the imaginative act of writing allows an author to be not only a Turkish author writing for a Turkish readership, but simultaneously a writer for the world. This sense of both here and there in her work encompasses a belief in literature's ability to partake in the cosmopolitan promise of a liberal world order, to cross-linguistic borders, and to act as a bridge of consciousness between Turkey and the world.

On the other hand, focusing on the literary prize in Turkey's contemporary culture also requires grappling with how the AKP government thinks about Turkish literature as a vehicle for projecting political power on the world stage. Much as the government has increasingly turned away from the EU ascension process in favor of neo-Ottoman political values which project Turkish power closer to home, a similar turn away from Euro-American cultural institutions as arbiters of Turkish cultural value can be seen. While James English records a general trend away from state-controlled literary prizes in the early twenty-first century, the newly established Necip Fazıl literary prize, supported by the Turkish Ministry of Culture and Tourism, subverts this tendency. Examining the recently established cultural prize, the second half of this chapter explores how the AKP's current cultural politics aim to create an alternative world for Turkish literature to circulate within. This in many ways runs counter to the academic understanding of world literature as a vehicle for the promotion of universal human rights and cosmopolitan values. Instead, examining the parallel infrastructure and alternative literary histories the current government promotes, we can see a different world literature emerging which actively eschews Western readerships, political values, and languages.

As cultural institutions which are frequently upheld as mediums of the circulation practices and cultural discernment that create world literature, literary prizes are central to the contestations over the world of world literature in contemporary Turkish letters. Furthermore, acknowledging the literary prize as an institution which "functions as a claim to authority and an assertion of that authority—the authority, at bottom, to produce cultural value" reveals the ways in which Turkish cultural values are "deeply interwoven with the international circuits of political, social, and economic power" (English 2005: 51, 261). Examining the ways in which literary prizes are deeply connected to the competing visions of Turkey's political, social, and economic conceptions of the global reveals how Turkey's bifurcated literary culture navigates competing claims to literary authority.

## Cultures of Polarization on the World Literary Stage

On February 28, 2018, the *Guardian* published an open letter to President Erdoğan signed by thirty-eight Nobel Laureates, including a large proportion of laureates of the Literature prize: Svetlana Alexievich, J. M. Coetzee, Kazuo Ishiguro, Elfriede Jelinek, Herta Müller, VS Naipaul, and Wole Soyinka (Coetzee et al. 2018). The letter discusses the detention and incarceration of novelist Ahmet Altan and his brother Mehmet, as well as journalist Nazlı Ilıcak. Outlining a larger trend of incarceration that "critically threatens journalism and with it the remnants of freedom of expression and media freedom in Turkey," the letter ends by linking Turkey's treatment of its authors to its standing as a "proud member of the free world." In doing so, the letter turns the international community of literary prizewinners into a committee which adjudicates who is included in the free world and who is not. The winners of the Nobel Prize thus become members of an exclusive group whose political and cultural role includes defining, in a very public and internationally focused way, the world to which Turkey belongs.

Obtaining membership to the free world (which is another way of saying the Western world) was the overarching objective of the Turkish government during the early Republican era. The role of literature, particularly the novel, in Turkey's Westernization process was largely one of complicity in the construction of Kemalist national ideology. Through the value ascribed to literary representation, early Republican novelists could help in the construction of a new national identity and effect a change in the material and spiritual dimensions of the lives of the Anatolian people. Given this history, the expression of literary values in Turkey has been unusually close to the communication of political values in ways that have an important resonance in contemporary discussions of Turkish cultural power.[3]

Returning to Pamuk's interview with Mishra, in the ensuing conversation Pamuk is confident that President Recep Tayyip Erdoğan's Justice and Development party does not feel its cultural powerlessness.[4] As Pamuk articulates, this nearly two decades of AKP political hegemony coincided with a flourishing of Turkish secular culture abroad. Not only did Orhan Pamuk himself win the Nobel Prize in 2006, but this same period also saw a renewed market for translated or Anglophone Turkish literature by contemporary authors like Elif Şafak and Ahmet Altan, as well as popular translations of canonical Turkish writers from the early twentieth century such as Ahmet Hamdi Tanpınar, Yaşar Kemal, and Sabahattin Ali.[5] Beyond the literary arts, Turkish artists and filmmakers were also highly successful in international exhibitions and film festivals. In the early decades of the twenty-first century, Turkish culture, and particularly Turkish literature, was visible with a renewed power in world cultural institutions.

As Pamuk's interview makes clear, this cultural power was seen as a barricade for secular Turkish culture against lifestyle encroachment from the AKP government by turning to the international community as arbiters of the literary and artistic merit of Turkish culture which circulated within this community. Pamuk's response to Mishra, the idea that Turkey's conservative government was powerful politically, but not culturally, was a narrative that dominated discussions of Turkish culture in the first years of the twenty-first century on all sides of the political spectrum. In his recent excavation of Turkey's new political vocabulary, Tanıl Bora excavates the phrase "kültürel hegemonya," or cultural hegemony, defining it as a rhetoric of opposition in which the Kemalists and secular leftists are pitted against a *yerli*, or local culture, in which "that hegemony crushes local and national culture, prevents it from flourishing, and renders it invisible" (2018: 56).[6]

The "local and national," or *yerli ve milli* culture mentioned here is also another aphorism coined by the AKP to denote the political-cultural values of their base supporters. *Yerlilik*, or localness, has become both a political and a cultural value which asserts an authentic, communitarian identity rooted in the locality of Turkey, while simultaneously denying that community or identity to those their political ideology views as *yabancı*, or foreign. Scholars have noted that it is not just secular, Republican nationalist cultural values that the AKP's populist rhetoric has represented as "other" to Turkish identity, but large groups including Kurds, Academics for Peace, Gülenists, leftists have all been "cast as traitors" and as "*moral* enemies to be purged, guilty of tainting 'the people'" (Çapana and Zarakol 2019: 276). AKP officials ascribe this foreignness to members of Turkish society whose values they disagree with, effectively denying their Turkishness, their ability to speak from a Turkish perspective, or to represent Turkey in the international realm.

In many respects, this rhetoric adheres to textbook definitions of classic populism as an ideology that separates society into "two homogenous and antagonistic groups, 'the pure people' and 'the corrupt elite'" (Mudde 2004: 23). These definitions, which characterize populism as an "antagonistic appropriation for political, mobilizational purposes of an 'unrepresentable Other,' itself historically created in the process of a specific 'proper' civilizational project" by a "current or previous well-educated and proper elite—often painted as hypocritical or false" map almost too easily onto the contours of Turkey's national history (Ostiguy 2017: 75). In this paradigm, the Kemalist government's civilizational projects of the early twentieth century empowered a cultural elite by implementing top-down sociocultural reforms. The role of the intellectual elite in this reform process was to model a modernity coded Western, progressive, and secular and to educate the *halk*, or the general public, mainly the Anatolian people, up to the civilizational standards of that modernity. The secularizing impulses of the Kemalist government aimed to repress Islam as a sociopolitical force through abolishing the caliphate, bringing religion under state purview, and suppressing the public expression of religious sentiment. While these histories are understood by those loyal to Kemalist values as narratives of emancipation and progress, which enabled the projection of Turkey's civilizational power on the world stage, these same historical details are cast as evidence of the "historical horrors [visited] on simple people in the name of Westernization or progress" (Çapana and Zarakol 2019: 276).

However, in studying the ways in which the AKP have consolidated power, scholars have emphasized how AKP policies draw on and emulate their Kemalist predecessors. This analysis focuses on the structural similarity of the two political projects, reading an emergent "Erdoğanism" as the "populist mirror image" of Kemalism (Çapan and Zarakol: 2019: 263). This mirroring can also be seen in the AKP's recent approach to literature and literary culture. In their administration of culture, as will be discussed in more detail in the following sections, there is an emphasis on the presumed influence literature has over the Turkish nation's identity formation and self-expression, which continues the highly political stakes of literary representation seen in the early Kemalist era. Lisel Hintz has explored how the moral values of the AKP center around "the constitutive norm of piety," which "prescribes clear standards of moral (*ahlaki*) behavior" (2018: 49). Her examination of AKP cultural production through the analysis of state-run television programs illustrates how the AKP conceives of the cultural realm as "a forum in which beliefs about identity are not only reflected but shaped and disseminated, regularly depict and thus repeatedly reinforce norms of piety, charity, reverence for a strong leader, and a family-centered focus" (2018: 51).

Thus, when the Nobel Laureate signatories of the letter published in the *Guardian* make reference to President Erdoğan's own imprisonment for reciting Islamically inflected poetry in 1997, they read it as a moment of hypocrisy. Turning Erdoğan's own words against him—his claim that "Turkey is no longer the same old Turkey who used to sentence its great writers to prison—this era is gone forever," the signatories of the letter fail to recognize that what President Erdoğan considers a "great writer" is motivated by entirely different criteria than the "greatness" they ascribe to authors. James English has explored how cultural awards such as the Nobel Prize explicitly "merge artistic and political considerations according to a defining but explicit ration between artistic value and the politics of "freedom" or "peace"" (2005: 60). English notes that the Nobel Literary prize has, in recent decades, increasingly favored "writers of strong political conviction who have become icons of moral leadership in their particular national or subnational communities" (59). While the political values of freedom of speech and universal human rights underlie the cultural standards that the Nobel Laureates proclaim in their adjudication of "great" literature, the AKP government, instead, professes that fundamental moral values lie not in the universality of human rights, but in the specific cultural practices of Turkishness and Islam as defined by the AKP political project.

Indeed, as the AKP has increasingly consolidated power in the wake of the Gezi Protests in 2013 and the attempted coup in 2016, it was these international literary voices which stood up for a cosmopolitan vision of Turkey, which included the affirmation of freedom of speech and participatory democracy. Yet, this also reveals the extent to which international literary values are highly tied to the specific literary institutions that set the standards for engagement and valuation of literature. This literature and the authors who write it take part in a global literary elite who value literature's ability to cross borders, participate in the free press, and affirm liberal humanitarian values. This kind of literary cosmopolitanism has long been of interest to literary scholars. Contingent with the rise of the globalization discourse in the 1990s, a renewed interest in the connections between literature and the global redefined cosmopolitanism as an intellectual stance which "endorses reflective distance from one's cultural affiliations, a broad understanding of other cultures and customs, and a belief in universal humanity" that defined itself, in contrast to cosmopolitanisms of earlier centuries, "as an alternative to nationalism in our contemporary era" (Anderson 1998: 267; Cheah 1998: 21). In proclaiming the cosmopolitan project as an alternative to nationalism, scholars registered cosmopolitanism primarily as a "moral politics or political morality" which "needs to be formulated beyond the polis or state form" (Cheah 1998: 23).

Yet, as Jessica Berman's study of literature and cosmopolitanism ethics reminds us, "the world does not simply occupy the outermost circle of a concentric cosmopolitan perspective" (2009: 27). While scholars have long been occupied with the connections between world literature, human rights discourse, and literary prizes, less attention has been paid to how alternative modes of international affiliation structure the circulation of world literature. A notable exception is Michael Allan's *In the Shadow of World Literature*, which highlights the ways in which world literature functions as a "normative force" circumscribed within "the limits of the cosmopolitan sensibilities it implies" (2016: 7). Articulating how world literature has historically been aligned with cosmopolitan values, Allan argues that more attention should be focused on "not only how literature is grounded in the world, but how it participates in the imagination of what this world is" through asking "What world does literature make imaginable?" (2016: 11, 18). The following two sections examine the kinds of worlds different literary prize cultures make imaginable and articulate the ways in which the cultural "norms" present in Turkey inform not only what is considered good literature, but also the proper relationship of that literature to the nation and to the world.

## Turkish World Literature under Attack

Pheng Cheah has described cosmopolitanism as "about viewing oneself as part of a world, a circle of political belonging that transcends the limited ties of kinship and country to embrace the whole of deterritorialized humanity" (2016: 3). His work highlights how recent theories of world literature following Franco Moretti, David Damrosch, and Pascale Casanova all assert literature's worldliness through emphasizing its status as an "object of circulation in a global market of print commodities" (2016: 24). In other words, scholars tend to highlight circulation in the global market as an assertion of literature's value, both economic and moral. On the surface this seems to be relatively straightforward: great literature is that which is recognized by national and international audiences for its literary merits. However, in the cosmopolitan literary sphere, particularly in reference to authors who have come under attack on the national level for their fiction's humanitarian impulses, there is an impulse to equate political and literary value. Examining the ways in which humanitarian and aesthetic categories merge to "expose the interdependence and ready convertibility of artistic with political capital," this section investigates how international coverage of Aslı Erdoğan's incarceration circulated alongside the justification of literary prizes she was awarded after her incarceration (English 2005: 310). What becomes clear are the ways in which the cosmopolitan world literary sphere works in opposition to Turkey's national literary sphere by explicitly valuing aspects of Aslı Erdoğan's work which are not tolerated within the nation.

A recent interview by Ceyda Nurtsch in which Nurtsch asks Aslı Erdoğan to address the contradiction between her international literary accolades and her reception in Turkey strikes at the heart of this discrepancy:

> Isn't it a contradiction that while you were imprisoned in your native country, you won awards abroad?
>
> Erdoğan: That actually started earlier, around the year 2000. My time in jail was a culmination of this contradiction. While the prison guard insulted me, lawmakers in the European Parliament demanded my release. My publisher is the current French culture minister. But here, a policeman can beat me, drag me away by my hair. I try not to take it too personally. (Nurtsch 2017)

This perceived contradiction between Erdoğan's imprisonment in 2016 for her role on the advisory board of the pro-Kurdish opposition newspaper *Özgür Gündem* and the simultaneous winning of cultural prizes illustrates how the logic of cosmopolitan-values-as-universal-values operates in the cultural sphere. It also highlights how cosmopolitanism perceives the relationship between the national "native country" and the global world "abroad." Returning to the metaphor of the perceived concentric circles of the culture, the interviewer here understands the proper relationship of the national to the international to be that of a prerequisite. In other words, a writer must first achieve prominence on the local or national scale before moving outward to commendation in the larger world. This also encompasses the idea that each widening circle also relates to an increased prestige, in which global standing always supersedes national standing.

The contradiction of Aslı Erdoğan's position lies not only in the fact that her work's literary merit is recognized abroad yet ignored at home, but also in the ways in which her literary value converts into the Turkish political realm. Her description of her imprisonment from this interview highlights the inherent conflict between the two visions of political values that underpin conceptions of the world within Turkey. In her statement, the European Parliament and the French culture minister emerge in opposition to Turkish prison guards and policemen. This highlights a curious feature of the relationship between the local and the global at work in the cosmopolitan circulation of Turkish literature. While the late-twentieth-century discussions of the relationship between global prizes and local-national literatures were inflected with postcolonial anxieties regarding the ways in which literary prizes reproduced the structural inequalities of taste between cultural centers and their ex-colonial peripheries, what goes unsaid in Aslı Erdoğan's response is the superior *moral* values of European governments. This morality is largely derived from their ability to recognize what is happening to Aslı Erdoğan as an infringement upon international human rights and the freedom of speech. In the figure of the publisher-as-culture-minister the traditional opposition between literature and politics is collapsed, necessitating the question of whether the merit of her literary work lies predominantly in the aesthetic or the political realm.

Perhaps in the case of Aslı Erdoğan's writing the distinction has been blurred all along. In 1998 she began writing a column in *Radikal*, a newspaper popular in Turkish leftist circles. Her column titled "The Others" addressed issues long considered taboo in the Turkish media, including the Kurdish issue, torture, and women's rights. In the same year, she saw her first major literary success with *Kırmızı Pelerinli Kent* (The City in Crimson Cloak). While the *Radikal* column was relatively short-lived (she was dismissed in 2001 and the newspaper ceased publication on June 21, 2014), the novel has had an impressive afterlife, with translations into French, Norwegian, German, Bosnian, Arabic, Bulgarian, Swedish, and English. Following her imprisonment, PEN International launched a campaign to release her, which drew upon her literature's ability to circulate internationally, highlighting at great length the successful translations of her writing and the recognition it has won beyond Turkey's borders.

This emphasis on recognition is exceptionally visible in biographies of Aslı Erdoğan that circulate on the websites of PEN's various national and international branches, which describe her as "an award-winning writer whose first book was published in 1994" and express concern at "the arrest of prize-winning novelist" Erdoğan (Akdeniz and Altıparmak 2018: 28). Yet, in Norwegian PEN's announcement of Erdoğan's honorary membership there is an explicit valuing of her political commitments over her literary accomplishments. While the announcement does praise the variety and versatility of her writing accomplishments, it concludes by describing her work as a journalist and columnist as "perhaps even more impressive" than her work as a writer of fiction ("Aslı Erdoğan: Norwegian PEN welcomes a new Honorary Member," 2016). Her value as a novelist is thus expressed either through her work's ability to circulate with the international realm of humanitarian cosmopolitanism, or as a derivative of her political work in which the political supersedes the literary.

This focus on the multilingual circulation—itself a form of cosmopolitanism—of Erdoğan's writing is all the more interesting in light of her own attachments to the Turkish language. In the same interview quoted earlier, when asked: "*Do you still feel at home in Istanbul, in Turkey? Many artists, academics and journalists are leaving*," Erdoğan responds that "My home, my native country, my umbilical cord is the language. I love to write in Turkish and have a very personal relationship with my language. If I lived in some other country, that relationship would be unhinged. If you don't hear your own language, you lose its rhythm, its sound" (Nurtsch 2017). Unlike Orhan Pamuk, who is frequently accused of writing in a Turkish that anticipates translation into English in a way that undermines the Turkishness of his language, the power of Erdoğan's language lies in the fact that her connection to Turkishness is imagined as a Turkishness that is highly personal, but also translatable.

The issue of circulation becomes increasingly relevant when the circulation of Erdoğan's work is contrasted with the ability of the author herself to circulate globally on the international literary prize circuit. As an incarcerated author and later as subject to a travel ban, Erdoğan was unable to attend the awards ceremonies for any literary prizes awarded during this time period, including the Kurt Tucholsky prize awarded by Swedish PEN; the Princess Margriet award conferred by the European Cultural Foundation; the Theodor Heuss Medal from Germany; the Bruno Kreisky Prize for Human Rights in Austria; and the ceremony held in celebration of her election as an Honorary Member of Norwegian PEN. In response to this, she commented:

The whole world has seen the treatment that Turkey sees fit for its authors. This country has until now thrown more than one hundred and sixty poets and writers in jail and has basically maintained a constant silence with an incomprehensible malice and has lacerated its own conscience by refusing to face the truth. ("Author Aslı Erdoğan unable to receive her award" 2017)

Her inability to be present at the awards ceremonies creates a formal stoppage in the global flow of literary cosmopolitanism. Yet, as she expresses, this blockage also illuminates the ways in which narratives of Turkish literature's inability to circulate within the cosmopolitan literary sphere creates a second narrative flow of its own which does circulate through global literary institutions: the narrative of Turkey's violations of freedom of speech and human rights.

## The Rhetorical Neo-Ottoman World of Literature

This section turns to the Necip Fazıl Cultural Prize to ask how the cultural politics of the AKP since the 2013 Gezi protests have aimed to establish new nodes of Turkish cultural power that promote Ottoman Islamist moral values. I propose that the cultural policies of the AKP government since 2013 have aimed to construct an alternative world for Turkish literature, one which relies upon moral values that are not explicitly tied to the discourse of human rights, but, rather, to Ottoman Islamic moral values. In doing so, these new cultural policies also work to project Turkish culture within neo-Ottoman borders and establish an alternative world in which Turkish literature can not only circulate but also achieve cultural superiority.

As the timeline Pamuk puts forward in his interview with Mishra suggests, the Gezi protests in 2013 were, if not a watershed moment for the AKP's administration of Turkish culture, certainly a larger part of an ongoing shift in the ruling party's relationship to Turkish cultural power. As Pamuk mentions, until 2013 the position of Minister of Culture and Tourism was held by Ertuğrul Günay, who Pamuk describes as a "secular, leftist guy." Günay had previously been an MP for the Republican People's Party (CHP) from 1977 to 2004, only leaving the CHP when he objected to what he termed the anti-democratic tendencies of CHP leader Deniz Baykal. In January 2013, Ömer Çelik, who had been an AKP party member since the beginning of his political career, was appointed to the position. While the change predates the Gezi Park protests which began in May 2013, the shift in cultural leadership is indicative of a larger change in the AKP's approach to administrating Turkish culture in the second decade of the twenty-first century that started to take high culture seriously as a means of political mobilization.

President Erdoğan, in a series of speeches at cultural prize-giving ceremonies has constructed the importance of literature not only as a means of gaining cultural power in Turkey, but also as a means of acquiring political power beyond Turkey's borders. Speaking at the 2018 Cumhurbaşkanlığı Kültür ve Sanat Büyük Ödülleri (Presidential Culture and Arts Grand Awards) Ceremony, he emphasized the connection between culture and global influence proclaiming that the "world's most powerful countries have reached their elevated status through cultural power rather than armies" ("President Erdoğan Emphasizes Cultural Resurrection Is a Must, 2018"). He reiterated this connection between Turkey's perceived cultural and political lack in January 2019 at the Turkish Culture and Tourism Ministry's Special Awards Ceremony where he stated that cultural development is as "important a matter of survival as the fight against terror, as foreign policy and basic areas of service. In the new era, we will address our shortcomings and elevate culture, arts, architecture and urbanization to their rightful place." Furthermore, he proclaimed that without literature and the arts, "it is not possible to sustain or create shared values." The message is that it is these government-sanctioned cultural events which will consolidate and promote this new version of Turkish culture, and the stakes for doing so is none other than Turkey's national survival in the face of national and international forces.

Erdoğan's repositioning of literature and culture takes place against a larger shift of Islamist discourse on the novel in the past fifty years. In contrast to earlier Turkish-Islamist thinkers such as Cemil Meriç and Ali Bulaç who viewed the novel as a sign of "social sickness" or a "trap" which prevented true believers from engaging in the reality of society, in the 1980s and 1990s there was a wave of publication of Islamic novels and Islamic novel criticism in Turkey (Çayır 2007: 6). Kenan Çayır, in his *Islamic Literature in Contemporary Turkey: From Epic to Novel*, highlights how these authors in the 1980s and 1990s brought about a new understanding of the novel, which saw the genre as "the most important means to construct and demolish a nation" and whose effect on society could be "more disruptive and more re-orienting than revolutions" (Yardım 2000: 170; Çayır 2007: 255). This stance toward the novel as a tool to construct a nation and national identity owes much to Republican-era initiatives which positioned the novel as a vehicle to bring about Kemalist modernity and establish Turkey's Western-oriented national identity. Indeed, this dialogic relationship between the status of the novel in Republican and Islamic novels is at the heart of Çayır's study, which reads the emergence of Islamic novels as "an alternative to and critique of 'secular Republican literature' whose themes and concepts are represented as the 'real source of moral degeneration'" (2007: 22). Given this dialogic nature, Çayır emphasizes that the novel in Islamist discourse is "much more than an expression of a literary imagination," but, rather, "a means of 'cultural war' in the Turkish political and literary fields" (2007: 22).

This concept of literature's specifically Islamic moral dimension is also in antagonistic dialogue with the literary values of secular fiction, which, as we saw in the previous section, tend to emphasize human rights as a precondition for circulation on the global literary sphere. This is particularly visible in the "compatibility debate" over Islam's compatibility with democracy and human rights. Çayır traces this debate, which "polarized those who claim that Islam is totally incompatible with democracy and human rights and those who claim that true democracy and human rights can only be achieved by Islam" (2007: xvi). Erdoğan's comments and the AKP's new cultural agenda, as part of a larger, collective effort to raise a pious generation, can be seen as an extension of these debates.

Additionally, AKP government officials, particularly President Recep Tayyip Erdoğan, Numan Kurtulmuş, the previous minister of culture and tourism, and Mehmet Ersoy, the current minister of culture and tourism, have promoted a different version of Turkish literary culture that emphasizes alternative histories, publishing networks, and crucially, competing literary values that directly reflect the ruling party's political and social interests. These alternative histories run counter to the Kemalist literary history that is prominent in many English-language volumes on Turkey and emphasize an Islamist literary culture that has engaged in its own debates over the proper relationship of literature to Turkey's national history; of literary form to Islamic moral principles; and of culture to national identity.

Taking its name from poet and writer Necip Fazıl Kısakürek, the Necip Fazıl Prize was first established in 2014. Kısakürek is best known in the Turkish literary sphere for his editorship of the journal "Büyük Doğu" or "The Great East," published between 1943 and 1978. His writings espoused the concept of "Islamization from above" as a counterpoint to secular, Kemalist ideas of Turkish nationalism, and his work remains highly influential for members of the AKP government, including Erdoğan. The poster for the 2018 ceremony includes a quote from Necip Fazıl, "Çilesiz dava olmaz," which can be translated as "there is no struggle free from suffering." The prize is jointly sponsored by *Star* newspaper and the Ministry of Culture and Tourism. The self-described "milli iradenin sesi," or the "voice of the national will," *Star* is a conservative newspaper supportive of the AKP government. While the categories for the prizes given out have not remained entirely consistent from year to year, each year the committee awards prizes for fiction and poetry to books published in the previous year, as well as a prize for research, a first book prize, and a life's work prize. There have also been prizes for a work of translation into Turkish and, since 2017, an award for International Art and Culture.

Cumulatively, the winners of these prizes represent an attempt to enshrine a new literary canon by focusing on the life's work of authors from previous generations and by selecting new authors to watch. It is notable that none of the winners from previous generations have won the Sait Faik Prize, and only two authors, Mustafa Kutlu and Rasim Özdenören, received the Presidential Culture and Arts Grand Awards for Literature awarded by the Presidency of Turkey in the same year they received the Necip Fazıl Cultural Prize.[7] In addition to these prizes honoring established writers, the Necip Fazıl Prize also awards an annual First Book Prize to two authors: one woman and one man. Since the First Book Prize was inaugurated in 2016, all female winners of the prize are pictured wearing headscarves, and with the exception of Cihan Aktaş's 2016 Story-Novel Award, women writers have been successful in winning only "the First Book Award" category. The language used to discuss these women's fiction emphasizes newness, freshness of voice, and connection to reality and tradition, while the men's writing emphasizes mastery of technique, innovation in language, and concern for the wider world.

Through a focus on translations and international prizes, the Necip Fazıl Prize also provides insight into how Turkey's new culture also constructs a different understanding of the world. Initiated in 2017, the prize was designed to recognize "intellectuals who act as a bridge between Turkey and their culture." Yet, it is striking to note that the winners to date have all come either from countries that were previously under Ottoman rule, or Muslim communities that recognized the Ottoman sultan as caliph, with the 2017 prize going to Bosnian poet Cemalettin Latiç, who is known for his religious poems and for writing the Bosnian national anthem; the 2018 prize going to Professor Muhammed Harb, an Egyptian academic who works on Ottoman history and Turkish literature, including authors Necip Fazıl Kısakürek, Ömer Seyfettin, and Mehmed Akif Ersoy; and the 2019 prize going to Emced İslâm Emced, a Pakistani poet. In doing so, we can read these prizes as an act of cultural self-assertion. If, as David Damrosch cautions "a work only has an effective life as world literature whenever, and wherever, it is actively present within a literary system beyond that of its original culture," what this prize attempts to enshrine is a world within which pious Turkish literature can circulate, and via that circulation, become a world of its own (2003: 4).

## Takeaways for World Literature

What becomes clear in examining Turkey's bifurcated literary spheres is that they are each predicated on different, and to some extent competing, visions of the global. While Damrosch's axiomatic assertion that world literature encompasses "all literary works that circulate beyond their culture of origin, either in translation or in their original language" (2003: 4) or

Franco Moretti's assertion that world literature "is the product of a unified market" (2011: 75) is highly applicable to the cosmopolitan, secular branch of Turkish literary culture, we also have to consider how the second literary world cultivates an uncirculatability in the cosmopolitan sphere through instituting alternative readers and marketplaces, eschewing the global platforms of literary flow that are coded as not-Turkish (4; 75).

While Pheng Cheah and Michael Allen share a commitment to reading world literature as a normative force that partakes in the process of making worlds, Cheah in particular is less consistent on how world literature should register world-making practices like those at work in the AKP's current cultural programming. Taking postcolonial fiction as that which "contests (neo)colonial and capitalist cartographies of the world with the normative aim of creating more progressive mappings," the emphasis on replacing the cosmopolitan world with that which contests capitalism in order to create a "more progressive" world for literature is clearly not the aim of the AKP's literary projects (Cheah 2016: 18).

On the one hand, President Erdoğan's desire to establish a new world literary center around Turkish literature can be read as a challenge to both world literature's Eurocentric valuative criteria and to the enduring hegemony of the Kemalist literary canon. In this reading, the formation of the Necip Fazil prize counters injustices regarding the literary representation of Islamic identity on a national level, while also tacking similar inequalities on a global scale. As such, it could be considered as a literary corollary to "the World is Bigger than Five" discourse, which originally developed as a critique against the structures of global governance led by the UN Security Council, but has evolved since into a more all-encompassing project which, in President Erdoğan's words, is the "biggest-ever rise against global injustice."[8]

Yet, this version of progress is cold comfort to those in Turkey who see the AKP's human rights violations and erosion of the freedom of speech as a distinct backsliding. While Turkey's cosmopolitan literature circulates visibly across and through Western literary institutions, its mirror image raises questions about how global ethno-nationalist authoritarianisms espouse alternative forms of circulation, but also how these alternatives seem to encompass a resistance to circulation as world literature has traditionally conceived of it as such. The next task of world literature in the twenty-first century is to explore these discrepancies.

# Notes

1 The Center for Turkish Studies has been tracking this data through the "Türkiye Sosyal-Siyasal Eğilimler Araştırması Sunumu" (Social and Political Trends in Turkey). For the specific breakdown of these percentages from 2016 to 2018, see pages 96–9 of the Center for Turkish Studies "Türkiye Sosyal-Siyasal

Eğilimler Araştırması – 2018, 30 Ocak 2019," Available online: http://ctrs.khas.edu.tr/sources/TSSEA-2018-TR.pdf

2  For more on the construction of other identity groups within Turkey, see Lisel Hintz, *Identity Politics Inside out: national identity contestation and foreign policy in Turkey*.

3  For more on this process see (Seyhan 2008).

4  Founded in 2001, the party first came to power in the 2002 general elections as the first party in eleven years to win a majority and it continues to hold a majority in the Turkish parliament at the time of writing.

5  Many of these translation projects were funded by the Republic of Turkey Ministry of Culture and Tourism TEDA Project, which was implemented in 2005 to foster the publication of Turkish literature in languages other than Turkish in order to increase the visibility of books by Turkish authors in the global book market. Two of Ahmet Hamdi Tanpınar's novels were translated into English in this time period, with Erdağ Göknar's translation of *Huzur* as *A Mind at Peace* in 2011 and Maureen Freely and Alexander Dawe's translation of *Saatleri Ayarlama Enstitüsü* as *The Time Regulation Institute* in 2013. Freely and Dawe also produced a highly anticipated translation of Sabahattin Ali's *Kürk Mantolu Madonna, Madonna in a Fur Coat*, in 2016. This same time frame saw a translation of Yaşar Kemal's *İnce Memed* as *Memed, My Hawk* reissued as a *New York Review of Books* paperback in 2005.

6  Unless otherwise noted, all translations from Turkish are my own.

7  Özdenören won the literature prize in 2015 and Kutlu in 2016; however, two other recipients of the Necip Fazıl Lifetime Achievement Award, Uğur Derman and Nevzat Atlığ, won prizes, Derman in 2009 for Traditional Arts (Geleneksel Sanatlar) and Atlığ in 1999 for music.

8  President Erdoğan first proclaimed "the World is Bigger than Five" at a UN General Assembly Meeting in 2013. The motto refers to the five permanent members of the UN Security Council – the UK, France, China, Russia and the US – and was originally used to address structural inequalities in global governance between those five powers and developing nations.

# References

Akdeniz, Yaman, and Kerem Altıparmak. (2018), "Turkey: Freedom of Expression in Jeopardy: Violations of the Rights of Authors, Publishers and Academics Under the State of Emergency." Tr. Ayşegül Bahcıvan, English PEN. Available online: https://www.englishpen.org/wp-content/uploads/2018/03/Turkey_Freedom_of_Expression_in_Jeopardy_ENG.pdf (accessed on January 10, 2020).

Allan, Michael. (2016), *In the Shadow of World Literature: Sites of Reading in Colonial Egypt*, Princeton: Princeton University Press.

Anderson, Amanda. (1998), "Cosmopolitanism, Universalism, and the Divided Legacies of Modernity," in P. Cheah and B. Robbins (eds.), *Cosmopolitics:*

*Thinking and Feeling Beyond the Nation*, 265–89, Minnesota: University of Minnesota Press.
"Author Aslı Erdoğan unable to receive her award," *Cumhuriyet*, April 30, 2017. Available online: http://www.cumhuriyet.com.tr/haber/english/730866/author-asl i-erdogan-unable-to-receive-her-award.html (accessed on January 10, 2020).
Berman, Jessica. (2009), *Modernist Fiction, Cosmopolitanism and the Politics of Community*, Cambridge: Cambridge University Press.
Bora, Tanıl. (2018), *Zamanın Kelimeleri: Yeni Türkiye'nin Siyasi Dili*, İstanbul: İletişim Yayınları.
Çapana, Zeynep Gülşah, and Ayşe Zarakol. (2019), "Turkey's Ambivalent Self: Ontological Insecurity in 'Kemalism' Versus 'Erdoğanism'," *Cambridge Review of International Affairs* 32 (3): 263–82.
Çayır, Kenan. (2007), *Islamic Literature in Contemporary Turkey: From Epic to Novel*, New York: Palgrave MacMillan.
Cheah, Pheng. (1998), "Introduction Part II: The Cosmopolitical – Today," in P. Cheah and B. Robbins (eds.), *Cosmopolitics: Thinking and Feeling Beyond the Nation*, 20–41, Minnesota: University of Minnesota Press.
Cheah, Pheng. (2016), *What Is a World?: On Postcolonial Literature as World Literature*, Durham: Duke University Press.
Coetzee, J. M. et al. (2018), "An Open letter to President Erdoğan from 38 Nobel Laureates," *The Guardian*, February 28, 2018. Available online: https://www.theguardian.com/commentisfree/2018/feb/28/nobel-laureates-president-erdogan-turkey-free-writers (accessed on January 10, 2020).
Damrosch, David. (2003), *What Is World Literature?* Princeton: Princeton University Press.
English, James. (2005), *The Economy of Prestige: Prizes, Awards, and the Circulation of Cultural Value*, Harvard: Harvard University Press.
Hintz, Liesel. (2018), *Identity Politics Inside Out: National Identity Contestation and Foreign Policy in Turkey*, Oxford: Oxford University Press.
Mishra, Pankaj. (2013), Interview with Orhan Pamuk. Available online: https://newrepublic.com/article/113948/orhan-pamuk-interview-taksim-square-erdogan-literature (accessed on January 10, 2020).
Moretti, Franco. (2011), "World-Systems Analysis, Evolutionary Theory, Weltliteratur," in D. Palumbo-Liu, B. Robbins, and N. Tanoukhi (eds.), *Immanuel Wallerstein and the Problem of the World: System, Scale, Culture*, 75, Duke: Duke University Press.
Mudde, Cas. (2004), "The Populist Zeitgeist," *Government and Opposition* 39 (4): 541–63.
Nurtsch, Ceyda. (2017), Interview with Aslı Erdoğan, "It's my country too," Qantara.de. July 26, 2017. Available online: https://en.qantara.de/node/28473 (accessed on January 10, 2020).
Ostiguy, Pierre. (2017), "Populism: A Socio-Cultural Approach," *The Oxford Handbook of Populism*, 73–97, Oxford: Oxford University Press.
"Our Motto 'the World is Bigger than Five' is the Biggest-Ever Rise against Global Injustice." Presidency of the Republic of Turkey. January 10, 2018. Available online: https://www.tccb.gov.tr/en/news/542/89052/our-motto-the-world-is-bigger-than-five-is-the-biggest-ever-rise-against-global-injustice

"President Erdoğan Emphasizes Cultural Resurrection Is a Must," *Daily Sabah.* December 20, 2018. Available online: https://www.dailysabah.com/duplicate/2018/12/20/president-erdogan-emphasizes-cultural-resurrection-is-a-must (accessed on January 10, 2020).

Seyhan, Azade. (2008), *Tales of Crossed Destinies: The Modern Turkish Novel in a Comparative Context*, New York: MLA.

Yardım, Mehmet N. (2000), *Romancılar Konuşuyor*, İstanbul: Kaknüs Yayınları.

# CONTRIBUTORS

**Burcu Alkan** is an Honorary Research Fellow at the University of Manchester, where she had also received her PhD in English and American Studies in 2009. She coedited (with Çimen Günay-Erkol) *Dictionary of Literary Biography 373: Turkish Novelists Since 1960* (2013) and its second series *DLB 379* (2016). She recently published her monograph *Promethean Encounters: Representation of the Intellectual in the Modern Turkish Novel of the 1970s* (2018). Her current research interests are in the field of medical humanities, particularly on the relationship between psychiatry and literature, focusing on the self, suicide, and mental illness.

**Fatih Altuğ** worked as assistant professor of Turkish Language and Literature at İstanbul Şehir University between 2009 and 2020. He was also the director of the Cultural Studies Program. Currently, he is associate professor at Johannes Gutenburg University Mainz, at the Institute of Slavic, Turkic and Circum-Baltic Studies. He earned his PhD from Boğaziçi University. His work focuses mostly on representations of subjectivity, agency, and gender in modern Ottoman-Turkish literature. His current research explores literary networks of women writers in the late-Ottoman period. He recently published *Kapalı İktisat Açık Metin* (Closed Economy Open Text) (2018). His articles on writers such as Namık Kemal, Fuad Köprülü, Sevgi Soysal, and Onat Kutlar have appeared in journals and essay collections in Turkey.

**Etienne E. Charrière** is an assistant professor in the Department of Turkish Literature at Bilkent University in Ankara. He received a BA in Modern Greek Studies from the University of Geneva and a PhD in Comparative Literature from the University of Michigan. His research focuses on the literary production of non-Muslims in the late-Ottoman Empire and, in particular, on the rise of novel writing during the Tanzimat Era. He is the co-editor of *Ottoman Culture and the Project of Modernity: Reform and the Tanzimat Novel* (2020).

**Peter Cherry** is an assistant professor in the Department of Turkish Literature at Bilkent University. He holds a PhD in Comparative Literature from the University of Edinburgh. Peter is the author of a forthcoming monograph *Muslim Masculinities in Literature and Film: Transcultural*

*Identity and Migration in Britain* (2021). His work has been published in the *Journal of Commonwealth Literature* and *Comparative Critical Studies*.

**Başak Çandar** is an assistant professor of English at Appalachian State University, North Carolina. She holds a PhD in Comparative Literature from the University of Michigan, Ann Arbor. Her research focuses on world literature theories and pedagogies, translation studies, and the relationship between political violence and literature, especially in contemporary Turkish and peninsular Spanish literatures. Previously, she has published on Turkish and Spanish authors including Orhan Pamuk, Erdal Öz, Murat Uyurkulak, Juan Marsé, and Juan Goytisolo. A work on teaching world literature during an age of refugee crises is forthcoming this year.

**Anirudha Dhanawade** studied at Magdalene College, Cambridge, and Birkbeck College, University of London. He has taught English and art history at the Universities of Mumbai, Manchester, and Genoa, and is currently an independent scholar.

**Simla Doğangün** works as an assistant professor in the Department of English Language and Literature at Doğuş University. She completed her PhD on a comparative study of cosmopolitanism in contemporary Anglo-Indian and Turkish novels at the Amsterdam School for Cultural Analysis (ASCA), University of Amsterdam. She has published on English, Indian, and Turkish literature. Her research interests include world literature, comparative postcolonial studies, and exile narratives.

**Mediha Göbenli** is Professor in the English Language and Literature Department of Yeditepe University. She received her PhD with her thesis on contemporary Turkish women's literature from Hamburg University in 1999. Since 2000, she has been teaching comparative literature, migration and exile literature, women's literature, European literature, and literary theory at Yeditepe University. Mediha Göbenli has published *Zeitgenössische türkische Frauenliteratur* (Contemporary Turkish Women's Literature) (2003) and *Direnmenin Estetiğine Güven* (Faith in the Aesthetic of Resistance) (2006), a comparative analysis of Peter Weiss's *Die Ästhetik des Widerstands* (The Aesthetic of Resistance), and Vedat Türkali's novel, *Güven* (Faith).

**Çimen Günay-Erkol** obtained her PhD in Literary Studies at Universiteit Leiden in 2008. Her PhD manuscript *Broken Masculinities: Solitude, Alienation and Frustration in Turkish Literature After 1970* (2016) reveals the complexity of the post-coup novels of the 1971 military intervention in Turkey. Since 2013, she has been a member of the ICSM (Initiative for the Critical Study of Masculinities) and works as an editor and board member for the *Masculinities Journal*. Currently, she teaches at Ozyegin University.

Her fields of interest are demilitarization, masculinity, trauma, narrations of self, post-conflict literature, and medical humanities.

**Irmak Ertuna Howison** teaches writing, world literature, and introduction to philosophy in Columbus College of Art and Design. Her research interests include world literature, feminist crime fiction, and literary criticism. She recently co-edited an essay collection on eco-criticism titled *Animals, Plants and Landscapes: An Ecology of Turkish Literature and Film* (2019). She has also coauthored two books on Jane Austen and Frankenstein in Turkish (2017 and 2018). She holds a BA degree in Sociology from Boğaziçi University (2004), and an MA (2006) and a PhD in Comparative Literature from Binghamton University (2010).

**Şima İmşir** worked as an assistant professor in the Department of English Language and Literature at Istanbul Şehir University between 2018–2020. She is currently teching at Ozyegin University. She received her BA degree from the Department of Comparative Literature at Istanbul Bilgi University and her MA degree from the Department of Women Studies at Istanbul University. Having received a School of Arts, Languages and Cultures fund from the University of Manchester, she completed her PhD studies at the University of Manchester in 2018. Her research interests include biopolitics, medical humanities, disability studies, gender, history of social Darwinism, nineteenth- and twentieth-century British literature, twentieth-century Turkish literature, and postcolonial theory.

**Kenan Behzat Sharpe** completed his PhD in Literature at the University of California, Santa Cruz, in 2019. His research focuses on the literature, music, and cinema produced by 1960s social movements in the United States, Turkey, and the eastern Mediterranean. He is currently completing a manuscript on psychedelic rock music and the Left in Turkey. His writings have been published in *The Routledge Handbook of the Global Sixties* and *Journal of the Ottoman and Turkish Studies Association*, as well as in *Al-Monitor*, *Jacobin*, and the Verso blog. He is a founder and co-editor of *Blind Field: A Journal of Cultural Inquiry*.

**Kaitlin Staudt** is a postdoctoral fellow in the Department of English at Auburn University. Her research focuses on how authors develop experimental aesthetics to counter-hegemonic narratives of political modernity, with an emphasis on the novels of the early Kemalist Republic and on contemporary fiction published since the rise of the AKP government in 2002. Her work has appeared in *Feminist Modernist Studies* and *Middle Eastern Literatures*, and she is the Turkish section editor of the anthology *Global Modernists on Modernism*. Her research has been supported by the DAAD, Türkiye Bursları, and the British Institute at Ankara.

**Mehmet Hakkı Suçin** is a professor in the Arabic Language and Literature Department of Gazi University. Suçin chaired the commission that prepared Arabic curricula based on CEFR for primary and secondary schools in Turkey (2012–14). He was a jury member for the International Prize for Arabic Fiction (IPAF) in 2014 and the Sheikh Hamad Award for Translation in 2015. He has translated writers such as Ibn Hazm, Ibn Tufail, Yahya Haqqi, Ali Duaji, Adonis (three books), Mahmoud Darwish (four books), Kahlil Gibran, Nizar Qabbani, and Muhammad Bennis into Turkish. He has authored several books related to translation studies and Arabic language and literature. His studies focus on translation studies, Arabic literature, and teaching Arabic to nonnative speakers.

**Joseph Twist** is a lecturer in German studies at University College Dublin, Ireland. In broad terms, he is interested in the intersection of philosophy, religion, and literature. He focuses on the interaction between mystical and postmodern thought in the work of contemporary German authors of varying Muslim backgrounds, such as Navid Kermani, Emine Sevgi Özdamar, SAID, Zafer Şenocak, and Feridun Zaimoğlu, analyzing the nonidentitarian spirituality of their fiction and its transnational contexts. He has numerous publications in this field, including the book *Mystical Islam and Cosmopolitanism in Contemporary German Literature: Openness to Alterity* (2018).

# INDEX

*Abdülhamid and Sherlock Holmes* 26
accessibility 3, 5
Adorno, Theodor W. 60–1, 66
*Akabi's Story (Akabi Hikayesi)*, see Vartanian, Hovsep
AKP 37, 221–2, 224–5, 231, 233
Aliye, Fatma 24
Anatolia 30, 38, 209
Ansari, Mukhtar Ahmed 93, 96
Apter, Emily 6, 11, 49–50, 77–8, 84–9, 184
Arabic
    Arabo-Persian script 40
    poetry 149
    readership 152, 159
    script 179
Aragon, Louis 115, 117–19, 131, 135, 151, 154
Armenian
    community in Turkey 29, 94, 206
    literature 19–20, 26
    script 38, 40–1
Asadur, Zabel 26
Asturias, Miguel Angel 122
Atatürk, Mustafa Kemal 63, 94
Atay, Oğuz 8
Auerbach, Erich 2, 6–7
Aydemir, Şevket Süreyya 138
Ayden, Erje 9
Aykol, Esmahan 9

Balkan Wars 26–7, 93
Batuman, Elif 9
Baybars, Taner 118
Behramoğlu, Ataol 33
Bektashism 60, 64–6, 68, *see also* Sufism

Beloyannis, Nikos 142–3
Bezirci, Asım 33
Bhabha, Homi 89, 205, 207
bibliomigrancy 7
border 39–40, 49–50, 176, 208
Brandes, Georg 27–8
Britain 75
Bseiso, Muin 155
Buchan, John 90
Butler, Judith 78–9

Canip, Ali 28–9, 31
canon
    countercanon 3
    hypercanon 3
    reformation 59
    Turkish literary canon 8, 10–11, 43, 95, 140, 224–5
    world literary canon 11, 32, 175, 178, 183
Casanova, Pascale 5–8, 12, 133, 136–7, 228, *see also* Republic of Letters
Caucasus 36
Celal, Mehmet 23
censorship 121, 138
Cevdet, Abdullah 26
Chang, Tina 123
Cheah, Pheng 190, 228
Choo, Susan 190
Chow, Rey 89–90
Christianity 66, 80, 83, 86, 94, 104
    Catholic 180
    Greek Orthodox 130
circulation 3, 13, 43–5, 49, 57, 176–84, 227
civilization
    colonial 100, 198–9

# INDEX

and culture 103
  divide 182–3
  Kemalist programs 225–6
close reading 4
Cold War 8, 12, 117, 120, 133
colonialism 207
  European 11, 60, 62, 76, 90
  of India 96–101, 107
Committee of Union and
    Progress 93–4
  Party 30, 93–4
commodification 191, 193–7
communism 117, 134, 138, 140,
    see also Soviet Union;
    Turkish, Left Wing
  in Greece 132
  literature 131, 133, 136
  in Soviet Russia 102
comparative literature 7, 27, 177
  comparative literary scholarship 3,
    37, 39, 193
Constantinople, see Istanbul
cosmopolitanism 4, 27–33, 190–1,
    205, 211–12, 217, 218, 227
Coşkun, Nusret Safa 31
criticism 19, 232
Cyprus 49–50, 130
  Turkish Cypriot literature 37,
    47, 51
Çayır, Kenan 232

Damrosch, David, see also
    scriptworlds
  cannon 2
  elliptical refraction 20, 175–7
  world literature 55, 77, 88, 234
Dare to Disappoint, see Samancı, Özge
Darwish, Mahmoud 152–4
decolonization 8
Diktaios, Aris 132, 135
Dimitriadi, Maria 130
discourse
  on cosmopolitanism 27–8
  on gender 82
  on globalization 205–6, 227
  Leftist 131–3
  literary 33
  on multiculturalism 56, 62

  nationalist 176
  Orientalist 76, 78–9, 84–5, 89
  postcolonial 211
  on script 38
  on translation 49
  Turkish cultural 222, 231–3
  on world literature 2–3, 76
distant reading 4–5
domestication 12–13
drama 19, 132, 192
Dussap, Srpouhi 26

East Asian scripts 39–40, 44
Eastern
  literature 21, 25
  modernity 103
East-West dichotomy 2, 63, 66, 222
  distortion 177–8, 180–1
  literary 134
  Pamuk, Orhan 175, 183–4
  Şafak, Elif 206, 208–11
Edib, Halide 11–12, 27, 82, 93, 108
  *Conflict of East and West in
    Turkey* 100–3
  *The Daughter of Smyrna* 97–9
  exile 94–5
  *Inside India* 103–7
  *New Turan (Yeni Turan)* 94
  *The Shirt of Flame (Ateşten
    Gömlek)* 95–100
Ekrem, Recaizade 23
Ellison, Grace 76–7, 79–83, 88–90
Emre, Yunus 56–62, 65
Enlightenment 56, 60–3, 67, 69
Erbil, Leyla 8
Erdoğan, Aslı 228–31
ethno-masquerade 76, 78–9, 86–7
Eurocentrism 235
  cosmopolitan 205
  literary 2–3, 5, 7, 12, 56, 175,
    178
  philosophical 67–9
  reading of history 103
European, see also Western
  colonialism 11, 60, 76, 90, 96–7
  intellectualism 14, 84, 107
  languages 6, 9
  literature 25, 27, 31

publishers 6
values 31, 229
writers 24
Evin, Ahmet 7

Fahrünnisa, Fatma 24
Farhi, Moris 9
Fast, Howard 113
feminism 75–6, 78, 82–3
Ferera, Isak 24
Fikret, Tevfik 23
First World War 94
Fisk, Gloria 175, 191–2
folk
    culture 149
    literature 30
    narrative 159–60
    poetry 56
    singer 113
    songs 142–3
Forché, Carolyn 123
foundational texts 2, 7
Frankfurt School 57, 62, 66
French literature 20, 22, 178

Gandhi, Mahatma 95–6, 102, 104–7
Gavriilidis, Ioannis 45–6
gender 78–81, 84
German literature 66
Germany 56, 63
    Germanness 61–2
    Jewish youth 67
    Turkish community 55, 63
Gezi protests 221, 231
global
    audience 2, 189
    capitalism 205
    impact 7
    issues 14
    literary market 174, 183
    village 206, 217
    works 13
globalization 2, 21, 189, 196, 212–14, 217
Goethe, Johann Wolfgang von 28, 55
Goytisolo, Juan 13, 171–3, 178–83
    *Don Julian* (*Count Julian*) 179

*Juan the Landless* (*Juan sin tierra*) 180
*Marks of Identity* (*Señas de identidad*) 179
*State of Siege* (*El sitio de los sitios*) 180
Gökalp, Ziya 28, 30–1, 103
Greek
    civil war 141–2
    literature 46–7, 132
    script 47–50
    Turkish literary representations 140
    War of Independence 130
Gronau, Dietrich 120–1
Gürçağlar, Şehnaz Tahir 32
Gürsel, Nedim 9

Halman, Talât Sait 7
Hamm, Peter 120
Hanım, Nigâr 24
Hanım, Zafer 24
Hanım, Zeyneb 75–7, 79, 83–9
Harem 11, 75, 77–8 80–2, 88
heterographics 10, 37, 46–7, 49
Hikmet, Nâzım 12–13, 112–13
    Arabic translation 148–50, 163–7
    Eastern Europe 115, 122, 136
    English translation 115–18
    French translation 118
    German translation 119–20
    Greek translation 130–2, 140, 142–3
    imprisonment 113, 115–17, 131
    Latin America 122
    memorialised 113, 119–20, 122–3, 161–3
    as political poet 113, 117, 122–3, 130–1, 136–8, 144
    as world literature 116–20, 123–4, 131, 134–5, 139, 161
Hirsch, Edward 116
Hölderlin, Friedrich 66
humanism 10, 28, 60–2, 154
humanities 4
hybridity 14–15, 19, 43, 50, 205–11, 218

identity politics 208, 214
ideology 4, 63, 224
　political 97, 102, 107–8, 139
India 96, 99, 101–2, 104–8
　Indian Hindus 104–6
　Indian Muslims 99–100, 104–6
İlhan, Attilâ 33
international
　dialogues 4
　internationalism 11–12, 30–1, 134–6, 139
intertextuality 183, 193
Islam 14, 59–64 66–8, *see also* Bektashism; Indian Muslims; Sufism
　Golden Age 56, 60, 62
　literature 32–3
　modernization 60, 63–4
　Turkey 221–2, 226, 233
Istanbul 29, 160
　Constantinople 173
　deconstantinopolization 171–2
　literary representations 178–9, 181–2
　Ottoman Era 10, 19–20
Izmir 97–8

Jamia Islamia 95, 100, 103, 106, 108
Jewish, *see* Ladino

Karaosmanoğlu, Yakup Kadri 27
Karay, Refik Halid 27
Kemal, Namık 20–2
Kemalism 63, 200, 222, 224–6
Khan, Muhammad Yakub 97–100
Kıvılcımlı, Hikmet 31
Konuk, Kader 86–7
Koutsoumpas, Dimitris 134
Köprülü, Fuad 26, 30

Ladino 19, 22, 38, 45, 143
language 5, 6, 19–23
Latin alphabet 36, 41–2
Leman, Makbule 24
Lewis, Reina 76–7
lingua franca 3, 4, 137
linguistic 4, 6–7, 39
Lisle, Debbie 79

literary
　awards 14, 223, 230
　historiography 19
　history 4–6, 10, 19, 22, 32, 223, 233
　scholarship 4, 227
　universality 5
　work 3, 7, 32–3, 55, 178, 218, 235
Loïzos, Manos 130
Loliée, Frederic 25
Longxi, Zhang 189, 218
Loti, Pierre 78, 84, 85
Lussu, Joyce 137

McCarthyism 113
Maltz, Albert 113–14
Marxism 104, 133, 135–7
Mayiopoulos, Stelios 132
Middle East 78, 178, 222
Mikroutsikos, Thanos 130
minor-scripting 38, 40, 42, 46–7, 50–1
Misailidis, Evangelinos 20, 46
Mithat, Ahmet 22–3, 45
mobility 9, 212
modernization 9, 33, 56
Moretti, Franco 4–5, 133, 177, 228, 235
Mouvafac, Nermine 115 116
multiculturalism 4, 208
　in Germany 61–2
　in the Ottoman Empire 20, 22, 206
multiethnicity 10
museums 198–9
mysticism 56, 66, 69
　Islamic 180, 206, 210
　Sufi 211

Naon, Avram 24
nationalism 98, 225
　authoritarian 14
　and cosmopolitanism 28, 30
　German 62
　Indian 93, 96–101, 103–8
　Turkish 27, 30, 33–4, 95–100, 103, 108

national literature 10, 177–8
nation-making 5, 99, 101–2
Nazif, Süleyman 26
Near East 95, 101
Necip Fazıl Literary Prize 231, 233–4
Nehru, Jawaharlal 96, 104
Neruda, Pablo 112, 114–17, 119, 122–4, 131, 136–8
*New Language (Yeni Lisan)* 28–9
Nobel Prize for Literature 173, 183, 224, 226–7
novel 19, 22, 224, 232

Odyan, Yervant 26
Orientalism 6, 56, 59, 76–7, 79, 81–90
Ottoman
  neo Ottomanism 14, 222–3, 231–5
  Ottoman Empire 11, 27, 30, 101–2
  Ottoman literature 9–10, 19–21, 27, 29–30, 33, 37
  Ottoman-Turkish language 27, 38–42
Özakın, Aysel 9
Özdamar, Emine Sevgi 9, 122

Palaiologos, Gregorios 46
Palestine 148, 151–2, 156
Pamuk, Orhan 13, 178–9, 188, 221, 224, 230
  *The Black Book (Kara Kitap)* 171–4, 179, 188
  *Istanbul: Memories and the City (İstanbul: Hatıralar ve Şehir)* 181–4
  *The Museum of Innocence* 191–4, 196–201
  Spanish translation 171 172
  *The White Castle (Beyaz Kale)* 181–2, 188
Paşa, Fatima 80–1
Paşa, Kamil 80
performativity 76–9, 89

periphery 27
peripheral European literature 27, 133
peripheral literatures 3, 175
peripheral national literatures 4, 136, 178
peripheral scholarship 3
periphery of former Ottoman Empire 222, 234, 235
*Persepolis*, see Satrapi, Marjane
poetry 19, 56, 116, 149
  readership 152
  as world literature 56, 116–19, 124, 139, 152, 167
populism 225–6
postcolonialism 59, 95–7, 207
  India 100–2, 108
  literature 137, 188, 211, 229, 235
postmodern 50, 183, 188
power relations 4, 14, 21, 77–8, 89, 221
Pratt, Mary Louise 78
publication
  industry 5
  journals 23–6, 28
  modern Turkey 232
  practices 3
  Second Constitution 25–6
  Translation and Publication Grant Program of Turkey (TEDA) 7

al-Qasim, Samih 156

Rasim, Ahmet 23
Rauf, Mehmet 23, 25
readership 3, 235
Republic of Letters 136–7, 139, 144, 173, see also Casanova, Pascale
Paris 5
Soviet Union 7, 131
Riffaud, Madeleine 120
Ritsos, Yannis 130–2, 134, 138–9
Robeson, Paul 115
*Romance of Talât and Fitnat, The (Taaşşuk-ı Talât u Fıtnat)*, see Sami, Şemsettin

Sabour, Salah Abdel  156–8
Sabri, Güzide  24
Said, Edward  79, 90
Sakai, Naoki  22
Salim, Hilmi  149
Samancı, Özge  194
Sami, Şemsettin  19
Sartinska, Theodossia  24–5
Satrapi, Marjane  194
Scandinavian literature  27
schema of cofiguration  22
Schimmel, Annemarie  60
Script Revolution  39
scriptworlds  41–4
Second Constitution  10, 25, 29, 80, 93–4
secularism  60–3, 67–8, 191, 221,
    see also Kemalism
Semiye, Emine  24
Seyfettin, Ömer  28
Sillen, Samuel  117
Soviet Union  102, 122, 133, 150, 158
    Republic of letters  7, 133, 136–7
Sowon S. Park  39
Sökmen, Müge Gürsoy  6
Spain  173, 179–80
spatial realm  3–4, 46
spirituality  10, 59, 63, 66–8
standardization  3, 207
Sufism  10
    Emre, Yunus  60, 64–8
    Hikmet, Nâzım  159–60
    Şafak, Elif  208–10
Sultan Abdülhamid II  25, 80, 83, 93–4
Süleyman, Şahabettin  26
Syriac  26, 38
Şafak, Elif  14, 204–8
    *The Forty Rules of Love: A Novel of Rumi*  206, 208–11, 217–18
    *The Saint of Incipient Insanities*  211–18
Şenocak, Zafer  55, 57–69, 121

Tahir, Kemal  33
*Tanzimat*  10, 33
*Tasavvuf*  149, 159–60

temporal  4, 68, 176
*Theatrum Mundi (Temaşa-i Dünya),*
    see Misailidis, Evangelinos
translation  44, 46, 57–9, 64
    industry  2
    practices  3
    translated works  2
    to Turkish  20, 32
    of Turkish literature  7, 150, 166–7, 172
    zone  11, 77, 84, 87, 89
transnational  5, 12
travel literature  11, 79, 89
Treaty of Sèvres  100–1
Tsambras, Giorgos  138
Tsipiras, Alex  129–30
Tuna, Fehmi Yahya  32
Turanism  94
Turkish
    left wing  32–3 132, 138–41,
        see also communism
    literature  29–31, 34, see also
        Ottoman Literature
    conception  21–3
    genres  19
    as world literature  1–3, 7–10, 15, 174, 222–3, 228–35
    readership  223
    Republic  11, 32, 100–3, 232
    War of Independence  94–5, 97–8, 100–1, 103, 108, 130

United States of America  212, 216
universal literature  21
Uşaklıgil, Halid Ziya  23, 25

Vartanian, Hovsep  20
Vecihi  23
Venuti, Lawrence  56–7
Vigorelli, Giancarlo  118

al-Wahhab al-Bayati, Abd  158–62
Wakabayashi, Judy  44
*Wealth of Sciences (Servet-i Fünun)*  23, 25, 28
Western, see also European
    cultural products  76
    languages  3

literature 20, 21, 28, 41
mindset 56, 59, 68–9, 214
modernity 103, 226
political systems 106–7
readership 11, 80–1, 88, 174, 210–11, 223
traditions 2
values 62–3
westernization 50, 191, 212, 216, 224
western-oriented scholars 4, 32
women's writing 77, 85, 234
  in the Ottoman Empire 24, 26
  in the Turkish Republic 95
world literature 1–6, 89, 218, 235
  center-periphery 133, 136–7, 227
  cosmopolitanism 188–9, 201
  debates 2, 31
  discourse 3
  East/West binary 174–8, 184
  in opposition to national literature 27–8, 139
  in the Ottoman Empire 25
  scholar 4
  in the Turkish republic 32
  world literariness 3
  world literary sphere 3

Xing, Yin 200

Yaşin, Mehmet 47–50
Yesayan, Zabel 26
Yeşilada, Karin 121
Yücel, Hasan Âli 32

Zayyād, Tawfīq 151–2